D0483572

ALSO BY THE AUTHOR, SIR WINSTON CHURCHILL

Story of the Malakand Field Force
The River War (2 volumes)*
Savrola*
London to Ladysmith via Pretoria
Ian Hamilton's March
Mr. Brodrick's Army*
Lord Randolph Churchill (2 volumes)*
For Free Trade*
My African Journey
Liberalism and the Social Problem
The People's Rights
The World Crisis (5 volumes)
My Early Life: A Roving Commission*
India
Thoughts and Adventures / Amid These Storms
Marlborough: His Life and Times (4 volumes)
Great Contemporaries
Arms and the Covenant / While England Slept
Step by Step 1936–1939
Into Battle / Blood Sweat and Tears
The Unrelenting Struggle
The End of the Beginning
Onwards to Victory
The Dawn of Liberation
Victory
War Speeches
Secret Session Speeches
Painting as a Pastime
The Second World War (6 volumes)*
The Sinews of Peace
Europe Unite
In the Balance
The War Speeches Definitive Edition (3 volumes)
Stemming the Tide
A History of the English-Speaking Peoples (4 volumes)
The American Civil War
The Island Race
Heroes of History
Joan of Arc
The Unwritten Alliance
Young Winston's Wars
Frontiers and Wars
Collected Works (34 volumes)
Collected Essays (4 volumes)
Complete Speeches (8 volumes)
The Boer War
The Dream

ALSO BY THE EDITOR, WINSTON S. CHURCHILL

First Journey
The Six-Day War (with Randolph S. Churchill)
Defending the West
Memories and Adventures
His Father's Son*

* currently in print

THE GREAT REPUBLIC

Edited by
Winston S. Churchill

THE MODERN LIBRARY   NEW YORK

THE
GREAT
REPUBLIC

A History of America

SIR WINSTON
CHURCHILL

2001 Modern Library Paperback Edition

Preface, additional text, and compilation copyright © 1999 by Winston S. Churchill
Maps copyright © 1999 by Anita Karl and Jim Kemp

All rights reserved under International and Pan-American Copyright
Conventions. Published in the United States by Random House, Inc.,
New York, and simultaneously in Canada
by Random House of Canada Limited, Toronto.

MODERN LIBRARY and colophon are registered trademarks
of Random House, Inc.

This work was originally published
in hardcover by Random House, Inc., in 1999.

The main text of this work is an abridgement of *A History of the
English-Speaking Peoples* by Winston Churchill, originally published
in four volumes in 1956, 1957, and 1958
by Cassell & Co. Ltd., London.

LIBRARY OF CONGRESS CATALOGING-IN-PUBLICATION DATA
Churchill, Winston, Sir, 1874–1965.
The great republic: a history of America/Sir Winston Churchill;
edited by Winston S. Churchill.
p.   cm.
"An abridgement of A history of the English-speaking peoples . . .
originally published in four volumes in 1956, 1957, and 1958
by Cassell & Co. Ltd., London."
Includes index.
ISBN 0-375-75440-7
1. United States—History.   I. Churchill, Winston, Sir, 1874–1965.
History of the English-speaking peoples.   II. Title.
E178 .C55   2000
973—dc21   00-62554

Modern Library website address: www.modernlibrary.com
Printed in the United States of America

1 2 3 4 5 6 7 8 9

Book design by Carole Lowenstein

To the hero generation
of the English-speaking peoples
who, by their courage and sacrifice,
and that of their allies,
liberated Europe
and saved the world from Hitler

EDITOR'S PREFACE

My grandfather, Winston Churchill, took enormous pride in his American heritage. This book stands as a tribute to him. It is also a testimony to the faith that he had in the theme of Anglo-American unity—a theme that transcended his life and achieved its apotheosis in World War II with the march to victory of the armies of Britain and her Commonwealth, the United States, Russia, and their allies. Thanks to their sacrifices the nations of Europe were liberated from Nazi tyranny.

Jennie Jerome, from the Duke of Marlborough's collection

Churchill was half American through his mother, the glamorous Miss Jennie Jerome of Brooklyn, New York, and, on the occasion of his first address to a joint session of the United States Congress, on December 26, 1941, he could not resist alluding to this fact, teasing the assembled senators and members of Congress with the mischievous suggestion: "If my father had been American and my mother British, instead of the other way

Leonard Jerome, from a
Churchill family portrait

round, I might have got here on my
own!" Through his maternal grandfather, Leonard Jerome, sometime
proprietor and editor of *The New
York Times,* he had at least two forebears who fought against the British
in the American War of Independence: one great-grandfather, Samuel
Jerome, served in the Berkshire County
Militia, while another, Major Libbeus
Ball of the 4th Massachusetts Regiment,
marched and fought with George Washington's
army at Valley Forge. Furthermore, Leonard Jerome's maternal grandfather, Reuben Murray, served as a lieutenant in the Connecticut and
New York Regiments, while his wife Clara's grandfather, Ambrose
Hall, was a captain in the Berkshire County Militia at Bennington.

Not only did he have Revolutionary blood in his veins but, it is believed, Native American as well. According to family tradition Jennie's
maternal grandmother, Clarisse Wilcox, was half Iroquois. Clarisse's
father, David Wilcox of Macedon, near Rochester, New York, is
recorded as having married Anna Baker of nearby Palmyra, New York,
in April 1791. In recent times genealogical researchers have cast scorn
on the suggestion that Jennie's descent is other than "American Colonial of English background," citing David Wilcox's wife as being the
daughter of Joseph Baker and Experience Martin, whose daughter
"Anne" was born in Rutland, Vermont, "about 1782." However, this is
implausible, given that she would have been only nine years old when
David Wilcox married his "Anna" and just fourteen when Clarisse was
born. Thus another myth bites the dust.

We Churchills take great pride in our Native American heritage and
are not lightly to be deprived of it. In opposition to those who doubt it,
I would merely assert that Winston's mother, Jennie, and her sister,
Leonie Leslie, were convinced of it. Furthermore, it is undisputed that
the densely wooded hills south of Lake Ontario had been the heartland
of the Iroquois nation. Anita Leslie, in *The Fabulous Leonard Jerome,*
quotes her grandmother Leonie, remarking on her exceptional energy,
as saying: *"That's my Indian blood, only don't let Mama know I told you!"*
Having inherited from my grandfather portraits of his maternal grand-
parents, Leonard and Clara Jerome, I have no doubt, judging by the

marked Native American features of
Clara, as to the truth of the matter.
Physical features speak louder than en-
tries in any Register of Births, but I
leave it to the reader to make his or her
own judgment of the matter.

While researching my family's American heritage on the Internet—thanks
to the Mormons who have recently
made available thirty years of their re-
searches on both sides of the Atlantic
(www.familysearch.org)—I   stumbled
on the fact that one of my ancestors,
John Cooke, who died in Plymouth,
Massachusetts, in 1694, had been born
in Leyden, Holland, in 1607. Knowing

*Clara Hall Jerome, from a
Churchill family portrait*

that half the pilgrims on the Mayflower had been known as the "Leyden Community"—Walloon Protestants escaping religious persecution—I was prompted to wonder if any of my forebears had made that
momentous voyage.

Within seconds, via the Mayflower website I was able to call up the
passenger manifest of all 102 passengers and was fascinated to discover
that Winston Churchill, at ten generations removed, had not one, but
three, ancestors who sailed on the Mayflower and who were among the
mere fifty who survived the rigours of that first winter on the inhos-
pitable shores of New England. John Cooke, a lad of just thirteen, was
one of those passengers, as was his father, Francis, and his future
father-in-law, Richard Warren. I was further intrigued to learn that,
through them, we are linked to no fewer than three Presidents of the
United States—Ulysses S. Grant, Franklin D. Roosevelt, and George
Bush—as well as to Alan B. Shepard, Jr., the first American in space
and the fifth man to walk on the moon.

It is no wonder that this injection of American Revolutionary blood
kick-started to new triumphs the Marlborough dynasty, which had
slumbered through seven generations since John Churchill, 1st Duke of
Marlborough, who, in a series of dazzling victories at the turn of the
eighteenth century, had humbled France's "Sun King," Louis XIV.

In November 1895, three weeks shy of his twenty-first birthday,
Winston, a lieutenant in the 4th Hussars, snatched a few weeks' leave
from his regiment to visit Cuba, with the aim of observing the Cuban
Revolutionary War against Spain. Getting there involved travelling by
way of New York. Thus, on November 9, Winston Churchill arrived in

*Young Winston, age twenty, in 1895, the year of his first visit
to the United States and Cuba. He is wearing the uniform of
a 2nd lieutenant in the 4th Hussars.*

New York harbor aboard the RMS *Etruria* and first set foot in his
mother's homeland and the city where she had been born and brought
up. It is evident that he did so with singularly little enthusiasm, for he
was impatient to get to Cuba. Indeed, the day before landing in New
York, he wrote to his mother from on board ship: "I look forward eagerly to reaching our destination and it is possible we may cut down our
stay in New York to a day and a half instead of three."

His visit, clearly, was a revelation and it did not take long for the young Winston to become captivated by the spirit and excitement of America. Within a day of his arrival, he was writing to his mother: "What an extraordinary people the Americans are! Their hospitality is a revelation to me and they make you feel at home and at ease in a way that I have never before experienced. On the other hand their press and their currency impressed me very unfavourably. . . ." It is no wonder that he extended his stay in New York to six days and that in each of his fifteen visits to America, over the span of sixty-five years, he derived the same delight and inspiration from America as on his first visit.

From an early age Winston rejoiced in his American ancestry and, as an enthusiastic student of history, the great events in the saga of the American nation held a powerful attraction for him. Indeed, so impassioned did he become that in 1929 he personally tramped several of the battlefields of the American Civil War—a fact that shows through in his brilliant chapters on this aspect of American history. His guide at the battlefields of Fredericksburg and the Chancellorsville, Wilderness and Spotsylvania had himself, at the age of eight, been an eyewitness of some of the heaviest fighting that had taken place there more than sixty-five years before. Winston was captivated: "Here is the Angle," recounted his guide. "Here is where the dead lay thickest. Yes! In this trench they were piled in heaps, both sides together, blue and grey. We came here while the firing was still going on a mile or two away. My father scolded me for trying to take the boots off a dead soldier who lay here. See that little gully here? It was pouring with rain, and all the water running along it was red. . . ."

Churchill's love of America endured throughout his lifetime until, by the chance of history, it fell to him to provide the leadership at a critical juncture in the greatest war of history, that crucially enabled Britain to hold out, though the rest of Europe had fallen beneath the Nazi jackboot, until in the fullness of time the United States was able to join the conflict. Though confident that Britain, sustained by her Empire and Commonwealth overseas, could hold out in her island, he was sufficient of a realist to acknowledge that only with the full-hearted commitment of the United States could the liberation of Europe be achieved and the defeat of Hitler accomplished.

It was in recognition of his contribution to victory in World War II that, on April 9, 1963, President John F. Kennedy conferred upon Churchill the remarkable distinction of honorary citizenship of the United States. By then eighty-eight years of age and infirm, he was not strong enough to make the journey to Washington in person but deputed my late father, Randolph, and me to represent him. In his reply

The author of The Great Republic *with his editor*

(read by my father) to the President's citation, my grandfather declared: "I am, as you know, half American by blood, and the story of my association with that mighty and benevolent nation goes back nearly ninety years to the day of my father's marriage. In this century of storm and tragedy I contemplate with high satisfaction the constant factor of the interwoven and upward progress of our peoples. Our comradeship and our brotherhood in war were unexampled. We stood together and because of that fact the free world now stands. . . . Mr. President, your action illuminates the theme of unity of the English-speaking peoples, to which I have devoted a large part of my life."

This book brings together for the first time Churchill's personal view of American history, from the voyages of discovery and the founding of the first colonies on the Eastern seaboard, through the Revolutionary and Civil Wars to the point where America stands on the threshold of world power. It is drawn from his *History of the English-Speaking Peoples,* a four-volume work, which he began in the mid-1930s but which, due to certain interruptions, he did not finish until the mid-1950s. The original work traced the fortunes of the British nation from the Roman invasion of Britain by Julius Caesar in 55 B.C. through the Dark Ages, the Viking raids, the Norman invasion of 1066, the Crusades, and on to the creation of the greatest empire the world has ever seen and the birth of the Industrial Revolution, that was the forerunner of the technological age in which we live today. Buried in this grand sweep of British history are many fascinating chapters unfolding the remarkable tale of the birth and development of the American nation; it is these that I now place before the American reader. I have also included, towards the end, a selection of Churchill's articles and speeches on twentieth-century America, as well as chapters on America's English constitutional and legal heritage.

I have called this work *The Great Republic,* the term my grandfather used with fondness to refer to the United States, upon which—in Britain's darkest hour—all his hopes of salvation and ultimate victory were focused. I have dedicated this work to the soldiers of the English-speaking world, whose heroism and tenacity through six long years of war brought Nazi Germany to unconditional surrender and the Allies to victory.

WINSTON S. CHURCHILL
London, April 23, 1999

Winston Churchill's *Mayflower* Ancestry

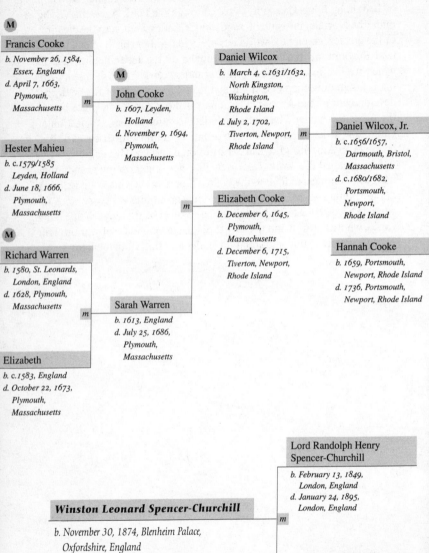

M **Francis Cooke**
b. November 26, 1584,
    Essex, England
d. April 7, 1663,
    Plymouth,
    Massachusetts

Hester Mahieu
b. c.1579/1585
    Leyden, Holland
d. June 18, 1666,
    Plymouth,
    Massachusetts

m

M **John Cooke**
b. 1607, Leyden,
    Holland
d. November 9, 1694,
    Plymouth,
    Massachusetts

m

M **Richard Warren**
b. 1580, St. Leonards,
    London, England
d. 1628, Plymouth,
    Massachusetts

Elizabeth
b. c.1583, England
d. October 22, 1673,
    Plymouth,
    Massachusetts

m

Sarah Warren
b. 1613, England
d. July 25, 1686,
    Plymouth,
    Massachusetts

Daniel Wilcox
b. March 4, c.1631/1632,
    North Kingston,
    Washington,
    Rhode Island
d. July 2, 1702,
    Tiverton, Newport,
    Rhode Island

m

Elizabeth Cooke
b. December 6, 1645,
    Plymouth,
    Massachusetts
d. December 6, 1715,
    Tiverton, Newport,
    Rhode Island

Daniel Wilcox, Jr.
b. c.1656/1657,
    Dartmouth, Bristol,
    Massachusetts
d. c.1680/1682,
    Portsmouth,
    Newport,
    Rhode Island

Hannah Cooke
b. 1659, Portsmouth,
    Newport, Rhode Island
d. 1736, Portsmouth,
    Newport, Rhode Island

**Lord Randolph Henry
Spencer-Churchill**
b. February 13, 1849,
    London, England
d. January 24, 1895,
    London, England

m

Winston Leonard Spencer-Churchill
b. November 30, 1874, Blenheim Palace,
    Oxfordshire, England
d. January 24, 1965, London, England

Jeanette ("Jennie") Jerome
b. January 9, 1854,
    Brooklyn, New York
d. June 29, 1921,
    London, England

M indicates those who voyaged on the *Mayflower*, 1620

m married

Daniel Wilcox

b. 1680,
  Dartmouth, Bristol,
  Massachusetts
d. February 2, 1720,
  Dartmouth, Bristol,
  Massachusetts

m

William Wilcox

b. November 27, 1711,
  Dartmouth, Bristol,
  Massachusetts
d. 1742, Dartmouth,
  Bristol, Massachusetts

m

William Wilcocks

b. August 8, 1739,
  Dartmouth, Bristol,
  Massachusetts
d. 1782

m

Sarah

b. c.1684, Dartmouth,
  Bristol, Massachusetts
d. January 7, 1755

Dorothy Allen

b. January 16, 1707,
  Dartmouth, Bristol,
  Massachusetts
d. 1742, Dartmouth,
  Bristol, Massachusetts

Sarah Smith

b. April 27, 1741,
  Dartmouth, Bristol,
  Massachusetts

Ambrose Hall

b. August 29, 1774,
  Lanesboro, Berkshire,
  Massachusetts
d. October 14, 1827,
  Palmyra, Wayne, New York

m

Leonard Walter Jerome

b. November 3, 1817,
  Pompey, Onondaga,
  New York
m d. March 1891,
  Brighton, Sussex,
  England

David Willcox

b. January 10, 1762,
  Dartmouth, Bristol,
  Massachusetts
d. August 23, 1828,
  Macedon, Wayne, New York

Clarisse Wilcox

b. September 10, 1796,
  Palmyra, Wayne, New York
d. July 1827,
  Palmyra, Wayne, New York

m

Clarissa ("Clara") Hall

b. July 16, 1825,
  Palmyra, Wayne,
  New York
d. April 2, 1895,
  Tunbridge Wells, Kent,
  England

Anna Baker

b. May 27, 1762,
  Massachusetts
d. December 28, 1813,
  Palmyra, Wayne, New York

CONTENTS

AUTHOR'S PREFACE

For the second time in the present century the British Empire and the United States have stood together facing the perils of war on the largest scale known among men, and since the cannons ceased to fire and the bombs to burst, we have become more conscious of our common duty to the human race. Language, law, and the processes by which we have come into being already afforded a unique foundation for drawing together and portraying a concerted task. I thought when I began this work in 1936 that such a unity might well notably influence the destiny of the world. Certainly I do not feel that the need for this has diminished in any way in the twenty years that have passed.

On the contrary, the theme of the work has grown in strength and reality and human thought is broadened. Vast numbers of people on both sides of the Atlantic and throughout the British Commonwealth of Nations have felt a sense of brotherhood. A new generation is at hand. Many practical steps have been taken which carry us far. There is a growing feeling that the English-speaking peoples might point a finger showing the way if things went right, and could of course defend themselves, so far as any of us have the power, if things went wrong.

This book does not seek to rival the works of professional historians. It aims rather to present a personal view on the processes whereby America has achieved its distinctive position and character. I write about the things that appear significant to me and I do so as one not without some experience of historical and violent events in our own time.

Every nation or group of nations has its own tale to tell. Knowledge of the trials and struggles is necessary to all who would comprehend the problems, perils, challenges, and opportunities which confront us today. It is not intended to stir a new spirit of mastery, or create a mood in the study of history which would favour national ambition at the expense of world peace. It may be indeed that an inner selective power may lead to the continuous broadening of our thought. It is in the hope that contemplation of the trials and tribulations of our forefathers may not only fortify the English-speaking peoples of today, but also play some small part in uniting the whole world, that I present this account.

W.S.C.
Chartwell,
Westerham,
Kent
January 15, 1956

PART I

FROM COLONIAL BEGINNINGS TO WORLD POWER

CHAPTER 1

THE ROUND WORLD

THE DISCOVERY of the New World by Christopher Columbus in 1492 heralded the dawn of the sixteenth century
(1500–1599), a period in which extraordinary changes affected the
whole of Europe. Some had been on the move for a long time, but
sprang into full operative force at this moment. For two hundred years
or more the Renaissance had been stirring the thought and spirit of
Italy, and now came forth in the vivid revival of the traditions of ancient Greece and Rome, in so far as these did not affect the foundations
of the Christian faith. The Popes had in the meanwhile become tempo-
ral rulers, with the lusts and pomps of other potentates, yet they
claimed to carry with them the spiritual power as well. The revenues of
the Church were swelled by the sale of "Indulgences" to remit Purga-
tory both for the living and the dead. The offices of bishop and cardinal were bought and sold, and the common people taxed to the limit of
their credulity. These and other abuses in the organisation of the
Church were widely recognised and much resented, but as yet they went
uncorrected. At the same time literature, philosophy, and art flowered
under classical inspiration, and the minds of men to whom study was
open were refreshed and enlarged. These were the humanists, who attempted a reconciliation of classical and Christian teachings, among
the foremost of whom was Erasmus of Rotterdam. To him is due a considerable part of the credit for bringing Renaissance thought to England. Printing enabled knowledge and argument to flow through the
many religious societies which made up the structure of medieval Europe, and from about 1450 onwards printing presses formed the core of

a vast ever-growing domain. There were already sixty universities in the Western world, from Lisbon to Prague, and in the early part of the new century these voluntarily opened up broader paths of study and intercourse which rendered their life more fertile and informal. In the Middle Ages education had largely been confined to training the clergy; now it was steadily extended, and its purpose became to turn out not only priests but lay scholars and well-informed gentlemen. The man of many parts and accomplishments became the Renaissance ideal.

This quickening of the human spirit was accompanied by a questioning of long-held theories. For the first time, in the course of the fifteenth century men began to refer to the preceding millennium as the Middle Ages. Though much that was medieval survived in their minds, men felt they were living on the brink of a new and modern age. It was an age marked not only by splendid achievements in art and architecture, but also by the beginnings of a revolution in science associated with the name of Copernicus. That the earth moved round the sun, as he conclusively proved, and Galileo later asserted on a celebrated occasion, was a novel idea that was to have profound effects upon the human outlook. Hitherto the earth had been thought of as the centre of a universe all designed to serve the needs of man. Now vast new perspectives were opening.

The urge to inquire, to debate, and seek new explanations spread from the field of classical learning into that of religious studies. Greek and even Hebrew texts, as well as Latin, were scrutinised afresh. Inevitably this led to the questioning of accepted religious beliefs. The Renaissance bred the Reformation. In 1517, at the age of thirty-four, Martin Luther, a German priest, denounced the sale of Indulgences, nailed his theses on this and other matters on the door of Wittenberg Castle church, and embarked on his venturesome intellectual foray with the Pope. What began as a protest against Church practices soon became a challenge to Church doctrine. In this struggle Luther displayed qualities of determination and conviction at the peril of the stake which won him his name and fame. He started or gave an impulse to a movement which within a decade swamped the Continent, and proudly bears the general title of the Reformation. It took different forms in different countries, particularly in Switzerland under Zwingli and Calvin. The latter's influence spread from Geneva across France to the Netherlands and Britain, where it was most strongly felt in Scotland.

There are many varieties of Luther's doctrine, but he himself adhered rigorously to the principle of "salvation by faith, not works." This meant that to lead a good and upright life on earth, as many pagans had done, was no guarantee of eternal bliss. Belief in the Christian revelation was vital. The words of Holy Writ and the promptings of individual conscience, not Papal authority, were Luther's guiding lights. He himself believed in predestination. Adam sinned in the Garden of Eden because Almighty God made him do so. Hence the original sin of man. About one-tenth of the human race might escape or have escaped consequential eternal damnation in the intervening years. All monks and nuns alike were, however, entitled to console themselves by getting married. Luther himself set the example by marrying a fugitive nun when he was forty, and lived happily ever after.

The Reformation affected every country in Europe, but none more than Germany. Luther's movement appealed to the nationalism of the German people, who were restive under the exactions of Rome. He gave them a translation of the Bible of which they have remained rightly proud. He also gave the German princes the opportunity to help themselves to Church property. His teachings in the hands of extremists led to a social war in Southern Germany, in which scores of thousands of people perished. Luther himself was passionately on the opposite side to the masses he had inflamed. Though he had used in the coarsest terms the language which roused the mob he did not hesitate to turn on them when they responded. He would go to all lengths to fight the Pope on doctrinal issues, but the oppressed multitude who gave him his strength did not make effective appeal to him. He called them "pigs," and grosser names, and rebuked the "overlords," as he described the aristocracy and well-to-do governing powers, for their slackness in repressing the Peasants' Rebellion.

Heresies there had always been, and over the centuries feeling against the Church had often run strong in almost every country of Europe. But the schism that had begun with Luther was novel and formidable. All the actors in it, the enemies and the defenders of Rome alike, were still deeply influenced by medieval views. They thought of themselves as restorers of the purer ways of ancient times and of the early Church. But the Reformation added to the confusion and uncertainty of an age in which men and states were tugging unwillingly and unwittingly at the anchors that had so long held Europe. After a period of ecclesiastical strife between the Papacy and the Reformation, Protestantism was established over a great part of the Continent under a variety of sects and schools, of which Lutheranism covered the larger area. The Church in Rome, strengthened by the heart-searching Catholic revival known as the Counter-Reformation and in the more worldly sphere by the activities of the Inquisition, proved able to maintain itself through a long series of religious wars. The division between the assailants and defenders of the old order threatened the stability of every state in modern Europe and wrecked the unity of some. England and France came out of the struggle scarred and shaken but in themselves united. A new barrier was created between Ireland and England, a new bond of unity forged between England and Scotland. The Holy Roman Empire of the German people dissolved into a dust of principalities and cities; the Netherlands split into what we now know as Holland and Belgium. Dynasties were threatened, old loyalties forsworn. By the middle of the century the Calvinists were the spearhead of the Protestant attack, the Jesuits the shield and sword of Catholic defence and counterattack. Not for another hundred years would exhaustion and resignation put an end to the revolution that began with Luther. It ended only after Central Europe had been wrecked by the Thirty Years War, and the Peace of Westphalia in 1648 terminated a struggle whose starting-point had been almost forgotten. It was not until the nineteenth century that a greater sense of toleration based upon mutual reverence and respect ruled the souls of men throughout the Christian world.

A well-known Victorian divine and lecturer, Charles Beard, in the 1880's poses some blunt questions:

> Was, then, the Reformation, from the intellectual point of view, a failure? Did it break one yoke only to impose another? We are obliged to confess that, especially in Germany, it soon parted company with free learning; that it turned its back upon culture, that it lost itself in a maze of arid theological controversy, that it held out no hand of welcome to awakening science. . . . Even at a later time it has been the divines who have most loudly declared their allegiance to the theology of the Reformation who have also looked most askance at science and claimed for their statements an entire independence of modern knowledge. I do not know how, on any ordinary theory of the Reformation, it is possible to answer the accusations implied in these facts. The most learned, the profoundest, the most tolerant of modern theologians, would be the most reluctant to accept in their fullness the systems of Melanchthon and of Calvin. . . . The fact is, that while the services which the Reformers rendered to truth and liberty by their revolt against the unbroken supremacy of medieval Christianity cannot be over-estimated, it was impossible for them to settle the questions which they raised. Not merely did the necessary knowledge fail them, but they did not even see the scope of the controversies in which they were engaged. It was their part to

open the flood-gates; and the stream, in spite of their well-meant efforts to check and confine it, has since rushed impetuously on, now destroying old landmarks, now fertilising new fields, but always bringing with it life and refreshment. To look at the Reformation by itself, to judge it only by its theological and ecclesiastical development, is to pronounce it a failure; to consider it as part of a general movement of European thought, to show its essential connection with ripening scholarship and advancing science, to prove its necessary alliance with liberty, to illustrate its slow growth into toleration, is at once to vindicate its past and to promise it the future.*

While the forces of Renaissance and Reformation were gathering strength in Europe the world beyond was yielding its secrets to European explorers, traders, and missionaries. From the days of the ancient Greeks some men had known in theory that the world was round and global. Now in the sixteenth century navigations were to prove it so. The story goes back a long way. In medieval times travellers from Europe had turned their steps to the East, their imagination fired with tales of fabulous kingdoms and wealth lying in regions which had seen the birth of man—stories of the realm of Prester John, variously placed between Central Asia and the modern Abyssinia, and the later, more practical account of the travels of Marco Polo from Venice to China. But Asia too was marching against the West. At one moment it had seemed as if all Europe would succumb to a terrible menace looming up from the East. Heathen Mongol hordes from the heart of Asia, formidable horsemen armed with bows, had rapidly swept over Russia, Poland, Hungary, and in 1241 inflicted simultaneous crushing defeats upon the Germans near Breslau and upon European chivalry near Budapest. Germany and Austria at least lay at their mercy. Providentially in this year the Great Khan died in Mongolia; the Mongol leaders hastened back the thousands of miles to Karakorum, their capital, to elect his successor, and Western Europe escaped.

Throughout the Middle Ages there had been unceasing battle between Christian and infidel on the borders of Eastern and Southern Europe. The people of the frontiers lived in constant terror, the infidel steadily advanced, and in 1453 Constantinople had been captured by the Ottoman Turks. Dangers of the gravest kind now jarred and threatened the wealth and economy of Christian Europe. The destruction of the Byzantine Empire and the Turkish occupation of Asia Minor im-

* *The Reformation of the Sixteenth Century,* by C. Beard (1927 edition), pp. 298–299.

perilled the land route to the East. The road which had nourished the towns and cities of the Mediterranean and founded the fortunes and the greatness of the Genoese and the Venetians was barred. The turmoil spread eastwards, and though the Turks wanted to preserve their trade with Europe for the sake of the tolls they levied, commerce and travel became more and more unsafe.

Italian geographers and navigators had for some time been trying to find a new sea-route to the Orient which would be unhampered by the infidel, but although they had much experience of shipbuilding and navigation from the busy traffic of the Eastern Mediterranean they lacked the capital resources for the hazard of oceanic exploration. Portugal was the first to discover a new path. Helped by English Crusaders, she had achieved her independence in the twelfth century, gradually expelled the Moors from her mainland, and now reached out to the African coastline. Prince Henry the Navigator, grandson of John of Gaunt, had initiated a number of enterprises. Exploring began from Lisbon. All through the later fifteenth century Portuguese mariners had been pushing down the west coast of Africa, seeking for gold and slaves, slowly extending the bounds of the known world, till, in 1487, Bartholomew Diaz rounded the great promontory that marked the end of the African continent. He called it "the Cape of Storms," but the King of Portugal with true insight renamed it "the Cape of Good Hope." The hope was justified; in 1498 Vasco da Gama dropped anchor in the harbour of Calicut; the sea-route was open to the wealth of India and the Farther East.

An event of greater moment for the future of the world was meanwhile taking shape in the mind of a Genoese named Christopher Columbus. Brooding over the dreamlike maps of his fellow-countrymen, he conceived a plan for sailing due west into the Atlantic beyond the known islands in search of yet another route to the East. He married the daughter of a Portuguese sailor who had served with the Navigator, and from his father-in-law's papers he learnt of the great oceanic ventures. In 1486 he sent his brother Bartholomew to seek English backing for the enterprise. Bartholomew was captured by pirates off the French coast, and when he finally arrived in England and won the notice of Henry Tudor, the new King, it was too late. Christopher, however, had gathered the support of the joint Spanish sovereigns, Ferdinand of Aragon and Isabella of Castile, and under their patronage in 1492 he set sail into the unknown from Palos, in Andalusia. After a voyage of three months he made landfall in one of the islands of the Bahamas.

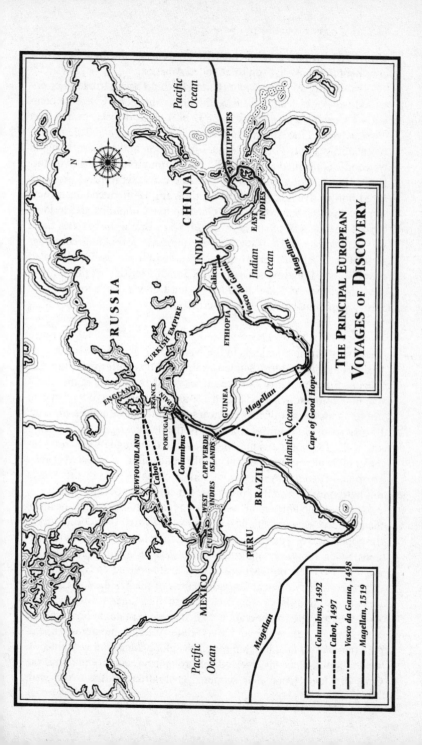

THE PRINCIPAL EUROPEAN
VOYAGES OF DISCOVERY

Pacific
Ocean

PHILIPPINES

CHINA

INDIA

EAST
INDIES

Calicut

Vasco da Gama

Indian
Ocean

Magellan

RUSSIA

N

ETHIOPIA

TURKISH EMPIRE

ENGLAND

FRANCE

SPAIN

PORTUGAL

GUINEA

Magellan

Cape of Good Hope

NEWFOUNDLAND

Cabot

Columbus

CAPE VERDE
ISLANDS

Atlantic
Ocean

WEST
INDIES

CUBA

MEXICO

PERU

BRAZIL

Magellan

Pacific
Ocean

——— Columbus, 1492
----- Cabot, 1497
—·—· Vasco da Gama, 1498
——— Magellan, 1519

Unwittingly he had discovered, not a new route to the East, but a new continent in the West, soon to be called America.

It was nearly a hundred years before England began to exert her potential sea-power. Her achievements during this period were by comparison meagre. The merchants of Bristol tried to seek a north-west passage beyond the Atlantic to the Far East, but they had little success or encouragement. Their colleagues in London and Eastern England were more concerned with the solid profits from trade with the Netherlands. Henry Tudor, however, appreciated private enterprise, provided it did not involve him in disputes with Spain. He financed an expedition by John Cabot, who was a Genoese like Columbus and lived in Bristol. In 1497 Cabot struck land near Cape Breton Island. But there was little prospect of trade, and an immense forbidding continent seemed to block further advance. On a second voyage Cabot sailed down the coast of America in the direction of Florida, but this was too near the region of Spanish efforts. Upon Cabot's death the cautious Henry abandoned his Atlantic enterprise.

The arrival of the Spaniards in the New World, and their discovery of precious metals, had led them into wordy conflict with the Portuguese. As one of the motives of both countries was the spreading of the Christian faith into undiscovered heathen lands they appealed to the Pope, in whose hands the gift of new countries was at this time conceived to lie. By a series of Bulls in the 1490's the Borgia Pope Alexander VI drew a line across the world dividing the Spanish and Portuguese spheres. This remarkable dispensation stimulated the conclusion of a treaty between Spain and Portugal. A north-south line 370 leagues west of the Azores was agreed upon, and the Portuguese felt entitled to occupy Brazil.

Although the Portuguese were first in the field of oceanic adventure their country was too small to sustain such efforts. It is said that half the population of Portugal died in trying to hold their overseas possessions. Spain soon overtook them. In the year of Columbus's first voyage, Granada, the only Moorish city which survived on Spanish soil, had fallen to the last great Crusading army of the Middle Ages. Henceforward the Spaniards were free to turn their energies to the New World. In less than a generation a Portuguese captain, in Spanish pay, Magellan, set out on the voyage to South America and across the Pacific that was to take his ship round the globe. Magellan was killed in the Philippines, but his chief officer brought his ship home round the Cape of Good Hope. The scattered civilisations of the world were being drawn together, and the new discoveries were to give the little kingdom in the northern sea a fresh importance. Here was to be the successor both of Portugal and Spain, though the time for entering into the inheritance was not yet. But already the spices of the East were travelling by sea to the European market at Antwerp. The whole course of trade was shifted and revolutionised. The overland route languished; the primacy of the Italian cities was eclipsed by North-West Europe; and the future lay not in the Mediterranean, but on the shores of the Atlantic, where the new Powers, England, France, and Holland, had ports and harbours which gave easy access to the oceans.

The wealth of the New World soon affected the old order in Europe. In the first half of the sixteenth century Cortes overcame the Aztec empire of Mexico and Pizarro conquered the Incas of Peru. The vast mineral treasures of these lands now began to pour across the Atlantic. By channels which multiplied gold and silver flowed into Europe. So did new commodities, tobacco, potatoes, and American sugar. The old continent to which these new riches came was itself undergoing a transformation. After a long halt its population was again growing and production on the farms and in the workshops was expanding. There was a widespread demand for more money to pay for new expeditions, new buildings, new enterprises, and new methods of government. The manipulation of finance was little understood either by rulers or by the mass of the people, and the first recourse of impoverished princes was to debase their currency. Prices therefore rose sharply, and when Luther posted his theses at Wittenberg the value of money was already rapidly falling. Under the impulse of American silver there now swept across the Continent a series of inflationary waves unparalleled until the twentieth century. The old world of landlords and peasants found it harder to carry on, and throughout Europe a new force gathered influence and honour with the overlords and began to exert its power. For merchants, traders, and bankers it was an age of opportunity. Most famous among them perhaps was the Fugger family of Germany, who gained a graceful reputation by placing their immense wealth at the service of Renaissance art. On their financial resourcefulness both Popes and Emperors at one time depended.

As ever in times of rapid inflation, there was much hardship and many difficulties in adjustment. But a strong sensation of new growth and well-being abounded, and ultimately every class benefited by the general amelioration. For a world which, a century before, had lost perhaps a third of its population by the Black Death there was a wonderful stimulus of mind and body. Men were groping their way into a larger age, with a freer interchange of more goods and services and with far greater numbers taking an effective part. The New World had opened its spacious doors, not only geographically by adding North and South America as places for Europe to live in, but by enlarging its whole way of life and outlook and the uses it could make of all it had.

CHAPTER 2

RIVALRY FOR
THE NEW WORLD

B Y THE LATTER PART of the sixteenth century, a deepening rivalry between England and Spain in the New World was inexorably leading the two European powers towards war. The chances were heavily weighted in favour of Spain. From the mines of Mexico and Peru there came a stream of silver and gold which so fortified the material power of the Spanish Empire that King Philip could equip his forces beyond all known scales. The position was well understood in the ruling circles of England. So long as Spain controlled the wealth of the New World she could launch and equip a multitude of Armadas; the treasure must therefore be arrested at its source or captured from the ships which conveyed it across the oceans. In the hope of strengthening her own finances and harassing the enemy's preparations against the Netherlands and ultimately against herself, [England's Queen] Elizabeth had accordingly sanctioned a number of unofficial expeditions against the Spanish coasts and colonies in South America. These had continued for some time, and as yet without open declaration of war, but she had come to realise that scattered raids of which she professed no prior knowledge could do no lasting harm to the Spanish Empire beyond the seas or the Spanish power in Northern Europe. Gradually therefore these expeditions had assumed an official character, and the Royal Navy surviving from the days of Henry VIII was rebuilt and reorganised by John Hawkins, son of a Plymouth merchant, who had formerly traded with the Portuguese possessions in Brazil. Hawkins had learnt his seamanship in slave-running on the West African coast and in shipping negroes to the Spanish colonies. In 1573 he was appointed Treasurer and Controller of the Navy. He had moreover educated an apt pupil, a young adventurer from Devon, Francis Drake.

This "Master Thief of the unknown world," as his Spanish contemporaries called Drake, became the terror of their ports and crews. His avowed object was to force England into open conflict with Spain, and his attacks on the Spanish treasure ships, his plundering of Spanish possessions on the western coast of the South American continent on his voyage round the world in 1577, and raids on Spanish harbours in Europe, all played their part in driving Spain to war. From their experiences on the Spanish Main the English seamen knew they could meet the challenge so long as reasonable equality was maintained. With the ships that Hawkins built they could fight and sink anything the Spaniards might send against them.

Meanwhile Elizabeth's seamen had been gaining experience in unexplored waters. Spain was deliberately blocking the commercial enterprise of other nations in the New World so far as it was then known. A Devon gentleman, Humphrey Gilbert, began to look elsewhere, and was the first to interest the Queen in finding a route to China, or Cathay as it was called, by the North-West. He was a well-read man who had studied the achievements of contemporary explorers. He knew there were plenty of adventurers schooled in the straggling fighting in France and in the Netherlands on whose services he could call. In 1576 he wrote *A Discourse to prove a Passage by the North-West to Cathaia and the East Indies.* His book closed with a notable challenge: "He is not worthy to live at all, that for fear or danger of death shunneth his country's service and his own honour; seeing death is inevitable and the fame of virtue is immortal." His ideas inspired the voyages of Martin Frobisher, to whom the Queen granted a licence to explore. The Court and the City financed the expedition, and two small ships of twenty-five tons sailed in search of gold. Having charted the bleak coasts round Hudson Strait Frobisher came back. High hopes were entertained that the samples of black ore he brought with him might contain gold. There was disappointment when the ore was assayed and proved worthless. No quick riches were to be gained from adventures in the North-West.

Gilbert, however, was undaunted. He was the first Englishman who realised that the value of these voyages did not lie only in finding precious metals. There were too many people in England. Perhaps they could settle in the new lands. The idea of planting colonies in America now began to take hold of men's imaginations. A few bold spirits were already dreaming of New Englands that would arise across the ocean. At first they had strictly practical aims in mind. In the hope of transporting the needy unemployed to the New World, and of finding new markets among the natives for English cloth, Gilbert himself obtained a charter from Elizabeth in 1578, "to discover . . . such remote heathen and barbarous lands not actually possessed by any Christian prince or people as to him . . . shall seem good and the same to hold occupy and enjoy. . . ." With six ships manned by many gentlemen adventurers, including his own half-brother, Walter Raleigh, of whom more hereafter, he made several hopeful voyages, but none met with success.

In 1583 Gilbert took possession of Newfoundland in the Queen's name, but no permanent settlement was made. Resolved to try again in the following year, he set out for home. The little convoy encountered terrible seas, "breaking short and high pyramid-wise." A narrative written by one Edward Hays survives: "Monday the 9th September in the afternoon, the frigate was near cast away, oppressed by waves, yet at that time recovered: and giving forth signs of joy, the General, sitting abaft with a book in his hand, cried out to us in the *Hind* so oft as we approached within hearing, 'We are as near to heaven by sea as by land.' " That night at twelve o'clock the lights of Gilbert's ship, the *Squirrel,* suddenly disappeared. The first great English pioneer of the West had gone to his death. Walter Raleigh tried to continue Gilbert's work. In 1585 a small colony was established on Roanoke Island, off the American continent, and christened Virginia in honour of the Queen. It was a vague term which came to include both the modern state and North Carolina. This venture also foundered, as did a second attempt two years later. But by now the threat from Spain was looming large, and to meet it all endeavour was concentrated at home. Colonial efforts were postponed for another twenty years by the Spanish War. In national resources the struggle that broke out was desperately unequal, but the Queen's seamen had received an unrivalled training which was to prove England's salvation.

The Spaniards had long contemplated an enterprise against England. They realised that English intervention threatened their attempts to reconquer the Netherlands and that unless England was overwhelmed the turmoil might continue indefinitely. Since the year 1585 they had been gathering information from many sources. English exiles sent lengthy reports to Madrid. Numerous agents supplied Philip with maps and statistics. The Spanish archives contain several draft plans for the invasion of England.

Troops were not the difficulty. If order were maintained for a while in the Netherlands an expeditionary force could be detached from the

Spanish army. A corps was deemed sufficient. The building and assembly of a fleet was a more formidable undertaking. Most of the King of Spain's ships came from his Italian possessions and were built for use in the Mediterranean. They were unsuited to a voyage round the western coasts of Europe and up the Channel. The galleons constructed for the trade routes to the Spanish colonies in South America were too unwieldy. But in the year 1580 Philip II had annexed Portugal, and the Portuguese naval constructors had not been dominated by the Mediterranean. They had experimented with classes of ships for action in the South Atlantic, and Portuguese galleons therefore formed the basis of the fleet which was now concentrated in the harbour of Lisbon. Every available vessel was summoned into Western Spanish waters, including even the privately owned galleons of the convoying force named the Indian Guard. Preparations were delayed for a year by Drake's famous raid on Cadiz in 1587. In this "singeing of the King of Spain's beard" a large quantity of stores and ships was destroyed. Nevertheless in May 1588 the Armada was ready. A hundred and thirty ships were assembled, carrying 2,500 guns and more than 30,000 men, two-thirds of them soldiers. Twenty were galleons, forty-four were armed merchantmen, and eight were Mediterranean galleys. The rest were either small craft or unarmed transports. Their aim was to sail up the Channel, embark the expeditionary corps of 16,000 veterans from the Netherlands under Alexander of Parma, and land it on the south coast of England.

The renowned Spanish Admiral Santa Cruz was now dead, and the command was entrusted to the Duke of Medina-Sidonia, who had many misgivings about the enterprise. His tactics followed the Mediterranean model of grappling with the enemy ships and gaining victory by boarding. His fleet was admirably equipped for carrying large numbers of men; it was strong in heavy short-range cannon, but weak in long-distance culverins—which was why the English kept out of range until the last battle. The seamen were few in proportion to the soldiers. These were recruited from the dregs of the Spanish population and commanded by army officers of noble families who had no experience of naval warfare. Many of the vessels were in bad repair; the provisions supplied under a corrupt system of private contract were insufficient and rotten; the drinking water leaked from butts of unseasoned wood. Their commander had no experience of war at sea, and had begged the King to excuse him from so novel an adventure.

The English plan was to gather a fleet in one of the south-western ports, intercept the enemy at the western entrance to the Channel, and concentrate troops in the south-east to meet Parma's army from the

Flemish shore. It was uncertain where the attack would fall, but the prevailing westerly winds made it likely that the Armada would sail up the Channel, join Parma, and force a landing on the Essex coast.

The nation was united in the face of the Spanish preparations. Leading Catholics were interned in the Isle of Ely, but as a body their loyalty to the Crown was unshaken. An army was assembled at Tilbury which reached twenty thousand men, under the command of Lord Leicester. This, with the muster in the adjacent counties, constituted a force which should not be underrated. While the Armada was still off the coasts of England Queen Elizabeth reviewed the army at Tilbury and addressed them in these stirring words:

> My loving people, we have been persuaded by some that are careful for our safety to take heed how we commit ourselves to armed multitudes, for fear of treachery. But I assure you I do not desire to live to distrust my faithful and loving people. Let tyrants fear. I have always so behaved myself that, under God, I have placed my chiefest strength and safeguard in the loyal hearts and goodwill of my subjects; and therefore I am come amongst you, as you see, resolved, in the midst and heat of the battle, to live or die amongst you all, to lay down for my God, and for my kingdom, and for my people, my honour and my blood, even in the dust. I know I have the body of a weak and feeble woman, but I have the heart and stomach of a king, and of a king of England too, and think foul scorn that Parma or Spain or any prince of Europe should dare to invade the borders of my realm; to which, rather than any dishonour shall grow by me, I myself will take up arms, I myself will be your general, judge and rewarder of every one of your virtues in the field. I know already for your forwardness you have deserved rewards and crowns; and we do assure you, in the word of a prince, they shall be duly paid you.

Hawkins's work for the Navy was now to be tested. He had begun over the years to revise the design of English ships from his experience of buccaneering raids in colonial waters. The castles which towered above the galleon decks had been cut down; keels were deepened, and design was concentrated on sea-worthiness and speed. Most notable of all, heavier long-range guns were mounted. Cannon were traditionally deemed "an ignoble arm," fit only for an opening salvo to a grappling fight, but Hawkins, with ships built to weather any seas, opposed hand-to-hand fighting and advocated battering the enemy from a distance with the new guns. The English sea-captains were eager to try these novel tactics against the huge overmasted enemy galleons, with their flat bottoms and a tendency to drift in a high wind. In spite of Hawkins's efforts only thirty-four of the Queen's ships, carrying six thousand men, could put to sea in 1588. As was the custom, however, all available privately owned vessels were hastily collected and armed for the service of the Government, and a total of a hundred and ninety-seven ships was mustered; but at least half of them were too small to be of much service.

The Queen had urged her seamen to "keep an eye upon Parma," and she was nervous of sending the main fleet as far west as Plymouth. Drake was for bolder measures. In a dispatch of March 30, 1588, he proposed sending the main body to attack a port on the Spanish coast—not Lisbon, which was well fortified, but somewhere near by, so as to force the Armada to sea in defence of the coastline. Thus, it was argued, the English would be certain of engaging the Spanish fleet and there would be no danger of its slipping past them on a favourable wind into the Channel.

The Government preferred the much more perilous idea of stationing isolated squadrons at intervals along the south coast to meet all possible lines of attack. They insisted on concentrating a small squadron of the Queen's ships at the eastern end of the Channel to keep watch on Parma. Drake and his superior, Lord Howard of Effingham, the commander of the English fleet, were alarmed and impatient, and with the greatest difficulty prevented a further dispersion of their forces. A southerly gale stopped their attacking the Spanish coast, and they were driven into Plymouth with their supplies exhausted and scurvy raging through the ships.

In the event they had plenty of time to consider their strategy. The Armada left the Tagus on May 20, but was smitten by the same storms which had repulsed Howard and Drake. Two of their 1,000-ton ships were dismasted. They put in to refit at Corunna, and did not set sail again until July 12. News of their approach off the Lizard was brought into Plymouth harbour on the evening of July 19. The English fleet had to put out of the Sound the same night against light adverse winds which freshened the following day. A sober nautical account of the operation is preserved in Howard's letter to Walsingham of July 21:

> Although the wind was very scant we first warped out of harbour that night, and upon Saturday turned out very hardly, the wind being at south-west; and about three o'clock of the afternoon descried the Spanish fleet, and did what we could to work for the wind, which [by this] morning we had recovered, descrying their fleet to consist of 120 sail, whereof there are four galleases [galleys] and many ships of

great burden. At nine of the clock we gave them fight, which continued until one.*

If Medina-Sidonia had attacked the English vessels to leeward of his
ships as they struggled to clear the land on the Saturday there would have
been a disaster. But his instructions bound him to sail up the Channel,
unite with Parma, and help transport to England the veteran troops assembled near Dunkirk. His report to Madrid shows how little he realised
his opportunity. By difficult, patient, precarious tacking the English fleet
got to windward of him, and for nine days hung upon the Armada as it
ran before the westerly wind up the Channel, pounding away with their
long-range guns at the lumbering galleons. They had gained the weather
gauge. On July 23 the wind sank and both fleets lay becalmed off Port-
land Bill. The Spaniards attempted a counter-attack with Neapolitan
galleys, rowed by hundreds of slaves, but Drake, followed by Howard,
swept in upon the main body, and, as Howard reported, "the Spaniards
were forced to give way and flocked together like sheep."

A further engagement followed on the 25th off the Isle of Wight. It
looked as if the Spaniards planned to seize the island as a base. But as
the westerly breeze blew stronger the English still lay to windward and
drove them once more to sea in the direction of Calais, where Medina,
ignorant of Parma's movements, hoped to collect news. The Channel
passage was a torment to the Spaniards. The guns of the English ships
raked the decks of the galleons, killing the crews and demoralising the
soldiers. The English suffered hardly any loss.

Medina then made a fatal mistake. He anchored in Calais Roads.
The Queen's ships which had been stationed in the eastern end of the
Channel joined the main fleet in the straits, and the whole sea-power of
England was now combined. A council of war held in the English flag-
ship during the evening of July 28 resolved to attack. The decisive engagement opened. After darkness had fallen eight ships from the
eastern squadron which had been filled with explosives and prepared as
fire-ships—the torpedoes of those days—were sent against the crowded
Spanish fleet at anchor in the roads. Lying on their decks, the Spanish
crews must have seen unusual lights creeping along the decks of strange
vessels moving towards them. Suddenly a series of explosions shook
the air, and flaming hulks drifted towards the anchored Armada. The
Spanish captains cut their cables and made for the open sea. Collisions
without number followed. One of the largest galleys, the *San Lorenzo,*

* Laughton, *Defeat of the Spanish Armada* (Navy Records Society, 1894), vol. i,
p. 273.

lost its rudder and drifted aground in Calais harbour, where the Governor interned the crew. The rest of the fleet, with a south-south-west wind behind it, made eastwards to Gravelines.

Medina now sent messengers to Parma announcing his arrival, and by dawn on July 29 he was off the sandbanks of Gravelines expecting to find Parma's troops ready shipped in their transports. But there was no sail to be seen. The tides in Dunkirk harbour were at the neap. It was only possible to sail out with a favourable wind upon a spring tide. Neither condition was present. The army and the transports were not at their rendezvous. The Spaniards turned to face their pursuers. A long and desperate fight raged for eight hours, a confused conflict of ships engaging at close quarters. The official report sent to the English Government was brief: "Howard in fight spoiled a great number of the Spaniards, sank three and drove four or five on the banks." The English had completely exhausted their ammunition, and but for this hardly a Spanish ship would have got away. Yet Howard himself scarcely realised the magnitude of his victory. "Their force is wonderful great and strong," he wrote on the evening after the battle, "yet we pluck their feathers by little and little."

The tormented Armada now sailed northwards out of the fight. Their one aim was to make for home. The horrors of the long voyage round the north of Scotland began. Not once did they turn upon the small, silent ships which followed them in their course. Neither side had enough ammunition.

The homeward voyage of the Armada proved the qualities of the Spanish seamen. Facing mountainous seas and racing tides, they escaped from their pursuers. The English ships, short of food and shot, their crews grumbling at their wretched outfits, were compelled to turn southwards to the Channel ports. The weather helped the Spaniards. The westerly wind drove two of the galleons as wrecks upon the coast of Norway; but then it shifted. As Medina recorded, "We passed the isles at the north of Scotland, and we are now sailing towards Spain with the wind at north-east." Sailing southwards, they were forced to make for the western coast of Ireland to replenish their supplies of water. They had already cast their horses and mules into the sea. The decision to put in on the Irish coast was disastrous. Their ships had been shattered by the English cannonades and now were struck by the autumn gales. Seventeen went ashore. The search for water cost more than five thousand Spanish lives. Nevertheless over sixty-five ships, about half of the fleet that had put to sea, reached Spanish ports during the month of October.

The English had not lost a single ship, and scarcely a hundred men. But their captains were disappointed. For the last thirty years they had believed themselves superior to their opponents. They had now found themselves fighting a much bigger fleet than they had imagined the Spaniards could put to sea. Their own ships had been sparingly equipped. Their ammunition had run short at a crucial moment. The gunnery of the merchant vessels had proved poor and half the enemy's fleet had got away. There were no boastings; they recorded their dissatisfactions.

But to the English people as a whole the defeat of the Armada came as a miracle. For thirty years the shadow of Spanish power had darkened the political scene. A wave of religious emotion filled men's minds. One of the medals struck to commemorate the victory bears the inscription *"Afflavit Deus et dissipantur"*—"God blew and they were scattered."

Elizabeth and her seamen knew how true this was. The Armada had indeed been bruised in battle, but it was demoralised and set on the run by the weather. Yet the event was decisive. The English seamen might well have triumphed. Though limited in supplies and ships the new tactics of Hawkins had brought success. The nation was transported with relief and pride. Shakespeare was writing *King John* a few years later. His words struck into the hearts of his audiences:

> *Come the three corners of the world in arms,*
> *And we shall shock them. Nought shall make us rue*
> *If England to itself do rest but true.*

With 1588 the crisis of the reign was past. England had emerged from the Armada year as a first-class Power. She had resisted the weight of the mightiest empire that had been seen since Roman times. Her people awoke to a consciousness of their greatness, and the last years of Elizabeth's reign saw a welling up of national energy and enthusiasm focusing upon the person of the Queen. In the year following the Armada the first three books were published of Spenser's *Faerie Queene*, in which Elizabeth is hymned as Gloriana. Poets and courtiers alike paid their homage to the sovereign who symbolised the great achievement. Elizabeth had schooled a generation of Englishmen.

The success of the seamen pointed the way to wide opportunities of winning wealth and fame in daring expeditions. In 1589 Richard Hakluyt published his magnificent book, *The Principal Navigations, Traffics and Discoveries of the English Nation*. Here in their own words the audacious navigators tell their story. Hakluyt speaks for the thrusting spirit of the age when he proclaims that the English nation, "in searching the most opposite corners and quarters of the world, and, to speak plainly, in compassing the vast globe of the earth more than once, have excelled all the nations and peoples of the earth." Before the reign came to a close another significant enterprise took its beginning. For years past Englishmen had been probing their way through to the East, round the Cape of Good Hope and overland across the expanses of the Middle East. Their ventures led to the founding of the East India Company. At the start it was a small and struggling affair, with a capital of only £72,000. Dazzling dividends were to be won from this investment. The British Empire in India, which was to be painfully built up in the course of the next three centuries, owes its origins to the charter granted by Queen Elizabeth to a group of London merchants and financiers in the year 1600.

The young men who now rose to prominence in the Court of the ageing Queen plagued their mistress to allow them to try their hand in many enterprises. The coming years resound with attacks upon the forces and allies of Spain throughout the world—expeditions to Cadiz, to the Azores, into the Caribbean Sea, to the Low Countries, and, in support of the Huguenots, to the northern coasts of France. The story is one of confused running fights, conducted with slender resources and culminating in few great moments. The war against Spain, which had never been officially declared, extended its heavy burden into the first year of the reign of Elizabeth's successor. The policy of the English Government was to distract the enemy in every quarter of the world, and by subsidising the Protestant elements in the Low Countries and in France to prevent any concentration of force against themselves. At the same time England intervened to prevent the Spaniards from seizing ports on the Norman and Breton coasts which might be used as bases for another invasion. As a result of these continued though rather meagre efforts the slow victory of the Dutch in Holland and the Huguenots in France brought its reward. The eventual triumph of Henry of Navarre, the Protestant champion and heir to the French throne, was due as much to his acceptance of the Catholic faith as to victories in the field. Paris, as he is supposed to have said, was worth a Mass. His decision put an end to the French religious wars and removed the danger to England of a Spanish-backed monarch in Paris. The Dutch too were beginning to hold their own. The Island was at last secure.

But there was no way of delivering a decisive stroke against Spain. The English Government had no money for further efforts. The total revenues of the Crown hardly exceeded £300,000 a year, including the fruits of taxation granted by Parliament. Out of this sum all expenses of Court and Government had to be met. The cost of defeating the Armada is reckoned to have amounted to £160,000, and the Netherlands expeditionary force at one stage was calling for £126,000 a year. The lights of enthusiasm slowly faded out. In 1595 Raleigh again tried his hand, this time in search of Eldorado in Guiana. But his expedition brought no profits home. At the same time Drake and the veteran Hawkins, now in his sixties, set out on a last voyage. Hawkins fell ill, and as his fleet was anchoring off Porto Rico he died in his cabin. Drake, cast down by the death of his old patron, sailed on to attack the rich city of Panama. With a dash of his former spirit he swept into the bay of Nombre de Dios. But conditions were now very different. The early days had gone for ever. Spanish government in the New World was well equipped and well armed. The raid was beaten off. The English fleet put out to sea, and in January 1596 Francis Drake, having assumed his armour to meet death like a soldier, expired in his ship. John Stow, a contemporary English chronicler, writes of him, "He was as famous in Europe and America as Tamburlaine in Asia and Africa."

As the conflict with Spain drew inconclusively on, and both sides struck at each other in ever-growing, offensive exhaustion, the heroic age of sea fights passed away. One epic moment has survived in the annals of the English nation—the last fight of the *Revenge* at Flores, in the Azores. "In the year 1591," says Bacon, "was that memorable fight of an English ship called the *Revenge,* under the command of Sir Richard Grenville, memorable (I say) even beyond credit and to the height of some heroical fable: and though it were a defeat, yet it exceeded a victory; being like the act of Samson, that killed more men at his death, than he had done in the time of all his life. This ship, for the space of fifteen hours, sate like a stag amongst hounds at bay, and was sieged and fought with, in turn, by fifteen great ships of Spain, part of a navy of fifty-five ships in all; the rest like abettors looking on afar off. And amongst the fifteen ships that fought, the great *San Philippo* was one; a ship of fifteen hundred ton, prince of the twelve *Sea Apostles,* which was right glad when she was shifted off from the *Revenge.* This brave ship the *Revenge,* being manned only with two hundred soldiers and marines, whereof eighty lay sick, yet nevertheless after a fight maintained (as was said) of fifteen hours, and two ships of the enemy sunk by her side, besides many more torn and battered and great slaughter of men, never came to be entered, but was taken by composition; the enemies themselves having in admiration the virtue of the commander and the whole tragedy of that ship."

It is well to remember the ordinary seamen who sailed in ships sometimes as small as twenty tons into the wastes of the North and South

Atlantic, ill-fed and badly paid, on risky adventures backed by inadequate capital. These men faced death in many forms—death by disease, death by drowning, death from Spanish pikes and guns, death by starvation and cold on uninhabited coasts, death in the Spanish prisons. The Admiral of the English fleet, Lord Howard of Effingham, spoke their epitaph: "God send us to sea in such a company together again, when need is."

CHAPTER 3

THE *MAYFLOWER*

T HE STRUGGLE with Spain had long absorbed the energies of Englishmen, and in the last years of Queen Elizabeth few fresh enterprises had been carried out upon the oceans. For a while little was heard of the New World. Hawkins and Drake in their early voyages had opened up broad prospects for England in the Caribbean; Frobisher and others had penetrated deeply into the Arctic recesses of Canada in search of a north-west passage to Asia; but the lure of exploration and trade had given way to the demands of war. The novel idea of founding colonies also received a setback. Gilbert, Raleigh, and Grenville had been its pioneers. Their bold plans had come to nothing, but they left behind them an inspiring tradition. Now after a lapse of time their endeavours were taken up by new figures, less glittering, more practical and luckier. Piecemeal and from many motives the English-speaking communities in North America were founded. The change came in 1604, when James I made his treaty of peace with Spain. Discussion that had been stimulated by Richard Hakluyt's *Discourse on Western Planting* was revived. Serious argument by a group of writers of which he was the head gained a new hearing and a new pertinence. For there were troubles in England. People reduced to beggary and vagabondage were many, and new outlets were wanted for the nation's energies and resources.

The steady rise in prices had caused much hardship to wage-earners. Though the general standard of living improved during the sixteenth century, a wide range of prices rose sixfold, and wages only twofold. Industry was oppressed by excessive Government regulation. The medieval system of craftsmen's guilds, which was still enforced, made the entry of young apprentices harsh and difficult. The squirearchy, strong in its political alliance with the Crown, owned most of the land and ran all the local government. The march of enclosures which they pursued drove many English peasants off the land. The whole scheme of life seemed to have contracted and the framework of social organisation had hardened. There were many without advantage, hope, or livelihood in the New Age. Colonies, it was thought, might help to solve these distressing problems.

The Government was not uninterested. Trade with lively colonies promised an increase in the customs revenue on which the Crown heavily depended. Merchants and the richer landed gentry saw new opportunities across the Atlantic for profitable investment, and an escape from cramping restrictions on industry and the general decline of European trade during the religious wars. Capital was available for overseas experiments. Raleigh's attempts had demonstrated the ill-success of individual effort, but a new method of financing large-scale trading enterprises was evolving in the shape of the joint stock company. In 1606 a group of speculators acquired a royal charter creating the Virginia company. It is interesting to see how early speculation in its broadest sense begins to play its part in the American field.

A plan was carefully drawn up in consultation with experts such as Hakluyt, but they had little practical experience and underestimated the difficulties of the profoundly novel departure they were making. After all, it is not given to many to start a nation. It was a few hundred people who now took the first step. A settlement was made at Jamestown, in the Chesapeake Bay, on the Virginian coast, in May 1607. By the following spring half the population was dead from malaria, cold, and famine. After a long and heroic struggle the survivors became self-supporting, but profits to the promoters at home were very small. Captain John Smith, a military adventurer from the Turkish wars, became the dictator of the tiny colony, and enforced harsh discipline. The marriage of his lieutenant John Rolfe with Pocahontas, the daughter of an Indian chief, caused a sensation in the English capital. But the London company had little control and the administration of the colony was rough-and-ready. The objects of the directors were mixed and ill-defined. Some thought that colonisation would reduce poverty and crime in England. Others looked for profit to the fisheries of the North American coast, or hoped for raw materials to reduce their dependence on the exports from the Spanish colonies. All were wrong, and Virginia's fortune sprang from a novel and unexpected cause. By chance a crop of tobacco was planted, and the soil proved benevolent. Tobacco had been introduced into Europe by the Spaniards and the habit of smoking was spreading fast. Demand for tobacco was great and growing, and the profits on the Virginia crop were high. Smallholders were bought out, big estates were formed, and the colony began to stand on its own feet. As it grew and prospered its society came to resemble the Mother Country, with rich planters in the place of squires. They were not long in developing independence of mind and a sturdy capacity for self-government. Distance from the authorities in London greatly aided their desires.

Beneath the drab exterior of Jacobean England, with favouritism at Court and humiliation in Europe, other and more vital forces were at work. The Elizabethan bishops had driven the nobler and tougher Puritan spirits out of the Established Church. But though they destroyed the organisation of the party small illegal gatherings of religious extremists continued to meet. There was no systematic persecution, but petty restrictions and spyings obstructed their peaceful worship. A congregation at Scrooby, in Nottinghamshire, led by one of their pastors, John Robinson, and by William Brewster, the Puritan bailiff of the manor of the Archbishop of York, resolved to seek freedom of worship abroad. In 1607 they left England and settled at Leyden, hoping to find asylum among the tolerant and industrious Dutch. For ten years these Puritan parishioners struggled for a decent existence. They were small farmers and agricultural workers, out of place in a maritime industrial community, barred by their nationality from the guilds of craftsmen, without capital and without training. The only work they could get was rough manual labour. They were persistent and persevering, but a bleak future faced them in Holland. They were too proud of their birthright to be absorbed by the Dutch. The authorities had been sympathetic, but in practice unhelpful. The Puritans began to look elsewhere.

Emigration to the New World presented itself as an escape from a sinful generation. There they might gain a livelihood unhampered by Dutch guilds, and practise their creed unharassed by English clerics. As one of their number records, "The place they had thoughts on was some of those vast and unpeopled countries of America, which are fruitful and fit for habitation; being devoid of all civil inhabitants;

where there are only savage and brutish men, which range up and down little otherwise than the wild beasts of the same."

Throughout the winter of 1616–17, when Holland was threatened with a renewal of war with Spain, there were many discussions among the anxious community. A mortal risk and high adventure lay before them. To the perils of the unknown, to famine, and the record of past failures were added gruesome tales of the Indians; how they flayed men with the shells of fishes and cut off steaks which they broiled upon the coals before the eyes of the victims. But William Bradford, who was to become Governor of the new colony, pleaded the argument of the majority. In his *History of the Plymouth Plantation* he has expressed the views they held at the time. "All great and honourable actions are accompanied with great difficulties, and must be both enterprised and overcome with answerable courages. The dangers were great, but not desperate; the difficulties were many, but not invincible. For though there were many of them likely, yet they were not certain; it might be sundry of the things feared might never befall; others by provident care and the use of good means might in a great measure be prevented; and all of them, through the help of God, by fortitude and patience, might either be borne or overcome. Such attempts were not to be made and undertaken without good ground and reason; not rashly or lightly, as many have done for curiosity or hope of gain. But their condition was not ordinary; their ends were good and honourable, their calling lawful, and urgent; and therefore they might expect the blessing of God in their proceeding. Yea, though they should lose their lives in this action, yet might they have comfort in the same, and their endeavours would be honourable. They lived here but as men in exile, and in a poor condition; and as great miseries might possibly befall them in this place, for the twelve years of truce were now out, and there was nothing but beating of drums, and preparing for war, the events whereof are always uncertain. The Spaniard might prove as cruel as the savages of America, and the famine and pestilence as sore here as there, and their liberty less to look out for remedy."

Their first plan was to settle in Guiana, but then they realised it was impossible to venture out upon their own. Help must come from England. They accordingly sent agents to London to negotiate with the only body interested in emigration, the Virginia company. One of the members of its council was an influential Parliamentarian, Sir Edwin Sandys. Supported by the London merchant backers of the company, he furthered the project. Here were ideal settlers, sober, hardworking, and skilled in agriculture. They insisted upon freedom of worship, and it would be necessary to placate the Anglican bishops. Sandys and the emissaries from Holland went to see the King. James was sceptical. He asked how the little band proposed to support itself in the company's territory in America. "By fishing," they replied. This appealed to James. "So God have my soul," he exclaimed in one of his more agreeable remarks, "'tis an honest trade! It was the Apostles' own calling."

The Leyden community was granted a licence to settle in America, and arrangements for their departure were hastened on. Thirty-five members of the Leyden congregation left Holland and joined sixty-six West Country adventurers at Plymouth, and in September 1620 they set sail in the *Mayflower,* a vessel of 180 tons.*

After two and a half months of voyaging across the winter ocean they reached the shores of Cape Cod, and thus, by an accident, landed outside the jurisdiction of the Virginia company. This invalidated their patent from London. Before they landed there was trouble among the group about who was to enforce discipline. Those who had joined the ship at Plymouth were no picked band of saints, and had no intention of submitting to the Leyden set. There was no possibility of appealing to England. Yet, if they were not all to starve, some agreement must be reached.

Forty-one of the more responsible members thereupon drew up a solemn compact which is one of the remarkable documents in history, a spontaneous covenant for political organisation. "In the name of God, Amen. We whose names are under-written, the loyal subjects of our dread sovereign Lord, King James, by the grace of God, of Great Britain, France, and Ireland King, Defender of the Faith, etc. Having undertaken, for the glory of God, and advancement of the Christian faith, and honour of our King and country, a voyage to plant the first colony in the northern parts of Virginia, do by these presents solemnly and mutually in the presence of God, and one of another, covenant and combine ourselves together into a civil body politic, for our better ordering and preservation and furtherance of the ends aforesaid; and by virtue hereof to enact, constitute, and frame such just and equal laws, ordinances, acts, constitutions, and offices, from time to time, as shall be thought most meet and convenient for the general good of the colony, unto which we promise all due submission and obedience."

In December on the American coast in Cape Cod Bay these men founded the town of Plymouth. The same bitter struggle with nature that had taken place in Virginia now began. There was no staple crop.

---

*Winston Churchill, when he wrote these words, was oblivious of the fact that no fewer than three of his ancestors were Pilgrims on the *Mayflower.*—Ed.

But by toil and faith they survived. The financial supporters in London reaped no profits. In 1627 they sold out and the Plymouth colony was left to its own resources. Such was the founding of New England.

For ten years afterwards there was no more planned emigration to America; but the tiny colony of Plymouth pointed a path to freedom. In 1629 Charles I dissolved Parliament and the period of so-called Personal Rule began. As friction grew between Crown and subjects, so opposition to the Anglican Church strengthened in the countryside. Absolutism was commanding the Continent, and England seemed to be going the same way. Many people of independent mind began to consider leaving home to find freedom and justice in the wilds.

Just as the congregation from Scrooby had emigrated in a body to Holland, so another Puritan group in Dorset, inspired by the Reverend John White, now resolved to move to the New World. After an unhappy start this venture won support in London and the Eastern Counties among backers interested in trade and fishing as well as in emigration. Influential Opposition peers lent their aid. After the precedent of Virginia a chartered company was formed, eventually named "The Company of the Massachusetts Bay in New England." News spread rapidly and there was no lack of colonists. An advance party founded the settlement of Salem, to the north of Plymouth. In 1630 the Governor of the company, John Winthrop, followed with a thousand settlers. He was the leading personality in the enterprise. The uneasiness of the time is reflected in his letters, which reveal the reasons why his family went. "I am verily persuaded," he wrote about England, "God will bring some heavy affliction upon this land, and that speedily; but be of good comfort. . . . If the Lord seeth it will be good for us, He will provide a shelter and a hiding place for us and others. . . . Evil times are coming when the Church must fly into the wilderness." The wilderness that Winthrop chose lay on the Charles river, and to this swampish site the capital of the colony was transferred. Here from modest beginnings arose the city of Boston, which was to become in the next century the heart of resistance to British rule and long remain the intellectual capital of America.

The Massachusetts Bay company was by its constitution a joint stock corporation, organised entirely for trading purposes, and the Salem settlement was for the first year controlled from London. But by accident or intent there was no mention in the charter where the company was to hold its meetings. Some of the Puritan stock-holders realised that there was no obstacle to transferring the company, directors and all, to New England. A general court of the company was held, and this momentous decision taken. From the joint stock company was born the self-governing colony of Massachusetts. The Puritan landed gentry who led the enterprise introduced a representative system, such as they had known in the days before King Charles's Personal Rule. John Winthrop guided the colony through this early phase, and it soon expanded. Between 1629 and 1640 the colonists rose in numbers from three hundred to fourteen thousand. The resources of the company offered favourable prospects to small emigrants. In England life for farm labourers was often hard. Here in the New World there was land for every newcomer and freedom from all restrictions upon the movement of labour and such other medieval regulations as oppressed and embittered the peasantry at home.

The leaders and ministers who ruled in Massachusetts, however, had views of their own about freedom. It must be the rule of the godly. They understood toleration as little as the Anglicans, and disputes broke out about religion. By no means all were rigid Calvinists, and recalcitrant bodies split off from the parent colony when such quarrels became strident. Outside of the settlement were boundless beckoning lands. In 1635 and 1636 some of them moved to the valley of the Connecticut river, and founded the town of Hartford near its banks. They were joined by many emigrants direct from England. This formed the nucleus of the settlement of the River Towns, later to become the colony of Connecticut. There, three thousand miles from home, enlightened rules of government were drawn up. A "Fundamental Order" or constitution was proclaimed, similar to the *Mayflower* compact about fifteen years before. A popular Government, shared in by all the freemen of the colony, was set up, and maintained itself in a modest way until its position was formally regularised after the Restoration of the Stuart monarchy.

The founders of Connecticut had gone out from Massachusetts to find new and larger lands in which to settle. Religious strife drove others beyond the bounds of the parent colony. A scholar from Cambridge, Roger Williams, had been forced to leave the university by Archbishop Laud. He followed the now known way to the New World, and settled in Massachusetts. The godly there seemed to him almost as oppressive as the Anglican Church in England. Williams soon clashed with the authorities, and became the leader of those idealists and humbler folk who sought escape from persecution in their new home overseas. The magistrates considered him a promoter of disorder, and resolved to send him back to England. Warned in time, he fled beyond their reach, and, followed at intervals by others, founded the town of Providence, to the south of Massachusetts. Other exiles from Massachusetts, some of them forcibly banished, joined his settlement in 1636, which became the colony of Rhode Island. Roger Williams was the first political thinker of America, and his ideas influenced not only his fellow colonists, but the revolutionary party in England. In many ways he foreshadowed the political conceptions of John Milton. He was the first to put into practice the complete separation of Church from lay government, and Rhode Island was the only centre at that time in the world where there was complete religious toleration. This noble cause was sustained by the distilling and sale of spirits, on which the colony thrived.

By 1640 five main English settlements had thus been established in North America: Virginia, technically under the direct rule of the Crown, and administered, somewhat ineffectually, by a standing committee of the Privy Council since the company's charter was abrogated in 1624; the original Pilgrim settlement at Plymouth, which, for want of capital, had not expanded; the flourishing Massachusetts Bay colony, and its two offshoots, Connecticut and Rhode Island.

The last four were the New England colonies. In spite of religious divergences they were much alike. All were coastal settlements, bound together by trade, fisheries, and shipping, and soon forced to make common cause against their neighbours. For the French were already reaching out from their earlier bases in Canada, having ousted an adventurous band of Scotsmen who had been ensconced for a time on the upper reaches of the St Lawrence. By 1630 the river was entirely in French hands. The only other waterway, the Hudson, was ruled by the Dutch, who had established at its mouth in 1621 the colony of New Netherland, later to become New York. By moving their company to the New World the English in Massachusetts had shelved relations with the home Government. The Plymouth colony was practically autonomous after the shareholders sold out in 1627. There was, however, no question of their demanding independence from England. That would have exposed them to attack and conquest by the French or the Dutch. But these dangers still lay in the future. England meanwhile was busy with her own affairs. For a moment in 1635 Charles I and his Council had considered sending an expedition to assert his authority in America. The colonists built forts and blockhouses and prepared to fight. But the Civil War in England suspended such designs, and they were left to themselves to grow for nearly a quarter of a century.

Two other ventures, both essentially commercial, established the English-speaking peoples in the New World. Since Elizabethan days they had often tried to get a foothold in the Spanish West Indies. In 1623, on his way back from a fruitless expedition to Guiana, a Suffolk gentleman named Thomas Warner explored one of the less inhabited West Indian islands. He deposited a few colonists on St. Christopher, and hurried home to get a royal patent for a more extensive enterprise. This achieved, he returned to the Caribbean, and, though much harassed by Spanish raids, he established the English in this disputed sea. By the 1640's Barbados, St. Christopher, Nevis, Montserrat, and Antigua were in English hands and several thousand colonists had arrived. Sugar assured their prosperity, and the Spanish grip on the West Indies was shaken. There was much competition and warfare in the succeeding years, but for a long time these island settlements were commercially much more valuable to England than the colonies in North America.

Another settlement of this period was sponsored by the monarchy. In theory all land settled by Englishmen belonged to the King. He had the right to grant such portions as he chose either to recognised companies or to individuals. Just as Elizabeth and James had granted industrial and commercial monopolies to courtiers, so now Charles I attempted to regulate colonial settlement. In 1632 George Calvert, Lord Baltimore, a Roman Catholic courtier who had long been interested in colonisation, applied for a patent for settling in the neighbourhood of Virginia. It was granted after his death to his son. The terms of the patent resembled the conditions under which land was already held in Virginia. It conferred complete proprietary rights over the new area, and tried to transport the manorial system to the New World. The government of the colony was vested in the Baltimore family, who had supreme power of appointment and regulation. Courtiers and merchants subscribed to the venture, and the new colony was named Maryland in honour of Charles's Queen, Henrietta Maria. Although the proprietor was a Roman Catholic there was a tolerant flavour about its government from the beginning, because Baltimore had only obtained his patent by proclaiming the religion of the Established Church as the official creed of the new settlement. The aristocratic nature of the régime was much modified in practice, and the powers of the local administration set up by Baltimore increased at the expense of his paper rights.

In these first decades of the great emigration over eighty thousand English-speaking people crossed the Atlantic. Never since the days of the Germanic invasions of Britain had such a national movement been seen. Saxon and Viking had colonised England. Now, one thousand years later, their descendants were taking possession of America. Many different streams of migrants were to make their confluence in the New

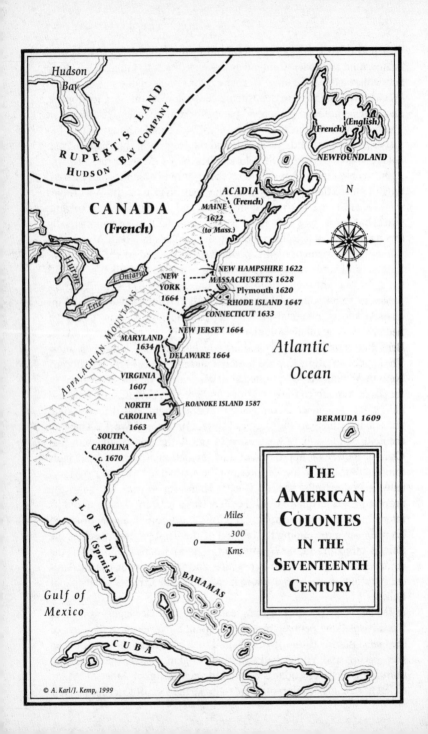

Hudson Bay

RUPERT'S LAND

HUDSON BAY COMPANY

CANADA
(French)

L. Huron

L. Ontario

L. Erie

APPALACHIAN MOUNTAINS

(French) (English)

NEWFOUNDLAND

ACADIA (French)

MAINE 1622 (to Mass.)

NEW HAMPSHIRE 1622
MASSACHUSETTS 1628
Plymouth 1620
RHODE ISLAND 1647
CONNECTICUT 1633

NEW YORK 1664

NEW JERSEY 1664

MARYLAND 1634

DELAWARE 1664

VIRGINIA 1607

NORTH CAROLINA 1663

ROANOKE ISLAND 1587

SOUTH CAROLINA c. 1670

FLORIDA (Spanish)

Atlantic Ocean

BERMUDA 1609

N

BAHAMAS

Gulf of Mexico

CUBA

Miles
0   300
0
Kms.

THE AMERICAN COLONIES IN THE SEVENTEENTH CENTURY

© A. Karl/J. Kemp, 1999

World and contribute to the manifold character of the future United States. But the British stream flowed first and remained foremost. From the beginning its leaders were out of sympathy with the Government at home. The creation of towns and settlements from the wilderness, warfare with the Indians, and the remoteness and novelty of the scene widened the gulf with the Old World. During the critical years of settlement and consolidation in New England the Mother Country was paralysed by civil war. When the English State again achieved stability it was confronted with self-supporting, self-reliant communities which had already evolved traditions and ideas of their own.

Even after Charles II's restoration to the throne in 1660 brought an end to eighteen years of fratricidal conflict, the widespread English thrusts across the seas came more often on the initiative of the men on the spot rather than by planned direction from London. English commerce was expanding in India and on the West Coast of Africa. The Hudson's Bay Company, launched in 1669, had set up its first trading posts and was building up its influence in the northern territories of Canada. On the coasts of Newfoundland English fishermen had revivified the earliest colony of the Crown. On the American mainland the British occupation of the entire eastern seaboard was almost complete. The capture of New York [from the Dutch in 1667] and the settlement of New Jersey had joined in contiguity the two existing groups of colonies that lay to the north and south. Inland the state of Pennsylvania was beginning to take shape as an asylum for the persecuted of all countries under the guidance of its Quaker proprietor, William Penn. To the south the two Carolinas had been founded and named in honour of the King Charles II. At the end of Charles's reign the American colonies contained about a quarter of a million settlers, not counting the increasing number of negro slaves, transhipped from Africa. The local assemblies of the colonists were sturdily asserting traditional English rights against the interventions of the King's Ministers from London. Perhaps not many Englishmen at the time, absorbed in the pleasures and feuds of Restoration London, foresaw the broad prospects that stretched out before these comparatively small and distant American communities. One who caught a glimpse was the first Sir Winston Churchill [father of John, 1st Duke of Marlborough]. Towards the close of his life he published a book called *Divi Britannici,* in praise of the greatness and antiquity of the British monarchy. Churchill wrote with pride of the new horizons of seventeenth-century Britain, "extending to those far-distant regions, now become a part of us and growing apace to be the bigger part, in the sunburnt America." But all this lay in the future.

CHAPTER 4

THE THIRTEEN COLONIES

THROUGHOUT the first half of the seventeenth century Englishmen poured into the American continent. Legally the colonies in which they settled were chartered bodies subordinate to the Crown, but there was little interference from home, and they soon learned to govern themselves. While distracted by the Civil War the Mother Country left them alone, and although Oliver Cromwell's Commonwealth asserted that Parliament was supreme over the whole of the English world its decree was never put into practice, and was swept away by the Restoration. But after 1660 the home Government had new and definite ideas. For the next fifty years successive English administrations tried to enforce the supremacy of the Crown in the American colonies and to strengthen royal power and patronage in the overseas possessions. Thus they hoped to gain credit and advantage. Committees were formed to deal with America. New colonies were founded in Carolina and Pennsylvania, and New Netherland was conquered from the Dutch. Precautions were taken to assure the Crown's authority in these acquisitions. There were efforts to rescind or modify the charters of the older colonies. All this led to unceasing conflict with the colonial assemblies, who resented the threat to royalise and unify colonial administration. Most of these assemblies were representative bodies of freeholders who claimed and exercised the same rights, procedure, and privileges as the Parliament at Westminster. The men who sat in them were many of them bred in a tradition hostile to the Crown. Their fathers had preferred exile to tyranny, and they regarded themselves as fighting for the same issues as had divided the English Parlia-

ment from Strafford and Charles I. They resisted the royal encroachments of the Board of Trade and Plantations. These were reckoned
overseas to be a direct attack on rights and privileges guaranteed by the
original colonial charters, and a tyrannical menace to vested rights.

For a long time the English Parliament played no part in the conflict. The struggle lay between the colonies and the King's Ministers in
the Privy Council. These officials were determined to call a halt to self-
government in America. In 1682 they were asked to grant a charter for
settling vacant lands on the borders of the Spanish possession of
Florida. The Council refused, saying it was the policy of the Crown
"not to constitute any new propriety in America nor to grant any further powers that might render the plantations less dependent on the
Crown." Under James II these royalist tendencies were sharpened. New
York became a royal province in 1685. The New England colonies were
united into a "dominion of New England" on the French model in
Canada. The main argument was the need for union against French expansion, but the move was fiercely resisted and the English Revolution
of 1688 was a signal for the overthrow and collapse of the "dominion
of New England."

England's motives were not entirely selfish. Slowly the menace of
French imperialism loomed upon the frontiers of her possessions. The
reforms of Colbert, the chief Minister of Louis XIV, had greatly
strengthened the power and wealth of France, and English statesmen
and merchants confronted a deadly competition upon the seas and in
the markets of the world. They saw the steady building up of French
colonial and commercial enterprise, backed by the centralised power of
absolute government. How could the British Empire fight off the threat
with a factious Parliament, fretful colonial assemblies, and a swarm of
committees?

The answer devised was an eminently practical one. British colonial
trade must be planned and co-ordinated in London. One of its main
objects must be to foster the British Merchant Navy, and to provide a
reserve of ships and seamen in the event of war. The foundation of the
whole system was the series of enactments known as the Navigation
Laws. Colonial trade must travel only in British bottoms, with British
crews and to British ports. The colonies were forbidden any outside
trade of their own that might hinder the growth of British shipping.
Moreover, the economic theories of the age supported this attack on
colonial independence. The prevailing view of trade was based on the
desire for self-sufficiency and on economic nationalism—or mercantil-
ism as it was called. The wealth of a country depended upon its trade
balance. An excess of imports over exports meant loss of bullion and

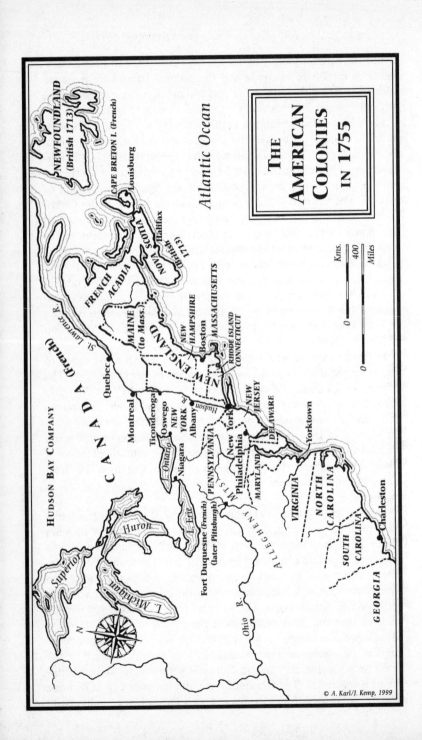

THE
AMERICAN
COLONIES
IN 1755

Atlantic Ocean

Kms.
0   400
Miles
0

NEWFOUNDLAND
(British 1713)

CAPE BRETON I. (French)
Louisburg

FRENCH
ACADIA

NOVA SCOTIA
British
(1713)
Halifax

St. Lawrence R.

CANADA (French)

HUDSON BAY COMPANY

Quebec

Montreal

Ticonderoga

MAINE
(to Mass.)

NEW ENGLAND

NEW HAMPSHIRE

MASSACHUSETTS
Boston

RHODE ISLAND
CONNECTICUT

Oswego

Ontario

NEW YORK
Albany

Hudson R.

NEW JERSEY

Niagara

Erie

PENNSYLVANIA

New York

Philadelphia

DELAWARE

Yorktown

L. Huron

L. Michigan

L. Superior

Fort Duquesne (French)
(later Pittsburgh)

MTS.

MARYLAND

VIRGINIA

ALLEGHENY

NORTH
CAROLINA

Ohio R.

SOUTH
CAROLINA

Charleston

GEORGIA

N

© A. Karl/J. Kemp, 1999

economic weakness. National prosperity required the control of plentiful natural resources. Colonies were vital. They must produce essential raw materials, such as timber for the Navy, and afford a market for the growing manufactures of the home country. The Empire must be a closed economic unit. Colonial manufactures must be stifled to prevent competition inside it, and trade between the colonies themselves must be strictly regulated. Such, in brief, was the economic conception enshrined in the legislation of the seventeenth century. There was no room in this scheme for the independent development of the colonies. They must remain the providers of raw materials, and the recipients of English manufactures.

The system was more irksome on paper than in practice. No seventeenth-century Government could enforce such a code over thousands of miles. American assemblies grumbled but went their own way, ingeniously evading the Westminster restrictions.

The English Revolution of 1688 changed the whole position. Hitherto the colonies had regarded the Parliament in England as their ally against the Crown. But the time was to come when Parliament, victorious over the Crown in the constitutional struggles at home, would attempt to enforce its own sovereignty over America. The clash was delayed by the War of the Spanish Succession. The long European struggle with France compelled the avoidance of fundamental issues elsewhere; and in the hope of marshalling the resources of the English-speaking peoples for the supreme conflict all efforts to impose the authority of the English Government in the New World were dropped. The Board of Trade and Plantations was allowed to subside and the colonies were largely left to themselves.

The spirit of amity which it was thus hoped to secure fell far short of expectation. There were ample reasons for this. Both in outlook and tradition the colonies had been steadily growing apart from the Mother Country. A colonial-born generation now inhabited the American plantations, trained in the harsh struggle with nature, expanding rapidly in the limitless lands stretching westwards from the seaboard, and determined to protect their individuality and their privileges. The doctrines of the English Revolution and the ideas of the seventeenth-century Whigs struck an even deeper echo in the New World than at home. The youthful energies of the Americans found paper obstacles at every turn to the development of their resources. All these causes indisposed them to any great effort on behalf of England. On the other hand, though quick to realise their potential strength and wealth, the colonists were slow to organise; and being still instinctively loyal to their nation and conscious of the French menace beyond their own frontiers they were as anxious as Britain to avoid a serious quarrel. They even took an active but ill-organised part in the attempts to conquer French Canada which culminated in the futile expedition of 1711. But, jealous as they were not only of the home Government but of each other, they soon lapsed into quarrelsome isolation.

These conditions persisted throughout the administration of Walpole, who perceived the necessity for avoiding friction at all costs. But in the course of time the colonists grew more and more resolved to press their advantage, and the middle years of the eighteenth century witnessed a vehement assault by the colonial Assemblies upon the authority of the Imperial Government. They were bent on making themselves into sovereign Parliaments, supreme in the internal government of the several colonies, and free of all restrictions or interference from London. Innumerable struggles took place between the Governors and the legislatures of the colonies. There were many complaints on both sides. The Crown looked upon posts overseas as valuable patronage for its servants, the Government for their supporters. Thus the whole colonial administration was tainted with the prevailing corruption of English public life. Governors, counsellors, judges, and many other officials were all appointed by the Crown, and they were seldom chosen with due regard to the interests of the colonists. "America," said one of her historians, "is the hospital of Great Britain for its decayed M.P.s and abandoned courtiers." By no means all the British officials were of such a type. Particularly in the North, the Governors often came from the leading colonial families, and the ablest men in colonial administration were of this class. But there were inevitable contests within the colonies themselves. The Governors were particularly vulnerable in matters of finance. Their salaries were fixed by the assemblies, and frequently the assemblies withheld their votes. Irritation between the officials and the assemblies grew and mounted as the years passed by.

Behind the squabbling of day-to-day administration lay vital developments. The Royal Prerogative, so drastically modified in England after the Revolution of 1688, still flourished in the New World. Though the colonial assemblies persistently tried to copy the English pattern, they were hampered at every turn. Not only were they bound by written charters or constitutions, but special customs, organisations, and Admiralty courts exercised their jurisdiction upon colonial soil, and although the English Government tried to avoid any open meddling matters went from bad to worse. America was still regarded as existing for the economic benefit of England. The mainland colonies supplied naval stores and tobacco, and the West Indies sent cargoes of sugar to English ports. But the energy and population of America were growing. There were signs that the colonies would produce their own manufactured goods and close their markets to the United Kingdom. As early as 1699 Parliament had legislated against the setting up of industries in the New World. The economic position, particularly in New England, was becoming more and more strained. The Americans could only pay for the increasing volume of English imports by selling their produce to their immediate neighbours and to the English and foreign possessions in the West Indies. This violated the provisions of the Navigation Acts. The economic pressure from England grew stronger with the years. The balance of trade turned steadily against the colonies, and by the middle of the century their annual deficit was over three million pounds. The colonial merchants could only scrape together enough cash by illegal methods. This drift of money from America was to help keep England solvent in the coming first world war. The City knew it; Pitt knew it, and on his monument in Guildhall we may still read how under his administration commerce had been unified and made to flourish by war. But the effect upon the New World was serious. The Americans had no mints, no regularised currency. Their unco-ordinated issues of paper money, which rapidly depreciated, made matters worse, and English merchants loudly complained of the instability of colonial credit.

The early eighteenth century saw the foundation of the last of the Thirteen Colonies. The philanthropist James Oglethorpe had been painfully moved by the horrible condition of the small debtors in English prisons. After much thought he conceived the idea of allowing these people to emigrate to a new colony. The Government was approached, and in 1732 a board of trustees was created to administer a large tract of territory lying below South Carolina. The following year the first settlement was founded at Savannah. Small estates were created, and religious toleration was proclaimed for all except Catholics. The first settlers were English debtors, but the foundation promised a new life for the oppressed in many parts of Europe. Bands of Jews quickly arrived, followed by Protestants from Salzburg, Moravians from Germany, and Highlanders from Skye. The polyglot community, named Georgia, soon attracted ardent missionaries, and it was here that John Wesley began his ministering work.

The high moral atmosphere of these beginnings was soon polluted by mundane quarrels. The settlers, like their brethren in the other colonies, coveted both rum and slaves. The trustees of the community wearied of their task of government; and their prolonged bickering with the rising merchants of Savannah ended in the cancellation of the charter. In 1752 Georgia came under royal control. This colony was the last foundation of the Mother Country in the territories that were later to become the United States. Emigration from England had now dwindled to a trickle, but new settlers arrived from other parts. Towards the end of the seventeenth century there had been an influx of Scottish-Irish refugees, whose industrial and commercial endeavours at home had been stifled by the legislation of the English Parliament. They formed a strong English-hating element in their new homes. Pennsylvania received a steady flow of immigrants from Germany, soon to number over two hundred thousand souls. Hard-working and prosperous Huguenots arrived from France in flight from religious persecution. People were also moving from colony to colony. The oases of provincial life were linked up. The population was rapidly doubling itself. Limitless land to the West offered homes for the sons of the first generation. The abundance of territory to be occupied encouraged large families. Contact with primeval conditions created a new and daring outlook. A sturdy independent society was producing its own life and culture, influenced and coloured by surrounding conditions. The Westward march had begun, headed by the Germans and the Irish in Pennsylvania. The slow trail over the mountains in search of new lands was opening. There was a teeming diversity of human types. In Kentucky and on the Western farms which bordered the Indian country were rugged pioneers and sturdy yeomen farmers, and in the New England colonies assertive merchants, lawyers, and squires, and the sons of traders. This varied society was supported in the North by the forced labour of indentured servants and men smuggled away from the press-gangs in English towns, in the South by a mass of slaves multiplied by yearly shiploads from Africa. Events in Europe, of which most Americans were probably scarcely conscious, now came to bear upon the destiny of the Thirteen Colonies.

CHAPTER 5

THE FIRST "WORLD WAR"

WHEN WILLIAM PITT first joined the British government as Secretary of State in November 1756 Frederick the Great declared, "England has long been in labour, but at last she has brought forth a man."

Nothing like it had been seen since Marlborough. From his office in Cleveland Row Pitt designed and won a war which extended from India in the East to America in the West. The whole struggle depended upon the energies of this one man. He gathered all power, financial, administrative, and military, into his own hands. He could work with no one as an equal. His position depended entirely on success in the field. His political enemies were numerous. He would tolerate no interference or even advice from his colleagues in the Cabinet; he made no attempt either to consult or to conciliate, and he irritated Newcastle and the Chancellor of the Exchequer by interfering in finance. But in the execution of his military plans Pitt had a sure eye for choosing the right man. He broke incompetent generals and admirals and replaced them with younger men upon whom he could rely: Wolfe, Amherst, Conway, Howe, Keppel, and Rodney. Thus he achieved victory.

But Pitt's success was not immediate. He had opposed the popular clamour for Admiral Byng's court-martial. He was at odds with his colleagues, and the Duke of Cumberland used his powerful and malevolent influence against him. The City merchants were still suspicious of the alliance with Prussia. In April 1757 Pitt was dismissed by the King. Nevertheless he had already made his mark with the nation. He received from the towns and corporations of England a manifestation of their deep feeling—"a shower of gold boxes." For three months there was no effective Government, though Pitt gave all the orders and did the day-to-day work. A stable war Ministry was not formed until June, but for the next four years Pitt was supreme.

Pitt did not confine himself to a single field of operations. By taking the initiative in every quarter of the globe Britain prevented the French from concentrating their forces, confused their plan of campaign, and forced them to dissipate their strength. Pitt had fiercely attacked Carteret for fighting in Europe, but he now realised that a purely naval and colonial war, such as he had advocated in the 1740's, could yield no final decision. Unless France were beaten in Europe as well as in the New World and in the East she would rise again. Both in North America and in Europe she was in the ascendant. At sea she was a formidable enemy. In India it seemed that if ever a European Power established itself on the ruins of the Mogul Empire its banner would be the lilies and not the cross of St. George. War with France would be a world war—the first in history; and the prize would be something more than a rearrangement of frontiers and a redistribution of fortresses and sugar islands.

Whether Pitt possessed the strategic eye, whether the expeditions he launched were part of a considered combination, may be questioned. Now, as at all times, his policy was a projection on to a vast screen of his own aggressive, dominating personality. In the teeth of disfavour and obstruction he had made his way to the foremost place in Parliament, and now at last fortune, courage, and the confidence of his countrymen had given him a stage on which his gifts could be displayed and his foibles indulged. To call into life and action the depressed and languid spirit of England; to weld all her resources of wealth and manhood into a single instrument of war which should be felt from the Danube to the Mississippi; to humble the house of Bourbon, to make the Union Jack supreme in every ocean, to conquer, to command, and never to count the cost, whether in blood or gold—this was the spirit of Pitt, and this spirit he infused into every rank of his countrymen, admirals and powder-monkeys, great merchants and little shopkeepers; into the youngest officer of the line, who felt that with Pitt in command failure might be forgiven but hesitation never; into the very Highlanders who had charged at Prestonpans and now were sailing across the Atlantic to win an empire for the sovereign who had butchered their brethren at Culloden.

On the Continent Britain had one ally, Frederick of Prussia, facing the combined power of Austria, Russia, and France. Sweden too had old grudges to avenge, old claims to assert against him. Frederick, by a rapid march through Saxony into Bohemia, sought to break through the closing circle. But in 1757 he was driven back into his own dominions; Cumberland, sent to protect Hanover and Brunswick, was defeated by the French and surrendered both. Russia was on the march; Swedish troops were again seen in Pomerania. Minorca had already fallen. From Canada Montcalm was pressing against the American frontier forts. Never did a war open with darker prospects. Pitt's hour had come. "I know," he had told the Duke of Devonshire, "that I can save this country and that no one else can." He sent back the foreign troops paid to protect England from invasion. He disavowed Cumberland's surrender. Life began to tingle in the torpid frame of English administration. Before the year was out it seemed as if Fortune, recognising her masters, was changing sides. Frederick, supported by the subsidies which Pitt had spent the eloquence of his youth in denouncing, routed the French at Rossbach and the Austrians at Leuthen.

So the great years opened, years for Pitt and his country of almost intoxicating glory. The French were swept out of Hanover; the Dutch, fishing in the murky waters of Oriental intrigue, were stopped by Clive and made to surrender their ships at Chinsura; Cape Breton was again taken, and the name of the "Great Commoner" stamped on the map at Pittsburg, Pennsylvania. France's two main fleets, in the Mediterranean and in the Channel, were separately defeated. Combined they might have covered an invasion of England. Admiral Boscawen, fresh from the capture of Louisburg, was detailed to watch the Toulon squadron. He caught it slipping through the Straits of Gibraltar, destroyed five ships and drove the rest into Cadiz Bay, blockaded and out of action. Three months later, in the short light of a November day, in a high gale and among uncharted rocks and shoals, Admiral Hawke annihilated the Brest fleet. For the rest of the war Quiberon was an English naval station, where the sailors occupied their leisure and maintained their health by growing cabbages on French soil. Between these victories Wolfe had fallen at Quebec, leaving Amherst to complete the conquest of Canada, while Clive and Eyre Coote were uprooting the remnants of French power in India. Even more dazzling prizes seemed to be falling into British hands. Pitt proposed to conquer the Spanish Indies, West and East, and to seize the annual Treasure Fleet. But at this supreme moment in his career, when world peace and world security seemed within his grasp, the Cabinet declined to support him and he resigned.

It is necessary to examine these triumphs and disasters at closer hand. In America Pitt faced a difficult and complex task. The governors of the English colonies had long been aware of the threat beyond their frontiers. The French were moving along the waterways beyond the mountain barrier of the Alleghenies and extending their alliances with the Red Indians in an attempt to link their colony of Louisiana in the South with Canada in the North. Thus the English settlements would be confined to the seaboard and their Westward expansion would stop. Warfare had broken out in 1755. General Braddock was sent from England to re-establish British authority west of the Alleghenies, but his forces were cut to pieces by the French and Indians in Pennsylvania. In this campaign a young Virginian officer named George Washington learnt his first military lessons. The New England colonies lay open to attack down the easy path of invasion, the Hudson valley. A struggle began for a foothold at the valley head. There was little organisation. Each of the colonies attempted to repel Red Indian raids and French settlers with their own militias. They were united in distrusting the home Government, but in little else. Although there were now over a million British Americans, vastly outnumbering the French, their quarrels and disunion extinguished this advantage. Only the tactful handling of Pitt secured their co-operation, and even so throughout the war colonial traders continued to supply the French with all their needs in defiance of the Government and the common interest.

The year 1756 was disastrous for England in America, and indeed upon all fronts. Oswego, the only English fort on the Great Lakes, was lost. The campaign of 1757 was hardly more successful. The fortress of Louisburg, which commanded the Gulf of St. Lawrence, had been taken by an Anglo-Colonial force in the 1740's and returned to France at the peace treaty of 1748 at Aix-la-Chapelle. English troops were now sent to recapture it. They were commanded by an ineffectual and unenterprising officer, Lord Loudon. Loudon prepared to attack by concentrating at Halifax such colonial troops from New England as the colonies would release. This left the Hudson valley open to the French. At the head of the valley were three small forts: Crown Point, Edward, and William Henry. The French, under the Governor of Canada, Montcalm, and his Red Indian allies, swept over the frontier through the wooded mountains and besieged Fort William Henry. The small colonial garrison held out for five days, but was forced to surrender. Montcalm was unable to restrain his Indians and the prisoners were massacred. The tragedy bit into the minds of the New Englanders. It was Loudon who was to blame. The British were not defending them; while New England was left exposed to the French, the troops which might have protected them were wasting time at Halifax. Indeed, by the end of July Loudon decided that Louisburg was impregnable and had given up the attempt.

Pitt now bent his mind to the American war. Throughout the winter he studied the maps and wrote dispatches to the officers and governors. A threefold strategic plan was framed for 1758. Loudon was recalled. His successor, Amherst, with Brigadier Wolfe, and naval support from Halifax, was to sail up the St. Lawrence and strike at Quebec. Another army, under Abercromby, was to seize Lake George at the head of the Hudson valley and try to join Amherst and Wolfe before Quebec. A third force, under Brigadier Forbes, would advance up the Ohio valley from Pennsylvania and capture Fort Duquesne, one of a line of French posts along the Ohio and the Mississippi. The Fleet was so disposed as to stop reinforcements leaving France.

A mind capable of conceiving and directing these efforts was now in power at Whitehall, but supervision at a distance of three thousand miles was almost impossible in the days of sail. Amherst and Wolfe hammered at the northern borders of Canada. In July Louisburg was captured. But Abercromby, advancing from Ticonderoga, became entangled in the dense woods; his army was badly beaten and his advance was halted. The Pennsylvanian venture was more successful. Fort Duquesne was taken and destroyed and the place renamed Pittsburg; but lack of numbers and organisation compelled the British force to retire at the end of the campaign. In a dispatch to Pitt Forbes gave a bitter description of the affair: "I vainly at the beginning flattered myself that some very good Service might be drawn from the Virginia & Pennsylvania Forces, but am sorry to find that, a few of their principal Officers excepted, all the rest are an extream bad Collection of broken Innkeepers, Horse Jockeys, & Indian traders, and that the Men under them are a direct Copy of their Officers, nor can it well be otherwise, as they are a gathering from the scum of the worst people, in every Country. . . ." These remarks reflect the worsening relations and woeful lack of understanding between British officers and American colonists.

There was little enough to show for such efforts, but Pitt was undaunted. He realised the need for a combined offensive along the whole frontier from Nova Scotia to the Ohio. Isolated inroads into French territory would bring no decision. On December 29, 1758, further instructions were accordingly sent to Amherst. The necessity for cutting across the French line of expansion was again emphasised. "It were much to be wished," the instructions continue, "that any Operations on the side of Lake Ontario could be pushed as far as Niagara, and that you may find it practicable to set on foot some Enterprize against the Fort there, the Success of which would so greatly contribute to establish the uninterrupted Dominion of that Lake, and at the same time effectually cut off the Communication between Canada and the French Settlements to the South."

There was also much talk about the need of acquiring Red Indian allies. Amherst thought little of this. Several months earlier he had written to Pitt that a large number of Indians were promised him: "They are a pack of lazy, rum-drinking people and little good, but if ever they are of use it will be when we can act offensively. The French are much more afraid of them than they need be; numbers will increase their Terror and may have a good Effect." Nevertheless it was fortunate for the British that the Six Nations of the Iroquois, who occupied a key position between the British and French settlements near the Great Lakes, were generally friendly; they, like the American colonists, were alarmed at French designs on the Ohio and the Mississippi.

According to the new plan, in the coming year the Navy would attack the French West Indies, and the invasion of Canada up the St. Lawrence would be pushed harder than ever in spite of the bitter experience of the past. Since the campaign of 1711 there had been several attempts to ascend the mighty river. Wolfe reported the Navy's "thorough aversion" to the task. It was indeed hazardous. But it was to be backed by a renewed advance up the Hudson against the French fort of Niagara on the Great Lakes, the importance of which Pitt had emphasised in his instructions.

The plan succeeded. The year 1759 brought fame to British arms throughout the world. In May the Navy captured Guadeloupe, the richest sugar island of the West Indies. In July Amherst took Ticonderoga and Fort Niagara, thus gaining for the American colonies a frontier upon the Great Lakes. In September the expedition up the St. Lawrence attacked Quebec. Wolfe conducted a personal reconnaissance of the river at night, and beguiled the officers by reciting Gray's "Elegy": "The paths of glory lead but to the grave." By brilliant co-operation between Army and Navy Wolfe landed his men, and led them by the unsuspected path, under cover of darkness, up the steep cliffs of the Heights of Abraham. In the battle that followed Montcalm was defeated and killed and the key fortress of Canada was secured. Wolfe, mortally wounded, lived until victory was certain, and died murmuring, "Now God be praised, I will die in peace."

But it needed another year's fighting to gain Canada for the English-speaking world. In May 1760 the British garrison in Quebec was relieved after a winter siege. With cautious and dogged organisation Amherst converged on Montreal. In September the city fell and the huge province of French Canada changed hands. These were indeed the years of victory.

The inactivity of the French Fleet is a remarkable feature of the war. If they had blockaded New York in 1759 while the English ships were gathered at Halifax they could have ruined Amherst's advance on Montreal. If they had attacked Halifax after Wolfe and the English ships had left for the St. Lawrence they could have wrecked the whole campaign for Quebec. But now it was too late. Further English naval reinforcements were sent to the New World. In 1761 Amherst dispatched an expedition to Martinique. The capture of yet another great commercial prize was received with jubilation in London. In one of his letters Horace Walpole wrote, "I tell you [the eloquence of Pitt] has conquered Martinico. . . . The Romans were three hundred years in conquering the world. We subdued the globe in three campaigns—and a globe as big again."

North America was thus made safe for the English-speaking peoples. Pitt had not only won Canada, with its rich fisheries and Indian trade, but had banished for ever the dream and danger of a French colonial empire stretching from Montreal to New Orleans. Little could he know that the extinction of the French menace would lead to the final secession of the English colonies from the British Empire.

Pitt's very success contributed to his fall. Just as Marlborough and Godolphin had been faced by a growing war-weariness after Malplaquet, so now Pitt, an isolated figure in his own Government, confronted an increasing dislike of the war after the great victories of 1759. To the people at large he was the "Great Commoner." This lonely, dictatorial man had caught their imagination. He had broken through the narrow circle of aristocratic politics, and his force and eloquence gained him their support. Contrary to the conventions of the age, he had used the House of Commons as a platform from which to address the country. His studied orations in severe classical style were intended for a wider audience than the place-holders of the Duke of Newcastle. Pitt had a contempt for party and party organisations. His career was an appeal to the individual in politics. His vast powers of work and concentration tired all who came in contact with him. Afflicted early in life with severe gout, he had to struggle with ill-health through the worst anxieties of war government. He hardly troubled to see his colleagues. All business was conducted from his office, except for weekly meetings with Newcastle and the Treasury Secretary to arrange the finances of his strategy, money and troops for Wolfe and Clive, subsidies for Frederick the Great. But his power was transient. There were not only enemies within the Government, stung by his arrogance and his secrecy, but also among his former political allies, the Princess of Wales and her circle at Leicester House. Here the young heir to the throne was being brought up amid the Opposition views of his mother and her confidant, the Earl of Bute. Pitt had been their chosen candidate for the sunshine days when the old King should die. They now deemed him a deserter. They branded his acceptance of office in 1746 as a betrayal. Bute, with his close position at this future Court, was the most dangerous of Pitt's opponents, and it was he who stimulated opinion and the Press against the war policy of the Minister.

Pitt's position was indeed perilous. He had destroyed France's power in India and North America and had captured her possessions in the West Indies. It seemed as if Britain had achieved everything she desired. All that was left was the unpopular commitment to Prussia, and Bute found it only too easy to convert the feelings of weariness into an effective opposition to Pitt. Among his colleagues there were some who honestly and patriotically doubted the wisdom of continuing the war, from which Britain had gained more than perhaps she could keep; a war which had raised her once more to the height at which she had stood after Ramillies. The war had to be paid for. It was already producing the inevitable consequences of even the most glorious war. Heavy taxation on the industrial and landed classes was matched by huge fortunes for the stock-jobber and the contractor. It was in vain that Pitt attempted to show that no lasting or satisfactory peace could be secured till France was defeated in Europe. Making terms before France was exhausted would repeat the Tory mistakes at Utrecht and only snatch a breathing-space for the next conflict. It was with bitterness that Pitt realised his position. His Imperial war policy had succeeded only too well, leaving him with the detested and costly subsidies to Prussia which he knew were essential to the final destruction of French power.

In October 1760 George II died. He had never liked Pitt, but had learnt to respect his abilities. The Minister's comment was pointed: "Serving the King may be a duty, but it is the most disagreeable thing imaginable to those who have that honour." The temper of the new ruler was adverse. George III had very clear ideas of what he wanted and where he was going. He meant to be King, such a King as all his countrymen would follow and revere. Under the long Whig régime the House of Commons had become an irresponsible autocracy. Would not the liberties of the country be safer in the hands of a monarch, young, honourable, virtuous, and appearing thoroughly English, than in a faction governing the land through a packed and corrupt House of Commons? Let him make an end of government by families, choose his own Ministers and stand by them, and end once and for all the corruption of political life. But in such a monarchy what was the place of a man like Pitt, who owed nothing to corruption, nothing to the Crown, and everything to the people and to his personal domination of the House of Commons? So long as he was in power he would divide the kingdom with Caesar. He could not help it. His profound reverence for the person and office of George III could not conceal from either of them the fact that Pitt was a very great man and the King a very limited man. Bute, "the Minister behind the curtain," was now all-powerful at Court. Newcastle, who had long chafed under the harsh, domineering ways of his colleague, was only too ready to intrigue against him. There was talk of peace. Negotiations were opened at The Hague, but broke down when Pitt refused to desert Prussia. The French War Minister, Choiseul, like Torcy fifty years before, saw his chance. He realised that Pitt's power was slipping. In 1761 he made a close alliance with Spain, and in September the negotiations with England collapsed. With the power of Spain behind her in the Americas, France might now regain her dominance in the New World.

Pitt hoped that war with Spain would rouse the same popular upsurge as in 1739. The chance of capturing more Spanish colonies might appeal to the City. His proposal for the declaration of war was put to the Cabinet. He found himself isolated. He made a passionate speech to his colleagues: "Being responsible I will direct, and will be responsible for nothing I do not direct." He met with a savage rebuke from the old enemy whose career he had broken, Carteret, now Lord Granville. "When the gentleman talks of being responsible to the people, he talks the language of the House of Commons, and forgets that at this board he is only responsible to the King." He had no choice but resignation.

William Pitt ranks with Marlborough as the greatest Englishman in the century between 1689 and 1789. "It is a considerable fact in the history of the world," wrote Carlyle, "that he was for four years King of England." He was not the first English statesman to think in terms of a world policy and to broaden on to a world scale the political conceptions of William III. But he is the first great figure of British Imperialism. Pitt too had brought the force of public opinion to bear upon politics, weakening the narrow monopoly of the great Whig houses. His heroic period was now over. "Be one people," he commanded the factions. Five years later he was to hold high office once more amid tragic circumstances of failing health. In the meantime his magnificent oratory blasted the policies of his successors.

Unsupported by the fame of Pitt, the Duke of Newcastle was an easy victim, and the administration slid easily into the hands of Lord Bute. His sole qualification for office, apart from great wealth and his command of the Scottish vote, was that he had been Groom of the Stole to the King's mother. For the first time since the assassination of the Duke of Buckingham the government of England was committed to a man with no political experience, and whose only connection with Parliament was that he had sat as a representative peer of Scotland for a short time twenty years before. The London mob delivered their verdict on the King's choice in the image of a Jack Boot and a Petticoat.

Within three months of Pitt's resignation the Government were compelled to declare war on Spain. This led to further successes in the West Indies and elsewhere. The British Fleet seized the port of Havana, which commanded the trade routes of the Spanish Main and the movement of the Treasure Fleets. In the Pacific Ocean an expedition from Madras descended upon the Philippines and captured Manila. At sea and on land England was mistress of the outer world. These achievements were largely cast away.

Fifty years after the Treaty of Utrecht Britain signed a new peace with France. Bute sent the Duke of Bedford to Paris to negotiate its terms. The Duke thought his country was taking too much of the globe and would be in perpetual danger from European coalitions and attacks by dissatisfied nations. He believed in the appeasement of France and Spain and the generous return of conquests. Pitt, on the other hand, demanded the decisive weakening of the enemy. To his mind there would be no secure or permanent peace until France and Spain were placed at a lasting disadvantage. He could take no part in the negotiations, and he vehemently denounced the treaty as undermining the safety of the realm.

Britain's acquisitions under the terms of the Peace of Paris in 1763 were nevertheless considerable. In America she secured Canada, Nova Scotia, Cape Breton, and the adjoining islands, and the right to navigate the Mississippi, important for Red Indian trade. In the West Indies

Grenada, St. Vincent, Dominica, and Tobago were acquired. From Spain she received Florida. In Africa she kept Senegal. In India the East India Company preserved its extensive conquests, and although their trading posts were returned the political ambitions of the French in the sub-continent were finally extinguished. In Europe Minorca was restored to England, and the fortifications of Dunkirk were at long last demolished.

Historians have taken a flattering view of a treaty which established Britain as an Imperial Power, but its strategic weakness has been smoothly overlooked. It was a perfect exposition of the principles of the Duke of Bedford. The naval power of France had been left untouched. In America she received back the islands of St. Pierre and Miquelon, in the Gulf of the St. Lawrence, with the right to fish upon the shores of Newfoundland. These were the nursery of the French Navy, in which about fourteen thousand men were permanently employed. Their commercial value was nearly half a million pounds a year. They might form naval bases or centres for smuggling French goods into the lost province of Canada. In the West Indies the richest prize of the war, the sugar island of Guadeloupe, was also handed back, together with Martinique, Belle Isle, and St. Lucia. Guadeloupe was so rich that the English Government even considered keeping it and in exchange returning Canada to the French. These islands were also excellent naval bases for future use against England.

Spain regained the West Indian port of Havana, which controlled the maritime strategy of the Caribbean. She also received back Manila, an important centre for the China trade. If the English had retained them the fleets of France and Spain would have been permanently at their mercy. In Africa, in spite of Pitt's protests, France got back Goree—a base for privateers on the flank of the East Indian trade routes. Moreover, the treaty took no account of the interests of Frederick the Great. This ally was left to shift for himself. He never forgave Britain for what he regarded as a betrayal, which rankled long afterwards in the minds of Prussian leaders.

These terms fell so short of what the country expected that, in spite of the general desire for peace, it seemed doubtful if Parliament would ratify them. By some means or other a majority had to be ensured, and the means were only too familiar. All the arts of Parliamentary management were employed. Lords and Commoners known to be hostile to the Government were dismissed from any office they had been fortunate enough to acquire. Vain was it that Pitt denounced the treaty and prophesied war. It was approved by 319 votes to 65. Appeasement and conciliation won the day. But the sombre verdict of the man who endured the deliberate maiming of his work contained the historic truth. He saw in its terms the seeds of a future war. "The peace was insecure, because it restored the enemy to her former greatness. The peace was inadequate, because the places gained were no equivalent for the places surrendered."

CHAPTER 6

THE QUARREL
WITH BRITAIN

THE ACCESSION of George III caused a profound change in English politics. In theory and in law the monarchy still retained a decisive influence and power in the making of policy, the choice of Ministers, the filling of offices, and the spending of money. In these and in many other fields the personal action of the King had for many centuries been far-reaching, and generally accepted, and only since the installation of the Hanoverian dynasty had the royal influence been largely exercised by the Whig Ministers in Parliament. Walpole and Newcastle had been much more than Ministers; they were almost Regents. There had been many reasons why they and their supporters had achieved and held such power for nearly half a century. Both George I and George II were aliens in language, outlook, upbringing, and sympathy; their Court was predominantly German; their interests and ambitions had centred on Hanover and on the Continent of Europe, and they owed their throne to the Whigs. Now all was changed. George III was, or thought he was, an Englishman born and bred. At any rate he tried to be. He had received a careful education in England from his mother and from the Earl of Bute, who was a Scotsman and in his opponents' eyes a Tory. George's earliest recorded literary achievement is a boyhood essay on Alfred the Great. "George, be King," his mother had said, according to tradition, and George did his best to obey. That he failed in the central problems of his reign may, in the long run of events, have been fortunate for the ultimate liberty of England. Out of the disasters that ensued rose the Parliamentary system of government as we now know it, but the disasters were nevertheless both formidable and far-reaching. By the time that George died America had separated herself from the United Kingdom, the first British Empire had collapsed, and the King himself had gone mad.

The contest with America had begun to dominate the British political scene. Vast territories had fallen to the Crown on the conclusion of the Seven Years War. From the Canadian border to the Gulf of Mexico the entire hinterland of the American colonies became British soil, and the parcelling out of these new lands led to further trouble with the colonists. Many of them, like George Washington, had formed companies to buy these frontier tracts from the Indians, but a royal proclamation restrained any purchasing and prohibited their settlement. Washington, among others, ignored the ban and wrote to his land agent ordering him "to secure some of the most valuable lands in the King's part [on the Ohio], which I think may be accomplished after a while, notwithstanding the proclamation that restrains it at present, and prohibits the settling of them at all; *for I can never look upon that proclamation in any other light (but this I say between ourselves) than as a temporary expedient to quiet the minds of the Indians.*"* This attempt by the British Government to regulate the new lands caused much discontent among the planters, particularly in the Middle and Southern colonies.

George III was also determined that the colonies should pay their share in the expenses of the Empire and in garrisoning the New World. For this there were strong arguments. England had supplied most of the men and the money in the struggle with France for their protection, and indeed their survival; but the methods used by the British Government were ineffective and imprudent. It was resolved to impose a tax on the colonies' imports, and in 1764 Parliament strengthened the Molasses Act. This measure was originally passed in 1733 to protect the West Indian sugar-growers. It created a West Indian monopoly of the sugar trade within the Empire and imposed a heavy duty on foreign imports. It had long been evaded by the colonists, whose only means of acquiring hard cash to pay their English creditors was by selling their goods for molasses in the French and Spanish West Indies. The new regulations were a serious blow. As one merchant put it, "The restrictions which we are laid under by the Parliament put us at a stand how to employ our vessels to any advantage, as we have no prospect of markets at our own islands and cannot send elsewhere to have anything that will answer in return."

* Author's italics.—W. S. C.

The results were unsatisfactory on both sides of the Atlantic. The British Government found that the taxes brought in very little money, and the English merchants, already concerned at the plight of their American debtors, had no desire to make colonial finance any more unstable. Indirect taxation of trade being so unfruitful, Grenville and his lieutenant Charles Townshend consulted the Law Officers about levying a direct tax on the colonies. Their opinion was favourable, and Grenville proposed that all colonial legal documents should be stamped, for a fee. The colonial agents in London were informed, and discussed the plan by post with the Assemblies in America. There were no protests, although the colonists had always objected to direct taxation, and in 1765 Parliament passed the Stamp Act.

With two exceptions it imposed no heavy burden. The stamps on legal documents would not in any case produce a large revenue. The English stamp duty brought in £300,000 a year. Its extension to America was only expected to raise another £50,000. But the Act included a tax on newspapers, many of whose journalists were vehement partisans of the extremist party in America, and the colonial merchants were dismayed because the duty had to be paid in bullion already needed for meeting the adverse trade balance with England. The dispute exposed and fortified the more violent elements in America, and gave them a chance to experiment in organised resistance. The future revolutionary leaders appeared from obscurity—Patrick Henry in Virginia, Samuel Adams in Massachusetts, and Christopher Gadsden in South Carolina—and attacked both the legality of the Government's policy and the meekness of most American merchants. A small but well-organised Radical element began to emerge. But although there was an outcry and protesting delegates convened a Stamp Act Congress there was no unity of opinion in America. The stamp-distributors were attacked and their offices and houses wrecked, but all this was the work of a few merchants and young lawyers who were trying their hand at rousing the unenfranchised mobs. The most effective opposition came from English merchants, who realised that the Act imperilled the recovery of their commercial debts and denounced it as contrary to the true commercial interests of the Empire and a danger to colonial resources.

The personality of George III was now exercising a preponderant influence upon events. He was one of the most conscientious sovereigns who ever sat upon the English throne. Simple in his tastes and unpretentious in manner, he had the superficial appearance of a typical yeoman. But his mind was Hanoverian, with an infinite capacity for mastering detail, and limited success in dealing with large issues and main principles. He possessed great moral courage and an inveterate obstinacy, and his stubbornness lent weight to the stiffening attitude of his Government. His responsibility for the final breach is a high one. He could not understand those who feared the consequences of a policy of coercion. He expressed himself in blunt terms. "It is with the utmost astonishment that I find any of my subjects capable of encouraging the rebellious disposition which unhappily exists in some of my colonies in America. Having entire confidence in the wisdom of my Parliament, the Great Council of the Nation, I will steadily pursue those measures which they have recommended for the support of the constitutional rights of Great Britain and the protection of the commercial interests of my kingdom."

But now, writhing under the domination of Grenville and his friends, alarmed at the growing disorder and disaffection of the country, aware at last of his folly in alienating the Whig families, the King sought a reconciliation. In July 1765 the Marquis of Rockingham, a shy, well-meaning Whig who was disturbed at George's conduct, undertook to form a Government, and brought with him as private secretary a young Irishman named Edmund Burke, already known in literary circles as a clever writer and a brilliant talker. He was much more. He was a great political thinker. Viewing English politics and the English character with something of the detachment of an alien, he was able to diagnose the situation with an imaginative insight beyond the range of those immersed in the business of the day and bound by traditional habits of mind.

The political history of the years following 1714 had led to a degeneration and dissolution of parties. The personal activity of the sovereign after 1760 and the emergence of great issues of principle found the Whigs helpless and divided into rival clans. The King's tactics had paralysed them. Burke's aim was to create out of the Rockingham group, high-principled but small in numbers and with no original ideas of its own, an effective political party. He could supply the ideas, but first he had to convince the Whigs that a party could be formed and held together on a ground of common principles. He had to overcome the notion, widely prevalent, that party was in itself a rather disreputable thing, a notion which had been strengthened by Pitt's haughty disdain for party business and organisation. It was an old tradition that politicians not in power need not bother to attend Parliament, but should retire to their country estates and there await the return to royal favour and a redistribution of the sweets of office. Individualists of different schools, such as Shelburne and Henry Fox, consistently opposed Burke's efforts to organise them into a party. "You think," Henry Fox had written to Rockingham, "you can but serve the country by continuing a fruitless Opposition. I think it impossible to serve it at all except by coming into office."

A consistent programme, to be advocated in Opposition and realised in office, was Burke's conception of party policy, and the new issues arising plainly required a programme. On Ireland, on America, on India, Burke's attitude was definite. He stood, and he brought his party to stand, for conciliation of the colonies, relaxation of the restraints on Irish trade, and the government of India on the same moral basis as the government of England. At home he proposed to deliver Parliament from its subservience to the Crown by the abolition of numerous sinecures and the limitation of corruption. What he lacked was, in his own words, "the power and purchase" which a strong and well-organised party could supply. For years Burke was a voice crying in the wilderness, and, too often rising to tones of frenzy. An orator to be named with the ancients, an incomparable political reasoner, he lacked both judgment and self-control. He was perhaps the greatest man that Ireland has produced. The same gifts, with a dash of English indolence and irony—he could have borrowed them from Charles James Fox, Henry Fox's famous son, who had plenty of both to spare—might have made him Britain's greatest statesman.

Rockingham's Government, which lasted thirteen months, passed three measures that went far to soothe the animosities raised by Grenville on both sides of the Atlantic. They repealed the Stamp Act, and induced the House of Commons to declare general warrants and the seizure of private papers unlawful. At the same time they reaffirmed the powers of Parliament to tax the colonies in a so-called Declaratory Act. But the King was determined to be rid of them, and Pitt, whose mind was clouded by sickness, was seduced by royal flattery and by his own dislike of party into lending his name to a new administration formed on no political principle whatever. His arrogance remained; his powers were failing; his popularity as the "Great Commoner" had been dimmed by his sudden acceptance of the Earldom of Chatham. The conduct of affairs slipped into other hands: Charles Townshend, the Duke of Grafton, and Lord Shelburne. In 1767 Townshend, against the opposition of Shelburne, introduced a Bill imposing duties on American imports of paper, glass, lead, and tea. There was rage in America. The supply of coin in the colonies would be still more depleted, and any surplus from the new revenue was not, as originally stated, to be used for the upkeep of the British garrisons but to pay British colonial officials. This threatened to make them independent of the colonial assemblies, whose chief weapon against truculent governors had been to withhold their salaries. Even so, revolt was still far from their minds.

Intelligent men, like Governor Hutchinson of Massachusetts, preferred not to impose taxes at all if they could not be enforced, and declared that another repeal would only "facilitate the designs of those persons who appear to be aiming at independency." John Dickinson, of Pennsylvania, in his *Letters from a Farmer,* voiced the opposition in the most widely read pamphlet of the time. It was studiously cautious in tone, and at this stage there were few people who desired secession. The authority of Parliament over the colonies was formally denied, but there was a general loyalty to King and Empire. Most of the opposition still came from respectable merchants, who believed that organised but limited resistance on the commercial plane would bring the British Government to reason.

The Massachusetts Assembly accordingly proposed a joint petition with the other colonial bodies against the new duties. Colonial resistance was now being organised on a continental scale and the barriers of provincialism and jealousy were being lowered. Non-importation agreements were concluded and there was a systematic and most successful boycott of English goods. But tempers began to rise. In May 1768 the sloop *Liberty,* belonging to John Hancock, the most prominent Boston merchant, was stopped and searched near the coast by Royal Customs officers. The colonists rescued it by force. By 1769 British exports to America had fallen by one-half. The Cabinet was not seriously apprehensive, but perturbed. It agreed to drop the duties, except on tea. By a majority of one this was carried. Parliament proclaimed its sovereignty over the colonies by retaining a tax on tea of threepence a pound.

Suddenly by some mysterious operation of Nature the clouds which had gathered round Chatham's intellect cleared. Ill-health had forced him to resign in 1768, and he had been succeeded in office by Grafton. The scene on which he reopened his eyes was lurid enough to dismay any man. In England, as we have seen, a senseless craving for revenge had driven the King and his friends in Parliament to an attempt to expel John Wilkes from the House, which was in fact an attack on the rights of electors throughout the country. The unknown "Junius" was flaying every Minister who provoked his lash. In America blood had not yet flowed, but all the signs of a dissolution of the Empire were there for those who could read them. But George III, after twelve years' intrigue, had at last got a docile, biddable Prime Minister. Lord North became First Lord of the Treasury in 1770. A charming man, of good abilities and faultless temper, he presided over the loss of the American colonies.

At first all seemed quiet. The American merchants were delighted at the repeal of the import duties, and by the middle of 1770 reconciliation seemed complete, except in Boston. Here Samuel Adams, fertile organiser of resistance and advocate of separation, saw that the struggle was now reaching a crucial stage. Hitherto the quarrel had been at bottom a commercial dispute, and neither the American merchants nor the English Ministers had any sympathy for his ideas. Adams feared that the resistance of the colonies would crumble and the British would reassert their authority unless more trouble was stirred up. This he and other Radical leaders proceeded to do.

News that the duties were withdrawn had hardly reached America when the first blood was shed. Most of the British garrison was stationed in Boston. The troops were unpopular with the townsfolk, and Adams spread evil rumours of their conduct. The "lobsters" in their scarlet coats were insulted and jeered at wherever they appeared. In March 1770 the persistent snowballing by Boston urchins of English sentries outside the barracks caused a riot. In the confusion and shouting some of the troops opened fire and there were casualties. This "massacre" was just the sort of incident that Adams had hoped for. But moderate men of property were nervous, and opinion in the colonies remained disunited and uncertain. The Radicals persisted. In June 1772 rioters burned a British Revenue cutter, H.M.S. *Gaspee,* off Rhode Island. "Committees of Correspondence" were set up throughout Massachusetts, and by the end of the year had spread to seventy-five towns. The Virginian agitators, led by the young Patrick Henry, created a standing committee of their Assembly to keep in touch with the other colonies, and a chain of such bodies was quickly formed. Thus the machinery of revolt was quietly and efficiently created.

Nevertheless the Radicals were still in a minority and there was much opposition to an abrupt break with England. Benjamin Franklin, one of the leading colonial representatives in London, wrote as late as 1773: ". . . There seem to be among us some violent spirits who are for an immediate rupture; but I trust that the general prudence of our country will see that by our growing strength we advance fast to a situation in which our claims must be allowed, that by a premature struggle we may be crippled and kept down, . . . that between governed and governing every mistake in government, every encroachment on right, is not worth a rebellion, . . . remembering withal that this Protestant country (our mother, though lately an unkind one) is worth preserving, and that her weight in the scales of Europe and her safety in a great degree may depend on our union with her." In spite of the Boston "massacre," the violence on the high seas, and the commercial squabbles, the agitations of Adams and his friends were beginning to peter out, when Lord North committed a fatal blunder.

The East India Company was nearly bankrupt, and the Government had been forced to come to its rescue. An Act was passed through Parliament, attracting little notice among the Members, authorising the company to ship tea, of which it had an enormous surplus, direct to the colonies, without paying import duties, and to sell it through its own agents in America. Thus in effect the company was granted a monopoly. The outcry across the Atlantic was instantaneous. The extremists denounced it as an invasion of their liberties, and the merchants were threatened with ruin. American shippers who brought tea from the British customs-houses and their middle-men who sold it would all be thrown out of business. The Act succeeded where Adams had failed: it united colonial opinion against the British.

The Radicals, who began to call themselves "Patriots," seized their opportunity to force a crisis. In December 1773 the first cargoes arrived in Boston. Rioters disguised as Red Indians boarded the ships and destroyed the cases. "Last night," wrote John Adams, Samuel's cousin, and later the second President of the United States, "three cargoes of Bohea tea were emptied into the sea. . . . This is the most magnificent movement of all. There is a dignity, a majesty and sublimity in this last effort of the Patriots that I greatly admire. . . . This destruction of the tea is so bold, so daring, so firm, intrepid, and inflexible, and it must have so important consequences, and so lasting, that I cannot but consider it as an epoch in history. This, however, is but an attack upon property. Another similar exertion of popular power may produce the destruction of lives. Many persons wish that as many dead carcases were floating in the harbour as there are chests of tea. A much less number of lives, however, would remove the causes of all our calamities."

When the news reached London the cry went up for coercion and the reactionaries in the British Government became supreme. In vain Burke and Chatham pleaded for conciliation. Parliament passed a series of "Coercion Acts" which suspended the Massachusetts Assembly, declared the colony to be in Crown hands, closed the port of Boston, and decreed that all judges in the colony were henceforth to be appointed by the Crown. These measures were confined to Massachusetts; only one of them, the Quartering Act, applied to the rest of the colonies, and this declared that troops were to be quartered throughout all of them to preserve order. Thus it was hoped to isolate the resistance. It had the opposite effect.

In September 1774 the colonial assemblies held a congress at Philadelphia. The extremists were not yet out of hand, and the delegates still concentrated on commercial boycotts. An association was formed to stop all trade with England unless the Coercion Acts were repealed, and the Committees of Correspondence were charged with carrying out the plan. A Declaration of Rights demanded the rescinding of some thirteen commercial Acts passed by the British Parliament since 1763. The tone of this document, which was dispatched to London, was one of respectful moderation. But in London all moderation was cast aside. The "sugar interest" in the House of Commons, jealous of colonial competition in the West Indies; Army officers who despised the colonial troops; the Government, pressed for money and blinded by the doctrine that colonies only existed for the benefit of the Mother Country: all combined to extinguish the last hope of peace. The petition was rejected with contempt.

Events now moved swiftly. The Massachusetts Military Governor, General Thomas Gage, tried to enforce martial law, but the task was beyond him. Gage was an able soldier, but he had only four thousand troops and could hold no place outside Boston. The Patriots had about ten thousand men in the colonial militia. In October they set up a "Committee of Safety," and most of the colonies started drilling and arming. Collection of military equipment and powder began. Cannon were seized from Government establishments. Agents were sent to Europe to buy weapons. Both France and Spain refused the British Government's request to prohibit the sale of gunpowder to the Americans, and Dutch merchants shipped it in large glass bottles labelled "Spirits."

The Patriots began accumulating these warlike stores at Concord, a village twenty miles from Boston, where the Massachusetts Assembly, which Parliament had declared illegal, was now in session. Gage decided to seize their ammunition and arrest Samuel Adams and his colleague John Hancock. But the colonists were on the alert. Every night they patrolled the streets of Boston watching for any move by the English troops. As Gage gathered his men messengers warned the assembly at Concord. The military supplies were scattered among towns farther north and Adams and Hancock moved to Lexington. On April 18, 1775, eight hundred British troops set off in darkness along the

Concord road. But the secret was out. One of the patrols, Paul Revere, from his post in the steeple of the North Church, warned messengers by lantern signals. He himself mounted his horse and rode hard to Lexington, rousing Adams and Hancock from their beds and urging them to flight.

At five o'clock in the morning the local militia of Lexington, seventy strong, formed up on the village green. As the sun rose the head of the British column, with three officers riding in front, came into view. The leading officer, brandishing his sword, shouted, "Disperse, you rebels, immediately!" The militia commander ordered his men to disperse. The colonial committees were very anxious not to fire the first shot, and there were strict orders not to provoke open conflict with the British regulars. But in the confusion someone fired. A volley was returned. The ranks of the militia were thinned and there was a general *mêlée*. Brushing aside the survivors, the British column marched on to Concord. But now the countryside was up in arms and the bulk of the stores had been moved to safety. It was with difficulty that the British straggled back to Boston, with the enemy close at their heels. The town was cut off from the mainland. The news of Lexington and Concord spread to the other colonies, and Governors and British officials were expelled. With strategic insight forts on Lake George, at the head of the Hudson valley, were seized by a Patriot force under Benedict Arnold, a merchant from Connecticut. The British were thus denied any help from Canada, and the War of Independence had begun.

CHAPTER 7

THE WAR OF INDEPENDENCE

IN MAY 1775 a congress of delegates from the American colonies met in the Carpenters' Hall of the quiet Pennsylvanian town of Philadelphia. They were respectable lawyers, doctors, merchants, and landowners, nervous at the onrush of events, and seemingly unfitted to form a revolutionary committee. The first shots had been fired and blood had been shed, but all hope of compromise had not yet vanished, and they were fearful of raising a military Power which might, like Cromwell's Ironsides, overwhelm its creators. They had no common national tradition except that against which they were revolting, no organisation, no industries, no treasury, no supplies, no army. Many of them still hoped for peace with England. Yet British troops under General Sir William Howe were on their way across the Atlantic, and armed, violent, fratricidal conflict stared them in the face.

The centre of resistance and the scene of action was Boston, where Gage and the only British force on the continent were hemmed in by sixteen thousand New England merchants and farmers. There was continual friction within the town, not only between Patriots and soldiery, but between Patriots and Loyalists. Derisive placards were hung outside the quarters of the troops and all was in ferment. On May 25 Howe, accompanied by Generals Clinton and Burgoyne, sailed into the harbour with reinforcements which brought the total English troops to about six thousand men.

Thus strengthened, Gage took the offensive. To the north, across a short tract of water, lay a small peninsula connected by a narrow neck with the mainland. Here Breed's Hill and Bunker Hill dominated the town. If the colonists could occupy and hold these eminences they could cannonade the English out of Boston. On the evening of June 16 Gage determined to forestall them, but next morning a line of entrenchments had appeared upon the heights across the water. Patriot troops, warned by messages from Boston, had dug themselves in during the night. Their position nevertheless seemed perilous. The English ships could bombard them from the harbour or put landing-parties on the neck of the peninsula and cut them off from their base. But neither course was attempted. Gage was resolved on a display of force. He had under his command some of the best regiments in the British Army, and he and his fellow-countrymen had acquired a hard contempt for the colonials in earlier wars. He decided to make a frontal attack on the hill, so that all Boston, crowded in its windows and upon its roofs, should witness the spectacle of British soldiers marching steadily in line to storm the rebel entrenchments.

On the hot afternoon of the 17th Howe, under Gage's orders, supervised the landing of about three thousand British regulars. He drew up his men and made them a speech. "You must drive these farmers from the hill or it will be impossible for us to remain in Boston. But I shall not desire any of you to advance a single step beyond where I am at the head of your line." In three lines the redcoats moved slowly towards the summit of Breed's Hill. There was silence. The whole of Boston was looking on. At a hundred yards from the trenches there was still not a sound in front. But at fifty yards a hail of buck-shot and bullets from ancient hunting guns smote the attackers. There was shouting and curses. "Are the Yankees cowards?" was hurled from the breastworks of the trenches. Howe, his white silk breeches splashed with blood, rallied his men, but they were scattered by another volley and driven to their boats. Howe's reputation was at stake and he realised that ammunition was running short on the hill-top. At the third rush, this time in column, the regulars drove the farmers from their line. It was now evening. The village of Charlestown, on the Boston side of the peninsula, was in flames. Over a thousand Englishmen had fallen on the slopes. Of the three thousand farmers who had held the crest a sixth were killed or wounded. Throughout the night carriages and chaises bore the English casualties into Boston.

This sharp and bloody action sent a stir throughout the colonies, and has been compared in its effects with Bull Run, eighty-six years later. The rebels had become heroes. They had stood up to trained troops, destroyed a third of their opponents, and wiped out in blood the legend of Yankee cowardice. The British had captured the hill, but the Americans had won the glory. Gage made no further attack and in

October he was recalled to England in disgrace. Howe succeeded to the command. On both sides of the Atlantic men perceived that a mortal struggle impended.

It was now imperative for the Patriots to raise an army. Massachusetts had already appealed to Congress at Philadelphia for help against the British and for the appointment of a Commander-in-Chief. Two days before the action at Breed's Hill Congress had agreed. There had been much talk of whom they were to choose. There was jealousy and dislike of the New Englanders, who were bearing the brunt of the fighting, and largely for political reasons it was decided to appoint a Southerner. Adams' eye centred upon a figure in uniform, among the dark brown clothes of the delegates. He was Colonel George Washington, of Mount Vernon, Virginia. This prosperous planter had fought in the campaigns of the 1750's and had helped extricate the remnants of Braddock's force from their disastrous advance. He was the only man of any military experience at the Congress, and this was limited to a few minor campaigns on the frontier. He was now given command of all the forces that America could raise. Great calls were to be made on the spirit of resolution that was his by nature.

The colonies contained about 280,000 men capable of bearing arms, but at no time during the war did Washington succeed in gathering together more than twenty-five thousand. Jealousy between the colonies and lack of equipment and organisation hampered his efforts. His immediate task was to provide the ragged band at Boston with discipline and munitions, and to this he devoted the autumn and winter months of 1775. Congress nevertheless resolved on an offensive. An expedition was dispatched to Canada under Benedict Arnold, who was to be for ever infamous in American history, and Richard Montgomery, who had once served under Wolfe. They marched along the same routes which the British troops had taken in the campaign of 1759, and they had only eleven hundred men between them. Montgomery captured and occupied Montreal, which was undefended. He then joined Arnold, who after desperate hardships had arrived with the ghost of an army before the fortifications of Quebec. In the depth of winter, in driving snow, they flung themselves at the Heights of Abraham, defended by Sir Guy Carleton with a few hundred men. Montgomery was killed and Arnold's leg was shattered. The survivors, even after this repulse, hung on in their wind-swept camp across the river. But in the spring, when the ice melted in the St. Lawrence, the first reinforcements arrived from England. Having lost more than half their men, the Patriots thereupon trudged back to Maine and Fort Ticonderoga. Canada thus escaped the revolutionary upsurge. French Canadians were on the whole content with life under the British Crown. Soon Canada was to harbour many refugees from the United States who were unable to forswear their loyalty to George III.

Meanwhile Howe was still confined to Boston. He shrank from taking reprisals, and for at least the first two years of the war he hoped for conciliation. Both he and his generals were Whig Members of Parliament, and they shared the party view that a successful war against the colonists was impossible. He was a gallant and capable commander in the field, but always slow to take the initiative. He now set himself the task of overawing the Americans. This, however, needed extensive help from England, and as none arrived, and Boston itself was of no strategic importance, he evacuated the town in the spring of 1776 and moved to the only British base on the Atlantic seaboard, Halifax, in Nova Scotia. At the same time a small expedition under General Clinton was sent southwards to the Loyalists in Charleston in the hope of rallying the Middle and Southern colonies. But the Patriot resistance was stiffening, and although the moderate elements in Congress had hitherto opposed any formal Declaration of Independence the evacuation of Boston roused them to a sterner effort. Until they acquired what would nowadays be called belligerent status they could get no military supplies from abroad, except by smuggling, and supplies were essential. The Conservative politicians were gradually yielding to the Radicals. The publication of a pamphlet called *Common Sense,* by Tom Paine, an English extremist lately arrived in America, put the case for revolution with enormous success and with far greater effect than the writings of intellectuals like Adams.

But it was the British Government which took the next step towards dissolving the tie of allegiance between England and America. Early in 1776 Parliament passed a Prohibitory Act forbidding all intercourse with the rebellious colonies and declaring a blockade of the American coast. At the same time, it being impossible to raise enough British troops, Hessians were hired from Germany and dispatched across the Atlantic. The resulting outcry in America strengthened the hands of the extremists. At Philadelphia on June 7 Richard Henry Lee, of Virginia, moved the following resolution: "That these united colonies are and of right ought to be free and independent states; that they are absolved from all allegiance to the British Crown, and that all political connection between them and the state of Great Britain is and ought to be totally dissolved." But six of the thirteen colonies still opposed an immediate Declaration. A large-scale British invasion was feared. No foreign alliances had yet been concluded. Many felt that a formal defiance would wreck their cause and alienate their supporters. But at last a committee was appointed, a paper was drafted by Thomas Jefferson, and on July 4, 1776, the Declaration of Independence was unanimously accepted by the Congress of the American colonies.

This historic document proclaimed the causes of the revolt, and enumerated twenty-eight "repeated injuries and usurpations" by the King of Great Britain. The opening is familiar and immortal: "When, in the course of human events, it becomes necessary for one people to dissolve the political bands which have connected them with another, and to assume among the powers of the earth the separate and equal station to which the Laws of Nature and of Nature's God entitle them, a decent respect to the opinions of mankind requires that they should declare the causes which impel them to the separation.

"We hold these truths to be self-evident: that all men are created equal, that they are endowed by their Creator with certain unalienable rights, that among these are life, liberty, and the pursuit of happiness. That to secure these rights Governments are instituted among men, deriving their just powers from the consent of the governed. That whenever any form of government becomes destructive of these ends it is the right of the people to alter or to abolish it, and to institute new government, laying its foundation on such principles and organising its powers in such form as to them shall seem most likely to effect their safety and happiness."

The Declaration was in the main a restatement of the principles which had animated the Whig struggle against the later Stuarts and the English Revolution of 1688, and it now became the symbol and rallying centre of the Patriot cause. Its immediate result was to increase the number of Loyalists, frightened by this splendid defiance. But the purpose of the colonies was proclaimed. The waverers were forced to a decision. There was now no turning back.

All this time the British had remained at Halifax awaiting reinforcements from England and meditating their strategy. Military success hinged on control of the Hudson valley. If they could seize and hold the waterway, and the forts which guarded it, New England would be sundered from the Middle and Southern colonies, which contained two-thirds of the population and most of the food and wealth. The first step was to capture New York, at the river-mouth. Howe could then move northwards, subdue the forts, and join hands with a force from Canada. Thereafter the South, where the settlements lay largely upon the rivers, could be crushed with the help of the Fleet. The plan seemed promising, for the colonists possessed no Navy and Great Britain

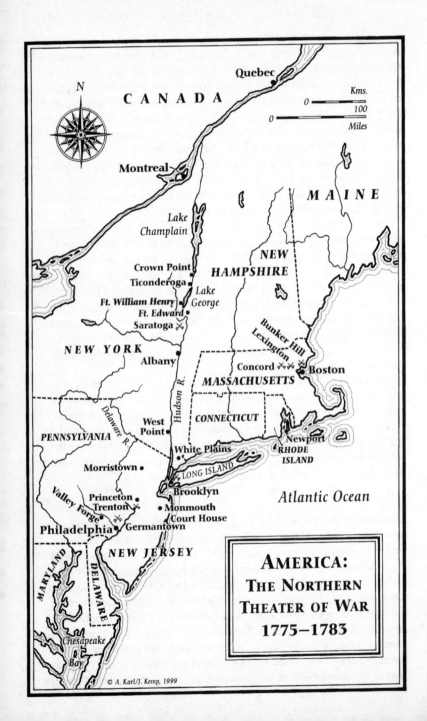

N

Quebec

C A N A D A

Kms.
0 _____ 100
0 _____
Miles

Montreal

M A I N E

Lake
Champlain

NEW
HAMPSHIRE

Crown Point
Ticonderoga
Lake
George
Ft. William Henry
Ft. Edward
Saratoga ⚔

Bunker Hill
Lexington

NEW YORK

Albany

Concord ⚔ ⚔   Boston

MASSACHUSETTS

Hudson R.

West
Point

CONNECTICUT

Delaware R.

PENNSYLVANIA

White Plains

Newport
RHODE
ISLAND

Morristown

LONG ISLAND

Brooklyn

Atlantic Ocean

Valley Forge

Princeton
Trenton ⚔

Monmouth
Court House

Philadelphia

Germantown

NEW JERSEY

MARYLAND

DELAWARE

AMERICA:
THE NORTHERN
THEATER OF WAR
1775–1783

Chesapeake
Bay

© A. Karl/J. Kemp, 1999

should have been able to blockade the Atlantic seaboard. But the Fleet was no longer in the high efficiency to which it had been raised by Chatham's admirals. It was able to bring reinforcements across the Atlantic, but in the event New England privateers did much damage to military operations on the coast and harassed transport vessels and supplies. In June 1776 Howe moved to New York, and began to invest the city, and in July his brother, Admiral Howe, arrived from England with a fleet of over five hundred sail and reinforcements. Howe was now in command of some twenty-five thousand men. This was the largest armed force that had yet been seen in the New World. But Washington was ready. He concentrated his army, now reduced by desertions and smallpox to about twenty thousand men, around the city. From the British camp on Staten Island the American lines could be seen across the bay on the spurs of Long Island, and on the heights of Brooklyn above the East River. In August Howe attacked. The slaughter of Bunker Hill, for thus the action at Breed's Hill is known, had taught him caution and this time he abstained from a frontal assault. He made a feint against the Long Island entrenchments, and then flung his main force to the left of the Americans and descended upon their rear. The stroke succeeded and Washington was compelled to retreat into New York City. Adverse winds impeded the British fleet and he and his army escaped safely across the East River.

In this disaster Washington appealed to Congress. It seemed impossible to make a stand in New York, yet to abandon it would dismay the Patriots. But Congress ordered him to evacuate the city without fighting, and after skirmishing on the Harlem heights he withdrew slowly northwards. At this juncture victory lay at Howe's finger-tips. He was master of New York and of the Hudson River for forty miles above it. If he had pursued Washington with the same skill and vigour as Grant was to pursue Lee eighty-eight years later he might have captured the whole colonial army. But for nearly a month Washington was unmolested. At the end of October he was again defeated in a sharp fight at White Plains; but once more the English made no attempt to pursue, and Washington waited desperately to see whether Howe would attack up the Hudson or strike through New Jersey at Philadelphia. Howe resolved to move on Philadelphia. He turned south, capturing as he went the forts in the neighbourhood of New York, and the delegates at Philadelphia fled. Thousands of Americans flocked to the British camp to declare their loyalty. The only hope for the Patriots seemed a mass trek across the Alleghenies into new lands, a migration away from British rule like that of the Boers in the nineteenth century. Even Washington considered such a course. "We must then [*i.e.*, if defeated] retire to Augusta County, in Virginia. Numbers will repair to us for safety and we will try a predatory war. If overpowered we must cross the Allegheny Mountains."* Meanwhile he traversed the Hudson and fell back southwards to cover Philadelphia.

The British were hard on his heels and began a rapid occupation of New Jersey. The Patriot cause seemed lost. But Washington remained alert and undaunted and fortune rewarded him. With an imprudence which is difficult to understand, and was soon to be punished, outposts from the British Army were flung about in careless fashion through the New Jersey towns. Washington determined to strike at these isolated bodies before Howe could cross the Delaware River. He selected the village of Trenton, held by a force of Hessians. On Christmas Night the Patriot troops fought their way into the lightly guarded village. At the cost of two officers and two privates they killed or wounded a hundred and six Hessians. The survivors were captured and sent to parade the streets of Philadelphia. The effect of the stroke was out of all proportion to its military importance. It was the most critical moment in the war. At Princeton Lord Cornwallis, a subordinate of Howe's of whom more was to be heard later, tried to avenge the defeat, but was foiled. Washington marched behind him and threatened his line of communications. The year thus ended with the British in winter quarters in New Jersey, but confined by these two actions to the east of the Delaware. Their officers spent a cheerful season in the society of New York. Meanwhile Benjamin Franklin and Silas Deane, first of American diplomats, crossed the Atlantic to seek help from France.

Posterity should not be misled into thinking that war on the American colonies received the unanimous support of the British people. Burke for one had no illusions. "No man," he had written after Bunker Hill, "commends the measures which have been pursued, or expects any good from those which are in preparation, but it is a cold, languid opinion, like what men discover in affairs that do not concern them. . . . The merchants are gone from us and from themselves. . . . The leading men among them are kept full fed with contracts and remittances and jobs of all descriptions, and are indefatigable in their endeavours to keep the others quiet. . . . They all, or the greatest number of them, begin to snuff the cadaverous *haut goût* of lucrative war. War is indeed become a sort of substitute for commerce. The freighting business never was so lively, on account of the prodigious taking

* J. Fisher, *The Writings of John Fisher* (1902), vol. i.

up for transport service. Great orders for provisions and stores of all kinds . . . keep up the spirits of the mercantile world, and induce them to consider the American war not so much their calamity as their resource in an inevitable distress." Powerful English politicians denounced not only the military and naval mismanagement, but the use of force against the colonists at all.

There was gloating over every setback and disaster to the British cause. "The parricide joy of some in the losses of their country makes me mad," wrote a Government supporter. "They do not disguise it. A patriotic duke told me some weeks ago that some ships had been lost off the coast of North America in a storm. He said a thousand British sailors were drowned—not one escaped—with joy sparkling in his eyes. . . . In the House of Commons it is not unusual to speak of the provincials as 'our Army.' " Such antics only made things worse. Indeed, but for the violence of the Opposition, which far outran the country's true feelings, it is probable that Lord North's administration would have fallen much sooner. As it was, he commanded large majorities in the House of Commons throughout the war. Not all the Opposition Members were so foolish or so extreme, but in the King's mind all were traitors. George III grew stubborn and even more intent. He closed his ears to moderate counsel and refused to admit into his Government those men of both parties who, like many American Loyalists, foresaw and condemned the disasters into which his policy was tottering and were horrified at the civil war between the Mother Country and her colonies. Even Lord North was half-hearted, and only his loyalty to the King and his sincere old-fashioned belief, shared by many politicians of his day, that a Minister's duty was to carry out the personal wishes of the sovereign stopped him resigning much sooner than he did. Though technically responsible as First Lord of the Treasury and Chancellor of the Exchequer, he had no grip on the conduct of affairs and allowed the King and the departmental Ministers to control the day-to-day work of government. George III tirelessly struggled to superintend the details of the war organisation, but he was incapable of co-ordinating the activities of his Ministers. These were of poor quality. The Admiralty was headed by Wilkes's comrade in debauch, the Earl of Sandwich. His reputation has been mauled, but recent research has shown that at least the Fleet was in much better condition than the Army.

Rarely has British strategy fallen into such a multitude of errors. Every maxim and principle of war was either violated or disregarded. "Seek out and destroy the enemy" is a sound rule. "Concentrate your force" is a sound method. "Maintain your objective" is common sense. The enemy was Washington's army. The force consisted of Howe's troops in New York and Burgoyne's columns now assembled in Montreal. The objective was to destroy Washington's army and kill or capture Washington. If he could be brought to battle and every man and gun turned against him, a British victory was almost certain. But these obvious truths were befogged and bedevilled by multiplicity of counsel. Howe was still determined to capture Philadelphia, the seat of the revolutionary Congress and the fountain-head of political resistance. Burgoyne, on the other hand, was hot for a descent from Canada into the upper reaches of the Hudson valley, and a seizure, with the aid of a thrust from New York, of the forts which dominated the waterway. Once in control of the Hudson, New England could be isolated and speedily subdued. Burgoyne had obtained leave of absence and journeyed to England late in the autumn of 1775. He offered his advice to the London Government. George III approved his plan and endorsed it in his own hand. Burgoyne was to advance from Montreal through the wooded borders of the frontier and seize the fort at Ticonderoga near the valley-head. At the same time a force from New York would strike north, capture the citadel of West Point, which had recently been strengthened with the help of French engineers, and join him at Albany.

Thus the London planners. The ultimate responsibility for co-ordinating these movements lay with the War Minister, Lord George Germain. Germain's career in the Army had ended in disgrace, though his military experience may not have been a fair guide to his capacities. Twenty years before he had refused to charge with his cavalry at the Battle of Minden, and been declared unfit to serve by a court-martial. But, secure in the favour of the young King, he had made himself into a politician. The Government were well aware that Howe intended to move in the opposite direction to Burgoyne, namely, southwards against Philadelphia, but did nothing to dissuade him. They gave him no orders to join forces at Albany and they stinted him of reinforcements. "The extraordinary spectacle was thus presented," writes an American historian, "of a subordinate general going to London and getting the King's approval to one plan of campaign; of the King's Minister sending full instructions to one general and none to the other who was to co-operate with him; and of this other general making his own independent plan. . . ."* On his return to Canada Burgoyne nevertheless sent Howe no fewer than three letters about the plan to meet at Albany, but in the absence of precise directions from England Howe saw no reason to abandon his project against Philadelphia. He held to

* F. V. Greene, *The Revolutionary War* (1911).

his course. Having tried and failed to bring Washington to battle, he left a garrison of eight thousand men in New York under Sir Henry Clinton and sailed in July 1777 with the main part of his army to Chesapeake Bay. Instead of concentrating their strength, the British forces were now dispersed over eight hundred miles of country, and divided between Burgoyne in Canada, Howe on the Chesapeake, and Clinton in New York.

Washington, from his winter quarters at Morristown, on the borders of New Jersey, moved hastily south-westwards to screen Philadelphia. Having abandoned New York without a serious fight, he could hardly do the same at the capital of the Congress, but with his ill-disciplined force, fluctuating in numbers, he could only hope to delay the British advance. At the beginning of September Howe advanced with about fourteen thousand men. Washington, with a similar force, drew up his lines on the north bank of the River Brandywine, barring the road to the capital. Howe perceived and exploited the faulty equipment of the army in front of him, its lack of an efficient staff and its inability to get quick information. He made the same feinting movements which had served so well at Long Island. On the morning of the 11th he divided his army, and, leaving a powerful body to make a frontal attack, marched up-river with Cornwallis, crossed it, and descended on Washington's right flank. His tactics went like clockwork. The attack was successful, disorder spread, and the British troops on the far bank crossed the river and drove the whole American force before them. By sunset Washington was in full retreat. As the Marquis de Lafayette, a young French volunteer in the American army, described it, "Fugitives, cannon, and baggage crowded without order into the road." But here, as at Long Island, Howe refused to pursue and capture the enemy. He was content. On September 26 his advance-guards entered Philadelphia. There was a confused fight to the north of the city at Germantown, but the British pressed on, and soon afterwards the capital fell.

By now however the London plans for the northern theatre were beginning to miscarry. Burgoyne, with a few hundred Indians and seven thousand regulars, of whom half were German, was moving through the Canadian forests expecting to join with the British forces from New York. After an arduous march he reached Fort Ticonderoga, and found that the Americans had retired, leaving their artillery behind them. He pushed eagerly southwards. If only Howe was moving up to West Point nothing could prevent an overwhelming success. But where was Howe? On the day that Burgoyne moved upon the next American fort Howe had sailed southwards from New York. All concerned were confident that after capturing Philadelphia Howe could quickly return to New York and reach out to the expedition from Canada. He failed to do so, and Burgoyne paid the price.

As Burgoyne advanced the New England militia gathered against him. He was a popular and dashing commander, but the country was difficult, he was harassed by raids, and his troops began to falter and to dwindle. He could still succeed if help came from New York. Clinton's garrison there had been halved, since Howe had called upon him for reinforcements. Nevertheless Clinton marched north and managed to capture West Point, but as the autumn rains descended Burgoyne was cornered at Saratoga, and the New Englanders, their strength daily increasing, closed in. He was only fifty miles from Albany, where he should have met the column from New York, but he could make no headway. Days of hard fighting in the woodlands followed. His supplies ran low, and he was heavily outnumbered. The Americans were operating in their own country by their own methods. Each man fighting mostly on his own initiative, hiding behind bushes and in the tops of trees, they inflicted severe casualties upon some of the best regiments that Europe could muster. The precise drill and formations of Burgoyne's men had no effect. An American deserter brought news that Clinton was moving northwards. It was too late. The Germans refused to fight any longer, and on October 17, 1777, Burgoyne surrendered to the American commander, Horatio Gates. The surrender terms were violated by Congress and the main body of his army were kept prisoners until the signing of the peace. Burgoyne returned to England to attack and be attacked by the Ministry.

At this point in the struggle the Old World stepped in to aid and comfort the New. Although militarily indecisive in America, Saratoga had an immediate effect in France. The French, though technically at peace with Britain, had been supplying the Patriots with arms, and French volunteers were serving in the colonial army. At Versailles Benjamin Franklin and Silas Deane had been urging an open alliance, but for a year both sides had wavered. The French Ministers hesitated to support the cause of liberty overseas while suppressing it at home, and many Americans feared that France would exact a heavy price for declaring war on England. Now all doubts were swept away. The colonists could not survive without French supplies, and the mass of Frenchmen were vehement to avenge the defeats of the Seven Years War. The French Navy had been strengthened; the British Fleet was disintegrating; and when the news arrived of Saratoga Louis XVI resolved on an official alliance. There was consternation in London, where the Whig Opposition had long warned the Government against harsh dealings with the colonists, and the British Ministry formulated a generous compromise. It was too late. On February 6, 1778, before the Congress could be apprised of the new offer, Benjamin Franklin signed an alliance with France.

Thus began another world war, and Britain was now without a single ally. She had lost one army as prisoners in America. There were no more troops to be hired in Germany. Old fears of invasion spread panic through the country. The Ministry was discredited. In the agony all minds except the King's turned to Chatham. On April 7 Chatham dragged himself upon crutches to make his last speech against an Opposition address for recalling the Army in America. He had always stood for conciliation and not for surrender. The corpse-like figure, swathed in flannel bandages, tottered to its feet. The House was hushed with the anticipation of death. In whispering sentences, shot through with a sudden gleam of fierce anger, he made his attack "against the dismemberment of this ancient and most noble monarchy." He warned the nation of the dangers of French intervention and the use of German mercenaries. He scourged his countrymen for their inhumanity. "My lords, if I were an American as I am an Englishman, while a foreign troop was landed in my country I never would lay down my arms—never, never, never." He dismissed the threat of invasion with contemptuous sarcasm. He struggled to speak again after the reply of the Opposition leader, the Duke of Richmond, but collapsed senseless in an apoplectic fit. On May 11 he died as his son William was reading to him from Homer the solemn scene of Hector's funeral and the deep despair of Troy. George III displayed his smallness of mind by opposing the plan to erect a monument, which would be, he said, "an offensive measure to me personally"; but the City of London defied him, and Burke's inscription was a fitting memorial: "The means by which Providence raises a nation to greatness are the virtues infused into great men." Such men were very few in the England of Lord North.

CHAPTER 8

THE UNITED STATES

W ASHINGTON IN 1777 took up his winter quarters at Valley Forge, to the north of Philadelphia. At the end of every campaign there were many desertions, and he was now reduced to about nine thousand men, of whom another third were to melt away by the spring. Short of clothing and shelter, they shivered and grumbled through the winter months, while in Philadelphia, a score of miles away, nearly twenty thousand well-equipped English troops were quartered in comfort. The social season was at its height, and the numerous Loyalists in the capital made the stay of Howe and his officers pleasing and cheerful. The British made no move to attack the Patriot army. While Washington could not count on provisions for his men even a day in advance, Howe danced and gambled in Philadelphia. As at Long Island, as at White Plains, as at the Brandywine River, he refused to follow up his victory in the field and annihilate his enemy. Unnerved perhaps by the carnage at Bunker Hill, and still hoping for conciliation, he did nothing. Some inkling of his reluctance may have reached the ears of the Government; at any rate, when news of the French alliance with the rebels reached England at the beginning of the New Year he was recalled.

Howe's successor was Sir Henry Clinton, the former commander of New York, who held very different views on the conduct of hostilities. He perceived that European tactics of march and counter-march and the siege and capture of towns and cities would never prevail against an armed and scattered population. The solution, he thought, was to occupy and settle the whole country. He also made a momentous change of strategy. He resolved to abandon the offensive in the North and begin the process of reduction by subduing the South. Here was the bulk of the population and the wealth, and the main repository of such supplies as the Continent could furnish. Here also were many Loyalists. They must be heartened and organised. A new base would be needed, for New York was too far away, and Clinton's eye rested on Charleston and Savannah. Much could be said for all this, and much might have been achieved if he had been allowed to try it out, but there now appeared a new force which abruptly checked and in time proved deadly to the realisation of these large plans. Savannah was eight hundred miles and fifty days' march from New York. Hitherto Britain had held command of the sea and could shift her troops by salt water far more speedily than the Patriots could move by land, but all was now changed by the intervention of France and the French Fleet. Sea-power was henceforth to dominate and decide the American struggle for independence, and Clinton soon received a sharp reminder that this was now in dispute.

In April 1778 twelve French ships of the line, mounting, with their attendant frigates, over eight hundred guns, set sail from Toulon. Four thousand soldiers were on board. News of their approach reached Clinton and it became his immediate and vital task to stop them seizing his main base at New York. If they captured the port, or even blockaded the mouth of the Hudson, his whole position on the Continent would be imperilled. On June 18 he accordingly abandoned Philadelphia and marched rapidly across New Jersey with ten thousand troops. Washington, his army swollen by spring recruiting to about equal strength, set off in parallel line of pursuit. At Monmouth Court House there was a confused fight. Clinton beat off the Americans, not without heavy loss, and did not reach New York till the beginning of July. He was only just in time. On the very day of his arrival a French fleet under d'Estaing appeared off the city. They were confronted by a British squadron under Admiral Howe, brother of the superseded military commander, and for weeks the two forces manœuvred outside the harbour. The French attempted to seize Rhode Island, but were frustrated, and Howe in a series of operations which has drawn high praise from American naval historians defeated all efforts by his opponent to intervene. In the autumn d'Estaing abandoned the struggle and sailed for the West Indies. Here also Clinton had managed to forestall the French. Earlier in the year he had sent troops to St. Lucia. D'Estaing arrived too late to intercept them, and this strategic island became a British base.

Nevertheless these successes could not disguise the root facts that

Clinton's campaign against the South had been delayed for a year and that Britain was no longer in undisputed command of the sea. The French Fleet dominated the Channel and hindered the transport to New York of men and supplies from Britain, while New England privateers waged a lively and profitable warfare against English commerce. Military operations in America came slowly to a standstill, and although three thousand of Clinton's troops occupied Savannah in Georgia on December 29 his plans for subduing the rebels from a Loyalist base in the South were hampered and curtailed. A furious civil war between Loyalists and Patriots had erupted in these regions, but he could do little to help. Stalemate continued throughout 1779, and for a time the main seat of war shifted from the New World. Both armies in America were crippled, the American from the financial chaos and weak credit of the Congress Government, and the British for want of reinforcements. Fear of invasion gripped the British Government and troops intended for Clinton were kept in the British Isles. The French, for their part, realised that they could get all they wanted in America by fighting Britain on the high seas, and this was anyway much more to the taste of the autocratic Government at Versailles than helping republican rebels. Except for a few volunteers, they did not at this stage send any military or naval help to their allies across the Atlantic; but stores of munitions and clothing preserved the Patriot cause from collapse. In June the world conflict spread and deepened and another European Power entered the struggle. French diplomacy brought Spain into the war. Britain was still further weakened, her naval communications in the Mediterranean were imperilled, and within a few months Gibraltar was besieged. In the New World she was forced to keep watch against a Spanish incursion into Florida, and American privateers based on the port of New Orleans harassed English commerce in the Caribbean.

In European waters one of these privateers provided a colourful episode. An American captain of Scottish birth named John Paul Jones was supplied by the French with an ancient East India merchantman, which he converted in French dockyards into a man-of-war. It was named the *Bonhomme Richard,* and in September Captain Jones, with a polyglot crew and in company with three smaller vessels, sailed his memorable craft into the North Sea. Off Flamborough Head he intercepted a convoy of merchantmen from the Baltic, and straightway attacked the English escorts, the men-of-war *Serapis* and *Scarborough.* The merchant ships escaped, and on the evening of the 23rd battle commenced between the *Serapis* and the *Bonhomme Richard.* The English vessel was superior in construction, equipment, and guns, but Jones manœuvred his vessel alongside and lashed himself to his adversary. Throughout the night the two vessels rocked together, the muzzles of their guns almost touching, mauling each other with broadsides, musketry volleys, and hand-grenades. At times both ships were on fire. Jones's three smaller vessels circled the inferno, firing broadsides into both ships. The English and American captains fought grimly on. At last towards dawn there was a violent explosion in the powder magazine of the *Serapis*. Her guns were wrecked and all abaft the mainmast were killed. The English were forced to surrender; but the *Bonhomme Richard* was so shattered that she sank two days later. The encounter made a lively stir in French and American society and Jones became a hero.

All this time Washington's army had remained incapable of action. They could do little except keep watch on Clinton. Simply to have kept his army in existence during these years was probably Washington's greatest contribution to the Patriot cause. No other American leader could have done as much. In December Clinton decided to try his hand once more at subduing the South. He resolved to capture Charleston, and on the 26th, having learned that the French fleet in the West Indies had been beaten by Admiral Rodney, he sailed for South Carolina with eight thousand men. For a time he prospered. Bad weather delayed him and the main siege did not begin till the end of March, but in May 1780 the town fell and five thousand Patriot troops surrendered in the biggest disaster yet sustained by American arms. Then fortune began to turn against Clinton. He had gained a valuable base, but he was confronted with civil war. He found himself faced, not with a regular army in the field, but with innumerable guerrilla bands which harassed his communications and murdered Loyalists. It became evident that a huge army would be needed to occupy and subdue the country. But again sea-power intervened. Rumours that French troops were once more crossing the Atlantic made Clinton hasten back to New York, leaving Cornwallis, his second-in-command, to do the best he could in the South. This was little enough. Washington sent a small force against him under Gates, the victor of Saratoga. Cornwallis defeated Gates at the Battle of Camden and marched into North Carolina, routing the guerrillas as he went, but the countryside rose in arms behind him. There was no crucial point he could strike at, and the only effect of his exertions was the destruction of a quantity of crops which the rebels might have traded to Europe for munitions.

In the North Clinton for the second time found himself in great peril. Another fleet had indeed arrived from France, and this time he was too late to forestall a landing. Over five thousand French troops under the Comte de Rochambeau had disembarked in July at Newport, in Rhode Island. Washington, vigilant and alert, was encamped at White Plains in the Hudson valley; Benedict Arnold, who had led the expedition to Canada in 1776 and fought with distinction at Saratoga, commanded the fort at West Point; at any moment the French might advance inland from the coast and join him. New York, Clinton's base and harbour, seemed lost. But events, in the form of treachery, ran for a time with the British. Arnold had long been dissatisfied with the conduct of the Patriots, and he had recently married a Loyalist lady. He was in debt, and he had lately been reprimanded by court-martial for misappropriating Government property. His discontent and his doubts were deepened by the news of Gates's defeat at Camden, and he now offered to surrender West Point to Clinton for the sum of twenty thousand pounds. Its loss would not only destroy Washington's grip on the Hudson valley, but might ruin the whole Patriot power. Clinton seized on the conspiracy as the one chance of retrieving his position in the North, and sent a young major named André in disguise to arrange the details of the capitulation.

On September 21, 1780, André sailed up the Hudson in a sloop, and met Arnold late at night on the west shore not far from Stony Point. Here Arnold gave him written descriptions of the forts, their armaments and stores, the strength of the garrisons, copies of their orders in case of attack, and copies of the proceedings of a council of war recently held at West Point. On his way back across the No Man's Land between the two armies André fell into the hands of some irregular scouts, and was delivered to the nearest American commander. The documents were found in his boots. The commander could not believe in Arnold's treachery, and a request for an explanation was sent to West Point. Arnold escaped, followed by his wife, and was rewarded with a general's commission in King George's service and the command of a British force. He died in disgrace and poverty twenty years after. André was executed as a spy. He wrote a graceful and dignified letter to Washington asking to be shot instead of hanged—in vain. He was a young man of great personal beauty, and in his scarlet uniform, standing upon the gallows, and himself arranging the noose round his neck, he made an appealing sight. His courage reduced to tears the rough crowd that had gathered to see him die. In all the anger of the struggle, with the exasperation of Arnold's desertion hardening every Patriot heart, no one could be found to perform the task of executioner, and in the end a nameless figure, with his face blackened as a disguise, did the work. Forty years later André was re-buried in Westminster Abbey.

Arnold's act of betrayal, though discovered in time, had a marked, if temporary, effect on the sentiment and cohesion of the Patriots. They had been very near disaster. Many Americans were strongly opposed to the war, and Loyalists throughout the country either openly or secretly supported the British. The South was already smitten with hideous civil strife in which American slew American and each man suspected his neighbour. Was the same frightful process to engulf the North, hitherto steadfast in the Patriot cause? If the commander of West Point was a traitor, then who could be trusted? These anxieties and fears were deepened by a reversal of the Patriot fortunes at sea. Admiral Rodney arrived before New York with a substantial fleet and blockaded the French in Newport till the end of the campaigning season. Then he struck again, this time in the West Indies, where the Dutch had been making large fortunes by shipping arms and powder to the Patriots. The centre of their trade was St. Eustatius, in the Leeward Islands. In the autumn news came that Holland had joined the coalition against Great Britain, and Rodney was ordered to seize the island. This he did early in 1781, and a large store of munitions and merchandise consigned to General Washington fell into the hands of the British Fleet.

Strategic divergences between Clinton and Cornwallis now brought disaster to the British and Loyalist cause. Cornwallis had long chafed under Clinton's instructions, which tethered him to his base at Charleston. Clinton judged that the holding of South Carolina was the main object of the war in the South, and that any inland excursion depended on naval control of the coast. Cornwallis on the other hand was eager to press forward. He maintained that the American guerrillas in North Carolina prevented any effective occupation of the South, and until and unless they were subdued the British would have to retire within the walls of Charleston. He held that Virginia was the heart and centre of the Patriot cause and that all efforts should be concentrated on its conquest and occupation. The first step therefore was to overrun North Carolina. There is no doubt he was wrong. Charleston, not Virginia, was the military key to the South. It was the only Southern port of any consequence, and the only place from which he could receive supplies for himself and deny them to the rebels. From here he could not only dominate the state of Georgia to the South, but by establishing small posts in North Carolina, and at Chesapeake Bay, "keep up the appearance," as Washington wrote at the time, "of possessing four hundred miles upon the coast, and of consequence have a pretext for setting up claims which may be very detrimental to the interest of

America in European councils."* But Cornwallis's military reputation had been in the ascendant since the Battle of Camden, and he was encouraged by the British Government to proceed with his plans, which largely depended for their success on the Southern Loyalists. In spite of their unpromising behaviour in the previous campaign, and in spite of the nomination of Washington's ablest general, Nathanael Greene, to command the Patriot forces in the South, Cornwallis resolved to advance. Thus he marched to destruction.

In January 1781 he moved towards the borders of North Carolina. His forward detachments clashed with the Americans at Cowpens on the morning of the 17th. The British tactics were simple and costly. Cornwallis had experienced the marksmanship of the American frontiersmen, and knew the inefficiency in musketry of his own troops. He therefore relied on sabre and bayonet charges. The American commander had placed his ill-organised and ill-disciplined militia with the Broad River behind them to stop them dispersing. Washington always doubted the value of these troops, and had declared that no militia would "ever acquire the habits necessary to resist a regular force." But this time, stiffened by Continental troops, they mauled the British.

Cornwallis nevertheless pressed on. He was now far from his base, and Greene's army was still in the field. His only hope was to bring Greene to battle and destroy him. They met at Guilford Court House on March 15. The American militia proved useless, but the trained nucleus of Greene's troops drawn up behind a rail fence wrought havoc among the British regulars. Again and again, headed by their officers, the regiments assaulted the American line. An English sergeant who kept a journal of the campaign thus describes the scene: "Instantly the movement was made, in excellent order, in a smart run with arms charged; when arrived within forty yards of the enemy's line it was perceived that this whole force had their weapons presented and resting on a rail fence, the common partitions in America. They were taking aim with nicest precision."† In the end this devoted and disciplined bravery drove the Americans from the field, but the slaughter was indecisive. The Patriot force was still active while the British were far from home and had lost nearly a third of their men. Cornwallis had no choice but to make for the coast and seek reinforcements from the Navy. Greene let him go. His army had done enough. In just under eight months they had marched and fought over nine hundred miles of swampy and desolate country. Outnumbered by three to one, he had reconquered the

* *The Writings of George Washington,* ed. W. C. Ford (1891), vol. ix.
† *The Journal of Sergeant Lamb* (Dublin, 1809).

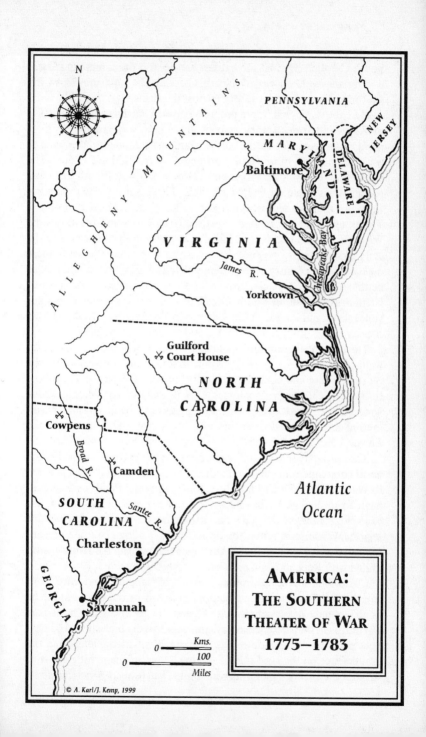

N

PENNSYLVANIA

NEW JERSEY

MARYLAND

DELAWARE

Baltimore

A L L E G H E N Y   M O U N T A I N S

VIRGINIA

James R.

Chesapeake Bay

Yorktown

Guilford
Court House

NORTH
CAROLINA

Atlantic
Ocean

Cowpens

Broad R.

Camden

SOUTH
CAROLINA

Santee R.

Charleston

GEORGIA

Savannah

Kms.
0 _____ 100
0 _____
Miles

**AMERICA:
THE SOUTHERN
THEATER OF WAR
1775–1783**

© A. Karl/J. Kemp, 1999

whole of Georgia except Savannah, and all but a small portion of South Carolina. He lost the battles, but he won the campaign. Abandoning the wide spaces of North Carolina, he now moved swiftly southwards to raise the country against the British.

Here the fierce civil war in progress between Patriots and Loyalists—or Whigs and Tories as they were locally called—was darkened by midnight raids, seizure of cattle, murders, ambushes, and atrocities such as we have known in our own day in Ireland. Greene himself wrote: "The animosities between the Whigs and Tories of this state [South Carolina] renders their situation truly deplorable. There is not a day passes but there are more or less who fall a sacrifice to this savage disposition. The Whigs seem determined to extirpate the Tories and the Tories the Whigs. Some thousands have fallen in this way in this quarter, and the evil rages with more violence than ever. If a stop cannot be put to these massacres the country will be depopulated in a few months more, as neither Whig nor Tory can live." While Greene began to subdue the isolated British posts in South Carolina, Cornwallis continued his advance to Virginia. He devastated the countryside in his march, but was fiercely and skilfully harried by Lafayette and a meagre Patriot band.

Throughout these months Clinton lay in New York, and as Cornwallis drew nearer it seemed possible that Clinton might evacuate the Northern base and concentrate the whole British effort on preserving the hold on the Southern colonies. This, if it had succeeded, might have wrecked the Patriot cause, for the Congress was bankrupt and Washington could scarcely keep his army together. But once again the French Fleet turned the scales, this time for ever.

The desperate situation of the Americans was revealed to the French naval commander in the West Indies, De Grasse. In July he sent word to Washington, who had now been joined at White Plains by Rochambeau from Newport, that he would attack the Virginian coast. He called for a supreme effort to concentrate the whole Patriot force in this region. Washington seized the opportunity. Taking elaborate precautions to deceive Clinton, he withdrew his troops from the Hudson and, united with Rochambeau, marched quickly southwards.

Cornwallis in the meantime, starved of supplies, and with ever-lengthening lines of communication, marched to the coast, where he hoped to make direct contact with Clinton by sea. In August he arrived at Yorktown, on Chesapeake Bay, and began to dig himself in. His conduct in the following months has been much criticised. He had no natural defence on the land side of the town, and he made little effort to strike at the enemies gathering round him. The Franco-American strategy was a feat of timing, and the convergence of force was carried out over vast distances. Nearly nine thousand Americans and eight thousand French assembled before Yorktown, while De Grasse blockaded the coast with forty ships of the line. For nearly two months Cornwallis sat and waited. At the end of September the investment of Yorktown began, and the bombardment of the French siege artillery shattered his earth redoubts. Cornwallis planned a desperate sortie as the defences crumbled. At the end one British cannon remained in action. On October 17, 1781, the whole army, about seven thousand strong, surrendered. On the very same day Clinton and the British squadron sailed from New York, but on hearing of the disaster they turned back.

Thus ended the main struggle. Sea-power had once more decided the issue, and but for the French blockade the British war of attrition might well have succeeded.

In November, his task accomplished, De Grasse returned to the West Indies and Washington was left unaided to face Clinton in New York and the menace of invasion from Canada. Two years were to pass before peace came to America, but no further military operations of any consequence took place.

The surrender at Yorktown had immediate and decisive effects in England. When the news was brought to Lord North his amiable composure slid from him. He paced his room, exclaiming in agonised tones, "Oh, God, it is all over!"

The Opposition gathered strongly in the Commons. There were riotous meetings in London. The Government majority collapsed on a motion censuring the administration of the Navy. An address to stop the American war was rejected by a single vote. In March North informed the Commons that he would resign. "At last the fatal day has come," wrote the King. North maintained his dignity to the last. After twelve years of service he left the House of Commons a beaten man. As the Members stood waiting in the rain for their carriages on that March evening in 1782 they saw North come down the steps and get into his own vehicle, which had been forewarned and was waiting at the head of the line. With a courtly bow to the drenched and hostile Members crowding round him he said, "That, gentlemen, is the advantage of being in the secret," and drove quickly away.

King George, in the agony of personal defeat, showed greater passion. He talked of abdication and retiring to Hanover. The violent feeling in the country denied him all hope of holding a successful election. He was forced to come to terms with the Opposition. Through the long years of the American war Rockingham and Burke had waited in patience for the collapse of North's administration. Now their chance had come. Rockingham made his terms with the King: independence for the colonies and some lessening of the Crown's influence in politics. George III was forced to accept, and Rockingham took office. It fell to him and his colleague, Lord Shelburne, to save what they could from the wreckage of the First British Empire.

CHAPTER 9

THE AMERICAN CONSTITUTION

T HE WAR OF INDEPENDENCE was over and the Thirteen
Colonies were free to make their own lives. The struggle had
told heavily upon their primitive political organisation. The Articles of
Confederation to which they had subscribed in 1777 set up a weak central Government enjoying only such authority as the Americans might
have allowed to the British Crown. Their Congress had neither the
power nor the opportunity in so vast a land of creating an ordered society out of the wreckage of revolution and war.

The strongest element behind the American effort had been the small
farmers from the inland frontier districts. It was they who had supplied
the men for the Army and who had in most of the states refashioned the
several constitutions on democratic lines. They now dominated the legislatures, and jealously guarded the privileges of their own states. With the
close of hostilities it seemed that the Union embodied in an unwieldy
Congress might snap or wither under the strain of post-war problems.
American society was rent by strong conflicting interests. The farmers
were heavily in debt to the city classes. The issue of too much paper
money by Congress had bred inflation. By 1780 one gold dollar was
worth forty paper ones. Every state was burdened with enormous debts,
and the taxes imposed to meet the interest fell heavily upon the land.
Small bankrupt farmers were everywhere being sold up. War profiteers
had emerged. A gulf was widening in American society between debtor
and creditor, between farmer and merchant-financier. Agitation and unrest marched with a deepening economic crisis. There were widespread
movements for postponing the collection of debts. In Massachusetts

farmers and disbanded soldiers who had been paid off in worthless paper notes rose in rebellion. In the autumn of 1786 Captain Daniel Shays, with a mob of armed farmers, attempted to storm the county courts. There was sharp fear that such incidents would multiply. Washington, himself as strong an upholder of property as Cromwell, wrote, "There are combustibles in every state which a spark might set fire to. I feel infinitely more than I can express for the disorders which have arisen."

It was not only internal conditions that clamoured for action. Some awkward points in the peace treaty were still unresolved. Debts to the British merchants, compensation for Loyalists, British evacuation of trading posts and forts on the Canadian boundary, all pressed for settlement. The British Government was legislating against American shipping. Spain was re-embedded in Florida and hostile to American expansion in the South-West. America was entangled in an official alliance with France, where the stir of great changes to come was already felt. Far-seeing men perceived the imminence of another world conflict. Distracted by internal disorder, without national unity or organisation, the American states seemed an easy prey to foreign ambitions.

Demand for revision of the Articles of Confederation grew among the people of the towns. Shays' rebellion was the spur to action, and in May 1787 a convention of delegates of the Thirteen States met at Philadelphia to consider the matter. The partisans of a strong national Government were in a large majority. Of the possible leaders of the farmers, or agrarian democrats as they were now called, Patrick Henry of Virginia refused to attend, and the greatest figure of them all, Thomas Jefferson, was absent as envoy in Paris. One of the leading personalities of the assembly was Alexander Hamilton, who represented the powerful commercial interests of New York City. This handsome, brilliant man, the illegitimate son of a West Indian planter, had risen rapidly on Washington's staff during the war. He had entered New York society and married well. He was determined that the ruling class, into which he had made his way by his own abilities, should continue to rule, and he now became the recognised leader of those who demanded a capable central Government and limitation of states' powers. A sense of the overhanging crisis in Europe and of the perils of democracy guided these men in their labours, and the debates in the Convention were on a high level. Most of the delegates were in favour of a Federal Government, but methods and details were bitterly contested. Many divisions cut across the discussions. The small states were anxious to preserve their equality in the great community of the Thirteen, and vehemently opposed any scheme for representation in a Federal Government on a simple basis of numbers.

All the delegates came from long-established centres on the Atlantic seaboard, but they realised with uneasiness that their power and influence would soon be threatened by the growing populace of the West. Here, beyond the Ohio and the Alleghenies, lay vast territories which Congress had ordained should be admitted to the Union on an equal footing with the original states as soon as any of them contained sixty thousand free inhabitants. Their population was already expanding, and it was only a question of time before they claimed their rights. Then what would happen to the famous Thirteen States? It was they who had expelled the British, and they felt with some justification that they knew more about politics and the true interests of the Union than the denizens of these remote, half-settled regions. As Gouverneur Morris of Pennsylvania put it—he owed his unusual Christian name to his mother, who had been a Miss Gouverneur—"The busy haunts of men, not the remote wilderness, is the proper school of political talents. If the Western people get the power in their hands they will ruin the Atlantic interests." Both principles were right. The Atlantic communities had the wealth and the experience, but the new lands were fully entitled to join the Union, and to the lasting credit of the Philadelphia delegates no step was taken to prevent them doing so. But one day the clash would come. The power and the future lay with the West, and it was with misgiving and anxiety that the Convention addressed itself to framing the Constitution of the United States.

This was a concise document defining the powers of the new central Government. It established a single executive: a President, appointed indirectly by electors chosen as the state legislatures might decide, and serving for four years, with the right of veto over the acts of Congress, but subject to impeachment; head of the Army and the administration, responsible only to the people, completely independent of the legislative power. The Lower House, or the House of Representatives as it was now called, was to be elected for two years, upon a population basis. But this concession to the democratic principle was tempered by the erection of a Senate, elected for six years by the state legislatures. The Senate was to restrain any demagogy of the Lower House, to defend the interests of property against the weight of a Lower House chosen upon the numerical principle, and by its share in the appointing and treaty-making powers of the President to control this powerful functionary. At the summit of the constitutional edifice stood a Supreme Court, composed of judges nominated for life by the President, subject to the ratification of the Senate. It assumed the task of judicial review—namely, a coercive supervision of the Acts not only of Congress, but also of the state legislatures, to ensure their conformity with the Constitution.

Such was the federal machinery devised at Philadelphia in September 1787. A national authority had been created, supreme within its sphere. But this sphere was strictly defined and limited; all powers not delegated under the Constitution to the Federal Government were to rest with the states. There was to be no central "tyranny" of the kind that King George's Ministers at Westminster had tried to exercise. The new nation that had with difficulty struggled into being was henceforth fortified with something unheard of in the existing world—a written Constitution. At first sight this authoritative document presents a sharp contrast with the store of traditions and precedents that make up the unwritten Constitution of Britain. Yet behind it lay no revolutionary theory. It was based not upon the challenging writings of the French philosophers which were soon to set Europe ablaze, but on Old English doctrine, freshly formulated to meet an urgent American need. The Constitution was a reaffirmation of faith in the principles painfully evolved over the centuries by the English-speaking peoples. It enshrined long-standing English ideas of justice and liberty, henceforth to be regarded on the other side of the Atlantic as basically American.

Of course, a written constitution carries with it the danger of a cramping rigidity. What body of men, however far-sighted, can lay down precepts in advance for settling the problems of future generations? The delegates at Philadelphia were well aware of this. They made provision for amendment, and the document drawn up by them was adaptable enough in practice to permit changes in the Constitution. But it had to be proved in argument and debate and generally accepted throughout the land that any changes proposed would follow the guiding ideas of the Founding Fathers. A prime object of the Constitution was to be conservative; it was to guard the principles and machinery of State from capricious and ill-considered alteration. In its fundamental doctrine the American people acquired an institution which was to command the same respect and loyalty as in England are given to Parliament and Crown.

It now remained to place the scheme before the people. The delegates foresaw that the democratic, isolationist state legislatures would probably reject it, and they accordingly advised that local conventions should be elected to vote upon the new project of government. Hamilton and Robert Morris, whose strong and well-organised group had become known as the Federalist Party, hoped that all men with a stake in the country, who had probably not wanted to sit on the revolutionary bodies formed during the war for the administration of the different states, would see the value and reason in the new Constitution and limit the influence of the more extreme elements.

To the leaders of agrarian democracy, the backwoodsmen, the small farmers, the project seemed a betrayal of the Revolution. They had thrown off the English executive. They had gained their local freedom. They were now asked to create another instrument no less powerful and coercive. They had been told they were fighting for the Rights of Man and the equality of the individual. They saw in the Constitution an engine for the defence of property against equality. They felt in their daily life the heavy hand of powerful interests behind the contracts and debts which oppressed them. But they were without leaders. Even so in Virginia, New York, and elsewhere there was a fierce and close contest upon the passing of the Constitution. Jefferson in his diplomatic exile in Paris brooded with misgiving on the new régime. But the party of Hamilton and Morris, with its brilliant propaganda, in a series of public letters called *The Federalist,* carried the day.

The Federalist letters are among the classics of American literature. Their practical wisdom stands pre-eminent amid the stream of controversial writing at the time. Their authors were concerned, not with abstract arguments about political theory, but with the real dangers threatening America, the evident weakness of the existing Confederation, and the debatable advantages of the various provisions in the new Constitution. Hamilton, Jay, and Madison were the principal contributors. The first two were New Yorkers, Madison a Virginian; none came from New England, which was losing its former predominance in the life of the nation. They differed widely in personality and outlook, but they all agreed upon one point, the importance of creating a collective faith in the Constitution as the embodiment of the American ideal. Only thus could the many discordant voices of the Thirteen States be harmonised. How well they succeeded and how enduring has been their success is testified by the century and three-quarters that have elapsed since they wrote. The faith generated by *The Federalist* has held and sustained the allegiance of the American people down to our own day.

Liberty, *The Federalist* argued, might degenerate into licence. Order, security, and efficient government must be established before disaster overtook America. In an article in this great political series one of the Federalists stated the eternal problem with breadth and power.

> The diversity in the faculties of men, from which the rights of
> property originate, is . . . an insuperable obstacle to a uniformity of

interests. The protection of these faculties is the first object of government. From the protection of different and unequal faculties of acquiring property the possession of different degrees and kinds of property immediately results; and from the influence of these on the sentiments and views of the respective proprietors ensues a division of the society into different interests and parties.

The latent causes of faction are thus sown in the nature of man; and we see them everywhere brought into different degrees of activity, according to the different circumstances of civil society. A zeal for different opinions . . . [has] divided mankind into parties, inflamed them with mutual animosity, and rendered them much more disposed to vex and oppress each other than to co-operate for their common good. . . . But the most common and durable source of factions has been the various and unequal distribution of property. Those who hold and those who are without property have ever formed distinct interests of society. Those who are creditors and those who are debtors fall under a like discrimination. A landed interest, a manufacturing interest, a mercantile interest, a moneyed interest, with many lesser interests, grow up of necessity in civilised nations, and divide them into different classes actuated by different sentiments and views. The regulation of these various and interfering interests forms the principal task of modern legislation, and involves the spirit of party and faction in the necessary and ordinary operations of the Government.

It was in vain that their opponents counter-attacked in print. "Because we have sometimes abused democracy I am not among those who think a democratic branch a nuisance," wrote Richard Henry Lee of Virginia. "Every man of reflection must see that the change now proposed is a transference of power from the many to the few." In the midst of faction fights and the collisions of Federalist and Radical mobs the Constitution was within eighteen months ratified by eleven of the states. Rhode Island and North Carolina stood aside for a little longer. Distrust of social revolution had bitten deep into the New World, and the gulf between the two elements that composed its society remained unbridged. The men who believed in the Rights of Man were forced to bide their time. Those, like Hamilton, who feared the mob in politics, and realised the urgent need for settlement, order, and protection for the propertied interests of the seaboard states, had triumphed.

In March 1789 elections were held for the new Federal bodies. Opponents of the Constitution exulted in the difficulties of gathering a quorum in the Upper and Lower House. There seemed little vigour and enthusiasm in the new régime. But by the end of the month sufficient people had arrived in New York, where the Government was to meet. The first step was to elect a President, and General Washington, the commander of the Revolution, was the obvious choice. Disinterested and courageous, far-sighted and patient, aloof yet direct in manner, inflexible once his mind was made up, Washington possessed the gifts of character for which the situation called. He was reluctant to accept office. Nothing would have pleased him more than to remain in equable but active retirement at Mount Vernon, improving the husbandry of his estate. But, as always, he answered the summons of duty. Gouverneur Morris was right when he emphatically wrote to him, "The exercise of authority depends on personal character. Your cool, steady temper is *indispensably necessary* to give firm and manly tone to the new Government."

There was much confusion and discussion on titles and precedence, which aroused the mocking laughter of critics. But the prestige of Washington lent dignity to the new, untried office. On April 30, 1789, in the recently opened Federal Hall in New York, he was solemnly inaugurated as the first President of the United States. A week later the French States-General met at Versailles. Another great revolution was about to burst upon a bewildered world. The flimsy, untested fabric of American unity and order had been erected only just in time.

Many details had yet to be worked out. The first step was the passing of a Bill of Rights. The lack of such fundamental assertions in the Constitution had been a chief complaint of its critics. They were now incorporated in ten Amendments. Next the Judiciary Act of 1789 made the Supreme Court the most formidable part of the Federal machinery. "With elaborate detail," wrote the historians Charles and Mary Beard,

> the law provided for a Supreme Court composed of a Chief Justice and five associates, and a Federal District Court for each state, with its own Attorney, Marshal, and appropriate number of deputies. Such were the agencies of power created to make the will of the national Government a living force in every community from New Hampshire to Georgia, from the seaboard to the frontier. . . . After contriving an ingenious system of appeal for carrying cases up to the Supreme Court, the framers of the Judiciary Act devised a process by which the measures of the local Governments could be nullified whenever they came into conflict with the Federal Constitution. . . . In a word, something like the old British Imperial control over provincial legislatures was re-established, under judicial bodies chosen indirectly and for life, within the borders of the United States.*

* Charles A. Beard and Mary R. Beard, *The Rise of American Civilization* (1930), vol. i.

As yet there were no administrative departments. These were quickly set up: Treasury, State, and War. The success of the new Federal Government depended largely upon the men chosen to fill these key offices: Alexander Hamilton, the great Federalist from New York; Thomas Jefferson, the Virginian democrat, now returned from Paris; and, to a lesser extent, General Knox of Massachusetts.

From 1789 to his resignation six years later Hamilton used his brilliant abilities to nourish the Constitution and bind the economic interests of the great merchants of America to the new system. A governing class must be created, and Hamilton proposed to demonstrate that Federal government meant a strong national economy. At his inspiration a series of great measures followed. In January 1790 his *First Report on Public Credit* was laid before the House of Representatives. State debts were to be assumed by Congress; public credit must depend on the assumption of past obligations. The war debts of the states were to be taken over by the Federal Government in order to woo the large class of creditors to the national interest. The whole debt was to be funded; all the old bonds and certificates which had been rotted by speculation were to be called in and new securities issued. A sinking fund was to be created and a national bank set up.

The moneyed interest was overjoyed by this programme, but there was bitter opposition from those who realised that the new Government was using its taxing powers to pay interest to the speculative holders of state debts now assumed by Congress. The clash between capitalist and agrarian again glared forth. The New England merchants had invested most of their war-time profits in paper bonds, which now gained enormously in value. Massachusetts, which had the largest state debt, profited most. The mass of public debt was concentrated in the hands of small groups in Philadelphia, New York, and Boston. The nation was taxed to pay them at par for what they had purchased at a tremendous discount. In Virginia there was fierce revolt against Hamilton's scheme. The planters distrusted the whole idea of public finance. They foresaw the worst elements of Whig plutocracy dominating the new Government. "They discern," wrote Patrick Henry,

a striking resemblance between this system and that which was introduced into England at the Revolution [of 1688], a system which has perpetuated upon that nation an enormous debt, and has, moreover, insinuated into the hands of the executive an unbounded influence, which, pervading every branch of the Government, bears down all opposition, and daily threatens the destruction of everything that appertains to English liberty. The same causes produce the same effects. In an agricultural country like this, therefore, to erect and concentrate and perpetuate a large moneyed interest is a measure which . . . must in the course of human events produce one or other of two evils, the prostration of agriculture at the feet of commerce, or a change in the present form of Federal Government, fatal to the existence of American liberty. . . . Your memorialists can find no clause in the Constitution authorising Congress to assume the debts of the states.

This cleavage is of durable importance in American history. The beginnings of the great political parties can be discerned, and they soon found their first leaders. Hamilton was quickly recognised as head of the financial and mercantile interest centring in the North, and his opponent was none other than Jefferson, Secretary of State. The two men had worked together during the first months of the new Government. Hamilton indeed had only secured enough votes for the passage of his proposals on state debts by winning Jefferson's support. This he did by agreeing that the new capital city which would house Congress and Government should be sited on the Potomac River, across the border from Virginia. In the meantime Philadelphia was to succeed New York as the temporary capital. But a wave of speculation which followed the financial measures of Hamilton now aroused the Secretary's opposition. The two leaders misunderstood each other fundamentally. Washington, impressed by the need to stabilise the new Constitution, exerted his weighty influence to prevent an open rupture. But by 1791 Jefferson and his Virginian planters were seeking alliance with the malcontents of Hamilton's party in New York and the North.

Before the break came Hamilton presented his *Report on Manufactures,* which was to be the basis of future American Protectionist theory. Protective duties and bounties were to be introduced to encourage home industries. A vision of a prosperous and industrial society in the New World, such as was rapidly growing up in England, was held before the eyes of the Americans.

The outward unity of the Federal administration was preserved for a few months by the re-election of Washington as President. But the conflict between Jefferson and Hamilton was not confined to economics. A profoundly antagonistic view of politics separated them. They held radically opposed views of human nature. Hamilton, the superbly successful financier, believed that men were guided by their passions and their interests, and that their motives, unless rigidly controlled, were evil. "The people!" he is supposed to have said. "The people is a great beast." Majority rule and government by the counting of heads were abhorrent to him. There must be a strong central Government and a powerful governing circle, and he saw in Federal institutions, backed by a ruling business class, the hope and future of America. The developing society of England was the ideal for the New World, and such he hoped to create across the Atlantic by his efforts at the Treasury Department. He represents and symbolises one aspect of American development, the successful, self-reliant business world, with its distrust of the collective common man, of what Hamilton himself in another mood called "the majesty of the multitude." But in this gospel of material success there was no trace of that political idealism which characterises and uplifts the American people. "A very great man," President Woodrow Wilson was to call him, "but not a great American."

Thomas Jefferson was the product of wholly different conditions and the prophet of a rival political idea. He came from the Virginian frontier, the home of dour individualism and faith in common humanity, the nucleus of resistance to the centralising hierarchy of British rule. Jefferson had been the principal author of the Declaration of Independence and leader of the agrarian democrats in the American Revolution. He was well read; he nourished many scientific interests, and he was a gifted amateur architect. His graceful classical house, Monticello, was built according to his own designs. He was in touch with fashionable Left-Wing circles of political philosophy in Europe, and, like the French school of economists who went by the name of Physiocrats, he believed in a yeoman-farmer society. He feared an industrial proletariat as much as he disliked the principle of aristocracy. Industrial and capitalist development appalled him. He despised and distrusted the whole machinery of banks, tariffs, credit manipulation, and all the agencies of capitalism which the New Yorker Hamilton was skilfully introducing into the United States. He perceived the dangers to individual liberty that might spring from the centralising powers of a Federal Government. With reluctance he came home from Paris to serve the new system. The passage of time and the stress of the Napoleonic wars were to modify his dislike of industrialism, but he believed in his heart that democratic government was only possible among free yeomen. It was not given to him to foresee that the United States would eventually become the greatest industrial democracy in the world.

"The political economists of Europe have established it as a principle," Jefferson declared,

> that every state should endeavour to manufacture for itself; and this principle, like many others, we transfer to America. . . . But we have an immensity of land courting the industry of the husbandman. Is it best then that all our citizens should be employed in its improvement, or that one half should be called off from that to exercise manufactures and handicraft arts for the other? . . . Corruption of morals in

the mass of cultivators is a phenomenon of which no age nor nation has furnished an example. It is the mark set on those who, not looking up to heaven, to their own soil and industry, as does the husbandman, for their subsistence, depend for it on casualties and caprice of customers. Dependence begets subservience and venality, suffocates the germ of virtue, and prepares fit tools for the designs of ambition. . . . While we have land to labour, then, let us never wish to see our citizens occupied at a work-bench or twirling a distaff. . . . *For the general operations of manufacture let our workshops remain in Europe. It is better to carry provisions and materials to workmen there than bring them to the provisions and materials and with them their manners and principles.* * . . . The mobs of great cities add just so much to the support of pure government as sores do to the strength of the human body. It is the manners and spirit of a people which preserve a republic in vigour. A degeneracy in these is a canker which soon eats to the heart of its laws and constitution.

Jefferson held to the Virginian conception of society, simple and unassailed by the complexity, the perils, and the challenge of industrialism. In France he saw, or thought he saw, the realisation of his political ideas—the destruction of a worn-out aristocracy and a revolutionary assertion of the rights of soil-tilling man. Hamilton, on the other hand, looked to the England of the Younger Pitt as the embodiment of his hopes for America. The outbreak of war between England and France was to bring to a head the fundamental rivalry and conflict between Hamilton and Jefferson and to signalise the birth of the great American parties, Federalist and Republican. Both were to split and founder and change their names, but from them the Republican and Democratic parties of today can trace their lineage.

* Author's italics.—W. S. C.

CHAPTER 10

WASHINGTON, ADAMS AND JEFFERSON

T HE CONFUSED and tumultuous issues of European politics reached America in black and white. Debate on the French Revolution raged throughout the country. Corresponding societies on the Revolutionary model sprang up wherever Jeffersonian principles were upheld, while the Federalist Press thundered against the Jacobins of the New World, and, like Edmund Burke in England, denounced them as destroyers of society.

Controversy became less theoretical and much more vehement as soon as American commercial interests were affected. Tempers rose as American ships and merchandise endured the commerce-raiding and privateering of France and Britain. Both parties demanded war—the Federalists against France and the Jeffersonians against England. President Washington was determined to keep the infant republic at peace. His task was smoothed by the antics of the French Revolutionary envoy to the United States, Citizen Genêt, who, finding the Government reluctant to honour the Franco-American alliance of 1778, meddled in American politics, attempted to raise troops, and greatly embarrassed his political allies. In August 1793 Washington demanded his recall. But, knowing the sharp activity of the guillotine in France, Genêt wisely married an American heiress and subsided peaceably in the New World.

Washington prevailed, and it was he who enunciated the first principle of traditional American foreign policy. In April 1793 his famous proclamation of neutrality declared that it was "the disposition of the United States to pursue a conduct friendly and impartial towards the belligerent Powers." Infringements would render American citizens liable to prosecution in the Federal courts. But relations with Britain were clouded by unsettled issues. Hamilton's Federalist Party was deeply committed to maintaining a friendly commerce with Britain. The overseas trade of New England was largely financed by London bankers. The carrying trade between the two countries brought great profit to the ship-owners of the Eastern states, and they strongly opposed any suggestion of war on the side of Revolutionary France. The farmers and pioneers of the frontier felt differently. To them Britain was the enemy who refused to honour the treaty of 1783 by evacuating the frontier posts on the Canadian border, and was pushing her fur trade from Canada southwards, inciting the Indians against American settlers, and threatening the flank of their own advance to the West. The British in their turn resented the failure of the American Government to settle the large debts still unpaid since before the Revolution. Meanwhile British interference with American shipping, on the plea that it was helping to sustain France, stung public opinion throughout the United States.

Washington decided that the whole field of Anglo-American relations must be revised and settled, and in 1794 he appointed John Jay, Chief Justice of the Supreme Court, as Envoy Extraordinary to London. The British Government felt little tenderness for their late rebels. They knew their military weakness, and Washington's need of the support of Hamilton's party. Moreover, they were considerably aided by Jay's ineptitude in negotiation. A treaty was drawn up which made few concessions to America. The frontier posts were evacuated, and the way to the West thus lay open and unmolested to American pioneers, but no guarantees were given about future British relations with the Indians. Britain paid some compensation for damage done to American ships on the high seas, but refused to modify her blockade or renounce the right to seize ships and cargoes destined for France and her allies. No satisfaction was obtained about the impressment of American seamen for service in the Royal Navy. Worst of all, Jay was forced to yield on the issue of the debts owing to British creditors, and the United States were bound to compensate British claimants for outstanding losses.

The effect on the Federalist Party was most damaging. The Western states were angered by the incomplete arrangements on the Canadian frontier. The Southerners were threatened with serious injury by the debts clause. The treaty revealed and exposed the superiority of British diplomacy and the weakness of the new American Government. The atmosphere was charged afresh with distrust, and the seeds were sown for another war between Britain and the United States.

Washington's second term of office expired at the end of 1796, and he prepared longingly for his retirement to Mount Vernon. His last days in power were vexed by the gathering assaults of the anti-Federalists and the din of preparations for the new Presidential election. Washington and many of his associates were alarmed by the growth of party spirit. They clung to the view that the diverse interests of the nation were best reflected in a balanced and all-embracing Government. The notion that two great parties should perpetually struggle for power was foreign and repellent to them. Only Jefferson, who had already resigned from the administration, had a clear vision of the rôle that parties should play. He saw the advantages of directing the strife of factions into broad streams and keeping an organised Opposition before the country as a possible alternative Government. But in Washington's mind the dangers of faction were uppermost when in September he issued his Farewell Address to the nation. This document is one of the most celebrated in American history. It is an eloquent plea for union, a warning against "the baneful effects of the Spirit of Party." It is also an exposition of the doctrine of isolation as the true future American policy. "Europe has a set of primary interests, which to us have none, or a very remote rela- tion. Hence she must be engaged in frequent controversies, the causes of which are essentially foreign to our concerns. Hence therefore it must be unwise in us to implicate ourselves by artificial ties in the ordinary vicis- situdes of her politics or the ordinary combinations and collisions of her friendships or enmities. Our detached and distant situation invites us to pursue a different course. . . . 'Tis our true policy to steer clear of permanent alliances with any portion of the foreign world. . . . Taking care always to keep ourselves, by suitable establishments, in a re- spectable defensive posture, we may safely trust to temporary alliances for extraordinary emergencies."

George Washington holds one of the proudest titles that history can bestow. He was the Father of his Nation. Almost alone his staunchness in the War of Independence held the American colonies to their united purpose. His services after victory had been won were no less great. His firmness and example while first President restrained the violence of faction and postponed a national schism for sixty years. His character and influence steadied the dangerous leanings of Americans to take sides against Britain or France. He filled his office with dignity and in- spired his administration with much of his own wisdom. To his terms as President are due the smooth organisation of the Federal Govern- ment, the establishment of national credit, and the foundation of a for- eign policy. By refusing to stand for a third term he set a tradition in

American politics which has only been departed from by President Franklin Roosevelt in the Second World War.

For two years Washington lived quietly at his country seat on the Potomac, riding round his plantations, as he had long wished to do. Amid the snows of the last days of the eighteenth century he took to his bed. On the evening of December 14, 1799, he turned to the physician at his side, murmuring, "Doctor, I die hard, but I am not afraid to go." Soon afterwards he passed away.

John Adams succeeded Washington as head of the American State. He had been nominated by the Federalist Party. Fear of chaos and disorder, a basic distrust of democracy, had cooled his revolutionary ardour and made him a supporter of Hamilton. Of independent mind, he was a thinker rather than a party politician, an intellectual rather than a leader. Though agreeing with Hamilton on the need for strong government and the preservation of property, Adams opposed using the Federal machine for the benefit of particular economic interests and was by no means a wholehearted Federalist. In his judgments he was frequently right, but he lacked the arts of persuasion. He was bad at handling men, and his reputation has suffered accordingly. He was nevertheless one of the ablest political thinkers among American statesmen.

In foreign affairs a new crisis was at hand. The rise of Napoleon Bonaparte dimmed the high regard of Americans for their first ally, France. Fears began to grow that the French might acquire from Spain the provinces of Louisiana and Florida. A vigorous and ambitious European Power would then replace a weak one as a barrier between the expanding United States and the Gulf of Mexico. News also came of extensive French propaganda among the French-speaking inhabitants of Canada. There was a strong reaction, and for the last time the Federalists managed to outdistance their opponents. War hysteria swept the country, and they seized the opportunity to push through legislation which gave the executive extraordinary powers over aliens. The Naturalisation Act of 1798 extended the qualifying period of residence from five to fourteen years, and the Aliens Act gave the President the right to expel foreigners from the country by decree. More pointed was the Sedition Act, which in effect imposed a rigid censorship on the Press and was aimed specifically at the Opposition newspapers. The result was an intense constitutional conflict. It was in vain that Hamilton exhorted his colleagues, "Let us not establish tyranny. Energy is a very different thing from violence." Jefferson was determined to take up the challenge. He drafted resolutions, which were passed both in Kentucky and Virginia, maintaining that a state could review acts of Congress and nullify any measure deemed unconstitutional. This fateful doctrine has been heard since in American history, and these resolves of 1798 became a platform of State Rights in later years.

The Federalists' attack on the liberty of the individual marked the beginning of their fall. Hamilton, who had resigned from the Treasury some years earlier, thought he could now regain power by forcing a war with France. He conceived a vast plan for dividing, in concert with Great Britain, the Spanish colonies in the New World. A grandiose campaign took shape in his mind, with himself leading the American Army southwards to the mouth of the Mississippi. But the person who extinguished these hopes was the President. Although he was no lover of the masses Adams hated both plutocracy and militarism. Until 1799 he had shown no signs of opposition to the Federalists, but he now realised that war was very near. His complete powers as President over foreign affairs made it easy for him to act swiftly. He suddenly announced the appointment of an envoy to France, and on October 1, 1800, an American mission in Paris concluded a commercial treaty with the French. On the very same day France in secret purchased Louisiana from Spain.

Adams's term of office was now expiring and the Presidential elections were due. They present a complicated spectacle, for there were dramatic splits on both sides. The Federalists had not forgiven Adams for stopping them from going to war with France. Nevertheless he was the only Federalist candidate with any hope of success, and so he won the nomination. Real power in the party, however, still lay with Hamilton, and he in his resentment hampered Adams in every way he could.

Ranged on the Republican side stood Jefferson, flanked for the office of Vice-President by Aaron Burr, a corrupt New York politician. By a curiosity of the American Constitution in those days, which was soon to be remedied, the man who won the largest number of votes became President, while the runner-up was declared Vice-President. Thus it was quite possible to have a President and a Vice-President belonging to opposite parties. Adams was beaten by both Jefferson and Burr, but Jefferson and Burr each gained an equal number of votes. There was little love lost between them. Burr tried to overthrow his chief when the deadlock was referred for decision to the House of Representatives. But here Hamilton stepped in to frustrate him. Local politics have always excited strong loyalties and antipathies in the United States, stronger often than Federal issues. Hamilton and Burr were at grips for power in New York. Hamilton could not stomach the thought of Burr becoming President, and in the House of Representatives he threw his weight behind Jefferson. Thus by a remarkable twist of fortune Hamilton's old opponent became the third President of the United States, and the centre of influence once more shifted from Massachusetts to Virginia. But the significance of the accession to power of Thomas Jefferson must not be exaggerated. The Supreme Court, headed by John Marshall, remained the zealous, impartial guardian and upholder of the rights and authority of the Federal Government. Jefferson himself, though a sincere agrarian democrat, was neither unrealistic nor sentimental, and events soon compelled him to follow the theme and methods of his predecessors.

The United States in which Jefferson was inaugurated as President on March 4, 1801, had grown fast during their short existence and were still growing. In the twenty-five years since the Declaration of Independence the population had nearly doubled and was now about five and a half millions. Three new inland states had been set up and admitted to the Union: Vermont in the North, Kentucky and Tennessee in the Central South. Red Indian confederacies that blocked the westward migration had been decisively defeated, and their lands divided into territories, which were in their turn to form states. Ohio was the first to do so in 1803. The nation was everywhere thrusting outward from its original Atlantic seaboard. Its commerce upon the high seas now flowed from China, round Cape Horn, to the countries of Europe by way of the fast-rising ports of Boston, Baltimore, and above all New York. Philadelphia remained the greatest of American cities, but it was gradually losing its position as the centre of the life of the Union. It now ceased to be the political capital. Jefferson was the first President to take his oath in the new city of Washington, for which spacious plans had been drawn up. As yet only one wing of the Capitol, which housed Congress, had been built and the White House was incomplete; there was a single convenient tavern, a few boarding-houses for Senators and Congressmen, and little else except quagmire and waste land. Jefferson was undaunted by the hardships of his backwoods capital. Thought of the fine city that would one day arise kindled his idealism, and its pioneering life suited his frugal, homely manner.

It was impossible for the President to ignore the world struggle. The farmers whom Jefferson represented depended for their markets upon the Old World, and the Western states and territories needed unhindered transport for their produce down the Mississippi to the Gulf of Mexico. At the mouth of the great river lay the port of New Orleans, and New Orleans was still in Spanish hands. Rumours of the secret French purchase of Louisiana were now circulating, and were soon given substance. Bonaparte dispatched an expedition to suppress a negro rising under Toussaint L'Ouverture in the French island colony of Haiti. This accomplished, it was to take possession of Louisiana in the name of the French Government. Thus while the Treaty of Amiens imposed an uneasy peace on Europe trained French troops had arrived once more off the North American continent, and would shortly, it seemed, proceed to the mainland. This, like the French menace from Canada in the eighteenth century, drew the English-speaking nations together. "The day that France takes possession of New Orleans . . ." wrote Jefferson to the American envoy in Paris, "we must marry ourselves to the British Fleet and nation. We must turn all our attention to a maritime force, and make the first cannon-shot which shall be fired in Europe a signal for . . . holding the two continents of America in sequestration for the common purposes of the united British and American nations. This is not a state of things which we seek or desire. It is one which this measure [the purchase of Louisiana], if adopted by France, forces on us." This was a surprising development in the views of Jefferson, hitherto an admirer of France and opponent of Great Britain. But theoretical opinions must often give way before the facts of international politics. At any rate, it is wise if they do, and Jefferson had his share of practical wisdom.

In the autumn of 1802 France compelled the Spaniards to close New Orleans to American produce. The whole West Country was ablaze with anger and alarm. As Jefferson wrote to his envoy in Paris, "There is on the globe one single spot the possessor of which is our natural and habitual enemy. It is New Orleans, through which three-eighths of our produce must pass to market." James Monroe was now sent on a special mission to Paris to try to purchase Louisiana, or at least New Orleans, from the French. While he was on his way American plans were suddenly forwarded by events elsewhere. The French expedition to Haiti ended in disaster, with the loss of thirty thousand men. The renewal of war between France and Britain after the Peace of Amiens was also imminent. With dramatic swiftness Napoleon abandoned all hopes of American empire, and to the astonishment of the American envoy offered to sell all the Louisiana territories which Spain had ceded to France. Monroe arrived in Paris in time to complete the purchase, and for fifteen million dollars Louisiana was transferred to the United States.

At a stroke of the pen the United States had thus doubled its area and acquired vast lands out of which a dozen states later arose. It was to prove the finest bargain in American history. Yet when the news crossed the Atlantic there was a vehement outcry. Had Napoleon the legal right to sign these lands away? Had the United States paid out an immense sum merely to acquire a faulty title-deed? Moreover, there was no express power in the Constitution for the Federal Government to carry out such an act. But it was necessary to confirm it at once lest Napoleon should change his mind. The Senate was called upon to ratify the cession, and Jefferson claimed that the negotiations were valid under his treaty-making powers in the Constitution. The Federalists loudly denounced the new acquisition, with its high purchase price and undefined frontiers. They realised it would provoke an extensive shift of power in the Union and a rapid growth of the agricultural interests of the West. But all the influence and pressure of the Eastern seaboard were marshalled in vain. In December 1803 the American flag was raised upon the Government buildings of New Orleans and the United States entered upon the possession of nine hundred thousand square miles of new territory.

The acquisition of Louisiana brought a new restlessness into American politics and a desire for further advance. West Florida, which stretched along the Gulf of Mexico, still belonged to Spain, and beyond the newly acquired lands the plains of Texas beckoned. Troubles were stirred up between the Western states and territories and the Federal capital. The evil genius of these years is Aaron Burr.

Burr, as we have seen, had missed a chance of becoming President in 1800 largely owing to Hamilton's intervention. Now in 1804 Hamilton's opposition stopped him being selected for the Governorship of New York. He challenged Hamilton to a duel. Hamilton accepted, intending to satisfy honour by firing wide. But Aaron Burr shot to kill, and thus put an end to the life of one of the outstanding figures in the founding years of the American Republic. Discredited in the eyes of all, Burr cast about for means of creating a new American realm of his own. He even sought a large bribe from the British Government. Whether he hoped to detach the Western states from the Union or to carve off a slice of the Spanish dominions is still obscure and disputed, but his career ended abruptly with his arrest and trial for treason. For lack of evidence he was acquitted, and went into voluntary exile.

Jefferson had been triumphantly re-elected President in 1804, but his second term of office was less happy than his first. Under the stress of Westward expansion his party in the East was splitting into local factions. The renewal of European war had also revived the old sinister issues of embargo, blockade, and impressment. Jefferson was faced with the provocations of the British Fleet, which continually arrested ships and took off sailors on the verge of American territorial waters, and sometimes even within them. The British were entitled by the customs of the time to impress British subjects who happened to be serving in American ships; but they also made a practice of impressing American citizens and many sailors whose nationality was doubtful. To this grievance was added another. In retaliation for Napoleon's Berlin Decrees, establishing a Continental blockade of Britain, Orders in Council were issued in London in 1807 imposing severe restrictions on all neutral trade with France and her allies. United States commerce was hard hit by both these belligerent measures. But, as the Battle of Trafalgar had proved, the Royal Navy was much more powerful than the French, and it was at the hands of the British that American shipping suffered most.

Amidst these troubles Jefferson remained serenely determined to preserve the peace. But public opinion was mounting against him. On his recommendation in 1807 Congress passed an Embargo Act which forbade American ships to sail for foreign waters. It prohibited all exports from America by sea or land, and all imports of certain British manufactures. Jefferson hoped that the loss of American trade would oblige the belligerents to come to terms, but in fact his measure proved far more damaging to American commerce than to either the British or French. The economy of New England and all the seaports of the Atlantic coast depended on trade with Britain. From everywhere in the Eastern states protests went up, New England being particularly vociferous. The Federalists were quick to rally their forces and join in the outcry. Jefferson's own party, the Republicans, revolted and divided against him. After it had been in operation for fourteen months he was forced to withdraw the embargo. Three days later his term of office expired and he retired to his Virginian estate of Monticello.

The failure of his policies in the last two years of his Presidency should not obscure the commanding position of Thomas Jefferson in the history of the United States. He was the first political idealist among American statesmen and the real founder of the American democratic tradition. Contact with the perils of high policy during the crisis of world war modified the original simplicity of his views, but his belief in the common man never wavered. Although his dislike of industrialism weakened in later years, he retained to the end his faith in a close connection between yeoman farming and democracy. His strength lay in the frontier states of the West, which he so truly represented and served in over thirty years of political life.

CHAPTER 11

THE WAR OF 1812

T HE NEW President of the United States in March 1809 was
    James Madison. As Jefferson's Secretary of State he had had
much experience of public office, and he was a political theorist of
note. There was a stubborn side to his nature, and his practical skill and
judgment were not always equal to that of his predecessor. Madison inherited an inflamed public opinion and a delicate state of relations with
Great Britain. At first there were high hopes of a settlement. Madison
reached a provisional agreement with the British Minister in Washington which was very favourable to British interests. But the Foreign Secretary, Canning, repudiated the document and recalled the Minister
responsible for it. He was never so happy in his handling of America as
he was in Europe. For three years Anglo-American relations grew
steadily worse. Madison was deceived by Napoleon's revocation of the
Berlin Decrees which had closed all European ports controlled by
France. He now tried to get England to reciprocate by annulling her
Orders in Council against trade with ports in French hands. In vain
wiser politicians warned him that Napoleon's action was merely a
diplomatic move "to catch us into a war with England."

The unofficial trade war with the United States was telling heavily
upon England. The loss of the American market and the hard winter of
1811–12 had brought widespread unemployment and a business crisis.
Petitions were sent to Parliament begging the Government to revoke the
Orders in Council. After much hesitation Castlereagh, now at the Foreign Office, announced in the House of Commons that the Government
had done so. But it was too late. The Atlantic crossing took too long for

the news to reach America in time. On June 18, 1812, two days after Castlereagh's announcement, Congress declared war on Great Britain.

In the following week Napoleon began his long-planned invasion of Russia.

The root of the quarrel, as American historians have pointed out, lay not in rival interpretations of maritime law, but in the problems of the Western frontier. The seaboard states, and especially New England, wanted peace. Their main concern was America's foreign trade, which had already gravely diminished. War with Britain would bring it to a stop. But American domestic politics had brought to power representatives of the West and South-West who were hostile to Britain, and it was they, not the merchants of the Atlantic coastline, who forced America into the conflict. On the frontiers, and especially in the North-West, men were hungry for land, and this could be had only from the Indians or from the British Empire.

Trouble with the Indians had been brewing for some time. The pioneers of the early nineteenth century were woodsmen. They had already occupied the forest lands held by Redskin tribes in Illinois and Indiana; they now coveted the forests of British Canada round the Great Lakes, with their unsettled Crown territory and tiny population of Loyalists. As the Western territories of America filled up, pressure mounted for a farther north-westerly move. In 1811 the Red Indians bordering on the Ohio united under their last great warrior leader, Tecumseh. On his orders the tribes now showed themselves impervious to the temptations of liquor and trade. Alarm spread along the frontier. A revival of Indian power would put an end to further expansion. Troops were called out by the Governor of Indiana, William Henry Harrison, who had been largely responsible for the recent westward push, and in November 1811 the Indian Confederacy was overthrown at the Battle of Tippecanoe.

It is one of the legends of American history that the resistance of the Indians was encouraged and organised from Canada—a legend created by the war party of 1812. A new generation was entering American politics, headed by Henry Clay from Kentucky and John C. Calhoun from South Carolina. These young men formed a powerful group in the House of Representatives, which came to be known as the "War Hawks." They had no conception of affairs in Europe; they cared nothing about Napoleon's designs, still less about the fate of Russia. Their prime aim and object was to seize Canada and establish American sovereignty throughout the whole Northern continent. Through the influence of Clay the President was won over to a policy of war. The causes of the conflict were stated in traditional terms: impressment, violations of the three-mile limit, blockades, and Orders in Council. Opinion in America was sharply divided, and New England voted overwhelmingly against the declaration of war, but the "War Hawks" with their vociferous propaganda had their way. The frontier spirit in American politics was coming in with a vengeance, and it was sure of itself. Moreover, the frontier farmers felt they had a genuine grievance. There was some good ground for the slogan of "Free Trade and Sailors' Rights" which they adopted. British restrictions on American shipping were holding up the export of their produce. A short expedition of pioneers would set things right, it was thought, and dictate peace in Quebec in a few weeks. Congress adjourned without even voting extra money for the American Army or Navy.

On paper the forces were very unequal. The population of the United States was now seven and a quarter millions, including slaves. In Canada there were only five hundred thousand people, most of them French. But there were nearly five thousand trained British troops, about four thousand Canadian regulars, and about the same number of militia. The Indians could supply between three and four thousand auxiliaries.

The American Regular Army numbered less than seven thousand men, and although with great difficulty over four hundred thousand state militia were called out few were used in Canada. On the American side never more than seven thousand men took part in any engagement, and the untrained volunteers proved hopeless soldiers. Nor was this all. The Seven Years War had shown that Canada could only be conquered by striking up the St. Lawrence, but the Americans had no sufficient Navy for such a project. They were therefore forced to fight an offensive war on a wide frontier, impassable at places, and were exposed to Indian onslaughts on their columns. Their leaders had worked out no broad strategy. If they had concentrated their troops on Lake Ontario they might have succeeded, but instead they made half-hearted and unco-ordinated thrusts across the borders.

The first American expedition ended in disaster. The ablest British commander, General Isaac Brock, supported by the Indian Confederacy, drove it back. By August the British were in Detroit, and within a few days Fort Dearborn, where Chicago now stands, had fallen. The American frontier rested once more on a line from the Ohio to Lake Erie. The remainder of the year was spent on fruitless moves upon the Niagara front, and operations came to an inconclusive end. The British in Canada were forced to remain on the defensive while great events were taking place in Europe.

The war at sea was more colourful, and for the Americans more cheering. They had sixteen vessels, of which three surpassed anything afloat. These were 44-gun frigates, the *Constitution,* the *United States,* and the *President.* They fired a heavier broadside than British frigates, they were heavily timbered, but their clean lines under water enabled them to outsail any ship upon the seas. Their crews were volunteers and their officers highly trained. A London journalist called them "a few fir-built frigates, manned by a handful of bastards and outlaws." This phrase was adopted with glee by the Americans, who gloried in disproving the insult. The British fleet on the transatlantic station consisted of ninety-seven sail, including eleven ships of the line and thirty-four frigates. Their naval tradition was long and glorious, and, with their memories of Trafalgar and the Nile, the English captains were confident they could sink any American. But when one English ship after another found its guns out-ranged and was battered to pieces the reputation of the "fir-built frigates" was startlingly made. The American public, smarting at the disasters in Canada, gained new heart from these victories. Their frigates within a year had won more successes over the British than the French and Spaniards in two decades of warfare. But retribution was at hand. On June 1, 1813, the American frigate *Chesapeake,* under Captain Lawrence, sailed from Boston harbour with a green and mutinous crew to accept a challenge from Captain Broke of H.M.S. *Shannon.* After a fifteen-minute fight the *Chesapeake* surrendered. Other American losses followed, and command of the ocean passed into British hands. American privateers, however, continued to harry British shipping throughout the rest of the war.

These naval episodes had no effect on the general course of the war, and if the British Government had abandoned impressment a new campaign might have been avoided in 1813. But they did not do so, and the Americans set about revising their strategy. The war was continuing officially upon the single issue of impressment, for the conquest of Canada was never announced as a war aim by the United States. Nevertheless Canada was their main objective. By land the Americans made a number of raids into the province of Upper Canada, now named Ontario. Towns and villages were sacked and burnt, including the little capital which has since become the great city of Toronto. The war was becoming fiercer. During the winter of 1812–13 the Americans had also established a base at Fort Presqu'ile, on Lake Erie, and stores were laboriously hauled over the mountains to furnish the American commander, Captain Oliver H. Perry, with a flotilla for fresh-water fighting. In the autumn Perry's little armada sailed to victory. A strange amphibious battle was fought in September 1813. Negroes, frontier scouts, and militiamen, aboard craft hastily built of new green wood, fought to the end upon the still waters of the lake. The American ships were heavier, and the British were defeated with heavy loss. "We have met the enemy," Perry reported laconically, "and they are ours."

Harrison, American victor at Tippecanoe, could now advance into Ontario. In October, at the Battle of the Thames, he destroyed a British army which had beaten him earlier in the year, together with its Indian allies. The Indian Confederacy was broken and Tecumseh was killed. Thus the United States were established on the southern shores of the Great Lakes and the Indians could no longer outflank their frontier. But the invasion of Upper Canada on land had been a failure, and the year ended with the Canadians in possession of Fort Niagara.

Hitherto the British in Canada had lacked the means for offensive action. Troops and ships in Europe were locked in the deadly struggle against Napoleon. Moreover the British Government was anxious not to irritate the New England states by threatening them from the North. Even the blockade was not extended to cover Massachusetts until 1814, and indeed the British forces were almost entirely fed from the New England ports. But by the spring of 1814 a decision had been reached in Europe. Napoleon abdicated in April and the British could at last send adequate reinforcements. They purposed to strike from Niagara, from Montreal by way of Lake Champlain, and in the South at New Orleans, with simultaneous naval raids on the American coast. The campaign opened before Wellington's veterans could arrive from the Peninsula. The advance from Niagara was checked by a savage drawn battle at Lundy's Lane, near the Falls. But by the end of August eleven thousand troops from Europe had been concentrated near Montreal to advance by Burgoyne's old route down the Hudson valley. In September, under Sir George Prevost, they moved on Plattsburg, and prepared to dispute the command of Lake Champlain. They were faced by a mere fifteen hundred American regulars, supported by a few thousand militia. All depended on the engagement of the British and American flotillas. As at Lake Erie, the Americans built better ships for freshwater fighting, and they gained the victory. This crippled the British advance and was the most decisive engagement of the war. Prevost and his forces retired into Canada.

At sea, in spite of their reverses of the previous years, the British were supreme. More ships arrived from European waters. The American coast was defenceless. In August the British General Ross landed in Chesapeake Bay at the head of four thousand men. The American militia, seven thousand strong, but raw and untrained, retreated rapidly, and on the 24th British troops entered the Federal capital of Washington. President Madison took refuge in Virginia. So hasty was the American withdrawal that English officers sat down to a meal cooked for him and his family in the White House. The White House and the Capitol were then burnt in reprisal for the conduct of American militiamen in Canada. Washington's home on the Potomac was spared and strictly guarded by the British. The campaign ended in an attempt to land at Baltimore, but here the militia were ready; General Ross was killed and a retreat to the ships followed.

In December the last and most irresponsible British onslaught, the expedition to New Orleans, reached its base. But here in the frontier lands of the South-West a military leader of high quality had appeared in the person of Andrew Jackson. As an early settler in Tennessee he had won a reputation in warfare against the Indians. When the British now tried to subsidise and organise them Jackson pursued them into Spanish West Florida, and occupied its capital, Pensacola.

Meanwhile eight thousand British troops had landed at New Orleans under Sir Edward Pakenham, who had commanded a division at Salamanca. The swamps and inlets in the mouth of the Mississippi made an amphibious operation extremely dangerous. All men and stores had to be transported seventy miles in rowboats from the Fleet. Jackson hastened back from Florida and entrenched himself on the left bank of the river. His forces were much inferior in numbers, but composed of highly skilled marksmen. On the morning of January 8, 1815, Pakenham led a frontal assault against the American earthworks—one of the most unintelligent manoeuvres in the history of British warfare. Here he was slain and two thousand of his troops were killed or wounded. The only surviving general officer withdrew the army to its transports. The Americans lost seventy men, thirteen of them killed. The battle had lasted precisely half an hour.

Peace between England and America had meanwhile been signed on Christmas Eve, 1814. But the Battle of New Orleans is an important event in American history. It made the career of a future President, Jackson, it led to the belief that the Americans had decisively won the war, and it created an evil legend that the struggle had been a second War of Independence against British tyranny.

On the American domestic scene events had been moving fast. New England, dependent upon shipping and commerce, was suffering heavily and her leaders were embarrassed. They had supported the Federal-

ist Party, now in disarray; they resented the predominance of the Western states and territories which had pushed them into war, and they
began to contemplate leaving the Union. In the summer of 1814
Massachusetts had been thrown upon her own resources. British troops
were in Maine; the harbours were blockaded by British ships. The burden of taxation fell largely upon the New England states, yet the Federal Government seemed incapable of providing even a local defence.
In October a Convention of delegates from Massachusetts, Rhode
Island, and Connecticut was summoned to meet. They assembled at
Hartford in December. They wanted a separate peace with Great
Britain and no further connection with the fast-growing West. They believed that the British expedition to New Orleans would succeed and
that the West, cut off from the sea, would probably leave the Union on
its own initiative. The President was alarmed and the war party feared
the worst. Fortunately for the United States the moderate New England politicians gained the upper hand at Hartford and the Convention only drew up a severe arraignment of Madison's administration.
For the time being secession was killed. "To attempt," they declared,
"upon every abuse of power to change the Constitution would be to
perpetuate the evils of revolution."

Andrew Jackson's victory at New Orleans and the success of the
peace negotiations produced an outcry against the disloyalty of New
England and attached a permanent stigma to the Federalist Party. Yet
the doctrine of State Rights, to which the Hartford delegates held, was
to remain a vivid force in American politics. The war had also done
much to diversify New England's economy. To her shipping and commercial interests were added great and rewarding developments in
manufacture and industry.

Peace negotiations had been tried throughout the war, but it was not
until January 1814 that the British had agreed to treat. The American
Commissioners, among them Henry Clay, reached Ghent in June. At
first the British refused to discuss either neutral rights or impressment,
and they still hoped for an Indian buffer state in the North-West. It was
Wellington's common sense which changed the atmosphere. The previous November he had been asked to take command in America, but he
had studied reports of the Battle of Plattsburg and realised that victory
depended on naval superiority upon the lakes. He saw no way of gaining it. He held moreover that it was not in Britain's interest to demand
territory from America on the Canadian border. Both sides therefore
agreed upon the *status quo* for the long boundary in the North. Other
points were left undetermined. Naval forces on the Great Lakes were
regulated by a Commission in 1817, and the disputed boundary of

Maine was similarly settled later. By the time the British Navy went to war again impressment had been abandoned.

Thus ended a futile and unnecessary conflict. Anti-American feeling in Great Britain ran high for several years, but the United States were never again refused proper treatment as an independent Power. The British Army and Navy had learned to respect their former colonials. When news of peace reached the British army in the New World one of the soldiers wrote, "We are all happy enough, for we Peninsular soldiers saw that neither fame nor any other military distinction could be acquired by this type of milito-nautico-guerrilla-plundering warfare."

The results of the peace were solid and enduring. The war was a turning-point in the history of Canada. Canadians took pride in the part they had played in defending their country, and their growing national sentiment was strengthened. Many disagreements were still to shake Anglo-American relations. Thirty years later in the dispute over the possession of Oregon vast territories were involved and there was a threat of war. But henceforward the world was to see a three-thousand-mile international frontier between Canada and the United States undefended by men or guns. On the oceans the British Navy ruled supreme for a century to come, and behind this shield the United States were free to fulfil their continental destiny.

CHAPTER 12

CANADA: THE BIRTH OF A NATION

O CCUPATION of the empty lands of the globe was vehemently accelerated by the fall of Napoleon. The long struggle against France had stifled or arrested the expansion of the English-speaking peoples, and the ships and the men who might have founded the second British Empire had been consumed in twenty years of world war. A generation of men and women had toiled or fought in their factories or on their farms, in the fleets and in the armies, and only a very few had had either the wish or the opportunity to seek a new life and new fortunes overseas. Their energies and their hopes had been concentrated on survival and on victory. There had been no time for dreams of emigration, and no men to spare if it had been possible. Suddenly all this was changed by the decision at Waterloo. Once again the oceans were free. No enemies threatened in Europe. Ships need no longer sail in convoy, and the main outlines of the continents had been charted. Once more the New World offered an escape from the hardships and frustrations of the Old. The war was over. Fares were cheap and transport was plentiful. The result was the most spectacular migration of human beings of which history has yet had record and a vast enrichment of the trade and industry of Great Britain.

Of course the process took time to gather way, and at first the flow of emigrants was very small. But the road had been pointed by the grim convict settlements in Australia, by the loyalists from the United States who had moved to Canada, and by traders, explorers, missionaries, and whalers all over the temperate zones of the earth. News began to spread among the masses that fertile unoccupied and habitable lands still existed, in which white men could dwell in peace and liberty, and perhaps could even better themselves. The increasing population of Great Britain added to the pressure. In 1801 it was about eleven millions. Thirty years later it was sixteen millions, and by 1871 it was ten millions more. Fewer people died at birth or in early childhood, and it has been established by a recent authority that despite the Industrial Revolution London was a healthier place to live in than rural Prussia or Bourbon Paris. The numbers grew, and the flow began: in the 1820's a quarter of a million emigrants, in the 1830's half a million, by the middle of the century a million and a half, until sixty-five years after Waterloo no fewer than eight million people had left the British Isles.

The motives, methods, and character of the movement were very different from those which had sustained the Pilgrim Fathers and the Stuart plantations of the seventeenth century. Famine drove at least a million Irishmen to the United States and elsewhere. Gold lured hardy fortune-hunters to Australia, and to the bleak recesses of Canada, where they discovered a more practical if less respectable El Dorado than had dazzled the Elizabethan adventurers. Hunger for land and for the profits of the wool trade beckoned the more sober and well-to-do. All this was largely accomplished in the face of official indifference and sometimes of hostility. The American War of Independence had convinced most of the ruling classes in Britain that colonies were undesirable possessions. They did not even have a departmental Secretary of State of their own until 1854. The Government was interested in strategic bases, but if ordinary people wanted to settle in the new lands then let them do so. It might cure unemployment and provide posts for penniless noblemen, but the sooner these communities became completely independent the better and cheaper for the tax-payer in England. Anyway, Greece was more interesting news than New Zealand, and the educated public were much more concerned about the slave-trade than the squalors of the emigrant ships. Thus, as in India, the Second British Empire was founded almost by accident, and with small encouragement from any of the main political parties.

Of the new territories Canada was the most familiar and the nearest in point of distance to the United Kingdom. Her Maritime Provinces had long sent timber to Britain, and rather than return with empty holds the shipowners were content to transport emigrants for a moderate fare. Once they landed, however, the difficulties and the distances were very great. The Maritime Provinces lived a life very much of their own, and many emigrants chose to push on into Lower Canada, or, as it is now called, the Province of Quebec. Pitt in 1791 had sought to solve the racial problems of Canada by dividing her into two parts. In Lower Canada the French were deeply rooted, a compact, alien community, led by priests and seigneurs, uninterested and untouched by the democratic ideas of liberal or revolutionary Europe, and holding stubbornly like the Boers in South Africa to their own traditions and language. Beyond them, to the north-west, lay Upper Canada, the modern Province of Ontario, settled by some of the sixty thousand Englishmen who had left the United States towards the end of the eighteenth century rather than live under the American republic. These proud folk had out of devotion to the British Throne abandoned most of their possessions, and been rewarded with the unremunerative but honourable title of United Empire Loyalists. The Mohawk tribe, inspired by the same sentiments, had journeyed with them. They had hacked a living space out of the forests, and dwelt lonely and remote, cut off from Lower Canada by the rapids of the St. Lawrence, and watchful against incursions from the United States. Then there was a vast emptiness till one reached a few posts on the Pacific which traded their wares to China.

These communities, so different in tradition, character, and race, had been rallied into temporary unity by invasion from the United States. French, English, and Red Indians all fought against the Americans, and repulsed them in the three-year struggle between 1812 and 1814. Then trouble began. The French in Lower Canada feared that the immigrants would outnumber and dominate them. The Loyalists in Upper Canada welcomed new settlers who would increase the price of land but were reluctant to treat them as equals. Moreover, the two Provinces started to quarrel with each other. Upper Canada's external trade had to pass through Lower Canada, and there pay taxes, and disputes occurred about sharing the proceeds. Differences over religion added to the irritations. From about 1820 the Assembly in Lower Canada began to behave like the Parliaments of the early Stuarts and the legislatures of the American colonies, refusing to vote money for the salaries of royal judges and permanent officials. French politicians made vehement speeches. In Upper Canada the new settlers struggled for political equality with the Loyalists. Liberals wanted to make the executive responsible to the Assembly and talked wildly of leaving the Empire, and in 1836 the Assembly in which they held a majority was dissolved.

In the following year both Provinces rebelled, Lower Canada for a month and Upper Canada for a week. There were mobs, firing by troops, shifty compromises, and very few executions. Everything was on a small scale and in a minor key, and no great harm was done, but it made the British Government realise that Canadian affairs required attention. The Whig leaders in London were wiser than George III. They perceived that a tiny minority of insurgents could lead to great troubles, and in 1838 Lord Durham was sent to investigate, assisted by Edward Gibbon Wakefield. His instructions were vague and simple, "To put things right," and meanwhile the Canadian constitution was suspended by Act of Parliament. Durham was a Radical, brilliant, decisive, and hot-tempered. Wakefield was an active theorist on Imperial affairs whose misconduct with a couple of heiresses had earned him a prison sentence and compelled him to spend the rest of his public life behind the scenes. Durham stayed only a few months. His high-handed conduct in dealing with disaffected Canadians aroused much criticism of him at Westminster. Feeling himself deserted by Lord Melbourne's Government, with which he was personally unpopular, but which should nevertheless have stood by him, Durham resigned and returned to England. He then produced the famous report in which he diagnosed and proclaimed the root causes of the trouble and advocated responsible government, carried on by Ministers commanding the confidence of the popular Assembly, a united Canada, and planned settlement of the unoccupied lands. These recommendations were largely put into effect by the Canada Act of 1840, which was the work of Lord John Russell.

Thereafter Canada's progress was swift and peaceful. Her population had risen from about half a million in 1815 to a million and a quarter in 1838. A regular steamship service with the British Isles and cheap transatlantic postage were established in the same year. There were hesitations and doubts in England at the novel idea of making colonies almost completely free and allowing their democratic Assemblies to choose and eject their own Ministers, but the appointment of Durham's son-in-law, Lord Elgin, as Governor-General in 1847 was decisive. Elgin believed, like Durham, that the Governor should represent the sovereign and remain in the background of politics. He appointed and dismissed Ministers according to the wishes of the Assembly. For this he was blamed or applauded, and even pelted with eggs and stones, according to how it pleased or angered either side. But when he laid down his office seven years later the principle had been firmly accepted by Canadians of all persuasions that popular power must march with popular responsibility, that Ministers must govern and be obeyed so long as they enjoyed the confidence of the majority and should resign when they had lost it. There was hardly any talk now of leaving the Empire or dividing Canada into separate and sovereign units or joining the American Republic. On the contrary, the Oregon

Treaty with the United States in 1846 extended the 49th parallel right across the continent as a boundary between the two countries and gave the whole of Vancouver Island to Great Britain.

In the mid-century a movement for the federation of all the Canadian Provinces began to grow and gather support. The Civil War in the United States helped to convince Canadians that all was not perfect in their neighbours' constitution, and the victory of the North also aroused their fears that the exultant Union might be tempted to extend its borders farther still. Canada had already turned her gaze westwards. Between the Province of Ontario and the Rocky Mountains lay a thousand miles of territory, uninhabited save by a few settlers in Manitoba, a roaming-place for Indians, trappers, and wild animals. It was a temptation, so it was argued, to the land-hunger of the United States. Discharged Irish soldiers from the Civil War had already made armed raids across the border which Congress had declared itself powerless to arrest. Might not the Americans press forward, occupy these vacant lands by stealth, and even establish a kind of squatter's right to the prairies? The soil was believed to be fertile and was said to offer a living for white men. In 1867 America purchased the remote and forbidding expanse of Alaska from the Russians for the sum of 7,200,000 dollars, but here, on the doorstep of the Republic, lay a prize which seemed much more desirable and was very easy of access. No one ruled over it except the Hudson's Bay Company, founded in the reign of Charles II, and the Company, believing that agriculture would imperil its fur-trade, was both hostile to settlers and jealous of its own authority. Eleven years before, however, the discovery of gold on the Fraser River had precipitated a rush of fortune-hunters to the Pacific coast. The Company's officials had proved powerless to control the turmoil, and the Government in London had been compelled to extend the royal sovereignty to this distant shore. Thus was born the Crown colony of British Columbia, which soon united with the Island of Vancouver and demanded and obtained self-rule. But between it and Ontario lay a no-man's-land, and something must be done if it was not to fall into the hands of the United States. How indeed could Canada remain separate from America and yet stay alive?

These considerations prompted the British North America Act of 1867, which created the first of the self-governing British Dominions beyond the seas. The Provinces of Ontario, Quebec, New Brunswick, and Nova Scotia were the founding members. They adopted a federal constitution of a very different shape from that of the United States. All powers not expressly reserved to the Provinces of Canada were assumed by the central Government: the Governor-General, representing the monarch, ruled through Ministers drawn from the majority in her Canadian House of Commons, and Members of the House were elected in numbers proportionate to the population they represented. Thus the way was made easy for the absorption of new territories and Provinces, and on the eve of her Railway Age and westward expansion the political stability of Canada was assured.

When the Parliament of the new Dominion first met, its chief anxiety was about the Western lands. Its members looked to the future, and it is convenient here to chart the results of their foresight. The obvious, immediate step was to buy out the Hudson's Bay Company. This was done two years later for the sum of £300,000. The Company kept its trading rights, and indeed retains them to this day, but it surrendered its territorial sovereignty to the Crown. The process was not accomplished without bloodshed. There was a brief revolt in Manitoba, where wild Indian half-breeds thought that their freedom was endangered, but order was soon restored. Manitoba became a Province of the Dominion in 1870, and in the next year British Columbia was also admitted. By themselves, however, these constitutional steps would not have sufficed to bind the broad stretches of Canada together. The challenging task that faced the Dominion was to settle and develop her empty Western lands before the immigrant tide from America could flood across the 49th parallel. The answer was to build a transcontinental railway.

When the Maritime Provinces joined the federation they had done so on condition they were linked with Ontario by rail, and after nine years of labour a line was completed in 1876. British Columbia made the same demand and received the same promise. It proved much more difficult to fulfil. Capital was scarce, investors were timid, politics were tangled, and much of the country was unknown. At length however a Scotsman, Donald Smith, better known as Lord Strathcona, carried out the plan. His company demanded ten years. Helped by Government funds, they finished their work in half the time, and the Canadian Pacific Railway was opened in 1885. Other lines sprang up, and corn, soon counted in millions of bushels a year, began to flow in from the prairies. Canada had become a nation, and shining prospects lay before her.

CHAPTER 13

AMERICAN EPIC

THE YEAR 1815 had marked the end of a period of American development. Up to this time the life of the continent had been moulded largely by forces from Europe, but with the conclusion of the war of 1812 against England America turned in upon herself and with her back to the Atlantic looked towards the West. The years following the Peace of Ghent are full of the din of the Westward advance. In politics the vehement struggles of Federalist and Republican were replaced by what a contemporary journalist called "the era of good feelings." But underneath the calm surface of the first decade lay the bitter rivalry of sectional interests which were soon to assume permanent and organised party forms. As in all post-war periods, the major political issue was that of finance. The ideas of Alexander Hamilton on Protection and banking were reluctantly accepted by the Republican administration under the stress of war conditions. The tariff of 1816 had created a régime of Protection under which New England turned from her shipping interests to manufacture and laid the foundations of her nineteenth-century prosperity. The old suspicions of Jefferson about a Federal banking system were overcome, and in 1816 a charter replacing the one which had expired was issued for the foundation of a new Federal Bank.

The ties with Europe were slowly and inexorably broken. Outstanding disputes between England and America were settled by a series of commissions. The boundaries of Canada were fixed, and both countries agreed to a mutual pact of disarmament upon that storm centre, the Great Lakes. In 1819, after straggling warfare in Spanish Florida, led by the hero of New Orleans, Andrew Jackson, the Spanish Government finally yielded the territory to the United States for five million dollars. Spain had withdrawn from the Northern continent for ever.

But the turmoils of European politics were to threaten America once again for the last time for many years to come. The sovereigns of the Old World were bound together to maintain the principle of monarchy and to co-operate in intervening in any country which showed signs of rebellion against existing institutions. The policy of this Holy Alliance had aroused the antagonism of Britain, who had refused to intervene in the internal affairs of Italy in 1821. The new crisis came in Spain. Bourbon France, burning to achieve respectability in the new Europe, sent an army across the Pyrenees to restore the Spanish monarchy. Russia would have liked to go farther. The Czar of Russia had world-wide interests, including large claims to the western coastline of North America, which he now reaffirmed by Imperial decree. Rumours also spread to Washington that the reactionary Powers of Europe, having supported the restoration of the Bourbons in Spain, might promote similar activities in the New World to restore Bourbon sovereignty there. In Southern America lay the Spanish colonies, which had in their turn thrown off the yoke of their mother country.

The British Government under Canning offered to co-operate with the United States in stopping the extension of this threatening principle of intervention to the New World. Britain announced that she recognised the sovereignty of the Latin republics in South America. Meanwhile President Monroe acted independently and issued his message to Congress proclaiming the principles later known as the Monroe Doctrine. This famous Doctrine was at once a warning against interference on the part of any European Powers in the New World and a statement of the intention of America to play no part in European politics. With this valedictory message America concentrated upon her own affairs. A new generation of politicians was rising. The old veterans of the days of the Constitution had most of them vanished from the scene, though Jefferson and Madison lingered on in graceful retirement in their Virginian homes.

Westward lay the march of American Empire. Within thirty years of the establishment of the Union nine new states had been formed in the Mississippi valley, and two in the borders of New England. As early as 1769 men like Daniel Boone had pushed their way into the Kentucky country, skirmishing with the Indians. But the main movement over the mountains began during the War of Independence. The migration of the eighteenth century took two directions: the advance westward towards the Ohio, with its settlement of Kentucky and Tennessee, and the occupation of the north-west forest regions, the fur-traders' domain, beyond Lake Erie. The colonisation of New England and the eastern coastline of America had been mainly the work of powerful companies, aided by the English Crown or by feudal proprietors with chartered rights. But here in the new lands of the West any man with an axe and a rifle could carve for himself a rude frontier home. By 1790 there were thirty-five thousand settlers in the Tennessee country, and double that number in Kentucky. By 1800 there were a million Americans west of the mountain ranges of the Alleghenies. From these new lands a strong, self-reliant Western breed took its place in American life. Modern American democracy was born and cradled in the valley of the Mississippi. The foresight of the first independent Congress of the United States had proclaimed for all time the principle that when new territories gained a certain population they should be admitted to statehood upon an equality with the existing partners of the Union. It is a proof of the quality and power of the Westerners that eleven of the eighteen Presidents of the United States between 1828 and 1901 were either born or passed the greater part of their lives in the valley of the Mississippi. Well might Daniel Webster upon an anniversary of the landing of the Pilgrim Fathers declaim the celebrated passage: "New England farms, houses, villages, and churches spread over and adorn the immense extent from the Ohio to Lake Erie and stretch along from the Alleghenies onwards beyond the Miamis and towards the falls of St. Anthony. Two thousand miles westward from the Rock where their fathers landed may now be seen the sons of pilgrims cultivating smiling fields, rearing towns and villages, and cherishing, we trust, the patrimonial blessings of wise institutions, of liberty and religion. . . . Ere long the sons of the pilgrims will be upon the shores of the Pacific."

America was swelling rapidly in numbers as well as in area. Between 1790 and 1820 the population increased from four to nine and a half millions. Thereafter it almost doubled every twenty years. Nothing like such a rate of growth had before been noted in the world, though it was closely paralleled in contemporary England. The settlement of great bodies of men in the West was eased by the removal of the Indian tribes from the regions east of the Mississippi. They had been defeated when they fought as allies of Britain in the war of 1812. Now it became Federal policy to eject them. The lands thus thrown open were made available in smaller units and at lower prices than in earlier years to the incoming colonists—for we might as well use this honourable word about them, unpopular though it may now be. Colonisation, in the true sense, was the task that engaged the Western pioneers. Farmers from stony New England were tilling the fertile empty territories to the south of the Great Lakes, while in the South the Black Belt of Alabama and Mississippi proved fruitful soil for the recent art of large-scale cotton cultivation.

But this ceaseless expansion to the West also changed the national centre of gravity, and intense stresses arose of interest as well as of feeling. The Eastern states, North and South alike, presently found their political power challenged by these settler communities, and the lure of pioneering created the fear of a labour shortage in the Eastern factories. In fact the gap was filled by new immigrants from Europe. As the frontier line rolled westward the new communities rising rapidly to statehood forced their own problems and desires upon the exhilarated but also embarrassed Federal Government. The East feared the approaching political dominance of the democratic West. The West resented the financial and economic bias of the Eastern moneyed classes. The forces of divergence grew strong, and only the elasticity of the Federal system around the core of state rights prevented the usual conflict between a mother country and its sturdy children.

The political history of these years between 1815 and 1830 is confused through the lack of adequate national party organisations to express the bitter sectional conflicts and hatreds in the North, South, and West. By 1830 the situation cleared and the great parties of the future stood opposed. With the growth of Federal legislation and the creation of a national economic framework of tariffs, banks, and land policies the Union felt the stress of state jealousies and rival interests. The expansion to the West tilted the political balance in favour of the new Western states, and strenuously the older forces in the North and South resisted the rising power of democracy within the Federal State. They had to confront not only the desires of the West, but also those of the small planters in the South and of the working men in the industrial North. Many of these people now for the first time began to receive the vote as universal manhood suffrage was more widely adopted. The electorate was expanding and eager to make its voice heard. At the same time the convention system was introduced into American politics. Candidates for the Presidency and for lesser public office in the states gradually ceased to be nominated by restricted party caucuses. Instead they were selected at meetings of delegates representing a variety of local and specialised opinion. This obliged the would-be President and other public office-holders to be more responsive to the divergences of popular will. Politicians of conservative mind like Henry Clay and John C. Calhoun feared the menacing signs of particularism and the consequent threat to the Union. These men formulated what they called the "American System." But their policy was merely a re-expression of the ideas of Hamilton. They sought to harmonise economic interests within a Federal framework. As Calhoun had said in 1817, "We are greatly and rapidly—I was about to say fearfully—growing. This is our pride and our danger, our weakness and our strength. . . . Let us then bind the Republic together with a perfect system of roads and canals. Protection would make the parts adhere more closely. . . . It would form a new and most powerful cement."

Public works were set on foot; steamboats appeared upon the Mississippi, and the concentration of trade in the Gulf of Mexico roused alarm in the Atlantic states, who saw themselves being deprived of profitable markets. But they hastened themselves to compete with this increasing activity. In 1817 the state of New York began the construction of the Erie Canal, which was to make New York City the most prosperous of the Eastern seaports. The great Cumberland high-road across the Ohio to Illinois was built with Federal money, and a network of roads was to bind the eager West to the Eastern states. But the history of the American nineteenth century is dominated by the continually threatened cleavage of East and West, and, upon the Atlantic seaboard, of the Northern and Southern states. In the early years of the century the keynote of politics was the rival bidding of Northern and Southern politicians for the votes and support of the Western states.

The issue of slavery was soon to trouble the relations of the North and South. In 1819 a Bill was tabled in Congress to admit Missouri as a state to the Union. This territory lay inside the bounds of the Louisiana Purchase, where the future of slavery had not so far been decided by Federal law. As the people of Missouri proposed to allow slavery in their draft constitution the Northerners looked upon this Bill as an aggressive move to increase the voting power of the South. A wild campaign of mutual recrimination followed. But with the increasing problem of the West facing them both, North and South could not afford to quarrel, and the angry sectional strife stirred up by this Bill ended in a compromise which was to hold until the middle of the century. Missouri was admitted as a slave-holding state, and slavery was prohibited north of latitude 36° 30′ within the existing territories of the Union which did not yet enjoy statehood. As part of the compromise Maine, which had just severed itself from Massachusetts, was admitted as a free state, making the division between slave and free equal, being twelve each. Far-seeing men realised the impending tragedy of this division. John Quincy Adams noted in his diary, "I considered it at once as the knell of the Union. I take it for granted that the present question is a mere preamble—a title-page to a great, tragic volume."

It was this cultured New Englander, son of the second President of the United States, who succeeded Monroe in 1825. The so-called era of good feelings was coming to a close, and the four years of his Presidency were to reveal the growth of lively party politics. All the political and economic interests of the Eastern states were forced on to the defensive by the rapid expansion of the West.

The West grouped itself around the figure of the frontier General Andrew Jackson, who claimed to represent the true Jeffersonian principles of democracy against the corrupt money interests of the East. Adams received the support of those classes who feared majority rule and viewed with alarm the growing power of the farmers and settlers of the frontier. The issue between the two factions was joined in 1828, when Jackson stood as rival candidate against Adams's re-election. In the welter of this election two new parties were born, the Democrats and the National Republicans, later called Whigs. It was the fiercest campaign since Jefferson had driven the elder Adams from office in 1800. As the results came in it was seen that Adams had won practically nothing outside New England, and that in the person of Andrew Jackson the West had reached controlling power. Here at last was an American President who had no spiritual contacts whatever with the Old World or its projection on the Atlantic shore, who represented at the White House the spirit of the American frontier. To many it seemed that democracy had triumphed indeed.

There were wild scenes at Washington at the inauguration of the new President, dubbed by his opponent Adams as "the brawler from Tennessee." But to the men of the West Jackson was their General, marching against the political monopoly of the moneyed classes. The complications of high politics caused difficulties for the backwoodsman. His simple mind, suspicious of his opponents, made him open to influence by more partisan and self-seeking politicians. In part he was guided by Martin Van Buren, his Secretary of State. But he relied even more heavily for advice on political cronies of his own choosing, who were known as the "Kitchen Cabinet," because they were not office-holders. Jackson was led to believe that his first duty was to cleanse the stables of the Republican régime. His dismissal of a large number of civil servants brought the spoils system, long prevalent in many states, firmly into the Federal machine.

Two great recurring problems in American politics, closely related, demanded the attention of President Andrew Jackson—the supremacy of the Union and the organisation of a national economy. Protection favoured the interests of the North at the expense of the South, and in 1832 the state of South Carolina determined to challenge the right of the Federal Government to impose a tariff system, and, echoing the Virginia and Kentucky resolutions of 1798, expounded in its most extreme form the doctrine of state rights. In the party struggles which followed the votes of the Western states held the balance. Their burning question was the regulation of the sale of public land by the Federal Government. As the historian S. E. Morison puts it, "It was all a game of balance between North, South, and West, each section offering to compromise a secondary interest in order to get votes for a primary interest. The South would permit the West to plunder the public domain, in return for a reduction of the tariff. The North offered the tempting bait of distribution [of the proceeds from land sales for public works in the West] in order to maintain protection. On the outcome of this sectional balance depended the alignment of parties in the future; even of the Civil War itself. Was it to be North and West against South, or South and West against North?"*

The debates on these themes in the American Senate contained the finest examples of American oratory. In this battle of giants the most imposing of them all was Daniel Webster, of Massachusetts, the best speaker of his day. He it was who stated the case for the Union and refuted the case of South Carolina in one of the most famous of American speeches. His words enshrined the new feeling of nation-wide patriotism that was gathering strength, at least in the North. They show that New England in particular was moving away from the sectional views which had prevailed in 1812. A broader sense of loyalty to the Union was developing. "It is to that Union," Webster declared in the Senate, "we owe our safety at home, and our consideration and dignity abroad. It is to that Union that we are chiefly indebted for whatever makes us most proud of our country. That Union we reached only by the discipline of our virtues in the severe school of adversity. It had its origin in the necessities of disordered finance, prostrate commerce, and ruined credit. Under its benign influences these great interests immediately awoke, as from the dead, and sprang forth with newness of life. Every year of its duration has teemed with fresh proofs of its utility and its blessings; and although our territory has stretched out wider and wider, and our population spread farther and farther, they have not outrun its protection, or its benefits. It has been to us all a copious fountain of national, social and personal happiness."

* *The Oxford History of the United States* (1927), vol. 1.

"I have not allowed myself, Sir," he went on, "to look beyond the Union, to see what might lie hidden in the dark recess behind. I have not coolly weighed the chances of preserving liberty when the bonds that unite us together shall be broken asunder. I have not accustomed myself to hang over the precipice of disunion to see whether, with my short sight, I can fathom the depth of the abyss below; nor could I regard him as a safe counsellor in the affairs of this Government, whose thoughts should be mainly bent on considering, not how the Union may be best preserved, but how tolerable might be the condition of the people when it should be broken up and destroyed. While the Union lasts we have high, exciting, gratifying prospects spread out before us, for us and our children. Beyond that I seek not to penetrate the veil. God grant that in my day at least that curtain may not rise! God grant that on my vision never may be opened what lies behind! When my eyes shall be turned to behold for the last time the sun in heaven, may I not see him shining on the broken and dishonoured fragments of a once glorious Union; on states dissevered, discordant, belligerent; on a land rent with civil feuds, or drenched, it may be, in fraternal blood! Let their last feeble and lingering glance rather behold the gorgeous ensign of the Republic, now known and honoured throughout the earth, still full high advanced, its arms and trophies streaming in their original lustre, not a stripe erased or polluted, not a single star obscured, bearing for its motto no such miserable interrogatory as 'What is all this worth?' nor those other words of delusion and folly, 'Liberty first and Union afterwards,' but everywhere, spread all over in characters of living light, blazing on all its ample folds, as they float over the sea and over the land, and in every wind under the whole heavens, that other sentiment, dear to every true American heart—Liberty *and* Union, now and for ever, one and inseparable!"

On the Indiana frontier a young man was moved by this speech. His name was Abraham Lincoln.

President Jackson himself was impressed, and in his warlike approach to politics was prepared to coerce South Carolina by force. But a tactful compromise was reached. The tariff was lowered but rendered permanent, and the Force Act, authorising the President to use the Army if necessary to collect the customs duties, was declared null and void by South Carolina. Here then for a space the matter was left. But the South Carolina theory of "nullification" showed the danger of the Republic, and with the prophetic instinct of the simple frontiersman Jackson pointed to the future: "The next pretext will be the negro or slavery question."

But the next serious issue was the Federal Bank, whose charter was due to come up for renewal in 1836: The National Republicans, or Whigs, now led by Clay, preferred to force it before the 1832 Presidential election. Jackson had long been expected to attack the moneyed power in politics. The position of the Bank illustrated the economic stresses which racked the American Republic. "It was an economic conflict," wrote Charles Beard, "that happened to take a sectional form: the people of the agricultural West had to pay tribute to Eastern capitalists on the money they had borrowed to buy land, make improvements, and engage in speculation." The contest was joined in the election. The triumphant return of Jackson to power was in fact a vote against the Bank of the United States. It was in vain that Daniel Webster was briefed as counsel for the Bank. Jackson informed the Bank president, "I do not dislike your bank more than all banks, but ever since I read the history of the South Sea Bubble I have been afraid of banks." He refused to consent to the passing of a Bill to renew the charter, and without waiting for the Bank to die a natural death in 1836 he decided at once to deprive it of Government deposits, which were sent to local banks throughout the states. When the charter expired it was not renewed, and for nearly thirty years there was no centralised banking system in the United States. The union of Western and Southern politicians had had their revenge upon the North. The Radicalism of the frontier had won a great political contest. Jackson's occupation of the Presidency had finally broken the "era of good feelings" which had followed the war with Britain, and by his economic policy he had split the old Republican Party of Jefferson. The Radicalism of the West was looked upon with widespread suspicion throughout the Eastern states, and Jackson's official appointments had not been very happy.

The election in 1836 of Jackson's lieutenant, Van Buren, meant the continuation of Jacksonian policy, while the old General himself returned in triumph to his retirement in Tennessee. The first incursions of the West into high politics had revealed the slumbering forces of democracy on the frontier and shown the inexperience of their leaders in such affairs.

The westward tide rolled on, bearing with it new problems of adjustment. The generation of the 1840's saw their culmination. During these years there took place the annexation of Texas, a war with Mexico, the conquest of California, and the settlement of the Oregon boundary with Great Britain. Adventurous Americans in search of land and riches had been since 1820 crossing the Mexican boundary into the Texas country, which belonged to the Republic of Mexico, freed from

Spain in 1821. While this community was growing, American sailors on the Pacific coast, captains interested in the China trade, established themselves in the ports of the Mexican Province of California. Pioneers pushed their way overland in search of skins and furs, and by 1826 reached the mission stations of the Province. The Mexicans, alarmed at the appearance of these settlers, vainly sought to stem the flood; for Mexican Governments were highly unstable, and in distant Provinces their writ hardly ran. But there appeared on the scene a new military dictator, Santa Anna, determined to strengthen Mexican authority, and at once a revolt broke out. In November 1835 the Americans in Texas erected an autonomous state and raised the Lone Star flag. The Mexicans, under Santa Anna, marched northwards. At the Mission House of the Alamo in March 1836 a small body of Texans, fighting to the last man, was exterminated in one of the epic fights of American history by a superior Mexican force. The whole Province was aroused. Under the leadership of General Sam Houston from Tennessee a force was raised, and in savage fighting the Mexican army of Santa Anna was in its turn destroyed and its commander captured at San Jacinto River. The Texans had stormed the positions with the cry "Remember the Alamo!" The independence of Texas was recognised by Santa Anna. His act was repudiated later by the Mexican Government, but their war effort was exhausted, and the Texans organised themselves into a republic, electing Sam Houston as President.

For the next ten years the question of the admission of Texas as a state of the Union was a burning issue in American politics. As each new state demanded entry into the Union so the feeling for and against slavery ran higher. The great Abolitionist journalist, William Lloyd Garrison, called for a secession of the Northern states if the slave state of Texas was admitted to the Union. The Southerners, realising that Texan votes would give them a majority in the Senate if this vast territory was admitted as a number of separate states, clamoured for annexation. The capitalists of the East were committed, through the formation of land companies, to exploit Texas, and besides the issue of dubious stocks by these bodies vast quantities of paper notes and bonds of the new Texan Republic were floated in the United States. The speculation in these helped to split the political opposition of the Northern states to the annexation. Even more important was the conversion of many Northerners to belief in the "Manifest Destiny" of the United States. This meant that their destiny was to spread across the whole of the North American continent. The Democratic Party in the election of 1844 called for the occupation of Oregon as well as the annexation of Texas, thus holding out to the North the promise of Oregon as a counterweight to Southern Texas. The victory of the Democratic candidate, James K. Polk, was interpreted as a mandate for admitting Texas, and this was done by joint resolution of Congress in February 1845.

It remained to persuade Mexico to recognise this state of affairs, and also to fix the boundaries of Texas. President Polk was determined to push them as far south as possible, and war was inevitable. It broke out in May 1846. Meanwhile a similar train of events was unfolding on the other side of the continent. All this time American penetration of the West had continued, often with grim experiences of starvation and winter snows. Nothing could stop the migration towards the Pacific. The lure of the rich China trade and the dream of controlling the Western Ocean brought the acquisition of California to the fore, and gave her even more importance in American eyes than Texas. In June 1846 the American settlers in California, instigated from Washington, raised the Bear Flag as their standard of revolt and declared their independence on the Texan model. Soon afterwards American forces arrived and the Stars and Stripes replaced the Bear.

The American advance was rapidly gathering momentum. The Mexican army of the North was twice beaten by General Zachary Taylor, a future President. A force under General Winfield Scott was landed at Vera Cruz and marched on Mexico City. The capital fell to the Americans after a month of street-fighting in September 1847. On this expedition a number of young officers distinguished themselves. They included Captain Robert E. Lee, Captain George B. McClellan, Lieutenant Ulysses S. Grant, and Colonel Jefferson Davis.

Mexico sued for peace, and by the treaty which followed she was obliged not only to recognise the annexation of Texas, but also to cede California, Arizona, and New Mexico. Lieutenant Grant confided his impressions to his memoirs: "I do not think there was ever a more wicked war than that waged by the United States on Mexico. I thought so at the time, when I was a youngster, only I had not moral courage enough to resign." But the expansive force of the American peoples was explosive. "Manifest Destiny" was on the march, and it was unfortunate that Mexico stood in the path. The legend of Imperialism and the belief in the right of the United States to exploit both continents, North and South, which sprang from the Mexican War henceforward cast their shadow on co-operation between the South American republics and the United States.

The immediate gains were enormous. While the commissioners were actually debating the treaty with Mexico an American labourer in California discovered the first nugget of gold in that region. The whole economy of a sleepy Mexican province, with its age-old Spanish culture, was suddenly overwhelmed by a mad rush for gold. In 1850 the population of California was about eighty-two thousand souls. In two years the figure had risen to two hundred and seven thousand. A lawless mining society arose upon the Pacific coast. From the cities of the East and from the adjoining states men of all professions and classes of society flocked to California, many being murdered, killed in quarrels, by cold and famine, or drowned in the sea voyage round Cape Horn. The gold of California lured numbers to their death, and a few to riches beyond belief.

> Oh! California,
> That's the land for me;
> I'm off to Sacramento
> With my washbowl on my knee.

The anarchy of the gold rush brought an urgent demand for settled government in California, and the old perplexing, rasping quarrel over the admission of a new state was heard again at Washington. For the moment nothing was done, and the Californians called their own state convention and drew up a temporary constitution.

During all this time, farther to the north, another territory had been coming into being. The "Oregon Trail" had brought many men from the more crowded states of the North-East to find their homes and establish their farms along the undefined Canadian frontier to the Pacific. With the prospect of war in the South for the acquisition of Texas and California, the American Government was not anxious to embark upon a quarrel with Great Britain upon its Northern frontier. There was strong opposition by the Southerners to the acquisition of Oregon, where the Northern pioneers were opposed to slavery. Oregon would be another "free soil state." Negotiations were opened with Britain, and in spite of electioneering slogans of "Fifty-four-forty or fight" the boundary was settled in June 1846 by peaceful diplomacy along the forty-ninth parallel. This solution owed much to the accommodating nature of the Foreign Secretary in Peel's Government, Lord Aberdeen. The controversy now died down, and in 1859 the territory of Oregon reached statehood.

Among the many settlements which lay dotted over the whole of the American continent the strangest perhaps was the Mormon colony at Salt Lake City. In the spring of 1847 members of this revivalist and polygamist sect started from the state of Illinois under their prophet leader, Brigham Young, to find homes free from molestation in the

West. By the summer they reached the country round Salt Lake, and two hours after their arrival they had begun establishing their homes and ploughing up the soil. Within three years a flourishing community of eleven thousand souls, combining religious fervour, philoprogenitiveness, and shrewd economic sense, had been established by careful planning in the Salt Lake country, and in 1850 the territory received recognition by the Federal Government under the name of Utah. The colony was established in a key position on the trail which led both to Oregon and California. The sale of food and goods to the travellers and adventurers who moved in both directions along this route brought riches to the Mormon settler, and Salt Lake City, soon tainted, it is true, by the introduction of more lawless and unbelieving elements, became one of the richest cities in America.

With the establishment of this peculiar colony the settlement of the continent was comprehensive. The task before the Federal Government was now to organise the Far Western territory won in the Mexican War and in the compromise with Britain. From this there rose in its final and dread form the issue of bond and free.

CHAPTER 14

SLAVERY AND SECESSION

I N THE YEARS FOLLOWING 1850 the prospects of the United States filled America with hope and Europe with envious admiration. The continent had been conquered and nourished. Exports, imports, and, most of all, internal trade, had been more than doubled in a decade. The American mercantile marine outnumbered the ships under the British flag. Nearly £50,000,000 in gold was added to the coinage in the years 1851 and 1852. More than thirty thousand miles of railway overcame the vast distances, and added economic cohesion to political unity. Here democracy, shielded by the oceans and the Royal Navy from European dangers, founded upon English institutions and the Common Law, stimulated by the impulse of the French Revolution, seemed at last to have achieved both prosperity and power. The abounding industrialism of the Eastern states was balanced and fed by an immense agriculture of yeomen farmers. In all material affairs the American people surpassed anything that history had known before.

Yet thoughtful men and travellers had for some years observed the approach of a convulsion which would grip not only the body but the soul of the United States. Of the three races who dwelt in North America, the Whites towered overwhelming and supreme. The Red Men, the original inhabitants, age-long product of the soil and climate, shrank back, pushed, exploited, but always disdainful, from the arms, and still more from the civilisation, of the transplanted European society by which they were ousted and eclipsed. The Black Men presented a problem, moral, social, economic, and political, the like of which had never before been known. It was said that both these races were downtrodden by White ascendancy as truly as animals are mastered, used, or exterminated by mankind. The proud Redskin was set upon his road to ruin by an excessive liberty. Almost all the four million negroes were slaves.

In regions so wide and varied as those of the Union extreme divergences of interest, outlook, and culture had developed. South of the fortieth parallel and the projecting angle formed by the Mississippi and the Ohio the institution of negro slavery had long reigned almost unquestioned. Upon this basis the whole life of the Southern states had been erected. It was a strange, fierce, old-fashioned life. An aristocracy of planters, living in rural magnificence and almost feudal state, and a multitude of smallholders, grew cotton for the world by slave-labour. Of the six million white inhabitants of the so-called slave states less than three hundred and fifty thousand owned slaves, and only forty thousand controlled plantations requiring a working unit of more than twenty field hands. But the three or four thousand principal slave-owners generally ruled the politics of the South as effectively as the medieval baronage had ruled England. Beneath them, but not dissociated from them, were, first, several hundred thousand small slave-owners, to whom "the peculiar institution," as it had already come to be called, was a domestic convenience; second, a strong class of yeomen farmers similar to that existing in the North; and, thirdly, a rabble of "mean whites" capable of being formed into an army.

There was a grace and ease about the life of the white men in the South that was lacking in the bustling North. It was certainly not their fault that these unnatural conditions had arisen. For two centuries the slave trade in African negroes with the New World had been a staple enterprise in Spain, in France, and above all in England. Vast numbers of black men, caught upon the west coast of Africa, had been transported like cattle across the Atlantic to be the property of their purchasers. They had toiled and multiplied. The bulk had become adapted to their state of life, which, though odious to Christian civilisation, was physically less harsh than African barbarism. The average negro slave, like the medieval serf, was protected by his market value, actual and procreative, as well as by the rising standards of society, from the more senseless and brutal forms of ill-usage.

The planters of the South, and the slaves they owned, had both grown up in wide, unkempt lands without ever having known any other relationship. Now, suddenly, in the midst of the nineteenth century, dire challenge was hurled at the whole system and the society in which it was engrained. A considerable, strongly characterised, and slowly matured community found itself subjected to the baleful and scandalised glare of the Christian world, itself in vigorous and self-confident progress. They had long dwelt comfortably upon the fertile slopes of a volcano. Now began the rumblings, tremors, and exhalations which portended a frightful eruption.

It is almost impossible for us nowadays to understand how profoundly and inextricably negro slavery was interwoven into the whole life, economy, and culture of the Southern states. The tentacles of slavery spread widely through the Northern "free" states, along every channel of business dealing and many paths of political influence. One assertion alone reveals the powerlessness of the community to shake itself free from the frightful disease which had become part of its being. It was said that over six hundred and sixty thousand slaves were held by ministers of the Gospel and members of the different Protestant Churches. Five thousand Methodist ministers owned two hundred and nineteen thousand slaves; six thousand five hundred Baptists owned a hundred and twenty-five thousand; one thousand four hundred Episcopalians held eighty-eight thousand; and so on. Thus the institution of slavery was not only defended by every argument of self-interest, but many a Southern pulpit championed it as a system ordained by the Creator and sanctified by the Gospel of Christ.

It had not always been so. During the Revolution against King George III many Southerners had expressed the hope that slavery would eventually be abolished. But as time passed "the peculiar institution" became, in the words of Morison and Commager, "so necessary that it ceased to appear evil."* By the 1830's Southerners were ready to defend slavery as a positive good and a permanent basis for society. This was a striking change of opinion for which there were several reasons. The rapid growth of cotton cultivation called for a large labour force which according to Southerners could only be provided by negroes in a state of slavery. Moreover, widespread fears had been aroused in the South by a number of slave insurrections in which some whites had been massacred. If the negro were freed, it was asked, would a white man's life be safe? or, to press the question more closely home, a white woman's honour? In earlier times hopeful philanthropists had thought to solve the problem by shipping the negroes back to Africa and setting them up in their own republic. The state of Liberia had thus come into existence. But attempts to carry this plan further were abandoned. It was too expensive. Besides, the negroes preferred America. For Southerners there was an alarming example near at hand of what happened when slaves were freed. In the British West Indies, as else-

* Morison and Commager, *The Growth of the American Republic* (1930), vol. i, p. 246.

where in the British Empire, slavery had been abolished by the Act passed in 1833. This was one of the great reforms achieved by the Whig Government of Earl Grey. The planters of the West Indies, who led a life much like that of Southern gentlemen, were paid compensation for the loss of their human property. Nevertheless their fortunes promptly and visibly declined. All this could be perceived by men of reflection on the neighbouring American mainland.

Meanwhile the North, once largely indifferent to the fate of slaves, had been converted by the 1850's to the cause of anti-slavery. For twenty years William Lloyd Garrison's newspaper, *The Liberator,* had been carrying on from Boston a campaign of the utmost virulence against the institution of slavery. This public print was not very widely read, but its language enraged the South. At the same time the American Anti-Slavery Society in New York and other humanitarian bodies were issuing vigorous tracts and periodicals. They employed scores of agents to preach Abolition up and down the land. The result was a hardening of sentiment on both sides of the question. It was hardened still further in 1852, when Harriet Beecher Stowe published *Uncle Tom's Cabin.* Her work was frankly propagandist; she used every weapon. On its pages the theoretical and religious arguments are bandied to and fro, but there was one method in which she excelled all other assailants of the evil. She presented to her readers a succession of simple, poignant incidents inseparable from a system of slavery: the breaking up of the negro's home and family, the parting of husband and wife, the sale of the baby from the breast of its mother; the indiscriminate auction of the slaves on the death of a good employer; the impotence of the virtuous slave-owner, the cruelties of the bad; the callous traffic of the slave-dealers, and the horrors of the remote plantations, the whipping establishments to which fine ladies sent their maids for chastisement for minor faults; the aggravated problem of the quadroon and the mulatto; the almost-white slave girl sold and resold for lust; the bringing into the world of slave children indistinguishable in their colour from the dominant race—all these features of the life of a civilised, educated, modern Christian community, occupying enormous fertile regions of the earth, were introduced with every trapping of art and appeal into her pages.

Such advocacy was devastating. By the end of the year hundreds of thousands of copies of *Uncle Tom's Cabin* had been sold in the United States. In September, it is said, ten thousand copies of it were being supplied every day to a single firm of English booksellers. By the end of 1852 more than a million copies had been sold in England, probably ten times as many as had ever been sold of any other work except the Bible and the Prayer Book. *Uncle Tom's Cabin* rolled round the world in every language and was read with passion and emotion in every country. It was the herald of the storm.

The moral surge of the age had first suppressed, by naval power, the slave trade on the seas, and thereafter—the young Mr. Gladstone notwithstanding—abolished the status of slavery throughout the British Empire. The same temper stirred alike the New England states of the Atlantic shore and the powerful, swiftly growing population of the Middle West of the American Union. A gulf of sentiment and interest opened and widened between the Northern and Southern states. Across this gulf there flashed for some years the interchanges of thought, of argument and parley. In the North many of the leaders, religious and secular, felt intensely that the whole future of the noble continent they had won lay under a curse. If it could not at once be lifted, at least it must be prevented from spreading. Nor was this passion in any degree excited, in its earliest phase, by commercial rivalry. There was no doubt that slave labour could not hold its own with free labour in tilling the soil where the climatic conditions were similar. The contrast between the activity and progress of a free state on the Ohio and the stagnation of a slave state on the opposite bank was glaringly apparent to all beholders. It was the contrast between the nineteenth century and the seventeenth. The Northern states were not undersold by the competition of the South. They also needed the cotton crop in which alone slave labour was an economic advantage. The issue was not economic, but moral. It was also social. The slave-owning aristocracy in much of the South felt a class-superiority to the business, manufacturing, and financial society of the North. The Puritan stock of the North regarded the elegant gentry of the South with something of the wrath and censure of Cromwell's Ironsides for Rupert's Cavaliers. Indeed, at many points the grim struggle which impended resembled and reproduced in its passions the antagonisms of the English Civil War.

But the actual occasion of quarrel was political and constitutional. The North held tenaciously to the Federal conceptions of Alexander Hamilton. In the South Jefferson's idea of sovereign state rights was paramount. Many of the Southern Generals, like Joseph E. Johnston, Ambrose P. Hill, and FitzHugh Lee, had never owned a slave. A Virginian colonel of the United States Army serving in Texas, Robert E. Lee, wrote that slavery was "a moral and political evil in any country," as few in an enlightened age could but acknowledge. But upon the constitutional issue all these men of the highest morale and virtue deemed themselves bound to the death to the fortunes and sovereign independence of their states. The North, it was said, was enriching itself at the expense of the South. The Yankees were jealous of a style and distinction to which vulgar commercialism could never attain. They had no right to use the Federal Constitution which the great Virginians Washington and Madison had largely founded, in order to bind the most famous states of the Union to their dictates. They did not understand the totally different conditions of Southern life. They maligned and insulted a civilisation more elevated in manners, if not in worldly wealth, than their own. They sought to impose the tyranny of their ideas upon states which had freely joined the Union for common purposes, and might as freely depart when those purposes had been fulfilled.

The old Missouri compromise of 1820, namely, that latitude 36° 30′ should divide freedom from slavery in the territories of the Louisiana Purchase, no longer satisfied the passions now aroused. By the Mexican War extensive new territories had been acquired; what principle should be applied to them? The Southerners, still dominated by that great figure of the 1812 generation, John C. Calhoun, held that the territories belonged to the states united, not to the United States, that slaves were Common Law property, and that Congress had no right to prohibit slavery in the Territories. The demand of California for admission to the Union precipitated the crisis. Many moderates had wanted to prolong the line of the Missouri compromise across the continent to the Pacific. But in California it did not meet the case. It would have run right through the middle of the state. Besides, the constitution of California prohibited slavery, and its introduction would set a precedent in those states which were to be created out of the conquests from Mexico. In January 1850 the gathering storm-clouds of slavery and secession evoked in the Senate the last of the great oratorical debates in which Calhoun, Clay, and Webster vied with one another. Henry Clay produced his last compromise in resolutions to postpone collision. California should be admitted to the Union immediately as a "free" state; the territorial Governments in New Mexico and Utah should be organised without mentioning slavery; a stringent Fugitive Slave Law would appease the South, and the assumption of the Texan National Debt by the Federal Government the bond-holders of the North. By these mutual concessions Clay hoped to preserve the political unity of the continent. On this last occasion he rose and spoke for nearly two days in the Senate. Calhoun was dying, and sat grimly silent in the house. One of his colleagues spoke his plea for him. "I have, Senators, believed from the first that the agitation of the subject of slavery would, if not prevented by some timely and effective measure, end in disunion. . . . The cords that bind the states together are snapping." Beneath the slavery problem lay the root fear of the Southern states that economically and politically they were being oppressed by the North and losing in the race for allies in the Western states.

Daniel Webster rose three days later: "I speak today for the preservation of the Union. Hear me for my cause." The voices of Webster and Clay prevailed and the compromise was adopted. Passions were for the moment stilled by what was called the "principle of popular sovereignty." This meant that when the new Territories became states the settlers should decide for themselves for or against slavery. Calhoun was already dead, and within two years Clay and Webster passed from the scene. They left behind them an uneasy calm. Meanwhile the continent developed at dizzy speed. By 1850 nine thousand miles of railway had been built; by 1861 over thirty thousand. German and Irish immigrants from Europe streamed into the new lands of the West. Agricultural machinery changed the settler type. The prairie farmer replaced the backwoodsman, and the cultivation of the Great Plains began in earnest.

A fresh cause of divergence sprang from the choice of the transcontinental railway route. The rival interests of North and South were decisively involved, and in the political dispute the North and West drew together. The southern route was the shortest to the Pacific coast, and passed through organised territories from New Orleans to Texas and thence by the Gila valley to San Diego. The northern followed the natural trail of emigration which bound California and Oregon to the states bordering the Great Lakes. In between lay a third route through regions as yet unorganised, but in which Northern capital was invested. Senator Stephen A. Douglas of Illinois, who ardently wished to promote the settlement of the West and was heavily committed to the central line, became the champion of Northern interests. In order to organise this central zone he proposed in January 1854 a Bill establishing the territory of Nebraska. As a bait for Southern votes he included a clause embodying the conception of "popular sovereignty." This changed the issue and aggravated the dispute. People in the North had taken the compromise of 1850 to apply only to the former Mexican territories. Now it was proposed to introduce it into regions where hitherto the line of the Missouri compromise had prevailed. As these areas of the Great Plains were north of latitude 36° 30′ the new Bill implicitly repealed the Missouri Compromise Act. The Southerners wished this to be done explicitly, and Douglas agreed. This might carry slavery north of the line.

The anti-slavery forces in the North, already furious with Douglas, were determined to resist the introduction of slavery into the new territories. In May the Kansas-Nebraska Act was passed by the Senate. The new territories of the Great Plains were to be divided into Kansas and Nebraska, and the principle of "popular sovereignty" was affirmed. This Act was a signal for outbursts of agitation and violence in the Northern states. Under the Fugitive Slave Law Federal agents had already been instructed to arrest and send back to their masters slaves who had escaped into the free states. There had been innumerable minor incidents, but now, on the morrow of the Kansas-Nebraska Act, the patience of the North was at an end. The day after it came into force a Boston mob attempted to rescue a fugitive slave, Anthony Burns, who was detained for deportation to the South. It took a battalion of artillery, four platoons of marines, the sheriff's posse, and twenty-two companies of the militia to line the streets and bring the slave to the ship at Boston wharf. "It cost the United States about a hundred thousand dollars to return that slave to his master. The real bill came later, and it was paid in blood."*

In the new territory of Kansas there was murderous faction fighting between the free-soil and pro-slavery partisans. Slavery-men sacked the free-soil town of Lawrence, and three days later John Brown, a Puritanical mystic and militant Abolitionist from Ohio, with his four sons, dragged five slavery-men from their beds and slaughtered them as a reprisal. Over two hundred lives were lost in this local reign of terror, but John Brown escaped. At every point, in every walk of life, the opposing causes came into conflict. A Senator from Massachusetts was beaten over the head with a cane in the Senate by a South Carolina Representative till he was unconscious. All the anti-slavery elements in the North and West had coalesced after the passing of the Kansas-Nebraska Act in a new Republican Party upon the platform of anti-slavery. Feeling ran high in the Presidential elections of 1856. But Democratic influences nominated "a Northern man with Southern principles," James Buchanan of Pennsylvania, and for the last time Southern influences had their voice at Washington.

Two days after the inauguration of the new President the Supreme Court published its decision upon the famous case of the slave Dred Scott versus his master, Sanford. Scott had been taken by his master

* Morison and Commager, *The Growth of the American Republic* (1930), vol. i, p. 622.

from slave-owning Missouri to the free state of Illinois and then to Wisconsin Territory. He sued for his freedom on the grounds that residence in those two places had made him a free man. The questions before the Court were two. Was Scott a citizen of Missouri, which he needed to be to have the right to bring an action? And had his residence elsewhere changed his established status? The Court decided against him on both points. Chief Justice Taney delivered a judgment which, while it expressed the law as it existed under the Constitution, provoked a storm throughout the North. "The negro," declared Taney, "was not a citizen in the eyes of the Constitution, which was 'made for white men only.' " He could not sue in any court of the United States. The negroes were regarded as "so far inferior that they had no rights which the white man was bound to respect." The slave was the property of his owner, and the National Government was nowhere given power over the property of the inhabitants of the United States. It had no right to prohibit slavery in the Territories, and the old Missouri compromise, on which Scott had in part relied for his freedom, was constitutionally wrong. Thus the Supreme Court. It is fair to add that Taney remarked it was not within the province of the Court to decide whether the Founding Fathers had been right to regard the negro in this way. And in fact Dred Scott was immediately freed after the verdict. His had been a case purposefully designed to test the law and inflame opinion. This it certainly did. The Republican Party, which had been launched to prevent slavery spreading into the Territories, saw its whole programme declared unconstitutional. "The people of the United States," cried William H. Seward, a Republican leader, "never can and never will accept principles so abhorrent."

The savage struggle between free-soil and slavery in the Great Plains brought from the backwoods into national politics a new figure. Abraham Lincoln, a small-town lawyer from Springfield, Illinois, was stirred to the depths of his being by the passing of the Kansas-Nebraska Act. He had already served a term in Congress; now he stood for the Senate. He espoused the duty of opposing by the moral force of his personality the principle of slavery. " 'A house divided against itself cannot stand.' I believe this Government cannot endure permanently half slave and half free. I do not expect the Union to be dissolved—I do not expect the house to fall—but I do expect it will cease to be divided. It will become all one thing or all the other. Either the opponents of slavery will arrest the further spread of it, and place it where the public mind shall rest in the belief that it is in the course of ultimate extinction; or its advocates will push it forward till it shall become alike lawful in all the states, old as well as new, North as well as South." In a series of public debates and speeches Lincoln fought Douglas throughout the prairie towns of Illinois in the summer and autumn of 1858, and although he was beaten for the Senatorship he had already become a national figure. He had made slavery a moral and not a legal issue, and he had propounded the disruptive idea of overriding the Supreme Court decision and of outlawing slavery in the new territories. He felt instinctively the weakness and impermanence of this new concession to the susceptibilities of the South. He realised that as the agitation for abolition grew, so the Southerners would demand further guarantees to protect their own peculiar slave society. President Buchanan and the Democratic circle around the White House talked of conquering Cuba and Nicaragua in the hope of adding new slave-owning territories to the Union. Southern businessmen urged reopening the slave trade owing to the high price of slaves, while all the time the North, in a series of disturbing incidents, defied the Fugitive Slave Act of 1850.

It needed but a spark to cause an explosion. In October 1859 the fanatic John Brown, with his sons and a dozen followers, seized the Federal arsenal at Harpers Ferry, on the slavery frontier, declared war upon the United States, and liberated a number of bewildered slaves. He was attacked by the Federal marines under Colonel Robert E. Lee, and after some loss of life was captured, severely wounded. He was tried and hanged with four of his adherents. The South, declaring the outrage the work of the Republican Party, was convulsed with excitement. In the North millions regarded John Brown as a martyr. His body lay mouldering in the grave, but his soul went marching on.

CHAPTER 15

THE UNION
IN DANGER

Now came the fateful Presidential election of 1860. In February the Southern Senator Jefferson Davis demanded that the Northern states should repeal their Personal Liberty Laws and cease to interfere with the Fugitive Slave Law of 1850. Chief Justice Taney's decision of the Supreme Court must be obeyed. Slavery could not be prohibited by the Federal Government in the Territories of the United States. Rather, Davis demanded, the Federal Government should protect slavery in those areas. Against this, Abraham Lincoln, in New York and elsewhere, unfolded in magnificent orations, calm, massive, and magnanimous, the anti-slavery cause. In this crisis the Democratic Party split. When Douglas, their Presidential candidate, carried a set of compromise proposals in the party meeting at Charleston the Alabama delegation marched out of the hall, followed by those of seven other cotton states. Lincoln would probably in any case have been elected, but the division among the Democrats made his victory certain. The cotton states put forward as their candidate John C. Breckinridge, of Kentucky, who was at that moment Vice-President. He stood as a Southern Rights Democrat. The scene was further complicated by the appearance of a fourth aspirant, Senator John Bell, of Kentucky, who called himself a Constitutional Unionist and was an old-fashioned Whig. Secession was not the issue, though everyone knew that the South would in fact secede if Lincoln won. Slavery was the dominating and all-absorbing topic. Lincoln and the Republicans wanted to reverse the Dred Scott decision, prohibit slavery in the Territories and confine it within its existing limits. Douglas and the official Democrats were for non-intervention in the

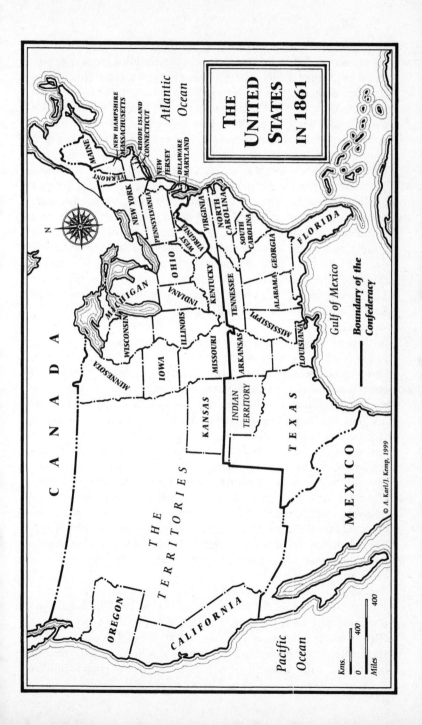

THE UNITED STATES IN 1861

Atlantic Ocean

MAINE
NEW HAMPSHIRE
MASSACHUSETTS
RHODE ISLAND
CONNECTICUT
VERMONT
NEW YORK
NEW JERSEY
DELAWARE
MARYLAND
PENNSYLVANIA
VIRGINIA
WEST VIRGINIA
NORTH CAROLINA
SOUTH CAROLINA
OHIO
KENTUCKY
TENNESSEE
GEORGIA
ALABAMA
FLORIDA
MICHIGAN
INDIANA
ILLINOIS
WISCONSIN
IOWA
MISSOURI
ARKANSAS
MISSISSIPPI
LOUISIANA
MINNESOTA
KANSAS
INDIAN TERRITORY
TEXAS

CANADA

MEXICO

Gulf of Mexico

Boundary of the Confederacy

THE TERRITORIES

OREGON

CALIFORNIA

Pacific Ocean

Kms.
0   400
Miles
0   400

N

© A. Karl/J. Kemp, 1999

Territories and "popular sovereignty" by the settlers. Breckinridge and his supporters demanded that slavery in the Territories should be protected by law. Bell tried to ignore the issue altogether in the blissful hope that the nation could be made to forget everything that had happened since the Mexican War. On November 6, 1860, Lincoln was elected. He had behind him only 40 per cent. of the voters. Douglas was the runner-up on the popular vote. Breckinridge, who was reputed to be the Secessionist candidate in spite of his assurances of loyalty to the Union, came third. Even in the slave states he failed to win a majority of the votes.

In spite of this great majority against breaking the Union, the state of South Carolina, where the doctrines of Calhoun were cherished, passed by a unanimous vote at Charleston on December 20 its famous Ordinance of Secession, declaring that the Union of 1788 between South Carolina and all other states, Northern and Southern alike, was dissolved. This precipitate and mortal act was hailed with delirious enthusiasm. The cannons fired; the bells rang; flags flew on every house. The streets were crowded with cheering multitudes. The example of South Carolina was followed by the states of Mississippi, Florida, Alabama, Georgia, Louisiana, and Texas. The delegates from the first six of these sovereign states, as they regarded themselves, met in Alabama in February and organised a new Confederacy, of which Jefferson Davis was chosen President. A new constitution, similar in almost all respects to that of the United States, but founded explicitly upon slavery, was proclaimed. A Confederate flag—the Stars and Bars—was adopted. President Davis was authorised to raise an army of a hundred thousand men, large sums were voted, and a delegation of three was sent abroad to seek recognition and friendship in Europe. All the leading figures concerned in this decision harboured grave illusions. They thought the North would not try to coerce them back into the Union. If it made the attempt they believed the Yankees would be no match for Southern arms. And if the North imposed a blockade the Confederates expected that the Powers of Europe would intervene on their behalf. They cherished the notion that "King Cotton" was so vital to Britain and France that neither country could peaceably allow its supplies to be cut off.

Buchanan was still President of the United States, and Lincoln, President-Elect, could not take office till March. For four months the dying administration gaped upon a distracted land. Floyd, Secretary of War, an ardent Southerner, showed no particular vigilance or foresight. He tamely allowed muskets which had been sent North for alterations to be returned to the Southern arsenals. Every facility was given to officers of the Regular Army to join the new forces being feverishly raised in the South. Buchanan, longing for release, tried desperately to discharge his duties and follow a middle course. All counter-preparations in the North were paralysed. On the other hand, he refused to recognise the validity of secession. Practically all the Federal posts, with their small garrisons, in the Southern states had passed without fighting into the possession of the Confederacy. But the forts of Charleston harbour, under the command of Major Anderson, a determined officer, continued to fly the Stars and Stripes. When called upon to surrender he withdrew to Fort Sumter, which stood on an island. His food ran low, and when a ship bearing supplies from the North arrived to succour him Confederate batteries from the mainland drove it back by cannon-fire. Meanwhile strenuous efforts at compromise were being made. Many Northerners were prepared for the sake of peace to give way to the South on the slavery issue. But Lincoln was inflexible. He would not repudiate the platform on which he had been elected. He could not countenance the extension of slavery to the Territories. This was the nub on which all turned. In this tense and tremendous situation Abraham Lincoln was sworn President on March 4, 1861. Around him the structure of Federal Government was falling to pieces. Officials and officers were every day leaving for their home states in the South. Hands were clasped between old comrades for the last time in friendship.

The North, for all its detestation of slavery, had by no means contemplated civil war. Between the extremists on both sides there was an immense borderland where all interests and relationships were interlaced by every tie of kinship and custom and every shade of opinion found its expression. So far only the cotton states, or Lower South, had severed themselves from the Union. Missouri, Arkansas, Kentucky, Tennessee, North Carolina, Maryland, Delaware, and above all the noble and ancient Virginia, the Old Dominion, the birthplace of Washington, the fountain of American tradition and inspiration, still hung in the balance. Lincoln appealed for patience and conciliation. He declared himself resolved to hold the forts and property of the United States. He disclaimed all intention of invading the South. He announced that he would not interfere with slavery in the Southern states. He revived the common memories of the North and South, which, like "mystic cords, stretch from every battlefield and patriot grave to every living heart . . . over this broad land." "In your hands," he exclaimed, "my dissatisfied fellow-countrymen, and not in mine, is this momentous issue of civil war. The Government will not assail you. You can have no conflict without yourselves being the aggressors. You have no oath registered in Heaven to destroy the Government, while I shall have the most solemn one to preserve, protect and defend it."

On April 8 Lincoln informed the Governor of South Carolina of his intention to re-victual Major Anderson and his eighty-three men in Fort Sumter. Thereupon President Davis ordered General Beauregard, who commanded seven thousand men at Charleston, to demand the immediate surrender of the fort. Anderson, admitting that famine would reduce him in a few days, nevertheless continued constant. Vain parleys were held; but before dawn on April 12 the Confederate batteries opened a general bombardment, and for two days fifty heavy cannon rained their shells upon Fort Sumter. Anderson and his handful of men, sheltering in their bomb-proof caverns, feeling that all had been done that honour and law required, marched out begrimed and half suffocated on the 14th, and were allowed to depart to the North. No blood had been shed, but the awful act of rebellion had occurred.

The cannonade at Fort Sumter resounded through the world. It roused and united the people of the North. All the free states stood together. Party divisions were effaced. Douglas, Lincoln's rival at the election, with a million and a half Democratic votes at his back, hastened to the White House to grasp Lincoln's hand. Ex-President Buchanan declared, "The North will sustain the administration almost to a man." Upon this surge and his own vehement resolve, Lincoln issued a proclamation calling for "the militia of the Union to the number of seventy-five thousand" to suppress "combinations" in seven states "too powerful to be suppressed by the ordinary course of judicial proceedings." Here, then, was the outbreak of the American Civil War.

Upon Lincoln's call to arms to coerce the seceding states Virginia made without hesitation the choice which she was so heroically to sustain. She would not fight on the issue of slavery, but stood firm on the constitutional ground that every state in the Union enjoyed sovereign rights. On this principle Virginians denied the claim of the Federal Government to exercise coercion. By eighty-eight votes to fifty-five the Virginia Convention at Richmond refused to allow the state militia to respond to Lincoln's call. Virginia seceded from the Union and placed her entire military forces at the disposal of the Confederacy. This decided the conduct of one of the noblest Americans who ever lived, and one of the greatest captains known to the annals of war.

Robert E. Lee stood high in American life. His father had been a colonel in the Revolution. By his marriage with Miss Custis, a descendant of Mrs. George Washington, he became the master of Arlington, the house overlooking the national capital which George Custis, Washington's adopted son, "the child of Mount Vernon," as he was called, had built for himself a few miles from Washington's own home. A graduate of West Point, General Scott's Engineer Staff-Officer in the Mexican War, Lee had served for more than twenty-five years in the United States Army with distinction. His noble presence and gentle, kindly manner were sustained by religious faith and an exalted character. As the American scene darkened he weighed carefully, while commanding a regiment of cavalry on the Texan border, the course which duty and honour would require from him. He was opposed to slavery and thought that "secession would do no good," but he had been taught from childhood that his first allegiance was to the state of Virginia. Summoned to Washington during February 1861, he had thus expressed himself to an intimate Northern friend: "If Virginia stands by the old Union, so will I. But if she secedes (though I do not believe in secession as a constitutional right, nor that there is sufficient cause for revolution), then I will follow my native state with my sword, and if need be with my life."

He reached the capital in the fevered days of March, and General Scott, his old chief, wrestled earnestly with him in a three hours' interview. By Lincoln's authority he was offered the chief command of the great Union army now being raised. He declined at once, and when a day later Virginia seceded he resigned his commission, bade farewell for ever to his home at Arlington, and in the deepest sorrow boarded a train for Richmond. Here he was immediately offered the chief command of all the military and naval forces of Virginia. He had resigned his United States commission on the Saturday, and on the Monday following he accepted his new task. Some of those who saw him in these tragic weeks, when sometimes his eyes filled with tears, emotion which he never showed after the gain or loss of great battles, have written about his inward struggle. But there was no struggle; he never hesitated. The choice was for the state of Virginia. He deplored that choice; he foresaw its consequences with bitter grief; but for himself he had no doubts at the time, nor ever after regret or remorse.

Those who hold that the fortunes of mankind are largely the result of the impact upon events of superior beings will find it fitting that Lee's famous comrade in arms, "Stonewall" Jackson, should be mentioned at this point. Lee was fifty-four in the crisis, Jackson but thirty-seven. Like Lee, he was a trained professional soldier who had served gallantly in the Mexican War. He had devoted himself to the theoretical study of the military art. He was at this time a professor at the Virginia Military Institute. Jackson came of Ulster stock, settled in

Virginia. His character was stern, his manner reserved and usually forbidding, his temper Calvinistic, his mode of life strict, frugal, austere. He might have stepped into American history from the command of one of Cromwell's regiments. There burned in him a hatred of Northern domination not to be found in Lee. Black-bearded, pale-faced, with thin, compressed lips, aquiline nose, and dark, piercing eyes, he slouched in his weather-stained uniform a professor-warrior; yet greatly beloved by the few who knew him best, and gifted with that strange power of commanding measureless devotion from the thousands whom he ruled with an iron hand.

Both these men, though they habitually spoke and no doubt convinced themselves to the contrary, loved war as a technical art to which their lives had been given. Their sayings and letters abound with expressions of sorrow at the terrible decrees of which they had now become the servants. But on a long night march to a desperate battle at dawn Jackson muttered to his companion, "Delightful excitement!"; and Lee, surveying a field of carnage, observed reflectively, "It is well that war is so terrible—we should grow too fond of it." Against Lee and his great lieutenant, united for a year of intense action in a comradeship which recalls that of Marlborough and Eugene, were now to be marshalled the overwhelming forces of the Union.

Both sides set to work to form armies. Trained officers and men were few, weapons and munitions scanty. The American people had enjoyed a long peace, and their warfare had been to reclaim the wilderness and draw wealth from the soil. On neither side was there any realisation of the ordeal that lay before them. The warlike spirit ran high in the South, and their gentry and frontier farmers, like the Cavaliers, were more accustomed to riding and shooting than their compeers in the commercial North. The Confederate states were defending hearth and home against invasion and overlordship. Proud and ardent, their manhood rallied to the newly forming regiments, confident that they would conquer, sure at least that they were unconquerable.

The North was at first astonished at the challenge. They could hardly realise that the wordy strife of party politics, the exciting turmoil of electioneering, must now give place to organised slaughter. When they surveyed the vast resources of the North they felt their power incomparable. All were resolved to maintain the Union whatever the cost; and beneath this august constitutional issue there glowed the moral fires of wrath against slavery.

At first sight, to foreign observers, the disparity between the combatants was evident. Twenty-three states, with a population of twenty-two millions, were arrayed against eleven states, whose population of nine millions included nearly four million slaves. But as the Southern states only claimed the right to go their own way their policy would be defensive; the North, which denied this right and was determined to keep them in the Union by force, had to take the offensive. A formidable task confronted the aggressors.

Nothing short of the subjugation of the entire South would suffice. The issue was not to be settled by two or three battles; the whole country would have to be conquered piecemeal. The Confederacy embraced an area which extended eight hundred miles from north to south and seventeen hundred from east to west. The railways were few and badly conditioned; the roads no better. The region was sparsely inhabited, and the invader would have for the most part to bring his own supplies. He would have enormously long lines of communication to guard in his march through a hostile country. Most of the slaves, who might have been expected to prove an embarrassment to the South, on the contrary proved a solid help, tending the plantations in the absence of their masters, raising the crops which fed the armies, working on the roads and building fortifications, thus releasing a large number of whites for service in the field.

In the North it might be suggested that a large proportion of the Democrats would oppose a policy of force. In the struggle of endurance, which seemed the shape which the war would ultimately take, the South might prove more staunch. In a war of attrition the North had the advantage of being a manufacturing community, and her best weapon against Southern agricultural strength, if it could blockade three thousand five hundred miles of Southern coast, might prove to be the Navy. But a resultant cotton famine in Europe might force Great Britain and France into intervention on the side of the South.

The seven states of the Lower South had seceded after Lincoln's election, and set up a Government of their own at Montgomery, Alabama, in February 1861. Lincoln's call for troops after Sumter was followed by the secession of four states of the Upper South, and the Confederate capital was moved to Richmond. There remained the attitude of the border slave states, Kentucky, Missouri, Maryland, and Delaware. Of these Kentucky was the most important on account of its geographical position, and because Missouri was likely to follow its example. Indeed, the issue of the war seemed perhaps to turn upon Kentucky. Lincoln, a Kentuckian by birth, like Jefferson Davis, is reported to have said, "I should like to have God on my side, but I must have Kentucky." But Kentucky, loyal to the memory of Henry Clay, "the

Great Compromiser," tried to remain neutral. Neither combatant could tolerate this attitude for long; yet both feared lest any violent act of aggression might throw the state into the other's arms. Lincoln proved the more astute diplomatist, and by keeping the control of policy in his own hands secured Kentucky for the Union in September. This was the first real victory for the North.

In Missouri, as in the sister state, there was a majority in favour of neutrality; but the extremists on both sides took control and civil war resulted. The Governor was a rabid Secessionist, and, supported by the legislature, endeavoured to take the state out of the Union. The Union leader was one of the powerful Blair family, and his brother a member of the Cabinet. He invoked the aid of General Lyon, commander of the Federal troops in St. Louis, and with his help the Governor's separatist designs were defeated, and he himself chased out of Jefferson City, the state capital, into the south-west corner of the state. But the intrusion of Federal troops into a domestic quarrel caused many citizens who had hitherto been neutral to join the ranks of Secession. Although a state Convention deposed the Governor and set up a Provisional Government at St. Louis months were to elapse before Missouri was fully brought under Federal control.

In Maryland the issue was more quickly settled. The Secessionists were strong in Baltimore, and gained temporary control of the city. They destroyed the railway bridges on the two northern lines, and for a few days Washington found itself dangerously isolated. Reinforcements from Massachusetts were assaulted in their march through the streets, and a bloody collision occurred. But without help from Virginia the Maryland Secessionists were not capable of making head against the national capital, and the Loyalist Governor gained time, until on May 13 General Butler, with a small Federal force, made a sudden dash, and, taking the Secessionists by surprise, occupied Baltimore. This ended the secession in Maryland. A fourth slave state, Delaware, also stayed in the Union. Its Legislature had Southern leanings, but geography ruled otherwise.

Lincoln not only secured four slavery states as allies, but also detached an important section from the seceding state of Virginia. West Virginia, separated by the Alleghenies from the rest of the state, and geographically and economically a part of the Ohio valley, had long chafed under the oppression of the state Government at Richmond, which ignored its interests and exploited it for the benefit of the "Tidewater" section. It now seized the opportunity to secede from Secession. When in May the popular vote ratified the Ordinance of Secession it broke away, and with the help of its powerful neighbour, Ohio, established its independence under the title of the state of Kanawha, which two years later was formally admitted to the Union as the state of West Virginia.

In the task of preparing for war the Southern President had advantages over his rival. A West-Pointer, he had served in the Regular Army for several years and had fought in the Mexican War; he had afterwards been Secretary of War in President Pierce's administration, and then chairman of the Senate Military Affairs Committee. He had an inside knowledge of the officer corps, and could make the best use of the material at his disposal. Not only did he select with a few exceptions the right men, but he supported them in adversity. The principal Confederate Generals who were in command at the beginning of the war, if not killed, were still in command at its end.

Lincoln, on the other hand, was without military experience; his profession of the law had not brought him in contact with Army officers. His appointments were too often made on purely political grounds. He was too ready, especially at first, to yield to the popular clamour which demanded the recall of an unsuccessful General. Few, having failed once, were given a second chance. After each defeat a change was made in the command of the Army of the Potomac. None of the Generals in command of Federal armies at the end of the war had held high commands at the beginning. The survivors were very good, but the Federal cause was the poorer for the loss of those who had fallen by the way. Others, fearing the President in the rear more than the foe in front, had been too nervous to fight their best. Nor did the War Department make the best use of the junior officers of the Regular Army. Too many were left with their detachments in the Far West instead of being utilised to train and lead the volunteers. But while the North attempted at first to organise its military strength as if it had been a confederacy of states, the Federal Government, gaining power steadily at the expense of the states, rapidly won unquestioned control over all the forces of the Union. The Southern "Sovereign States," on the other hand, were unable even under the stress of war to abandon the principle of decentralisation for which they had been contending. Some State Governors, though loyal to the Confederate cause, were slow to respond to central direction, and when conscription was decided upon by the Confederate Congress in 1862 there was much opposition and evasion by the state authorities.

By what paths should the North invade the South to reconquer it for the Union? The Allegheny Mountains divided the Mississippi valley from the broad slopes which stretched eastward to the Atlantic. The

Mississippi and its great tributary, the Ohio, with the Cumberland and the Tennessee Rivers, offered sure means of carrying the war into the heart of the Confederacy and rending it asunder. The mechanical and material resources of the North ensured the control of these water-ways. The South could not organise any river forces capable of coping with the Federal flotillas. The one lateral line of communication within Confederate territory, the Charleston-Memphis railroad, which passed through the key position of Chattanooga on the Tennessee, at the junc-tion of four railway lines, would be speedily threatened. Waterways could not be cut by cavalry raids; the current of the rivers was with the North, and there was no limit except shipping to the troops and the supplies which could be carried. Old Winfield Scott, the Federal General-in-Chief, saw in this Western theatre the true line of strategic advance. But the initial neutrality of Kentucky confused the Northern view, and when at the end of September Kentucky was gained the main Union forces were differently engaged.

Upon Virginia joining the Confederacy Jefferson Davis made Rich-mond the Southern capital. It was within a hundred miles of Washing-ton. It controlled, or might control, the estuaries of the James and York Rivers, with their tributaries. It covered the powerful naval base at Nor-folk. Between Richmond and the enemy flowed in successive barriers the broad outlets of the Potomac and the Rappahannock, with its trib-utary the Rapidan. Here, then, upon this advanced battleground, rather than in the interior, must the Confederacy maintain itself or fall. Thus the two capitals stood like queens at chess upon adjoining squares, and, sustained by their combinations of covering pieces, they endured four years of grim play within a single move of capture.

The Confederates hoped at first to defend the line of the Potomac, which marked the northern frontier of Virginia. They had seized the Federal arsenal and army depot at Harpers Ferry, where the Shenan-doah joins the Potomac, and for several months, while the Union forces were gathering, Colonel Jackson, and later General Joseph E. Johnston, with a few thousand men, maintained themselves there. In front of the railway junction of Manassas, by the Bull Run stream, only thirty miles from Washington, stood General Beauregard, of Sumter repute, with the main Confederate army. Thus the summer of 1861 came. "How long," cried the politicians in Washington, and the turbulent public opinion behind them in the North, "should the United States tolerate this insolent challenge?" The three-months volunteers whom Lincoln had summoned at the end of April must be made to strike a blow before their time expired. General Scott wished to wait till trained armies were formed. But do not all regulars despise militia and volunteers? Pressed beyond resistance, Scott yielded to the entreaties of Lincoln and his Cabinet. Harpers Ferry had already been recovered, and Joseph E. Johnston, with eleven thousand men, had withdrawn up the Shenandoah. Scott therefore sent fifteen thousand men to hold off Johnston in the valley, while Irvin McDowell, a competent soldier, with thirty-five thousand, moved to attack Beauregard, who mustered twenty-two thousand. The essence of this plan was that Johnston's army, held by superior force, should not join Beauregard before McDowell attacked him. Some have suggested that if Scott, who was still robust of mind, if not in body, could have been conveyed to the field of battle in a litter or ambulance, as Marshal Saxe had been at Fontenoy, the Federal army might have been spared the disaster which overtook it. Knowledge and experience in command outweigh mere physical disability.

The Federal advance had originally been fixed for July 9, but it was not till a week later that it actually began. The two Confederate Generals were both expecting to be attacked by the superior forces on their respective fronts, and each was asking for reinforcements from the other. But the Union General in the valley, Patterson, allowed Johnston to slip away unobserved, and he joined Beauregard with two brigades on the day before the battle. Both McDowell and Beauregard had planned the same manœuvre, to turn the enemy's left flank. McDowell got his blow in first; on the Confederate right orders miscarried and the offensive faltered. With such troops the side standing on the defensive might be expected to hold its ground. But McDowell virtually achieved a surprise, and his much superior force threatened to overwhelm the weak Confederate left before reinforcements could arrive. In this crisis Jackson's brigade, standing "like a stone wall" on the Henry Hill, stopped the Federal advance, until the arrival by rail of another of Johnston's brigades turned the tide of battle.

The combat, though fierce, was confused, and on both sides disjointed. The day was hot, the troops raw, the staffs inexperienced. The Northerners retreated; the Confederates were too disorganised to pursue; but the retreat became a rout. Members of the Cabinet, Senators, Congressmen, even ladies, had come out from Washington to see the sport. They were involved in a panic when thousands of men, casting away their arms and even their coats, fled and never stopped till they reached the entrenchments which surrounded Washington. Not more than five thousand men were killed or wounded on both sides in the action, but the name Bull Run rang far and wide. Europe was astonished; the South was overjoyed; and a wave of fury swept the Union, before which the passions which had followed the attack on Fort Sumter seemed but a ripple.

It is still argued that the Confederates should have struck hot-foot at Washington. But Johnston at the time thought the Confederate army more disorganised by victory than the Federals by defeat. He had not seen the rout. Jackson and other Confederate Generals were eager to advance on Washington. Who shall say?

The day after this ignominious affair a new commander replaced McDowell. One of Lee's comrades on Scott's staff in Mexico, General George B. McClellan, a Regular officer with many remarkable qualities, was summoned from West Virginia, where he had been active and forward, to take command. Congress had voted the enlistment of five hundred thousand volunteers and a grant of two hundred and fifty million dollars for the prosecution of the war. A week after his assumption of command McClellan laid before the President the grandiose scheme of forming an army of two hundred and seventy-three thousand men, which, in combination with a strong naval force and a fleet of transports, should march through the Atlantic states, reducing the seaports from Richmond to New Orleans, and then move into the interior and stamp out the remnants of the rebellion. In war matters are not settled so easily. Public opinion, vocal through a thousand channels, demanded quick results. The scythe of Time cut both ways. The Confederacy was becoming consolidated. Every month increased the peril of foreign recognition of the South, or even of actual intervention. However, when at the end of October General Scott retired, McClellan became General-in-Chief of all the armies of the Republic, and bent himself with zeal and capacity to forming brigades, divisions, army corps, with artillery, engineers, and supply trains, according to the best European models.

The year 1861 ended with the Confederacy intact and almost unmolested. Along the immense front, with its deep borderlands and debatable regions, more than a hundred and fifty skirmishes and petty actions had been fought without serious bloodshed. Although the Confederate commanders realised that the time would soon come when McClellan would take the field against them with an army vastly superior in numbers, well disciplined and well equipped, they did not dare, with only forty thousand men, however elated, to invade Maryland and march on Baltimore. They did not even attempt to recover West Virginia. Lee, who was sent to co-ordinate defence on this front, could not prevail over the discord of the local commanders. Although he still retained his commission from the state of Virginia, he ranked below both Joseph E. Johnston and Albert Sidney Johnston in the Confederate hierarchy. Beauregard, though junior to him, had gained the laurels. Lee returned from Western Virginia with diminished reputation, and President Davis had to explain his qualities to the State Governors when appointing him to organise the coast defences of the Carolinas.

So far the American Civil War had appeared to Europe as a desultory brawl of mobs and partisans which might at any time be closed by politics and parley. Napoleon III sympathised with the Confederates, and would have aided them if the British Government had been agreeable. Queen Victoria desired a strict neutrality, and opinion in England was curiously divided. The upper classes, Conservative and Liberal alike, generally looked with favour upon the South, and in this view Gladstone concurred. Disraeli, the Conservative leader, was neutral. The Radicals and the unenfranchised mass of the working classes were solid against slavery, and Cobden and Bright spoke their mind. But the Northern blockade struck hard at the commercial classes, and Lancashire, though always constant against slavery, began to feel the cotton famine. The arrest on a British ship, the *Trent,* of the Confederate agents, Mason and Slidell, by a United States cruiser roused a storm. The Foreign Secretary, Lord John Russell, penned a hard dispatch which the Prince Consort persuaded the Prime Minister, Lord Palmerston, to modify. A clause was inserted which enabled the Federal Government without loss of honour to declare their cruiser's action unauthorised. President Lincoln took some persuading, but in the end he sagely remarked "One war at a time," liberated the captives, and all remained in sullen suspense. Blockade-running, both in cotton outwards and arms inwards, developed upon a large scale; but not a single European Government received the envoys of the Confederate states. No one in Europe imagined the drama of terrific war which the year 1862 would unfold. None appraised truly the implacable rage of the antagonists. None understood the strength of Abraham Lincoln or the resources of the United States. Few outside the Confederacy had ever heard of Lee or Jackson.

CHAPTER 16

THE CAMPAIGN AGAINST RICHMOND

THE NEW YEAR opened grievously for the South, and a bitter tide of disillusion chilled its people. In the Cabinet and headquarters at Richmond, where facts and figures told their sombre tale, the plight of the Confederacy already seemed grave. The Union blockade froze the coasts. Hostile armies, double or triple the numbers the South could muster, were assuming shape and quality, both in the Atlantic and Mississippi theatres. The awful weight of the North, with its wealth and munition-making power, lay now upon the minds of President Davis, his colleagues and Generals. The Southern states had no arsenals, little iron and steel, few and small factories from which boots, clothing, equipment could be supplied. The magazines were almost empty. Even flintlock muskets were scarce. The smooth-bore cannon of the Confederate artillery was far out-ranged by the new rifled guns of the Union. Nor was there any effectual means by which these needs could be met. It is upon this background that the military prodigies of the year stand forth.

Disaster opened in the Mississippi valley. Here Albert Sidney Johnston commanded the Confederate forces. Davis believed him to be his finest General. He was certainly a man of boundless devotion, whose daring was founded upon a thorough knowledge of his art. In the autumn of 1861 he had advanced to Bowling Green, a railway junction of high strategic value to the south of the Green River, a tributary of the Ohio. Here he stood brazenly, hoping to rouse Kentucky and marshal Tennessee, while to the westward Leonidas Polk, who in peace-time was Bishop of Louisiana, with another small army barred the Mississippi at Columbus. The Federal forces, with their fleets of armoured river gun-boats, descending the Mississippi from St. Louis and the Ohio from Louisville, outnumbered both these Confederate Generals by four to one. Still, for months they had remained unmolested in their forward positions, covering enormous territories from whose population and resources much might be drawn. Now with the turn of the year the Union leaders set their men in motion. Masses of blue-clad soldiers began to appear upon the three-hundred-mile front from the great river to the mountain ranges, and all kinds of queer craft cased in steel and carrying cannon and mortars glided slowly down the riverways from the north. The bluff could be played no longer. Polk abandoned Columbus, and Johnston retreated from Bowling Green. This carried the fighting line southwards to the Cumberland and Tennessee Rivers, and to a Confederate fortress called Island No. 10 on the Mississippi.

The Federal General, Henry W. Halleck, who commanded the Western Department was a model of caution. Fortunately among his generals there was a retired Regular officer, Ulysses S. Grant, who since the Mexican War had lived in obscurity, working for a time in his father's leather store in Illinois. The Confederates sought to block the Mississippi at Island No. 10, the Tennessee at Fort Henry, and the Cumberland at Fort Donelson, and their advanced forces garrisoned these armed posts. Fort Henry was weak, and Fort Donelson was an entrenched camp which required a considerable army for its defence. Grant proposed a winter advance up the Tennessee River and an attack upon Fort Henry. Halleck approved. Grant made the advance, and the advance made Grant. Albert Sidney Johnston foresaw with perfect clarity a Federal winter offensive while the rivers were well filled. He clamoured for reinforcements, both to President Davis and the Governors of the Western states. The former could not and the latter did not supply them. In February 1862 Grant seized Fort Henry. It was but ten miles across the tongue of land between the rivers to Fort Donelson, on the Cumberland. Without authority, and in severe frost, Grant struck at Fort Donelson, which was defended by seventeen thousand Confederates under Floyd, the former United States Secretary for War, who in the interval between Lincoln's election and inauguration had allowed the muskets to be transferred to the South. After four days' fighting and confrontation Fort Donelson surrendered, with fourteen thousand prisoners and sixty guns. Floyd, apprehending a charge of treason, escaped the night before. He was probably wise.

The fall of Fort Donelson on February 16 was the first great military disaster of the Confederacy; but others followed quickly in the West. Albert Sidney Johnston, now at last furnished with the beginnings of an army, gathered the remnants of his former front at Corinth, behind the Tennessee, and Polk fell back down the Mississippi to Memphis.

═══

At Washington McClellan, General-in-Chief, laboured to prepare his army, and resisted by every means the intense political pressures which demanded an advance "on to Richmond." He exaggerated the strength of the enemy, and furnished Lincoln with endless reports from Pinkerton's Private Detective Agency, which he used as his secret service, showing very heavy forces at Richmond and behind Joseph E. Johnston's entrenchments thirty miles away at Centerville. He strove to gain time to drill his men by repeated promises to advance. As month succeeded month and the swarming Army of the Potomac made no movement the enthusiasm which had greeted McClellan in July 1861 waned. The Radical Republicans began to attack this Democrat General who had been preferred to their own candidate, John C. Frémont. McClellan was known to be opposed to the Radical policy of proclaiming the emancipation of all slaves. Early in December he informed the President that he did not favour a frontal attack on Joseph E. Johnston and a march along the straight road through Fredericksburg to Richmond. He had long been devising a plan for an amphibious movement down Chesapeake Bay to some point on the coast of Virginia close to the rebel capital. He imparted these ideas to Lincoln in general terms early in December. Then in the middle of the month he contracted typhoid fever and was absent for several weeks. The Republican Party leaders had already procured the appointment of a Joint Committee on the conduct of the war, consisting of three Senators and four Congressmen. It was dominated by the Radical enemies of the General-in-Chief. Lincoln and the Cabinet, during McClellan's absence from duty, called into council several Generals of the Army, and invited constructive suggestions. But their conferences were abruptly disturbed by the reappearance of McClellan himself. A few days later he explained his plan to the President in detail. Availing himself of sea-power, he proposed to transport an army of a hundred and fifty thousand men down Chesapeake Bay and disembark it at Urbanna, on the Lower Rappahannock, where it would be only one day's march from West Point and two more marches from Richmond. He expected to cut off General J. B. Magruder and the Confederate troops defending the Yorktown peninsula, and he hoped to reach Richmond before Johnston could retreat thither.

No one can asperse the principle of this conception. It utilised all the forces of the Union Government; it turned the flank of all the Confederate positions between Washington and Richmond; it struck at the forehead of the Confederacy. Its details were substantially modified on examination. Fortress Monroe, at the tip of the peninsula, between the York and James Rivers, was held by the Union, and was finally chosen as a safe landing-place. President Lincoln had one overpowering objection to the whole idea of a maritime expedition. It would uncover Washington; and Joseph E. Johnston, for the strength of whose army he probably accepted McClellan's own figures, to say nothing of "Stonewall" Jackson, would at once swoop down on the defenceless capital. Hard bargaining ensued upon the number of troops to be left to guard the capital and the mouth of the Shenandoah valley, where at Harpers Ferry the river flows into the Potomac. This was agreed at forty thousand. Eventually towards the end of February Lincoln gave a reluctant assent, and everything was set in train for the tremendous enterprise. At the same time Lincoln resolved to keep supreme control, relieved McClellan of the general direction of the United States armies, and restricted him to the command of the Army of the Potomac. For this there were also sound military reasons. Feeling that he required a military adviser, he decided to summon General Halleck from the West. McClellan learnt of his removal from the higher command through the medium of the newspapers before Lincoln's emissary reached him. Thus the President appeared guilty of a grave discourtesy, so unusual in him that the suspicion naturally arose that the "hidden hand" of the Joint Committee was here at work.

It was a far worse mistake not to appoint a new General-in-Chief. All the generals in command of armies were ordered to take their instructions from the Secretary of War. For the last two months this office had been held by Edwin M. Stanton, who had replaced the incompetent and perhaps corrupt Cameron. Stanton, like McClellan, was a Democrat, and during the last days of the Buchanan administration had held the post of Attorney-General. Possibly Lincoln had appointed him because he thought that he would be acceptable to McClellan. It was no doubt his intention to reappoint McClellan as General-in-Chief, if he succeeded in his Richmond campaign, and at the time he could think of no one to fill the vacancy, which he hoped would be only temporary. At the outset Stanton had professed unbounded devotion to McClellan, but the General soon began to doubt the sincerity of his professions and thought that he detected a deliberate design to debar him from free access to the President. It was not very long before Stanton appeared to be in collusion with the Joint Committee. The Attorney-General had given the opinion that "the order of the Secretary of War is the President's order." There now began to issue from the Secretary's office a series of orders seriously crippling McClellan's operations. McClellan's scope was reduced by the creation of the Military Departments of the Rappahannock under McDowell, who had commanded at Bull Run, and of the Shenandoah under Nathaniel P. Banks. A whole corps was thus taken from him. He claimed that he was leaving behind him no less than seventy-three thousand men, of whom but thirty-five thousand belonged to Banks's command in the Shenandoah valley. McClellan was justified in regarding this force as available for the protection of the capital. However, he did not clearly explain his arrangements to Lincoln, and his failure to take the President into his confidence had an unfortunate result. For Lincoln in misunderstanding ordered the First Corps, under McDowell, to remain in front of Washington, thus reducing the force on which McClellan had counted by forty thousand men, at the moment of launching his tremendous operation.

The Confederates lost their best chance of victory when they failed to use the autumn and winter of 1861. Their success at Bull Run proved as injurious as a reverse. Believing with their President that foreign intervention was near at hand, and arrogantly confident that they could beat the North in the field if need arose, they relaxed their efforts. The volunteers who came forward after the first battle could not be armed. Recruiting fell off; the soldiers in the field began to go home. Efforts to fill the ranks by grants of bounties and furloughs were ineffectual. By the beginning of 1862 the position was desperate. Nearly two-thirds of the Confederate Army consisted of one-year volunteers. In May the terms of enlistment of the hundred and forty-eight regiments which they formed would expire. These regiments were the backbone of the Army. Invasion was imminent. Conscription was contrary to the theory of state independence and sovereignty. But the Confederate Congress rose manfully to the occasion, and on April 16 by a vote of more than two to one passed an Act declaring every able-bodied white man between the ages of eighteen and thirty-five subject to military service. The armies were nevertheless filled by volunteers seeking to escape the stigma of serving under compulsion rather than by the Act itself. Indeed, the Act proved unpopular in the States and was difficult to enforce. Full use was made of its exemption clauses by the disaffected in order to escape service.

Throughout this period President Jefferson Davis rigorously adhered to the passive-defensive. He made no attempt to exploit the victories of Bull Run and Wilson's Creek. Determined to keep the control of military operations in his own hands, he devoted his attention to the East, and largely ignored the West, where chaos reigned until Albert Sidney Johnston's appointment to the supreme command in September. He obstinately refused to draw upon the "seasoned soldiers" who formed the garrisons on the Atlantic coastline. Hatteras Inlet, which afforded the best approach to the North Carolina Sounds, and Port Royal and Beaufort in South Carolina, which threatened both Charleston and Savannah, had been captured by small Federal forces and sea-power. Lee after his return from Western Virginia was sent to organise the coast defences. When a large expedition under the Union General Ambrose E. Burnside entered the inland waters of North Carolina the Confederates were ill-prepared, and lost Roanoke Island and New Bern. President Davis was more than ever determined to maintain at their full strength the garrisons in the threatened states. He recalled General Lee from his coastal defence work in the Carolinas, and employed him in a somewhat ill-defined capacity as his chief military adviser at headquarters.

In the middle of March Halleck, who had been appointed to the sole command in the Western theatre, directed Don Carlos Buell, who had occupied Nashville, to march with the greater part of his army to Savannah, on the Tennessee, thirty miles from Corinth, to combine with Grant, who had William T. Sherman with him, on the western bank near Shiloh, and attack Albert Sidney Johnston. But before Buell's men were across the river Johnston struck. In the early morning of April 6 he surprised the advanced Federal troops in their tents near Shiloh, and the largest and most bloody battle yet seen in the war was fought. Johnston at first carried all before him; and Grant, who was late in reaching the field, was by nightfall in grave danger. But Johnston, exposing himself with reckless gallantry at the head of an infantry charge, was wounded and bled to death from a main artery in a few minutes. Whatever results his great personality and wonderful energy could have gained on the morrow were lost. Beauregard, who succeeded him, drew off the Confederate troops, much to the disgust of his subordinate, Braxton Bragg. Each side lost in this furious action ten thousand men; but the proportion of loss was far heavier in the thinner Confederate ranks. The arrival of the cautious Halleck, although he brought Federal reinforcements, stopped any thought of pursuit. Island No. 10 was reduced by General John Pope on April 8, and seven thousand Confederates became prisoners of war. It now seems that a combined naval and military expedition could easily at this time have lunged far to the south and secured the fortress of Vicksburg in Mississippi. But Halleck accommodated himself readily to the President's wish for action in

East Tennessee. He moved slowly against Corinth, and spent a month in trying to surround Beauregard, who escaped by a swift and long retreat. By the summer the Union line in the West had moved southwards by two hundred miles on a three-hundred-mile front.

The stage was now set for the military drama of the Richmond-Yorktown peninsula. At the beginning of April McClellan's army began to land in large numbers at the Federal Fortress Monroe, which served as a bridgehead. As soon as this movement, about which there could be no secrecy, became evident Joseph E. Johnston, to the surprise and relief of the Federal Government, withdrew from Centerville, abandoned Manassas Junction, crossed the Upper Rappahannock, and stood in the rugged wilderness country behind its tributary the Rapidan. It may seem confusing that there should be two Confederate Generals named Johnston; but after the gallant death of Albert Sidney at Shiloh only one remained. He was Joseph E. Now behind the Rapidan he was in close touch with Richmond, so that McClellan's strategy, vindicated in principle, was baulked in practice. In the middle of April Johnston, leaving his main army eighty miles to the westward, arrived at Yorktown, and assumed the additional command of the troops in the peninsula. He thus enjoyed interior lines and could concentrate all his forces for the defence of Richmond. The Union Navy, after a heavy combat, found itself unable to face the plunging fire of the batteries on the bluffs of the York River on McClellan's right flank. The Confederate entrenchments, manned by Magruder's troops, stretched before him across the peninsula. He conceived himself outnumbered by the enemy, and if Davis had consented to give Johnston the garrisons of the Atlantic towns he would have been.

In these depressing circumstances McClellan acted with more than his habitual deliberation. He spent a month in a formal siege of Yorktown, incessantly appealing to Lincoln for McDowell's corps. Lincoln, on the other hand, urged him to vigorous action. "I always insisted," he wrote drily, on April 9, "that going down the bay in search of a field instead of fighting at or near Manassas was only shifting and not surmounting a difficulty; that we would find the same enemy, and the same or equal entrenchments, at either place." And a month later: "By delay the enemy will relatively gain upon you—that is, he will gain faster by fortifications and reinforcements than you can gain by reinforcements alone." Eventually, after the surrender of Yorktown, which opened the York River to his ships, McClellan advanced upon the Confederate lines. Magruder, who had only eleven thousand men, made no resistance, and though mauled in a rearguard action at Williamsburg on May 5 extricated himself successfully. By the middle of May McClellan had advanced sixty miles up the York, and arrived at White House, on the Richmond–West Point railway, twenty-five miles from the rebel capital. He formed a new base at West Point and became independent of Fortress Monroe. Could he at this moment have brought McDowell from Fredericksburg into his combination the fate of Richmond might well have been sealed.

However, President Davis had in April been persuaded by Lee to reinforce "Stonewall" Jackson for an offensive diversion in the Shenandoah valley. With only sixteen thousand men against four Federal Generals, Banks, Shields, Frémont and Milroy who disposed of over forty thousand, Jackson fought the brief, brilliant campaign which reinforced his first renown. Striking right and left at the superior forces on either side of him, running daily risks of capture, making enormous marches, sometimes dividing his small force, he gained a series of sharp actions, which greatly perturbed President Lincoln and his advisers. Lincoln had at last promised McClellan McDowell's corps; but six days later, when the Union Army was half across the swampy river Chickahominy, a telegram brought the General the news that McDowell's movement was "suspended." McClellan paused in his advance; violent rains flooded the Chickahominy, and the Union Army found itself divided, with two corps only on the southern side. This was clearly Johnston's opportunity. With his whole force he attacked the two isolated Union corps. President Davis, with Lee at his side, rode out to watch the resulting battle of Seven Pines, or Fair Oaks as it is sometimes called. They had not been consulted by the Commander-in-Chief, who had given all his orders verbally to his Generals. The Confederate attack miscarried. The battle was severe but indecisive, costing each side about six thousand men. McClellan was checked, and heavy rains made him all the more ready to remain inactive. He stood fast with his outposts five miles from Richmond. Lincoln, having learned that Jackson was now in retreat up the valley, again promised McDowell's corps. But when Jackson turned on his pursuers and defeated them on two successive days, June 8 and 9, at Cross Keys and Port Republic, he changed his mind again and would not let McDowell go. It was certainly desirable to guard against any risk of the Federal capital's falling even temporarily into rebel hands, for the effect would have been shattering, though hardly disastrous. But Lincoln's vacillations are a classic instance of the dangers of civilian interference with generals in the field.

Far more important than the fighting was the fact that General Joseph E. Johnston was severely wounded on the first day at Seven Pines, and

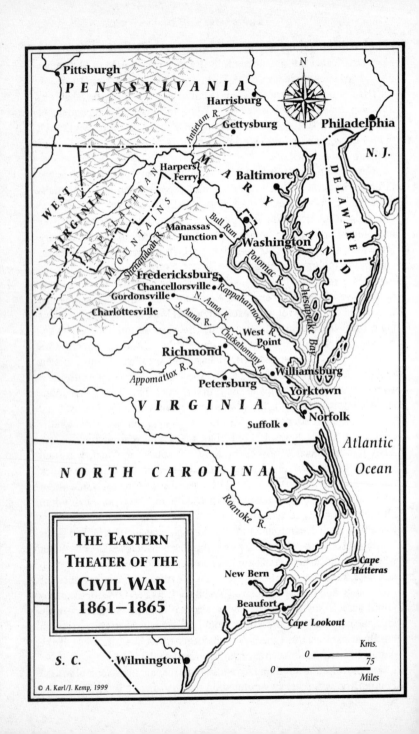

Pittsburgh

P E N N S Y L V A N I A

Harrisburg

Antietam R.

Gettysburg

Philadelphia

N. J.

Harpers
Ferry

**WEST
VIRGINIA**

M A R Y L A N D

Baltimore

A P P A L A C H I A N M O U N T A I N S

Shenandoah R.

Bull Run

Manassas
Junction

Washington

Potomac R.

Fredericksburg

Chancellorsville

Rappahannock

Gordonsville

N. Anna R.

S. Anna R.

Charlottesville

Chickahominy R.

West
Point

DELAWARE

Chesapeake Bay

Richmond

Appomattox R.

Petersburg

Williamsburg

Yorktown

V I R G I N I A

Suffolk

Norfolk

*Atlantic
Ocean*

N O R T H   C A R O L I N A

Roanoke R.

**Cape
Hatteras**

THE EASTERN
THEATER OF THE
CIVIL WAR
1861–1865

New Bern

Beaufort

Cape Lookout

Kms.

0 ——————— 75

0

Miles

S. C.   **Wilmington**

© A. Karl/J. Kemp, 1999

President Davis on June 1 appointed Lee to command what was hence-forward to bear the deathless title of the Army of Northern Virginia.

Lee now made the first of his offensive combinations, and immediately his hand was felt in the whole conduct of the war. He procured from Davis the gathering of the Atlantic garrisons which Johnston had been denied. He played upon the fears of Washington by sending seven thousand men to strengthen Jackson in the valley. This ensured the fur-ther paralysis of McDowell. Jackson rode in from his army to concert the plans. He was ordered to leave his "enfeebled troops" in the valley, and come secretly with his main force to Ashland, fifteen miles north of Richmond on the Richmond-Fredericksburg railway. He could thence by advancing turn the flank and the rear of the Union armies and cut their communications with West Point. He was to be ready to act by dawn on June 26. In the interval J. E. B. Stuart, the young Confederate cavalry leader, with twelve hundred horse, made a remarkable recon-naissance of McClellan's right. He actually traversed his communica-tions, and, being unable to return, rode right round the Union Army, arriving south of Richmond with several hundred captives. This was more than Lee had wished, and Stuart's exploit might well have warned the enemy. But McClellan made no change in his array, which still lay in sight of Richmond astride the Chickahominy. Lee's army, counting Jackson, was now over seventy-five thousand strong. McClellan mus-tered eighty-seven thousand; but of these only the corps of General Fitz-John Porter, twenty-five thousand strong, was now north of the Chickahominy. Lee resolved to move the bulk of his force across that river, and, joined by Jackson, to concentrate fifty-six thousand men against Porter's corps, turn its right flank, destroy it, sever McClellan's communications with West Point, and thereafter cross the Chicka-hominy in his rear and bring him to ruin. There would be left in the en-trenchments defending Richmond only sixteen thousand men under Magruder. It would be open to McClellan, when he saw what was afoot, to march with sixty thousand men straight upon the Richmond lines and assault them with a superiority of nearly four to one. Lee, who knew McClellan well, and judged him rightly, was sure he would not do this. "Anyhow," he said to Davis, "I shall be hard on his heels"—meaning that he would be attacking the Union Army from the rear while it was fighting its way into Richmond. This remark illustrates the agile, flexible grasp which Lee had of war, and how great commanders seem to move their armies from place to place as if they were doing no more than riding their own horses.

During the night of June 25 two Confederate corps crossed the Chickahominy, formed to their right, and fell upon Porter at Mechanicsville. Porter, surprised, made a stubborn resistance. His batteries of rifled cannon wrought havoc in the Confederate ranks. Jackson did not appear upon the scene. The difficulties of the route had delayed him by a day. Porter, having inflicted a loss of over two thousand men upon his assailants, was able to fall back upon his reserves at Gaines's Mill, four miles farther downstream, where the onslaught was renewed with the greatest fury on June 27. Gaines's Mill was the first battle in which Lee commanded personally. It was bitterly contested. Again the power of the Union artillery was manifest. The Confederates were several times repulsed at all points, and the country on Porter's right was so obstructed with forest and swamp that when Jackson came into action in the late afternoon he could not turn the flank. Lee, however, did not despair. He appealed to his troops. He launched John B. Hood's gallant Texans at the centre, and as the shadows lengthened ordered the whole army to attack. The Texans broke the centre of Porter's hard-tried corps. The Union troops were driven from the field. Twenty guns and several thousand prisoners were already taken when night fell. Where would Porter go? McClellan had remained immobile opposite Magruder during the two days' fighting. What would he do? His communications were cut. His right wing was crushed. Lee's long, swinging left arm, of which Jackson was at last the fist, must curve completely round the right and rear of the Federal Army. Surely the stroke was mortal?

But McClellan was a skilful soldier. When his generals met him at headquarters on the night of Gaines's Mill he informed them that he had let go his communications with West Point and the York River; that, using sea-power, he was shifting his base from the York to the James; that the whole army would march southwards to Harrison's Landing on that river, where all supplies would await them. He had, we now know, made some preparations for such a change beforehand. But he ran a grave risk in leaving the decision till the last moment. What was called, from its shape, a "grape-vine bridge" had been built across the swamps and stream of the Chickahominy, and by this tortuous, rickety structure Porter made good his escape, while the whole Federal Army prepared to make a difficult and dangerous flank march across the White Oak Swamp to the southern side of the peninsula. It was now Magruder's turn to advance and strike at this vulnerable army. He broke in upon them on the 28th at Savage Station, capturing their field hospitals and large supplies. But Lee could not yet be sure that McClellan was really making for the James. He might as well be retreating by the Williamsburg road on Fortress Monroe. Lee therefore delayed one day before crossing the Chickahominy in pursuit. It was not till the 30th that he brought McClellan to battle at Glendale, or Frayser's Farm. This was the main crisis.

It is almost incredible that McClellan spent the day conferring with the Navy and arranging the new base on the James. He left the battle to fight itself. On the Confederate side many things went wrong. The maps were faulty; the timing failed; the attacks were delivered piecemeal; Jackson, from whom so much had been hoped, appeared in physical eclipse. Out of seventy-five thousand men with whom Lee had proposed to deal the final blow barely twenty thousand were really launched. These, after frightful losses, broke the Union centre; but night enabled the army to continue its retreat. At Malvern Hill, in a position of great strength, with the James River behind them to forbid further retreat, and the fire of the Navy and its gunboats to cover their flanks, McClellan stood at bay. Once again at the end of this week of furious fighting Lee ordered the attack, and his soldiers charged with their marvellous impetuosity. Loud roared the Union cannonade; high rose the rebel yell, that deadly sound "Aah-ib!" so often to be heard in these bloody years. But all was in vain. McClellan was saved. Frustrated, beaten, driven into retreat, his whole campaign wrecked, with a loss of enormous masses of stores and munitions, sixty cannon and thirty-six thousand rifles, with Richmond invincible, McClellan and his brave army nevertheless finished the Battle of the Seven Days by hurling back their pursuers with the loss of five thousand men.

Victory in the Seven Days Battle rested with Lee. The world saw the total failure of the immense Federal plan. This also was the impression at Washington. McClellan, who was undaunted, proposed to move across the James to Petersburg and attack Richmond "by the back door," as Grant was to do in 1865. His proposals were not accepted. But to Lee the adventure was hardly less disappointing. He had failed by a succession of narrow chances, arising largely from the newness of his staffs, to annihilate his foe. He had lost over twenty thousand of the flower of his army, against seventeen thousand on the Union side with its overflowing manpower.

Lincoln and his advisers now sought to return to their original plan of massing overwhelming forces on the overland route between Washington and Richmond and breaking through by weight of numbers. But their armies were divided, and Lee at Richmond stood directly between them. The President ordered McClellan to withdraw from the peninsula and bring his troops up the Potomac to the neighbourhood of Washington. Halleck, who was then credited with the successes gained against his orders in the Western theatre, was appointed General-in-Chief. He brought General Pope, who had done well in the Mississippi valley, to command what was to be called "the Army of Virginia." Pope was a harsh, vainglorious man, puffed up with good fortune in the Western theatre, and speaking in derogatory terms of the armies of the East and their achievements. He would show them how war should be waged. McClellan was ordered to hand over his troops, who parted from him in outspoken grief, and was relegated to the defence of the Washington lines. Pope now would be the champion of the Union. He signalised his appointment by severities upon the civil population of Western Virginia not yet used in the war. All male inhabitants in the zone of his army must either swear allegiance to the Union or be driven from their homes on pain of death if they returned. Jackson only with difficulty preserved his habitual calm on hearing this news about his beloved native state.

The strategic situation offered advantages to Lee and his lieutenant. Before McClellan's army could be brought round from the Yorktown peninsula they would deal with Pope. How they treated him must be recounted.

An historic naval episode had meanwhile occurred. When in the spring of 1861 the Federal Government had lightly abandoned the Navy yard at Norfolk to the seceding state of Virginia some stores and several vessels of the United States Navy had been burned. One of these, the frigate *Merrimac,* was repaired and refashioned in a curious way. It was given steam-engines to propel it, and above its deck a low penthouse of teak was erected. This was covered with two layers of railway iron hammered into two-inch plates. These layers were riveted transversely upon each other, making an ironclad shelter four inches thick. A heavy metal ram was fastened to the prow, and a battery of ten 7-inch rifled guns, firing through portholes, was mounted in the penthouse. Many had thought of this sort of thing before; now it came upon the scene.

This strange vessel was only finished on March 7, 1862. She had never fired a gun, nor had her engines been revolved, when on March 8 she went into action against the all-powerful Navy of the United States, which from Fortress Monroe was blockading the estuaries of the York and James Rivers. The engines, described as the worst possible, were found to make only five knots an hour, and the vessel swam and steered like a waterlogged ship. Out she came, and with no hesitation engaged the two nearest ships of the blockading fleet, the *Cumberland* and the *Congress.* These delivered broadsides which would have sunk an ordinary frigate. Besides this, all other United States ships in range and the shore batteries at Sewell's Point concentrated their fire upon her. Without paying the slightest attention to this bombardment, the *Merrimac,* rechristened the *Virginia,* steered straight for the *Cumberland,* and struck her almost at right angles. On board the *Merrimac* the collision was hardly perceptible. The ram broke off; the *Cumberland* heeled over, and, firing her cannon to the last, soon foundered, with most of her crew. The *Merrimac* then turned upon the *Congress,* and at two hundred yards range smashed her to pieces and set her on fire. After an hour the *Congress* hoisted the white flag, and every effort was made by various small Confederate ships to rescue her crew. The *Minnesota,* which was aground, would have shared her fate if the ebb tide had not prevented the *Merrimac,* which drew twenty-two feet of water, from approaching her. Although the *Merrimac* was for a long time under the fire of at least a hundred heavy guns her armour was hardly damaged. Nothing outside the armour escaped. The funnel and two of the muzzles of the guns were shot off. Inside only twenty-one men were killed or wounded by splinters through the portholes. Her triumphant crew lay down by the side of their guns, expecting to destroy the rest of the United States fleet the next morning.

But when daylight came and steam was raised a strange-looking vessel was seen to be protecting the *Minnesota.* "She appeared," wrote one of the *Merrimac*'s crew, "but a pigmy compared with the lofty frigate which she guarded." This was Ericsson's *Monitor,* of which there had been much talk, now at last ready. The *Merrimac* had made the naval revolution, but the *Monitor,* one day later, was a whole lap ahead of her. She carried only two guns; but they were eleven-inch, and mounted in a revolving iron turret nine inches thick. She had a turtle deck, heavily protected, almost flush with the water-line. As she drew only twelve feet of water she had an advantage in manœuvre.

Both these ironclad monsters approached each other, while the stately ships of the United States fleet watched spellbound. They came to the closest quarters, and the *Merrimac,* now ramless, struck the *Monitor.* None of the *Merrimac*'s shells pierced the *Monitor*'s armour; but when the two eleven-inch guns hit the *Merrimac* amidships the whole side was driven in several inches, and all the guns' crews bled at the nose from concussion. For six hours these two ironclads battered each other with hardly any injury or loss on either side, and both withdrew at close of day, never to meet again. As the *Merrimac* had no armour below the water-line her crew considered her lucky. She returned to the dockyard to have this defect and many others repaired. The *Monitor,* which was so unseaworthy that she had nearly foundered on the way to the fight, also required attention. As soon as the news reached Europe it was realised that all the war-fleets of the world were obsolete. The British Admiralty, by an intense effort, in the course of a few years reconstructed the Royal Navy so as to meet the altered conditions. But even now there are fools who build large ships to fight at sea with hardly any armour.* The combat of the *Merrimac* and the *Monitor* made the greatest change in seafighting since cannon fired by gunpowder had been mounted on ships about four hundred years before.

When Norfolk was evacuated by the Confederates efforts were made to take the *Merrimac* up the James River for the defence of Richmond; but although she was so lightened as to become defenceless her draught prevented her escape. By the orders of her captain she was therefore burned and sunk. The joy which her exploit had evoked throughout the Confederacy now turned to grief and anger. But the Confederate court-martial upon the captain declared that "The only alternative, in the opinion of the court, was to abandon and burn the ship then and there; which in the judgment of the court was deliberately and wisely done by order of the accused."

* Written in 1939.

CHAPTER 17

LEE AND McCLELLAN

GENERAL POPE reached the front on August 1, 1862. The new commander's task was plainly to gain as much ground as he could without being seriously engaged until McClellan's army could return from the James River and join him. Aquia Creek, not far south of the capital, was appointed for the landing of this army, and further large reinforcements were moving from Washington, through Alexandria, and along the railroad. Pope had already forty thousand men; in six weeks he would have a hundred and fifty thousand. He was full of energy, and very sanguine. He hoped to capture both Gordonsville and Charlottesville even before his main force arrived, and then finish off Richmond.

As soon as Lee saw that McClellan had no further bite he sent Jackson, in the middle of July, with two divisions (eleven thousand men) to Gordonsville, and raised him by the end of the month to twenty-four thousand. This was a lot for Jackson, who had barely two to one to face. He found Pope's army moving hopefully towards him by the three roads which joined at Culpeper. On August 9 he fell upon General Banks, commanding Pope's leading corps, seven miles south of Culpeper, at Cedar Mountain. He used twenty thousand men against Banks's nine thousand, drove them from the field with the loss of a quarter of their number, and left the rest in no condition to do more than guard the baggage. But before Culpeper he found himself confronted with the other two corps of Pope's army, and in harmony with Lee's conceptions he fell back to Gordonsville.

On August 13 Lee learnt that McClellan's army was being re-embarked at Fortress Monroe. This was the signal for which he was waiting. Before this splendid army could make its weight tell with Pope in Northern Virginia, a period of a month at the outside, he must win a great battle there. He at once ordered General James Longstreet with twelve brigades, the bulk of the Richmond forces, to join Jackson at Gordonsville, and by the 17th he had fifty-five thousand men concentrated in the woods behind Clark's Mountain, within striking distance of Culpeper, where Pope was now established. Pope was unaware of his peril, and might well have been destroyed. But Lee waited a day to bring up his cavalry, and in the meantime a Confederate officer was captured with papers which opened Pope's eyes. Favoured by the morning mist, he retreated forthwith behind the Rappahannock. Lee's first right-handed clutch had failed. He now scooped with the left hand. Jackson crossed the Upper Rappahannock by Sulphur Springs. But the river rose after his first brigade was over, and a second time Pope was saved.

Lee now knew that his brief period of superiority had passed, and that he must expect, in a week or ten days, overwhelming forces to be massed against him. He knew that the leading divisions of McClellan's former army were already ashore at Aquia Creek. How could the Army of Northern Virginia cope with a hundred and fifty thousand men, once they were concentrated? He therefore resolved with Jackson upon a daring and, since it was successful, brilliant manœuvre. In the face of a superior and rapidly growing enemy he divided his army. Before dawn on August 25 Jackson began another of his famous marches. With twenty thousand men, after covering twenty-six miles, he reached Salem, far behind Pope's right flank, and the next day by another twenty-five-mile march through Thoroughfare Gap in the hills he cut the Alexandria–Orange railway, upon which Pope depended for his supplies, a few miles south of Manassas Junction. On the 27th he seized the junction. Here the whole supply of Pope's army was heaped. Food, equipment, stores of every kind, dazzling to the pinched Confederates, fell into his hands. He set guards upon the liquor and let his men take what they could carry. Most of them reclothed themselves. But this booty might be bought at a fatal price. On every side superior Federal forces lay or were approaching. The cutting of Pope's communications was an incident and not the aim of Jackson and his chief. Nothing short of a great battle won was of any use to them. He therefore delivered the junction and its depot to the flames. Looking northwards, Pope perceived the night sky reddened by the immense conflagration. It was Jackson's part to keep him puzzled and occupied till Lee could come round with Longstreet and the main army and join him.

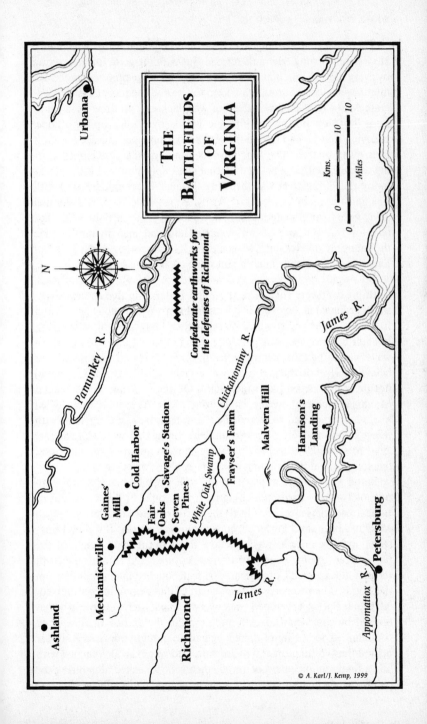

THE BATTLEFIELDS OF VIRGINIA

Kms.
Miles

N

Confederate earthworks for the defenses of Richmond

Pamunkey R.

Urbana

Chickahominy R.

James R.

Ashland

Mechanicsville

Gaines' Mill

Cold Harbor

Savage's Station

Fair Oaks

Seven Pines

White Oak Swamp

Frayser's Farm

Malvern Hill

Harrison's Landing

Richmond

James R.

Petersburg

Appomattox R.

© A. Karl/J. Kemp, 1999

There was now no danger of Pope marching on towards Richmond. He was hamstrung. He must retreat. But with the great forces arriving by every road to join him he would still have a large preponderance. He might even close Thoroughfare Gap to Lee and the rest of the Confederate Army. It was a dire hazard of war. Jackson withdrew from Manassas Junction northward into the woods by Sudley Springs. Pope, believing that he had him in his grip at the Junction, marched upon it from every quarter. The Junction was found in ashes and empty. During the 28th neither side knew all that was happening; but Jackson was aware that Longstreet was thrusting through Thoroughfare Gap with Lee and the main Confederate Army. Pope's orders to his disjointed army were to annihilate Jackson, now located south of Sudley Springs, and for this purpose he set seventy thousand men in motion. He thought only of Jackson. He seemed to have forgotten Longstreet and Lee, who were already massing into line on Jackson's right.

On August 29 began the Second Battle of Bull Run, or Manassas. With great bravery fifty-three thousand Federals in five successive assaults grappled in the open field with Jackson's twenty thousand. To and fro the struggle swayed, with equal slaughter. Longstreet, already in line, but still unperceived, was painfully slow in coming into action. He always wished to look before he leapt; and this sound maxim was far below the level of the event. He was a great war-horse, and Lee would not press him beyond a certain point. On the first day of the Second Manassas Jackson bore the whole brunt alone. As evening came, when his last reserves had delivered their counter-attack, a clergyman with whom he was friendly expressed his fears for the thin-worn Confederate left. "Stonewall," measuring the struggle from minute to minute, took one long look at the field and said, "They have done their worst."

Battle was renewed at dawn on the 30th. Pope had received the support of two new corps, marching up from Aquia. Still unconscious of Longstreet's presence, he ordered the ill-starred General, Porter, to turn Jackson's right, and Porter's troops responded loyally. But now Longstreet, massive once he was in action, threw in the main weight of the Confederate Army. Pope's array was ruptured. On a four-mile front the new, unexpected Confederate Army debouched magnificently from the woods. The two corps of Pope's left, outnumbered and outflanked, retreated. Porter, enveloped, was overwhelmed, and subsequently victimised by court-martial. Although even at the end of the day Pope commanded 70,000 faithful men, he had no thought but to seek shelter behind the Washington entrenchments, into which he also carried with him a final reinforcement of 10,000 men which reached him during the night. Lee had captured thirty guns, 20,000 precious rifles, and 7,000 prisoners, and had killed and wounded 13,500 Federals, at a total cost to the Confederacy of 10,000 men. He had utterly defeated 75,000 Union troops with less than 55,000 in his own hand. It was exactly four months since President Davis had given him command. Then McClellan was within five miles of Richmond. Now Lee's outposts were within twenty miles of Washington. In this decisive manner the tables were turned.

Ill-treatment was meted out to General McClellan by the Washington politicians and Cabinet, with the cautious, pliant General Halleck as their tool. For this Lincoln cannot escape blame. He wanted an aggressive General who would energetically seek out Lee and beat him. McClellan, for all his qualities of leadership, lacked the final ounces of fighting spirit. Lincoln with his shrewd judgment of men knew this. But he also knew that McClellan was probably the ablest commander available to him. His instinct had been to stand by his chosen General. Instead he had yielded to political outcry. He had swapped horses in midstream. He found he had got a poorer mount. As the different corps of McClellan's army were landed at Aquia they were hurried off to join Pope, until McClellan had not even his own personal escort with him. Yet he was never removed from the command of the Army of Virginia, which had been renamed the Army of the Potomac. He made voluble and justified complaints, to which no attention was paid. But on September 2, when Pope and his beaten army seemed about to collapse upon Washington, and panic lapped around the President, a different attitude was shown. While McClellan was breakfasting that morning he was visited by the President and the General-in-Chief. Halleck declared that Washington was lost, and offered McClellan the command of all the forces. The flouted commander at once undertook to save the city. As he had never been dismissed officially, he was never reappointed. He had been deprived of all his troops; they were now restored. History has never allowed McClellan to rise above the level of competent and courageous mediocrity; but it must not be forgotten that when he rode out to meet the retreating army they received him with frantic enthusiasm. The long, jaded, humiliated columns of brave men who had been so shamefully mishandled broke their ranks and almost dragged their restored commander from the saddle. The soldiers embraced and kissed his horse's legs. Thus fortified, McClellan restored order to the army and turned its face again to the foe.

Lee, after the second Confederate victory at Manassas, did what ought to have been done after the first. He invaded Maryland to give that state a chance to come over, if it still would or could. Always seeking the decisive and final battle which he knew could alone save the Confederacy, he marched north by Leesburg, crossed the Potomac, and arrived in the neighbourhood of Frederick, abreast of Baltimore. He knew he had never the slightest chance of taking Washington; but there were prizes to be won in the open field. Three Federal garrisons occupied Martinsburg, Winchester, and Harpers Ferry, in the Shenandoah valley. At Harpers Ferry there was a great Union depot of supply. In the three places there were about fifteen thousand men. Halleck had refused to withdraw them while time remained. They became a substantial objective to Lee, and his design was to capture Harpers Ferry, into which the two smaller garrisons withdrew. Accordingly he marched west from Frederick through the range of hills called the South Mountains, sent Jackson looping out by Martinsburg, and on September 13 closed down on Harpers Ferry from all sides.

The Washington politicians, in their hour of panic, had clung to McClellan. They did not mean to sink with him. He was originally given orders only to defend the Washington fortifications. However, on his own responsibility, or, so he later claimed, "with a rope round his neck," he took charge of his old army, quitted "the Washington defences," and set out after Lee, whom he outnumbered by two to one. McClellan's account of this episode is widely contested, for in fact Lincoln discussed with him the Army's movement into Maryland and verbally gave him "command of the forces in the field" as well as around the capital. McClellan's political prejudices may well have coloured his memory. He had reason to feel aggrieved. His innumerable critics in high places never ceased to harry him. Their attitude to the commander in the field at this juncture was dishonouring to them.

McClellan, hoping to save Harpers Ferry, now started after Lee with nearly ninety thousand men, including two fine corps that had not yet suffered at all. By a stroke of luck a Northern private soldier picked up three cigars wrapped in a piece of paper which was in fact a copy of Lee's most secret orders. McClellan learned on the 13th that Lee had divided his army and that the bulk of it was closing on Harpers Ferry. He therefore advanced with very good assurance to attack him. Everything now became a matter of hours. Could Jackson, with Walner and McLaws, capture Harpers Ferry before Lee was beaten in the passes of the South Mountains?

McClellan wasted many of these precious hours. But considering that members of the Government behind him could only gape and gibber and that his political foes were avid of a chance to bring him to ruin it is not surprising that he acted with a double dose of his habitual caution. By overwhelming forces Lee was beaten back from the two gaps in the South Mountain range on the 14th. He now had to take a great decision. At first he thought to gather his spoils and laurels and re-cross the Potomac into Virginia. But later, feeling that nothing but victory would suffice, he resolved to give battle behind the Antietam stream, with his back to the Potomac, believing that Jackson would capture Harpers Ferry in the meanwhile and rejoin him in time.

Harpers Ferry surrendered early on the 15th. Seventy-three guns, thirteen thousand rifles, and twelve thousand five hundred prisoners were gathered by Jackson's officers. He was himself already marching all through the afternoon and night to join Lee, who stood with but twenty thousand men against the vast approaching mass of McClellan. This worthy General was unable to free himself from the Washington obsession. Had he been as great a soldier or as great a man as Lee he would have staked all on the battle. But he could not free his mind from the cowardly and personally malignant political forces behind him. To make sure of not running undue risks, he lost a day, and failed to win the battle.

It was not till the 17th that he attacked. By this time Jackson had arrived and was posted on Lee's left, and the rest of the Confederate divisions, having cleaned up Harpers Ferry, were striding along to the new encounter. Lee fought with his back to the Potomac, and could scarcely, if defeated, have escaped across its single bridge by Sharpsburg. This horrible battle was the acme of Federal mismanagement. McClellan, after riding down the line, fought it from his headquarters on what was called "the Commander-in-Chief idea." This meant that he made his dispositions and left the battle to fight itself. But Jackson stood in the line, and Lee rode his horse about the field controlling the storm, as Marlborough, Frederick the Great, and Napoleon were wont to do. The Confederate left, under Jackson, was practically destroyed, but only after ruining double their numbers, two whole corps of the Federal Army. All here came to a standstill, till Jackson was reinforced by Lee from his hard-pressed right and centre. The Union centre then attacked piecemeal, and their leading division was torn to pieces, half falling smitten. Burnside, who with the Union left was to cross the Antietam and cut Lee's line of retreat, would have succeeded but for the arrival of Lee's last division, under A. P. Hill, from Harpers Ferry. Striking the right flank of the assailants from an unexpected direction, he ended this menace; and night fell upon a drawn battle, in which the Federals had lost thirteen thousand men, a fourth of the troops they engaged and one-sixth of those they had on the field, and the Confederacy nine thousand, which was about a quarter.

When darkness fell Lee faced his great lieutenants. Without exception they advised immediate retreat across the Potomac. Even Jackson, unconquerable in action, thought this would be wise. But Lee, who still hoped to gain his indisputable, decisive battle, after hearing all opinions, declared his resolve to stand his ground. Therefore the shattered Confederates faced the morning light and the huge array of valiant soldiers who seemed about to overwhelm them. But McClellan had had enough. He lay still. Before the slightest reproach can fall on him the shabby War Department behind him must shoulder their share. There was no fighting on the 18th. Lee put it hard across Jackson to take the offensive; but when Jackson, after personal reconnaissance with the artillery commander, declared it impossible Lee accepted this sagacious judgment, and his first invasion of Maryland came to an end.

War had never reached such an intensity of moral and physical forces focused upon decisive points as in this campaign of 1862. The number of battles that were fought and their desperate, bloody character far surpassed any events in which Napoleon ever moved. From June 1, when Lee was given the command, the Army of Northern Virginia fought seven ferocious battles—the Seven Days, Cedar Run, the Second Manassas, South Mountain, Harpers Ferry, the Antietam, and later Fredericksburg—in as many months. Lee very rarely had three-quarters, and several times only half, the strength of his opponents. These brave Northerners were certainly hampered by a woeful political direction, but, on the other side, the Confederates were short of weapons, ammunition, food, equipment, clothes, and boots. It was even said that their line of march could be traced by the bloodstained footprints of unshod men. But the Army of Northern Virginia "carried the Confederacy on its bayonets" and made a struggle unsurpassed in history.

Lincoln had hoped for a signal victory. McClellan at the Antietam presented him with a partial though important success. But the President's faith in the Union cause was never dimmed by disappointments. He was much beset by anxieties, which led him to cross-examine his commanders as if he were still a prosecuting attorney. The Generals did not relish it. But Lincoln's popularity with the troops stood high. They put their trust in him. They could have no knowledge of the relentless political pressures in Washington to which he was subjected. They had a sense, however, of his natural resolution and generosity of character. He had to draw deeply on these qualities in his work at the White House. Through his office flowed a stream of politicians, newspaper editors, and other men of influence. Most of them clamoured for quick victory, with no conception of the hazards of war. Many of them cherished their own amateur plans of operation which they confidently urged upon their leader. Many of them too had favourite Generals for whom they canvassed. Lincoln treated all his visitors with patience and firmness. His homely humour stood him in good stead. A sense of irony helped to lighten his burdens. In tense moments a dry joke relieved his feelings. At the same time his spirit was sustained by a deepening belief in Providence. When the toll of war rose steeply and plans went wrong he appealed for strength in his inmost thoughts to a power higher than man's. Strength was certainly given him. It is sometimes necessary at the summit of authority to bear with the intrigues of disloyal colleagues, to remain calm when others panic, and to withstand misguided popular outcries. All this Lincoln did. Personal troubles also befell him. One of his beloved sons died in the White House. Mrs. Lincoln, though devoted to her husband, had a taste for extravagance and for politics which sometimes gave rise to wounding comment. As the war drew on Lincoln became more and more gaunt and the furrows on his cheeks and brow bit deep. Fortitude was written on his countenance.

The Antietam and the withdrawal of Lee into Virginia gave the President an opportunity to take a momentous step. He proclaimed the emancipation of all the slaves in the insurgent states. The impression produced in France and Britain by Lee's spirited and resolute operations, with their successive great battles, either victorious or drawn, made the Washington Cabinet fearful of mediation, to be followed, if rejected, by recognition of the Confederacy. The North was discouraged by disastrous and futile losses and by the sense of being outgeneralled. Recruitment fell off and desertion was rife. Many urged peace, and others asked whether the Union was worthy of this slaughter, if slavery was to be maintained. By casting down this final challenge and raising the war to the level of a moral crusade Lincoln hoped to rally British public opinion to the Union cause and raise a new enthusiasm among his own fellow-countrymen.

It was a move he had long considered. Ever since the beginning of the war the Radicals had been pressing for the total abolition of slavery. Lincoln had misgivings about the effects on the slave-owning states of the border which had remained loyal. He insisted that the sole object of the war was to preserve the Union. As he wrote to the New York publisher, Horace Greeley, "My paramount object is to save the Union, and is not either to save or to destroy slavery. . . . What I do about slavery and the coloured race, I do because it helps to save the Union; and what I forbear, I forbear because I do not believe it would help to save the Union." Meanwhile he was meditating on the timing of his Proclamation and on the constitutional difficulties that stood in the way. He believed he had no power to interfere with slavery in the border states. He felt his Proclamation could be legally justified only as a military measure, issued in virtue of his office as Commander-in-Chief of the Army and Navy. Its intention was to deprive the Confederacy of a source of its strength. When the Proclamation was published, with effect from January 1st, 1863, it therefore applied only to the rebel states. Slavery in the rest of the Union was not finally abolished until the passing of the Thirteenth Amendment in December 1865. In the South the Proclamation only came into force as the Federal armies advanced. Nor were the broader results all that Lincoln had hoped. In Britain it was not understood why he had not declared Abolition outright. A political manœuvre on his part was suspected. In America itself the war assumed an implacable character, offering to the South no alternative but subjugation. The Democratic Party in the North was wholly opposed to the Emancipation Edict. In the Federal armies it was unpopular, and General McClellan, who might be expected to become the Democratic candidate for the Presidency, had two months earlier sent Lincoln a solemn warning against such an action. At the Congressional elections in the autumn of 1862 the Republicans lost ground. Many Northerners thought that the President had gone too far, others that he had not gone far enough. Great, judicious, and well-considered steps are thus sometimes at first received with public incomprehension.

The relations between the Washington Government and its General remained deplorable. McClellan might fairly claim to have rendered them an immense service after the panic at Manassas. He had revived the Army, led it to the field, and cleared Maryland. For all the Government knew, he had saved the capital. In fact he had done more. Lord Palmerston in England had decided that summer on mediation. News of the Antietam made him hesitate. This averted the danger to the North that the Confederacy would be recognised by the Powers of Europe. But it was not immediately apparent in the Union. Gladstone, Chancellor of the Exchequer in Palmerston's Government, delivered a speech at Newcastle in the autumn which enraged Northern opinion. He said: "We know quite well that the people of the Northern states have not yet drunk of the cup—they are still trying to hold it far from their lips—which all the rest of the world see they nevertheless must drink of. We may have our own opinions about slavery, we may be for or against the South, but there is no doubt that Jefferson Davis and other leaders of the South have made an Army; they are making, it appears, a Navy; and they have made what is more than either, they have made a Nation." Gladstone had not been informed that Palmerston had changed his mind.

Meanwhile between the politicians and the Commander-in-Chief upon the Potomac there was hatred and scorn on both sides. Bitter party politics aggravated military divergence. The President desired a prompt and vigorous advance. McClellan, as usual, magnified Confederate numbers and underrated their grievous losses. He was determined to run no unmilitary risks for a Government which he knew was eager to stab him in the back. Five weeks passed after the battle before he began to cross the Potomac in leisurely fashion and move forward from Harpers Ferry to Warrenton.

Lee withdrew by easy marches up the Shenandoah valley. He had sent "Jeb" Stuart on his second romantic ride round McClellan in mid-October, had harried the Federal communications and acquired much valuable information. He now did not hesitate to divide his army in the face of McClellan's great hosts. He left Jackson in the valley to keep Washington on tenterhooks, and rested himself with Longstreet, near Culpeper Court House. If pressed he could fall back to Gordonsville, where he judged Jackson could join him in time. McClellan, however, had now at length prepared his blow. He planned to strike Lee with overwhelming strength before Jackson could return. At this moment he was himself taken in rear by President Lincoln. On the night of November 7, 1862, he was ordered to hand over his command to General Burnside, and at the same time Porter, his most competent subordinate, was placed under arrest. The Government had used these men in their desperation. They now felt strong enough to strike them down. McClellan was against the abolition of slavery, and he never changed his view. The dominant Radical wing of the Republican Party was out for his blood. They were convinced that McClellan would never set himself to gain a crushing victory. They suspected him of tender feelings for the South and a desire for a negotiated peace. They also feared that the General would prove to be a potent Democratic candidate for the Presidency. Lincoln allowed himself to be persuaded by the Radical Republicans that McClellan had become a liability to his Government. He had long stood up for his commander against the attacks and whisperings of the politicians. Now he felt he must give way. But it was without animosity, for that viper was never harboured in Lincoln's breast.

There was almost a mutiny in the Union Army when McClellan's dismissal was known. He himself acted with perfect propriety, and used all his influence to place his successor in the saddle. He was never employed again. Thus the General who, as Lee after the war told his youngest son, was by far the best of his opponents disappeared from command. No one can be blind to McClellan's limitations, but he was learning continually from his collisions with Lee and Jackson. His removal was a wrong done to the Union Army, which never gave its love to any other leader. There remained for McClellan a vivid political struggle where numbers, which alone count in such affairs, were found upon the other side. General Porter, although he had rendered good service in the intervening Maryland campaign, was tried by court-martial for his conduct at the Second Manassas, condemned, and dismissed the United States Army. This injustice was repaired after the lapse of years. A re-trial was ordered and he received honourable acquittal.

We have seen several times in this obstinate war President Lincoln pressing for battle and for frontal attack. "On to Richmond" was his mood; and now at last in Burnside he had found a General who would butt straight at the barrier. Burnside, a charming personality, but a thoroughly bad General, was, to his honour, most reluctant to take command. Once in charge he followed a simple plan. He chose the shortest road which led on the map to Richmond, and concentrated his army along it upon the crossing of the Rappahannock at Fredericksburg.

He took a fortnight in order to do this as well as possible. Meanwhile Lee brought in Jackson and other reinforcements. Hitherto Lee had always fought in the open field; even against the heavy odds of the Antietam he had not used the spade. He now applied the fortnight accorded him to fortify his position above Fredericksburg with every then-known device. Breastworks revetted with logs and stone walls covered by solid earth were prepared. Nearly a hundred and fifty cannon were comfortably sited. Rifle-pits abounded, and good lateral roads were cut through the scrubby forest behind the line. On December 11 Burnside occupied Fredericksburg, crossed the river with a large part of his army, and deployed for battle. He had a hundred and eighteen thousand men, against Lee's eighty thousand. On the 13th he delivered his assault. He attacked both the Confederate left wing and its right piecemeal. Then he attacked in the centre. The Northern soldiers showed an intense devotion. Brigade after brigade, division after division, they charged up the slopes under a murderous fire. As evening fell the Union army recoiled with a loss of nearly thirteen thousand men. The Confederate casualties, mostly in Jackson's command, were under six thousand. Burnside, who now thought chiefly of dying at the head of his troops, wished to renew the battle next day. He was restrained by universal opinion at the front and at the capital; and soon after was superseded in chief command by one of his lieutenants, General Joseph Hooker.

Lee had not wished to fight at Fredericksburg at all. The Federal Army was so near its salt-water base at Aquia Creek that no counter-stroke was possible. He had advised President Davis to let him meet Burnside thirty miles back on the North Anna River, where there was room for him to use Jackson and Stuart in terrible revenge upon the communications of a repulsed army. But although Davis's relations with the Confederate Generals were on a high plane he had hampered his champion most sadly, cramping him down to a strict defensive, and thus the shattering blow of Fredericksburg had no lasting consequences. If these two Presidents had let McClellan and Lee fight the quarrel out between them as they thought best the end would have been the same, but the war would have been less muddled, much shorter, and less bloody.

In the West nothing decisive had happened up till the end of 1862. By November General Joseph E. Johnston, having recovered from the wounds he got at Seven Pines, was appointed to the chief Confederate command in this theatre, but with only a partial authority over its various armies. In Tennessee General Bragg, with forty-four thousand men in the neighbourhood of Murfreesboro, faced the Federal General William S. Rosecrans, who had forty-seven thousand. General J. C. Pemberton, who commanded the department of the Mississippi, had a field army of about thirty thousand men, apart from the garrisons of Vicksburg and Port Hudson. Lastly, still farther west, in Arkansas, the Confederate General Holmes was encamped near Little Rock with an army raised in that state of fifty thousand men, against whom there were now no active Federal forces. When it was evident that Grant was preparing for the invasion of Mississippi and an attack upon Vicksburg Johnston urged that the Arkansas army should cross the Mississippi and join Pemberton. This would have secured a Confederate superiority. Jefferson Davis vetoed this desirable, and indeed imperative, measure. He knew the violent hostility which an order to the Arkansas forces to serve east of the Mississippi would excite throughout the Western states. No doubt this objection was substantial; but the alternative was disastrous. The President insisted instead that Bragg should send ten thousand men from Chattanooga to strengthen Pemberton in defending Vicksburg. This was accordingly done.

Early in December Grant made a renewed attempt against Vicksburg, sending General Sherman from Memphis, with about thirty thousand men, and Admiral Porter's Naval Squadron, to enter the Yazoo River and occupy the heights to the north of the city. Sherman assaulted the Confederate defences at Chickasaw Bluff on December 29, and in less than an hour was repulsed with the loss of nearly two thousand men, the Confederates losing only a hundred and fifty. He consoled himself with ascending the Arkansas River and capturing a garrison of five thousand Confederates at Arkansas Post. Meanwhile the weakening of Bragg's army in Tennessee brought about, on the last day of the year, a severe battle at Murfreesboro, in which the greatest bravery was displayed by both sides. The Federals, under Rosecrans, lost over nine thousand killed and wounded, as well as nearly four thousand prisoners and twenty-eight guns. But for this Bragg paid over ten thousand men. The Federal hold on Tennessee and its capital Nashville was unshaken. Bragg withdrew his disappointed troops into winter quarters covering Chattanooga.

The armies in the different states still confronted each other on fairly equal terms, and although the Union Navy declared its ability to run the gauntlet of the Confederate batteries when required the great riverway remained barred to Federal transports and traffic. Murfreesboro gave the impression of a drawn battle, and Chickasaw Bluff was an undoubted Confederate success. But now there was to be a profound change in the balance.

CHAPTER 18

CHANCELLORSVILLE AND GETTYSBURG

THE SPRING OF 1863 found the Army of the Potomac and the Army of Northern Virginia still facing each other across the Rappahannock. Hooker, "Fighting Joe," had distinguished himself as a corps commander at the Antietam. He was not the next senior and had intrigued against his chief. He owed his present advancement to Lincoln, who knew him to be a good fighter and hoped the best of him as a commander. The obvious course, to restore McClellan again, was politically impossible and would have weakened the President's authority. At the end of January, when he was appointed, Hooker found the Federal Army in a sorry plight, which his own previous discontent had fomented. More than three thousand officers and eighty thousand men were either deserters or absent with or without leave. Blows like Fredericksburg are hard to sustain. It was not till April that reorganisation was complete; reinforcements had poured in, and the absentees had returned from their Christmas at home. He was now at the head of over a hundred and thirty thousand men, rested and revived, splendidly equipped, and organised in six army corps. He formed besides a cavalry corps ten thousand strong, and he felt himself able to declare that he led "the finest army on the planet."

In meeting the offensive, which he knew must come, Lee was gravely hampered by President Davis's policy of the strict defensive and the dispersal of the Confederate troops to cover a number of places. The continued pressure of the war rendered the defence of the ports of Wilmington and Charleston in South Carolina of vital importance, though only blockade-runners could enter them. They and the railways connecting them with Richmond were threatened in the President's eyes by the somewhat near presence of Federal forces which had been landed in March 1862 at New Bern, in North Carolina, and others which had advanced to Suffolk in the estuary of the James River and only seventy-five miles from Richmond. These parties, owing to the nature of the ground near the coast, had been dealt with by local forces. But Lee, also bearing in mind the difficulty of feeding his troops near the Rappahannock, sent first one, then a second and a third detachment, under Longstreet, to deal with them. It was one of Lee's mistakes. Longstreet, who was always striving for an independent command, unnecessarily sat down to besiege Suffolk. Thus Lee's nine divisions were reduced by three, and two of his four cavalry brigades were south of the James to gather forage. His infantry was less than half and his cavalry a quarter of the forces he had to encounter. He therefore abandoned the idea of an offensive into Pennsylvania by way of the Shenandoah valley, which he had had in mind, and awaited events.

Hooker's preponderance enabled him to act with two armies. His plan was, first, a fortnight in advance of the main move, to send his cavalry round Lee's left by the upper fords of the Rappahannock; then to turn Lee's left with three corps, while the two others, under General John Sedgwick, crossed the river below Lee's right at Fredericksburg. Even then he had another corps in reserve. He expected that Lee would be forced to abandon his lines and retreat, in which case he meant to follow him up by the direct road to Richmond. In the middle of April these movements began. The Federal cavalry corps, under a second-rate commander, General George Stoneman, was delayed by floods, and only crossed the Upper Rappahannock simultaneously with the right column of the main army.

At first all went well with Hooker. His three army corps, about seventy thousand strong, crossed the Rappahannock, and, on the morning of April 30, its tributary the Rapidan. As they marched eastward they took in flank and rear the fortified line which Lee had formed. The Confederates guarding United States Ford on the Rappahannock had to retire, and the reserve Federal corps passed over unmolested. By the night of the 30th a Federal army of ninety thousand men was concentrated at or near Chancellorsville behind all these defences. The Federal cavalry, in enormous, though not as it proved overwhelming strength, were already moving towards the Virginia Central Railway, forty-five miles in rear of Lee's army, and one of his main lines of supply, which it was their mission not only to cut but to destroy. At the same time General Sedgwick, commanding the two corps opposite Fredericksburg, crossed the river and deployed to attack Jackson's three divisions under General Jubal A. Early, which held the old trenches of the former battle.

Lee was thus taken in pincers by two armies, each capable of fighting a major battle with him, while at the same time his rear was ravaged and his communications assailed. The advance of either Federal Army would render his position untenable, and their junction or simultaneous action in a single battle must destroy him. Nothing more hopeless on the map than his position on the night of the 30th can be imagined, and it is this which raises the event which followed from a military to an historic level.

The great commander and his trusty lieutenant remained crouched but confident amid this tremendous encirclement. Beset upon both flanks by hostile armies which were for the moment disconnected, and unable to retreat without yielding vital positions, Lee naturally sought to hold off one assailant while striking at the other. Which to choose? Jackson was for falling upon Sedgwick and driving him into the river; but Lee knew that nothing less than the defeat of the main Union army would save him. Hooker had taken command in person of this mighty array, and Lee, as soon as he learned where he was, left only a division to delay Sedgwick and marched at once to attack him. Meanwhile "Jeb" Stuart manœuvred against Stoneman's cavalry over a wide front to such good purpose that though he was outnumbered by four to one he was able to render perfect service to Lee, while the Federal cavalry General, Stoneman, played no part in the battle.

Chancellorsville stands on the edge of a wild region of forest and tangled scrub which still deserves the name of Wilderness. Roads or paths cut through this alone rendered movement possible. On May 1 Hooker, having brought up all his troops, ordered a general advance eastward along the Turnpike and the Plank road. His numerous cavalry were breaking up the Virginia Central Railway at Louisa Court House, thirty miles to the southward. He had three balloons and numerous signal stations, and even a field electric telegraph for communication with Sedgwick. But the mist of the morning lay in fog-banks over the valley of the Rappahannock. The balloons and signal stations could see nothing, and the electric telegraph broke down. As he advanced into the Wilderness he met large enemy forces, who began at once to attack him. These were Stonewall Jackson's corps, handled with its general's usual vigour. Now "Fighting Joe," so famous as a subordinate, bent under the strain of supreme command. He had expected that his well-executed strategy would compel Lee to retreat. He now conceived himself about to be attacked by the whole Confederate Army. He turned at once and fell back upon the entrenched line he had already prudently prepared before Chancellorsville. It was late in the afternoon of the 1st when the advancing Confederates, emerging from the woodland, came within sight of this formidable position with its masses of troops. All the time Sedgwick, at Fredericksburg, receiving no orders by the electric telegraph, and, baffled by Early's brave show on the fatal heights, already dyed with Union blood, although he heard the firing, made no effort. How did he know that Longstreet might not have arrived, as would indeed have been only proper? Thus the night set in.

Lee and Jackson sat together, and knew that they had one day before them. Unless they could beat Hooker at odds of two to one during May 2 they would be attacked front and rear by overwhelming forces. Frontal attack was impossible. Their only chance was to divide their small army and swing round Hooker's right. Search had been made for a road or track for such a movement; and in the small hours one of Jackson's staff officers reported that there was a private road used for hauling wood and ore to a furnace which would serve. Jackson at once proposed to lead his whole corps along it, and Lee after a moment's reflection assented. This meant that Jackson with twenty-six thousand men would march round Hooker's right to attack him, while Lee faced nearly eighty thousand Federals with seventeen thousand.

At 4 A.M. Jackson was on the march. It seemed vital that his movement should be unperceived, but an unexpected gap in the forest revealed about eight o'clock to the Federal troops at Hazel Grove a long column moving towards the right of their wide front. This exposure actually helped the Confederate manœuvre. Two divisions of General Daniel E. Sickles's corps advanced after some delay to strike at these processionists and find out their purpose. They came into contact with Jackson's rearguard, who fought stubbornly, and then vanished in the woods. The two divisions, now joined by Sickles himself, feeling they had a retreating enemy before them, pushed on hopefully, and Sickles thought he had cut the Confederate Army in twain. This was indeed true. Lee and Jackson were now separated, and only victory could reunite them. Had Hooker set his army in motion against Lee he must have driven Lee ever farther from Jackson and ever nearer to Sedgwick, who had now at length forced the heights of Fredericksburg, and, little more than eight miles away, was, with thirty thousand men, driving Early back upon Lee's rear. But Hooker, convinced that he was safe within his fortifications and that his strategy was successful, made no move, while the hours slipped away. It was six o'clock in the evening before Jackson reached the end of his march. He had not only turned

Hooker's flank, but was actually in rear of his right-hand corps. He deployed into line, facing Lee about four miles away on the other side of the Federal Army. The surprise was complete. The soldiers of the Eleventh Federal Corps were eating their supper and playing cards behind their defences when suddenly there burst from the forest at their backs the Confederate line of battle. In one hour the Eleventh Corps, attacked by superior forces in this battle, although as a whole their army was two to one, was dashed into rout and ruin.

Night was falling, but Jackson saw supreme opportunity before him. He was within half a mile of the road leading to United States Ford, the sole line of retreat for Hooker's whole army, and between him and this deadly thrust no organised force intervened. He selected the point which he must gain by night and hold to the death at dawn. The prize was nothing less than the destruction of the main Federal Army. They must either overwhelm him the next day or starve between the Wilderness and his cannon. All this he saw. He rode forward with a handful of officers along the Plank road to the skirmish line to see what he could of the ground. He had often risked his life in this way, and now the forfeit was claimed. As he returned, his own men, Carolinians proud to die at his command, mistaking in the darkness the small party for hostile cavalry, fired a volley. Three bullets pierced the General's left arm and shoulder. He fell from his horse, and when, after an agonising passage, he reached the field hospital he was too much weakened by loss of blood to concentrate his mind. His staff officer, who was to lead A. P. Hill's division to the vital point, had been killed by the same volley. Hill, on whom the command devolved, hastening forward after vainly questioning his swooning chief, was almost immediately himself wounded. It was some hours before Stuart, from the cavalry, could be brought to the scene. No one knew Jackson's plan, and he was now unconscious. Thus on small agate points do the balances of the world turn.

Stuart fought a fine battle during the night, and on May 3, with wild shouts of "Remember Jackson!" the infuriated Confederates assaulted the Federal line. They drove it back. They captured Hazel Grove. They joined hands again with Lee. But the chance of the night was gone for ever. Hooker now had masses of men covering his line of retreat. He now thought of nothing but retreat. He did not even keep Lee occupied upon his front. He was morally beaten on the 2nd, and during the battle of the 3rd a solid shot hitting the pillar of a house by which he stood stunned him, which was perhaps a merciful stroke.

Lee now turned on Sedgwick, whose position south of the river was one of great peril. He had fought hard during the whole of the 3rd, and found himself on the 4th with the river at his back and only twenty thousand effective men, attacked by Lee, with at least twenty-five thousand. But the Confederate soldiers were exhausted by their superhuman exertions. Sedgwick, though beaten and mauled, managed to escape by his pontoons at Fredericksburg. Here he was soon joined by the Commander-in-Chief and the rest of the magnificent army which nine days before had seemed to have certain success in their path, but now stood baffled and humbled at their starting-point. They were still twice as numerous as their opponents. They had lost 17,000 men out of 130,000 and the Confederates 12,500 out of 60,000.

Chancellorsville was the finest battle which Lee and Jackson fought together. Their combination had become perfect. "Such an executive officer," said Lee, "the sun never shone on. Straight as the needle to the pole, he advances to the execution of my purpose." "I would follow General Lee blindfold" is a remark attributed to Jackson. Now all was over. "Could I have directed events," wrote Lee, ascribing the glory to his stricken comrade, "I should have chosen for the good of the country to be disabled in your stead." Jackson lingered for a week. His arm was amputated. Pneumonia supervened. On the 10th he was told to prepare for death, to which he consented with surprise and fortitude. "Very good, very good; it is all right." Finally, after some hours, quietly and clearly: "Let us cross over the river and rest under the shade of the trees." His loss was a mortal blow to Lee and to the cause of the South.

Nevertheless in these months the scales of war seemed to turn against the Union. A wave of discouragement swept across the North. Desertion was rife in the Federal ranks. Conscription, called "the draft," was violently resisted in many states. Many troops had to be withdrawn from the front to enforce the law. Many hundreds of lives were lost in New York City in the draft riots. Clement L. Vallandigham, the leader of the peace party, or "Copperheads" as they were called, after a particularly poisonous snake, declared in Congress, "You have not conquered the South; you never will. Money you have expended without limit, blood poured out like water. . . . Defeat, death, taxation, and sepulchres . . . these are your only trophies." The legislatures of Indiana and Illinois threatened to acknowledge the Confederacy. "Everybody feels," wrote Medill, the editor of the *Chicago Tribune,* and a close friend of the President's, "that the war is drawing to a disastrous and disgraceful termination. Money cannot be supplied much longer to a beaten democracy and homesick army." It was indeed the darkest hour. But the heart of Lincoln did not fail him.

Problems on the seas and across the ocean also perplexed and agitated the North. The small Confederate Navy was active and successful in the Gulf of Mexico and on the Atlantic coast. On the high seas Confederate commerce-raiders, built in Britain, were taking a heavy toll of Northern shipping. The most famous of them, the *Alabama,* had stolen out of the River Mersey in June 1862. She sailed under a false name, and in spite of the protests of the American Minister in London. After a glorious career, lasting two years, she was brought to bay by a Federal cruiser in the English Channel. A gallant engagement was fought off Cherbourg. It was witnessed by a number of French artists, one of whom, Manet, has left a remarkable painting of the scene. The *Alabama* was outgunned and sunk. The Federal Government pressed Britain hard for compensation for the damage done by the Southern raiders. Negotiations were long and disputatious. They were not concluded until six years after the end of the war, when Gladstone's Government agreed to pay the United States fifteen million dollars.

Throughout the spring and summer of 1863 anxiety grew in Washington because of the building in the British yard which had launched the *Alabama* of two new ironclad Confederate warships. They were fitted with nine-inch rifled guns and formidable underwater rams, thus combining the offensive merits of the *Merrimac* and the *Monitor.* These ships were known as the Laird rams, after their builders. The American Minister bombarded the Foreign Secretary, Lord John Russell, with demands that the Laird rams must not be allowed to escape as the *Alabama* had done. Russell eventually realised that the construction of such vessels by a neutral would set a bad precedent which might work to Britain's disadvantage in future wars. In September he ordered their seizure. Thus was closed the last of the war-time diplomatic crises between Britain and the Union.

The initiative in the field now passed to Lee, who resolved to carry out his long-planned invasion of Pennsylvania. But Vicksburg, on the Mississippi, was in dire straits, and unless Joseph E. Johnston could be largely reinforced its fall was imminent. A proposal was made to stand on the defensive in Virginia, to send Lee himself with Longstreet's two divisions to the Mississippi, and other troops to Middle Tennessee to defeat the covering forces under Rosecrans south of Nashville and threaten the commercial cities of Louisville and Cincinnati, perhaps forcing Grant to abandon his campaign against Vicksburg. Lee refused point-blank to go. Squarely he put the issue before the Council of War: the risk had to be taken of losing Mississippi or Virginia. His view prevailed, and on May 26, three weeks after Chancellorsville, the invasion of Pennsylvania was sanctioned. The Army of Northern Virginia was reorganised in three corps of three divisions each, commanded by Longstreet, Richard S. Ewell, and A. P. Hill. Lee's object in 1863, as in the previous year, was to force the Army of the Potomac to fight under conditions in which defeat would spell annihilation. In this he saw the sole hope of winning Southern independence.

The movement commenced on June 3. Longstreet concentrated his corps at Culpeper, and behind it the other two corps passed into the Shenandoah valley, marching straight for the Potomac. Longstreet meanwhile moved up on the east of the Blue Ridge with his front and flank screened by Stuart's cavalry, eventually entering the valley behind the other two corps through the northern "Gaps." On the 9th, before the movement was well under way, there was an indecisive cavalry battle at Brandy Station, in which the Federal cavalry, under their new commander, Alfred Pleasanton, regained their morale.

At first the campaign went well for Lee. Ewell on the 10th left Culpeper for the valley, and, marching with a speed worthy of "Stonewall" Jackson, cleared the Federal garrisons out of Winchester and Martinsburg, capturing four thousand prisoners and twenty-eight guns, and on the 15th was crossing the Potomac. He established his corps at Hagerstown, where it waited for a week, till the corps in the rear was ready to cross, and his cavalry brigade pushed on to Chambersburg, in Pennsylvania, to collect and send back supplies. On the 22nd he was ordered to advance farther into Pennsylvania and capture Harrisburg, a hundred miles north of Washington, if it "came within his means."

On the 27th Ewell reached Carlisle, and his outposts next day were within four miles of Harrisburg. The other two Confederate corps were at Chambersburg. As far as Chambersburg Lee had been following the Cumberland valley, with his right flank shielded by the South Mountain range, and as yet he knew nothing of Hooker's movements. He accepted Stuart's plan of making a raid through the mountains and joining Ewell in Pennsylvania. Stuart, who started on the 25th, believed that Hooker was still in his encampments on the east side of the mountains, and expected to be able to ride through his camp areas and cross the Potomac near Leesburg. But Hooker had broken up his camps and was marching that same morning for the Potomac. Stuart had to make a third ride round the Federal rear, crossed the Potomac within twenty miles of Washington, failed to make contact with Ewell's right division, and only rejoined Lee with his men and horses utterly exhausted on the afternoon of July 2. Thus for a whole week Lee had been deprived of the "eyes" of his army; and much had happened meanwhile.

As soon as Lee began his movement to the north Hooker proposed to march on Richmond. But Lincoln forbade him, and rightly pointed out that not Richmond but Lee's army was his proper objective. In thus deciding the President did what Lee had expected. After crossing the Potomac Hooker made his headquarters near Frederick, where he covered Washington and threatened Lee's line of communications. Halleck and Stanton had agreed after Chancellorsville that Hooker must not be in command of the army in the next battle. When therefore the General, denied the use of the Harpers Ferry garrison, tendered his resignation it was promptly accepted. Early in the morning of June 28 General George G. Meade, commander of the Fifth Corps, who was now appointed to the chief command, decided to move his whole army by forced marches northwards to the Susquehanna to prevent Lee from crossing that river, and at the same time to cover Baltimore and Washington. Meade was a safe, dogged commander, with no political affiliations. He could be relied upon to avoid acts of folly, and also anything brilliant. Expecting that Lee would come south from the Susquehanna to attack Baltimore, he now prepared to meet him on the line of Pipe Creek, ten miles beyond Westminster.

Lee had been greatly perplexed by Stuart's failure to report, but, having implicit confidence in him, had concluded that Hooker must still be south of the Potomac. On learning the truth during the 28th he ordered a concentration at Cashtown, close to the eastern foot of South Mountain. He did not hurry, and "the march was conducted with a view to the comfort of the troops." At the outset of the campaign he had been in agreement with Longstreet that the strategy should be offensive and the tactics defensive, and he had no intention of fighting a battle except under favourable conditions. But chance ruled otherwise.

On June 30 a brigade of Hill's corps advanced eight miles from Cashtown to Gettysburg, partly to look for shoes, partly to reconnoitre a place through which Ewell's corps might be moving next day. Gettysburg was found in the hands of some Federal cavalry, which had just entered. The Confederate brigade thereupon turned back without ascertaining the strength of the hostile force. Buford, the Federal cavalry commander, who bore the Christian names of Napoleon B., seems to have been the first man in either army to appreciate the strategical importance of Gettysburg, the meeting-place of some dozen roads from all points of the compass. He moved his division to the west of the town, where he found a strong position behind a stream, and called upon the commander of the First Corps to come to his aid with all speed. The First Corps was followed by the Eleventh Corps.

On July 1 severe fighting began with the leading Confederate troops, and presently Ewell, coming down from the north-east, struck in upon the Federal flank, driving the Eleventh Corps through Gettysburg to seek shelter on higher ground three miles southwards, well named Cemetery Ridge. On this first day of battle fifty thousand men had been engaged, and four Confederate divisions had defeated and seriously injured two Federal corps. It now became a race between Lee and Meade, who could concentrate his forces first. Neither Lee nor Meade wished to fight decisively at this moment or on this ground; but they were both drawn into the greatest and bloodiest battle of the Civil War. Lee could not extricate himself and his supply trains without fighting Meade's army to a standstill, and Meade was equally committed to a field he thought ill-chosen.

Lee wished to open the second day of the battle with an attack by Ewell and Hill on Cemetery Ridge, which he rightly regarded as the key to the Federal position. He was deterred by their objections. Longstreet, when he arrived, argued at length for a manœuvre round Meade's left to place Lee's army between Meade and Washington. Such a movement in the absence of Stuart's cavalry would certainly have been reckless, and it is not easy to see how Lee could have provisioned his army in such a position. Finally Lee formally ordered Longstreet to attack the Federal left at dawn. Longstreet, who entirely disapproved of the rôle assigned to him, did not come into action till four in the afternoon. While he waited for an additional brigade two corps joined the Union Army. Lee, who imagined that the Federal left rested upon the Emmetsburg road, expected that Longstreet's advance up this road would roll up the Federal line from left to right. But at this point the Federal corps commander, Sickles, had taken up an advanced position on his own authority, and his flank was not the end of the Federal line. When this was discovered Longstreet obstinately refused to depart from the strict letter of his orders, though he knew that Lee was not aware of the true position. All that he achieved after several hours' fierce fighting was to force Sickles back to Meade's main line. On this day the greater part of Hill's corps took no part in the battle. Ewell, who was to have attacked the north end of the ridge as soon as he heard Longstreet's guns, did not get into action till 6 P.M. There were no signs of any co-ordination of attacks on the Confederate side on July 2. Although Lee had failed to make his will prevail, and the Confederate attacks had been unconnected, the losses of the Federal Army were terrible, and Meade at the Council of War that night was narrowly dissuaded from ordering a general retreat.

The third day began. Lee still bid high for victory. He resolved to launch fifteen thousand men, sustained by the fire of a hundred and

THE
GETTYSBURG
CAMPAIGN

PENNSYLVANIA

Harrisburg
Carlisle
Chambersburg
Cashtown
Gettysburg

Susquehanna R.

N

WEST
VIRGINIA

Hagerstown
Westminster
Sharpsburg
Martinsburg
Frederick
Harpers
Ferry
Baltimore

MARYLAND

Winchester

B L U E   R I D G E   M T S.

Leesburg
Potomac R.

Shenandoah R.

Washington

Manassas Junction
Alexandria

V I R G I N I A

Brandy Station
Aquia
Creek

Rapidan R.
Fredericksburg
Spotsylvania
Rappahannock R.

Gordonsville

Kms.
0   30
Miles
0   30

© A. Karl/J. Kemp, 1999

twenty-five guns, against Meade's left centre, at the point where one of Hill's brigades had pierced the day before. Ewell's corps would at the same time attack from the north, and if the assault under General George E. Pickett broke the Federal line the whole Confederate Army would fall on. Again the attack was ordered for the earliest possible hour. It was the Federals, however, who opened the third day by recapturing in the grey of the dawn some of the trenches vacated the previous evening, and after hard fighting drove the Confederates before noon entirely off Culp's Hill. Exhausted by this, Ewell made no further movement. Longstreet was still arguing vehemently in favour of a wide turning movement round Meade's left. The heavy losses which his corps had suffered on the 2nd made this more difficult than ever.

The morning passed in utter silence. It was not till one in the afternoon that the Confederates began the heaviest bombardment yet known. Longstreet, unable to rally himself to a plan he deemed disastrous, left it to the artillery commander, Alexander, to give the signal to Pickett. At half-past two the Confederate ammunition, dragged all the way from Richmond in tented wagons, was running short. "Come immediately," Alexander said to Pickett, "or I cannot give you proper support." "General," said Pickett to Longstreet, who stood sombre and mute, "shall I advance?" By an intense effort Longstreet bowed his head in assent. Pickett saluted and set forty-two battalions against the Union centre. We see to-day, upon this battlefield so piously preserved by North and South, and where many of the guns still stand in their firing stations, the bare, slight slopes up which this grand infantry charge was made. In splendid array, all their battle flags flying, the forlorn assault marched on. But, like the Old Guard on the evening of Waterloo, they faced odds and metal beyond the virtue of mortals. The Federal rifled artillery paused till they were within seven hundred yards; then they opened again with a roar and cut lanes in the steadfastly advancing ranks. On they went, without flinching or disorder; then the deadly sound, like tearing paper, as Lee once described it, rose under and presently above the cannonade. But Pickett's division still drove forward, and at trench, stone wall, or rail fence closed with far larger numbers of men, who if not so lively as themselves, were at least ready to die for their cause. All three brigadiers in Pickett's division fell killed or mortally wounded. General L. A. Armistead with a few hundred men actually entered the Union centre, and the spot where he died with his hand on a captured cannon is to-day revered by the manhood of the United States.

But where were the reserves to carry through this superb effort? Where were the simultaneous attacks to grip and rock the entire front?

Lee at Gettysburg no more than Napoleon at Waterloo could win dominance. The victorious stormers were killed or captured; the rest walked home across the corpses which encumbered the plain amid a remorseless artillery fire. Less than a third came back. Lee met them on his horse Traveller with the only explanation, which they would not accept, "It is all my fault." Longstreet, in memoirs written long afterwards, has left on record a sentence which is his best defence: "As I rode back to the line of batteries, expecting an immediate counter-stroke, the shot and shell ploughed the ground around my horse, and an involuntary appeal went up that one of them would remove me from scenes of such awful responsibility."

But there was no counter-stroke. The Battle of Gettysburg was at an end. Twenty-three thousand Federals and over twenty thousand Confederates had been smitten by lead or steel. As after the Antietam, Lee confronted his foe on the morrow and offered to fight again. But no one knew better that it was decisive. With every personal resource he gathered up his army. An immense wagon train of wounded were jolted, springless, over sixteen miles of crumpled road. "Carry me back to old Virginia." "For God's sake kill me." On the night of the 4th Lee began his retreat. Meade let him go. The energy for pursuit had been expended in the battle. The Potomac was found in flood; Lee's pontoon bridge had been partially destroyed by a raid from Frederick City. For a week the Confederates stood at bay behind entrenchments with their backs to an unfordable river. Longstreet would have stayed to court attack; but Lee measured the event. Meade did not appear till the 12th, and his attack was planned for the 14th. When that morning came, Lee, after a cruel night march, was safe on the other side of the river. He carried with him his wounded and his prisoners. He had lost only two guns, and the war.

The Washington Government were extremely discontented with Meade's inactivity; and not without reason. Napoleon might have made Lee's final attack, but he certainly would not have made Meade's impotent pursuit. Lincoln promoted Meade only to the rank of Major-General for his good service at Gettysburg. Lee wended his way back by the Shenandoah valley to his old stations behind the Rappahannock and the Rapidan. The South had shot its bolt.

Up to a certain point the Gettysburg campaign was admirably conducted by Lee, and some of its objects were achieved; but the defeat with which it ended far more than counterbalanced these. The irreparable loss of twenty-eight thousand men in the whole operation out of an army of seventy-five thousand forbade any further attempts to win Southern independence by a victory on Northern soil. Lee believed that his own army was invincible, and after Chancellorsville he had begun to regard the Army of the Potomac almost with contempt. He failed to distinguish between bad troops and good troops badly led. It was not the army but its commander that had been beaten on the Rappahannock. It may well be that had Hooker been allowed to retain his command Lee might have defeated him a second time. Fortune, which had befriended him at Chancellorsville, now turned against him. Stuart's long absence left him blind as to the enemy's movements at the most critical stage of the campaign, and it was during his absence that he made the fatal mistake of moving to the east side of the mountains. Lee's military genius did not shine. He was disconcerted by Stuart's silence, he was "off his balance," and his subordinates became conscious of this mood. Above all he had not Jackson at his side. Longstreet's recalcitrance had ruined all chance of success at Gettysburg. On Longstreet the South laid the heavy blame.

There was no other battle in the East in 1863, and the armies were left for the winter facing each other on the Rapidan.

We must now turn to the West, where great battles were fought, and many fell. But since a decisive victory by Lee's army would have enabled him to march where he pleased, and to hold New York and every great city of the Atlantic coast to ransom or surrender, this secondary though spacious theatre need not be precisely lighted. From the West, it is true, the eventual thrust came which split and devastated the South. But its importance in 1862 and 1863 lay chiefly in the advance of Grant to the supreme unified command of the Union armies. The objective was the clearance or barrage of the Mississippi. In April 1862 Admiral Farragut, a Southerner, who adhered to the Union, had become prominent at the head of the Federal Navy. In April, with a fleet of all kinds of vessels, partly armoured or naked, he had run past the forts guarding the approaches to New Orleans, the largest city and the commercial capital of the Confederacy, which fell next day. He had then continued the ascent of the river, and reached Vicksburg on May 18. Finding no Federal troops at hand to support him, he retired to run the batteries again on June 25, and join hands with the Federal flotilla at Memphis. It was therefore known by the end of 1862 that the Confederate batteries could not stop the Union ships. As for the torpedoes, a new word, of which there was then much talk, Farragut was to say, "Damn the torpedoes!" and be justified. Thenceforward the Union flotillas could move up and down the great river, through its entire course, by paying a toll. This was a substantial aid to the Federal Army on either bank. Here in the Mississippi valley was almost a separate war. The Western states of the Confederacy claimed a great measure of autonomy from Jefferson Davis and his Government at Richmond, while clamouring for its help. At Washington the Western theatre was viewed in much the same way as was the Eastern front by the Allied and associated Powers in the First World War. It was secondary, but also indispensable. It was not the path to victory, but unless it was pursued victory would be long delayed.

After the failure of the river expedition in December 1862 Grant reassembled his army on the right bank of the Mississippi. Vicksburg was still his first aim, but the floods of the Yazoo basin prevented at this season all operations except by water. Having by numerous feints deceived the Confederate General, Pemberton, who with a field army was defending Vicksburg, Grant successfully ferried forty-five thousand men across the Mississippi below the Grand Gulf batteries thirty-six miles down-stream from Vicksburg. He surprised and drove back Pemberton's troops, and on May 3 established himself at Grand Gulf, in a safe position on the uplands, with his left flank protected by the wide Black River, and in touch with the Federal flotillas. Here he was joined four days later by his third corps, under Sherman. He now began a cautious movement towards Vicksburg and the railway which joined it to the town of Jackson. General Joseph E. Johnston, reinforced too late by President Davis, was hurried, ill though he was, to the scene. His only thought now was to extricate Pemberton's army. He ordered that General to march at once to join him before Grant could interpose his three corps between them. Pemberton resolved to disobey this order. He conceived that a movement across Grant's communications with Grand Gulf would compel a Federal retreat. He not only disobeyed, he miscalculated; for Grant, like McClellan before Richmond in 1862, with his command of the rivers, was not dependent upon any one particular base. Dropping his links with Grand Gulf, he pressed Johnston back with his right hand, and then turned on Pemberton in great superiority. After a considerable battle at Champion's Hill, in which over six thousand men fell, Pemberton was driven back into Vicksburg. With the aid of the flotilla the Union General opened a new base north of the city, and after two attempts to storm its defences, one of which cost him four thousand men, commenced a regular siege. Large reinforcements presently raised his army to over seventy thousand men. Johnston, with twenty-four thousand, could do nothing to relieve Pemberton. Vicksburg was starved into surrender, and its Confederate garrison and field army, more than thirty thousand strong, capitulated on July 4, at the very moment of Lee's defeat at Gettysburg. Five days later Port Hudson, in Louisiana, also reduced by famine, surrendered with seven thousand men to General Banks, and the whole course of the Mississippi was at last in Federal hands. "The Father of Waters," said Lincoln, "again goes unvexed to the sea." These were stunning blows to the South.

The main fury of the war was now transferred to the West. Until the fall of Vicksburg was certain the highly competent Rosecrans, with about sixty thousand men, forming the Union Army of the Cumberland, was content from the scene of his success at Murfreesboro to watch Bragg, who stood across the railway line between him and Chattanooga. This city and railway centre, protected by the deep and wide Tennessee River on the north and the high ridges of the Appalachian Mountains, a western chain of the Alleghenies, on the south, was the key not only to the mastery of the Mississippi valley, but to the invasion of prosperous, powerful, and hitherto inviolate Georgia. The waiting period was marked by fierce Confederate cavalry raids to break up the railways behind the Union army, and by Federal counter-strokes against important ironworks and munitions factories in the southern part of Tennessee. In these the Confederates had the advantage. But when Rosecrans, at the end of June, advanced along the railway to Chattanooga, and Burnside, with another army of forty thousand men, a hundred miles to the east, struck at Knoxville, great and far-reaching operations were afoot. Burnside captured Knoxville, cutting one of the sinew railways of the Confederacy. Rosecrans manœuvred Bragg out of all his defensive lines astride the Nashville–Chattanooga railway, and by September 4 gained Chattanooga without a battle.

Until this moment Rosecrans had shown high strategic skill. He now made the disastrous mistake of supposing that the resolute, agile army in his front was cowed. Bragg, who was one of the worst generals, hated by his lieutenants, and nearly always taking the wrong decision, was none the less a substantial fighter. South of Chattanooga the mountain ridges spread out like the fingers of a hand. Bragg lay quiet at Lafayette with an army now reinforced to sixty thousand men. By September 12 Rosecrans realised the appalling fact that his three corps were spread on a sixty-mile front, and that Bragg lay in their midst three times as strong as any one of them. Bragg, overbearing and ill-served, missed this opportunity, which Lee or Jackson would have made decisive for the whole of the West. Rosecrans recoiled, and concentrated towards

N

Nashville

T E N N E S S E E

Memphis Shiloh

Corinth

Arkansas R.

A R K A N S A S

Mississippi R.

Tennessee R.

Yazoo R.

Yazoo City

A L A B A M A

Vicksburg

Grand Gulf

L O U I S I A N A

M I S S I S S I P P I

Port Hudson

Mobile FLORIDA

Mississippi R.

New
Orleans

Gulf of Mexico

Kms.
0 ⸺ 100
0 ⸺
Miles

THE
MISSISSIPPI
THEATER
OF THE
CIVIL WAR

© A. Karl/J. Kemp, 1999

Chattanooga; but he was too late, even against Bragg, to escape a battle on ground and under conditions far from his choice.

At Chickamauga, across the border of Georgia, on September 18 Bragg fell upon his enemy. Longstreet, from Virginia, with two divisions and artillery, had reached him, together with other heavy reinforcements, so that he had the rare fortune for a Confederate General of the weight of numbers behind him. Seventy thousand Confederates attacked fifty-five thousand Federals. The two days' battle was fought with desperate valour on both sides. Bragg tried persistently to turn the Federal left and cut Rosecrans from Chattanooga, but when this wing of the Union Army, commanded by General George H. Thomas, had drawn to its aid troops from the centre and right, Longstreet, with twenty thousand Virginian veterans, assaulted the denuded parts of the Union front, and drove two-thirds of Rosecrans's army, with himself and the corps commanders, except Thomas, in ruin from the field. Longstreet begged Bragg to put all his spare weight behind a left-handed punch; but the Commander-in-Chief was set upon his first idea. He continued to butt into Thomas, who had built overnight breastworks of logs and railway iron in the woodland. Night closed upon a scene of carnage surpassed only by Gettysburg. Thomas, "the rock of Chickamauga," extricated himself and his corps and joined the rest of the Federal Army in Chattanooga.

The casualties in this battle were frightful. Sixteen thousand Federals and over twenty thousand Confederates were killed, wounded, or missing. The Confederates, who had captured forty guns and the battlefield, and who for the moment had broken the enemy's power, had gained the victory. It might have been Ramillies, or Waterloo, or even Tannenberg. It was Malplaquet.

Bragg now blockaded and almost surrounded Rosecrans and the Army of the Cumberland in Chattanooga. He held the two heights which dominated, Look-out Mountain and Missionary Ridge. For a time he barred all supplies by the Tennessee River. In early October it looked as if the Army of the Cumberland would be starved into surrender. Meanwhile the position of Burnside at Knoxville, against whom Longstreet had been sent, appeared no less deadly.

The Washington Government now began to lean heavily upon General Ulysses Grant. His faults and weaknesses were apparent; but so also was his stature. On the Union side, baffled, bewildered, disappointed, weary of bloodshed and expense, Grant now began to loom vast and solid through a red fog. Victory had followed him from Fort Donelson to Vicksburg. Here were large rebel surrenders—troops, cannon, territory. Who else could show the like? On October 16 Grant was given command of the departments of the Ohio, Cumberland, and Tennessee Rivers, with his lieutenant, Sherman, under him at the head of the Army of the Tennessee.

Rosecrans was dismissed. He had lost a great battle, and under the Washington administration no General survived defeat. He had, however, played a distinguished part in the West, and his military record was clean. Long before Chickamauga he had lost favour with Halleck. That poor figure, who stood at the portals of the grim politics of these days, who sought to tell the armies what the politicians wanted and the politicians as much as they could understand of the military needs, showed his measure clearly when in February 1863 he wrote to Grant and Rosecrans that the vacant Major-Generalship would be given to whoever won the first notable success. Grant left his letter unanswered. Rosecrans wrote in stern rebuke that "a patriot and a man of honour should require no additional incentive to make him do his duty." Thus when he tripped he fell on stony ground.

By a series of intricate measures Grant freed the Tennessee River, stormed both Missionary Ridge and Look-out Mountain, and drove Bragg and the Confederate Army in thorough disorder away from Chattanooga. At the same time he relieved Burnside at Knoxville. The frontiers of the Confederacy rolled southwards in another long lap. Vicksburg had cut it in two along the line of the Mississippi. Chattanooga cut the eastern half again along the range of the Alleghenies. By December 1863 the Confederates were driven back into Georgia, and the whole Mississippi valley was recovered for the Union. All these convulsive events might have taken a different grip if President Davis had made Lee Supreme Commander of the Confederate Army after Chancellorsville, or, better still, in 1862, and if he had devoted his authority and fine qualities wholly to the task of rallying behind the chief General the loyal, indomitable, but woefully particularist energies of the South.

By the end of 1863 all illusions had vanished. The South knew they had lost the war, and would be conquered and flattened. It is one of the enduring glories of the American nation that this made no difference to the Confederate resistance. In the North, where success was certain, they could afford to have bitter division. On the beaten side the departure of hope left only the resolve to perish arms in hand. Better the complete destruction of the whole generation and the devastation of their enormous land, better that every farm should be burned, every city bombarded, every fighting man killed, than that history should record that they had yielded. Any man can be trampled down by superior force, and death, in whatever shape it comes, is only death, which comes to all. It might seem incredible when we survey the military consequences of 1863 that the torments of war should have been prolonged through the whole of 1864 and into 1865. "Kill us if you can; destroy all we have," cried the South. "As you will," replied the steadfast majority of the North.

CHAPTER 19

THE VICTORY OF THE UNION

THE CONFEDERACY was defeated, and the last long phase of the war was one of conquest and subjugation. During the winter of the year which had witnessed Chancellorsville and Gettysburg, Vicksburg, Chattanooga, and Chickamauga, there was a pause. The North gathered its overwhelming strength for a sombre task. The war-leadership of President Davis was gravely questioned in the South. He had kept in his own hands not only the enormous business of holding the Confederacy together and managing its political and economic life, but he had exercised an overriding control upon its military operations. He had obdurately pursued a defensive policy and strategy, against odds which nothing but decisive victory in the field could shorten. This had led logically and surely to ruin. Lee and Longstreet were now asked for a general plan for 1864. They proposed that Beauregard, with twenty thousand men drawn from the forts in South Carolina, should be joined to Longstreet's army in East Tennessee, and, invading Kentucky, strike at the Louisville railway, the sole line of supply for the main Federal Army, which was expected to advance southward from Chattanooga against Joseph E. Johnston. Thereafter Johnston and all Confederate forces in the West would unite, fighting such battles as might be necessary, in a northward march towards the Ohio. This, they declared, would rupture all Federal combinations in the West. As for the East, Lee and the Army of Northern Virginia would be answerable. When this great scheme was laid before Davis at a Council of War, Bragg, of all men, pressed an alternative plan, with the result that there was no plan. Johnston must fight as best he could in the West, and Lee would continue to defend Richmond.

On March 9 President Lincoln appointed Ulysses Grant to the command of all the armies of the United States, raising him to the rank of Lieutenant-General. At last on the Northern side there was unity of command, and a general capable of exercising it. Grant's plan was brutal and simple. It was summed up in the word "Attrition." In intense fighting and exchange of lives weight of numbers would prevail. To Meade, who nominally retained the command of the Army of the Potomac, he gave the order, "Wherever Lee goes there you will go." To Sherman, his friend and brother officer, who had risen with him, he confided the command in the West with similar instructions, but with an addition: "To move against Johnston's army, to break it up, and to get into the interior of the enemy's country as far as you can, inflicting all the damage you can against their war resources." If either Johnston or Lee, profiting by interior lines, showed signs of trying to join the other no exertion was to be spared to follow him.

Grant also ordered three secondary operations: an attack, aided by the Navy, upon Mobile, on the Gulf of Mexico; pressure from Fortress Monroe towards Richmond; and the devastation of the Shenandoah valley, the granary of the South, and its oft-used route towards Maryland and Washington. Of these diversions the first two failed, and the Shenandoah plan only succeeded late in the year, when two corps and three cavalry divisions were applied to it under General Philip H. Sheridan.

With the approach of spring Grant, having launched the Union Army, came to grips with Lee on the old battle-grounds of the Rappahannock and the Rapidan, where the traces of Chancellorsville remained and memories of "Stonewall" Jackson brooded. He took the field at the beginning of May with a hundred and twenty thousand men against Lee with sixty thousand. He crossed the Rapidan by the fords which "Fighting Joe" Hooker had used the year before. There in the savage country of the Wilderness was fought a battle worthy of its field. In two days of intricate and ferocious fighting, May 5 and 6, Grant was repulsed with a loss of eighteen thousand men, Lee himself losing about ten thousand, the most part in a vehement counter-stroke. Grant then passaged to his left, and in a series of confused struggles from the 8th to the 19th sought to cut the Confederates from their line of retreat upon Richmond. This was called the Battle of Spotsylvania Court House, in which the Federal armies suffered another loss of over eighteen thousand men, or double that of their opponents. Undeterred by this slaughter, Grant repeated his movement to the left, and prolonged heavy fighting followed in the wild regions of the South Anna stream and afterwards on the Pamunkey River. Grant, for all the courage of his men, could never turn Lee's right flank, and Lee and his devoted soldiers could never overcome odds of two to one. They could only inflict death and wounds in proportion to their numbers. According to Grant's war-thought, this process, though costly, had only to be continued long enough to procure the desired result. "I purpose to fight it out on this line," he wrote to Halleck at Washington, "if it takes all summer." But other factors, less arithmetical in their character, imposed themselves.

At Cold Harbour, on the ground of the "Seven Days" in 1862, the Federal Commander-in-Chief hurled his army through the blasted, undulating woodland against the haggard, half-starved, but elated Confederate lines. It was at this battle that Lee conversed with the Postmaster-General of the Confederacy, who had ridden out to see the fighting, and asked, "If he breaks your line what reserve have you?" "Not a regiment," said Lee, "and that has been my condition ever since the fighting commenced. If I shorten my lines to provide a reserve he will turn me; if I weaken my lines to provide a reserve he will break them." But the result of the day ended Grant's tactics of unflinching butchery. After seven thousand brave blue-coated soldiers had fallen in an hour or so the troops refused to renew the assault. More is expected of the high command than determination in thrusting men to their doom. The Union dead and wounded lay between the lines; the dead soon began to stink in the broiling sun, the living screamed for water. But Grant failed to secure a truce for burial and mercy. It was not till the third day after the battle that upon a letter from Lee, saying he would gladly accord it if asked, formal request was made, and for a few hours the firing ceased. During the World Wars through which we have lived no such indulgences were allowed, and numbers dwarfing the scale of the American Civil War perished in "no-man's-land," in long, helpless agony where they fell. But in that comparatively civilised and refined epoch in America Cold Harbour was deemed a horror almost beyond words.

The Army of Northern Virginia had inflicted upon Grant in thirty days a loss equal to its own total strength. He now saw himself compelled to resort to manœuvre. He did exactly what McClellan had done on this same ground two years earlier. By a skilful and daring march, which Lee was too weak to interrupt, he moved his whole army across the peninsula, and, again using sea-power, crossed the James River and established a new base on the south bank. He set himself to attack

Richmond by the "back-door," as McClellan had wished to do. Re-pulsed at Petersburg, he laid siege with an army now reinforced to a hundred and forty thousand men to the trench lines covering that stronghold and the lines east of Richmond. He failed again to turn Lee's right flank by movements south of the James, and at the end of June resigned himself to trench warfare attack by spade, mine, and can-non. There was no investment, for Lee's western flank remained open. There static conditions lasted till April 1865. These performances, al-though they eventually gained their purpose, must be regarded as the negation of generalship. They were none the less a deadly form of war.

Meanwhile, in the West, Sherman, who enjoyed a superiority of almost two to one, had begun in May to fight his way south along the railway from Chattanooga to Atlanta, deep in Georgia. He was faced by Joseph E. Johnston, with three strong Confederate corps. A remarkable duel ensued between skilful adversaries. Sherman avoided frontal at-tacks, and by flanking movements manœuvred Johnston out of one strong position after another. Fierce fighting was continuous on the outpost lines, and in a minor engagement one of Johnston's corps com-manders, General Leonidas Polk, was killed by a cannon-shot. Only at Kenesaw Mountain did Sherman assault. He was repulsed with the loss of two thousand five hundred men. But meanwhile the spectacle of this remorseless advance and his unwillingness to force a battle cost John-ston the confidence of Jefferson Davis. At the moment when he had re-solved to stand at Peach Tree Creek he was superseded by John B. Hood. The Confederate Army, impatient of long retreats, acclaimed the change; but military opinion has always regarded the removal of Johnston as one of the worst mistakes of President Davis in his anxious office. Hood felt himself under obligation to attack, and at Peach Tree Creek, Decatur, and East Point he gave full range to the passion for an offensive which inspired the Government he served and the army he led. The Confederates, defending their native soil, hurled themselves against the invader, and suffered irreparable losses. At Decatur alone they lost ten thousand men, without inflicting a third of that loss upon the enemy. After East Point, where five thousand Confederates fell, both the Army of the West and the Richmond Government were con-vinced that Johnston had probably been right. Hood was directed to re-turn to the defensive, and after some weeks of siege was driven from Atlanta. In the four months' fighting Sherman had carried the Union flag a hundred and fifty miles into the Confederacy, with a loss of

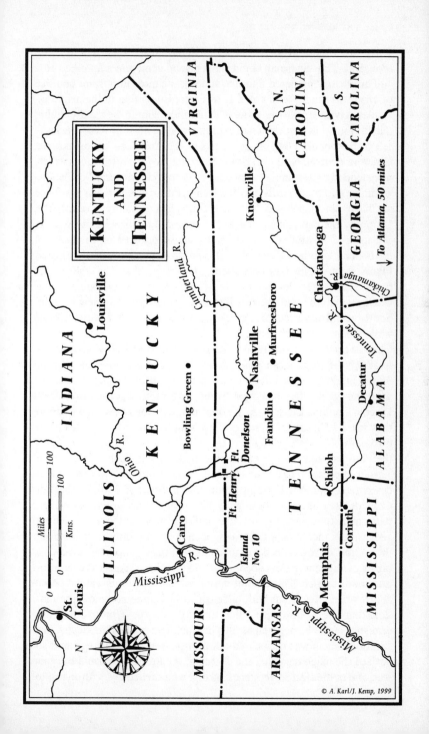

KENTUCKY AND TENNESSEE

VIRGINIA

N. CAROLINA

S. CAROLINA

GEORGIA

→ To Atlanta, 50 miles

Knoxville

Chattanooga

Chickamauga R.

Tennessee R.

Cumberland R.

INDIANA

Louisville

KENTUCKY

Bowling Green

Nashville

Murfreesboro

Franklin

Ohio R.

Ft. Henry

Ft. Donelson

TENNESSEE

Decatur

ALABAMA

Shiloh

ILLINOIS

Cairo

Ohio R.

Island No. 10

Corinth

Memphis

MISSISSIPPI

Miles

Kms.

0   100

0   100

St. Louis

Mississippi R.

MISSOURI

ARKANSAS

Mississippi R.

N

© A. Karl/J. Kemp, 1999

thirty-two thousand men. The Confederate loss exceeded thirty-five thousand. Thus Sherman could claim a solid achievement.

This victory prepared another. Indeed, the most important conflict of 1864 was fought with votes. It was astonishing that in the height of ruthless civil war all the process of election should be rigidly maintained. Lincoln's first term was expiring, and he must now submit himself to the popular vote of such parts of the American Union as were under his control. Nothing shows the strength of the institutions which he defended better than this incongruous episode. General McClellan, whom he had used hardly, was the Democratic candidate. His platform at Chicago in August was "that after four years of failure to restore the Union by the experiment of war . . . immediate efforts be made for a cessation of hostilities . . . and peace may be restored on the basis of the Federal Union of the states." This proposal was known as the Peace Plank. Republicans had no difficulty in denouncing it as disloyal. In fact it represented the views of only a section of the Democrats. The worst that can be said about it is that it was absurd. All knew that the South would never consent to the restoration of the Federal Union while life and strength remained. In Lincoln's own Cabinet Salmon P. Chase, Secretary of the Treasury, a man of proved ability, became his rival for the Republican nomination. This was one of a number of moves made by Republican malcontents to displace their leader by someone whom they imagined would be a more vigorous President. Lincoln's political foes, gazing upon him, did not know vigour when they saw it. These were hard conditions under which to wage a war to the death. The awful slaughters to which Grant had led the Army of the Potomac and the prolonged stalemate outside Richmond made a sinister impression upon the North. But the capture of Atlanta, and a descent by Admiral Farragut upon the harbour of Mobile, the last Confederate open port, both gave that surge of encouragement which party men know how to use. Four million citizens voted in November 1864, and Lincoln was chosen by a majority of only four hundred thousand. Narrow indeed was the margin of mass support by which his policy of the remorseless coercion of the Southern states to reincorporation was carried. This did not mean that all Democrats wanted peace at any price. McClellan had made it plain when he accepted nomination that the South must offer to return to the Union before an armistice could be negotiated. But the founders of the American Constitution, which was now based upon the widest male suffrage, had so devised the machinery that the choice of the President should be indirect; and in the electoral college Lincoln, who carried every Union state except New Jersey, Delaware, and Kentucky, commanded two hundred and twelve delegates against only twenty-one.

In order to placate or confuse the pacifist vote Lincoln had encouraged unofficial peace parleys with the South. Horace Greeley, of the *New York Tribune,* was the President's representative. He met the Southern emissaries in Canada at Niagara Falls. Greeley soon discovered that they had no authority to negotiate a peace. The move would in any case have failed, since Lincoln's conditions now included the abolition of slavery as well as Reunion. The fourth winter of this relentless moral and physical struggle between communities who now respected and armies who had long admired one another came on.

Although Atlanta had fallen Hood's army of forty-four thousand bitter men was still active in the field and free to strike at Sherman's communications. With him were also ten thousand cavalry under Nathan B. Forrest, a new figure who gleamed in the sunset of the Confederacy. Forrest could hardly read or write, but by general account he possessed military qualities of the highest order. His remark that the art of war consists of being "Firstest with mostest" is classic. All these forces were at large around and behind Sherman. On November 12 that General, having persuaded a naturally anxious Washington Cabinet, cast his communications to the winds and began his grim march through Georgia to the shores of the Atlantic. When the Northern blockade had practically stopped the export of cotton from the Confederacy the women, with the slaves, who obeyed and respected them, had sowed the fields with corn. Georgia was full of food in this dark winter. Sherman set himself to march through it on a wide front, living on the country, devouring and destroying all farms, villages, towns, railroads, and public works which lay within his wide-ranging reach. He left behind him a blackened trail, and hatreds which pursue his memory to this day. "War is hell," he said, and certainly he made it so. But no one must suppose that his depredations and pillage were comparable to the atrocities which were committed during the World Wars of the twentieth century or to the barbarities of the Middle Ages. Searching investigation has discovered hardly a case of murder or rape. None the less a dark shadow lies upon this part of the map of the United States.

Meanwhile Hood, with the Confederate Army of the West, not only tore up Sherman's communications with the United States, so that he was not heard of for a month, but with an army of nearly sixty thousand men struck deep into the Northern conquests. He invaded Tennessee, Thomas, who had been left by Sherman to watch him, retiring. His soldiers, infuriated by the tales of what was happening in their homes, drove the Federals from Franklin, though at the cost of nearly seven thousand men. It looked as if the Confederates might once more break through to the Ohio. But, pressing on, they were defeated and routed by Thomas on December 15 in the Battle of Nashville. Hood returned in much disorder to the South. Sherman, after vicissitudes, reached Savannah on the ocean coast in time to send the news of its fall as a "Christmas present" to the re-established President Lincoln.

The end was now in sight. Sherman planned for 1865 a more severe punishment for South Carolina than had been inflicted upon Georgia. Here was a state which by its arrogance had let loose these years of woe upon the American people. Here were the men who had fired upon the Stars and Stripes at Fort Sumter. In Lincoln's Cabinet Ministers spoke of obliterating Charleston and sowing the foundations with salt. Sherman marched accordingly with extreme vigour. But meanwhile outside Richmond Lee's powers of resistance were exhausted. He had not been deterred by Grant's arrival on the south bank of the James from sending General Early with a strong detachment into the Shenandoah valley. In July 1864 Early defeated the Federal commanders in the Jackson style, and once again Washington had heard the cannon of an advancing foe. But now the Shenandoah had been cleared and devastated by Sheridan with overwhelming forces. The Petersburg lines before Richmond had long repelled every Federal assault. The explosion of a gigantic mine under the defences had only led to a struggle in the crater, in which four thousand Northerners fell. But the weight which lay upon Lee could no longer be borne.

It was not until the beginning of February 1865, in this desperate strait, that President Davis appointed him Commander-in-Chief. In the same month another attempt was made at negotiation. The Vice-President of the Confederacy, A. H. Stephens, was empowered to meet the President of the United States on board a steamer in Hampton Roads, at the mouth of the James River. It offers a strange spectacle, which has not been repeated since, that two opposed belligerent leaders should thus parley in the midst of war. Moreover, the Southern representative had not so many years ago been an acquaintance of Lincoln's. But neither side had the slightest intention of giving way on the main issue. Jefferson Davis in his instructions spoke of a treaty "whereby our two countries may dwell in peace together." Lincoln offered a wide generosity, but only if the United States were again to be one country. It was as he had predicted. The South could not voluntarily re-accept the Union. The North could not voluntarily yield it.

Lee meanwhile had at once restored Joseph E. Johnston to the command of the Western Army. No rule can be laid down upon the High Command of states and armies in war. All depends upon the facts and the men. But should a great General appear the civil Government would be wise to give him full scope at once in the military sphere. After the Second Manassas, or after Chancellorsville at the latest, Lee was plainly discernible as the Captain-General of the South. But that was in the spring of '62; it was now the spring of '65. Every Confederate counter-offensive had been crushed. The forces of the North ravaged the doomed Confederacy, and at last Grant closed upon its stubborn capital.

On Sunday, April 2, after the Battle of Five Forks and the turning of the Petersburg lines, President Davis sat in his pew in the church at Richmond. A messenger came up the aisle. "General Lee requests immediate evacuation." Southward then must the Confederate Government wander. There were still some hundreds of miles in which they exercised authority. Nothing crumbled, no one deserted; all had to be overpowered, man by man and yard by yard. Lee had still a plan. He would march swiftly south from Richmond, unite with Johnston, break Sherman, and then turn again to meet Grant and the immense Army of the Potomac. But all this was for honour, and mercifully that final agony was spared. Lee, disengaging himself from Richmond, was pursued by more than three times his numbers, and Sheridan, with a cavalry corps almost equal to the Confederate Army, lapped around his line of retreat and broke in upon his trains. When there were no more half-rations of green corn and roots to give to the soldiers, and they were beset on three sides, Grant ventured to appeal to Lee to recognise that his position was hopeless. Lee bowed to physical necessity. He rode on Traveller to Appomattox Court House to learn what terms would be offered. Grant wrote them out in a few sentences. The officers and men of the Army of Northern Virginia must surrender their arms and return on parole to their homes, not to be molested while they observed the laws of the United States. Lee's officers were to keep their swords. Food would be provided from the Union wagons. Grant added, "Your men must keep their horses and mules. They will need them for the spring ploughing." This was the greatest day in the career of General Grant, and stands high in the story of the United States. The Army of Northern Virginia, which so long had "carried the Confederacy on its bayonets," surrendered, twenty-seven thousand strong; and a fortnight later, despite the protests of President Davis, Johnston accepted from Sherman terms similar to those granted to Lee. Davis himself was captured by a cavalry squadron. The armed resistance of the Southern States was thus entirely subdued.

Lincoln had entered Richmond with Grant, and on his return to Washington learned of Lee's surrender. Conqueror and master, he towered above all others, and four years of assured power seemed to lie before him. By his constancy under many varied strains and amid problems to which his training gave him no key he had saved the Union with steel and flame. His thoughts were bent upon healing his country's wounds. For this he possessed all the qualities of spirit and wisdom, and wielded besides incomparable authority. To those who spoke of hanging Jefferson Davis he replied, "Judge not that ye be not judged." On April 11 he proclaimed the need of a broad and generous temper and urged the conciliation of the vanquished. At Cabinet on the 14th he spoke of Lee and other Confederate leaders with kindness, and pointed to the paths of forgiveness and goodwill. But that very night as he sat in his box at Ford's Theatre a fanatical actor, one of a murder gang, stole in from behind and shot him through the head. The miscreant leapt on the stage, exclaiming, *"Sic semper tyrannis,"* and although his ankle was broken through his spur catching in an American flag he managed to escape to Virginia, where he was hunted down and shot to death in a barn. Seward, Secretary of State, was also stabbed at his home, though not fatally, as part of the same plot.

Lincoln died next day, without regaining consciousness, and with him vanished the only protector of the prostrate South. Others might try to emulate his magnanimity; none but he could control the bitter political hatreds which were rife. The assassin's bullet had wrought more evil to the United States than all the Confederate cannonade. Even in their fury the Northerners made no reprisals upon the Southern chiefs. Jefferson Davis and a few others were, indeed, confined in fortresses for some time, but afterwards all were suffered to dwell in peace. But the death of Lincoln deprived the Union of the guiding hand which alone could have solved the problems of reconstruction and added to the triumph of armies those lasting victories which are gained over the hearts of men.

> *Who overcomes*
> *By force hath overcome but half his foe.*

Thus ended the great American Civil War, which must upon the whole be considered the noblest and least avoidable of all the great mass-conflicts of which till then there was record. Three quarters of a million men had fallen on the battlefield. The North was plunged in debt; the South was ruined. The material advance of the United States was cast back for a spell. The genius of America was impoverished by the alienation of many of the parent elements in the life and history of the Republic. But, as John Bright said to his audience of English working folk, "At last after the smoke of the battlefield had cleared away the horrid shape which had cast its shadow over the whole continent had vanished and was gone for ever."

CHAPTER 20

AMERICAN "RECONSTRUCTION"

THE VICTORY of Northern arms had preserved American unity, but immense problems had now to be faced. The most urgent was that of restoring order and prosperity to the defeated Confederacy. Great areas in the South, along the line of Sherman's march, and in the valley of Virginia, had been devastated. Atlanta, Columbia, Charleston, Richmond and other cities had been grievously damaged by bombardment and fire. The life of the South had come to a standstill. Farming, denied a market by the Northern blockade, had fallen into stagnation, despite the heroic efforts of Southern women and the faithful slaves to keep the land in cultivation. The blockade had also caused severe shortages in many common goods, and the breakdown of transport within the Confederacy had brought all within the grip of famine. The entire and inflated Southern banking system had collapsed. Confederate paper money and securities were now worthless. The whole region was reduced to penury. As the ragged, hungry soldiers of the Confederacy made their way homeward after Appomattox they were everywhere confronted by scenes of desolation and ruin.

Reconstruction was the word. But a prime difficulty in reconstructing the South was the future of the negro. In spite of Lincoln's Proclamation of 1863, which nominally freed the slaves in the rebellious states, millions of them had continued throughout the war to work loyally for their old owners. At the end of the war many of them believed that Emancipation meant that they need no longer work. They made off to the nearest town or army camp, depriving the plantations of their labour and presenting the Union authorities with an alarming problem.

There was another reason for tackling the question of the negro, for in some parts of the Union he was legally still a slave. Lincoln's Proclamation had abolished slavery only in those areas under Confederate control. It had not applied either to the parts of the Confederacy occupied by the Union or to the four slave states which had remained loyal. Only two of these states, Maryland and Missouri, had outlawed slavery within their limits. Further action was needed, especially since doubts were expressed in many quarters about the constitutional rightness of Lincoln's Proclamation and of the Act passed by Congress in 1862 abolishing slavery in the Territories. The Thirteenth Constitutional Amendment was therefore proposed, prohibiting slavery in all areas within the jurisdiction of the United States.

But here was a complication. The American Constitution provided that no amendment was valid until it had been ratified by three-quarters of the states. As the Union now consisted of thirty-six states, some at least of the eleven former Confederate states would have to ratify if the Thirteenth Amendment was to become effective. The position of the states which had seceded from the Union had to be defined. If they had in fact left the Union should they return as the equals of their conquerors? If so, on what conditions?

While the war was still in progress Lincoln had dismissed the question of the legal status of the Confederate states as a "pernicious abstraction." He had been concerned only with restoring them to their "proper practical relation with the Union." In December 1863 he had set out a plan for their readmission. Pardon was offered, with a few exceptions, to all adherents of the Confederacy who would take an oath of loyalty to the Union. When such oaths had been taken by 10 per cent. of the electorate of any state it remained only for state Governments to be established which were prepared to abolish slavery. Then they would be readmitted. Lincoln's "10 per cent. plan" was never carried out. Reconstructed Governments were set up in 1864 in three of the Confederate states which had fallen under the control of Union armies, but Congress refused to seat the Senators and Representatives whom they sent to Washington.

Congress believed that Reconstruction was its business, and not the President's. The Radical Republicans who dominated Congress did not wish to smooth the path of the South's return to her allegiance. They wanted a harsh and vengeful policy, and they especially desired the immediate enfranchisement of the negro. Radical vindictiveness sprang from various causes. The most creditable was a humanitarian concern for the welfare of the negro. These feelings were shared only by a minority. More ignoble motives were present in the breasts of such Radical leaders as Zachariah Chandler and Thaddeus Stevens. Loving the negro less than they hated his master, these ill-principled men wanted to humiliate the proud Southern aristocracy, whom they had always disliked, and at whose door they laid the sole blame for the Civil War. There was another and nearer point. The Radicals saw that if the negro was given the vote they could break the power of the Southern planter and preserve the ascendancy over the Federal Government that Northern business interests had won since 1861. To allow the Southern states, in alliance with Northern Democrats, to recover their former voice in national affairs would, the Radicals believed, be incongruous and absurd. It would also jeopardise the mass of legislation on tariffs, banking, and public land which Northern capitalists had secured for themselves during the war. To safeguard these laws the Radicals took up the cry of the negro vote, meaning to use it to keep their own party in power.

Even if Lincoln had lived to complete his second term he would have met with heavy opposition from his own party. The magnanimous policy he had outlined in April 1865, in the classic address delivered from the White House, was shattered by the bullet that killed him a few days later. The new President, Andrew Johnson of Tennessee, though sharing Lincoln's views on Reconstruction, was markedly lacking in political gifts. Nevertheless, from Lincoln's death until the end of the year, while Congress was in recess, Johnson was able to put into effect a Reconstruction plan closely resembling Lincoln's. Each Southern state, in conventions chosen by loyal electors, could qualify for readmission to the Union by repealing the Ordinances of Secession, repudiating the Confederate war debt, and abolishing slavery. The South, anxious, in the words of General Grant, "to return to self-government within the Union as soon as possible," was quick to comply. Southerners then proceeded to elect state legislatures and officials, chose Senators and Representatives to go to Washington, and ratified the Thirteenth Amendment, which went into force in December 1865.

When Congress reconvened in that same month it declined to seat the elected Representatives of the South. Ignoring Johnson's work, Congress went on to put its own ideas into practice. Its first step was to set up a Joint Committee on Reconstruction, charged with the task of collecting information about Southern conditions. Later in the new year this body, under Radical control, reported that drastic measures were necessary to protect the emancipated negro. Congress promptly took action. First came the Freedmen's Bureau Bill, which prolonged the life and greatly extended the powers of an agency set up earlier to assist negroes to make the transition to freedom. This was followed by a Civil Rights Bill, conferring citizenship on the negroes and granting them equality of treatment before the law. Both these measures were vetoed by Johnson as unconstitutional infringements of the rights of the states. The Civil Rights Bill was repassed over Johnson's veto and became law. The Radicals meanwhile aimed at making doubly sure of their purposes by incorporating its provisions in the Fourteenth Amendment.

The quarrel between Johnson and the Radicals was now open and bitter, and the Congressional elections of 1866 witnessed a fierce struggle between them. The Radicals were much the more astute in presenting their case to the electorate. They pointed to a serious race riot in New Orleans as proof of Southern maltreatment of the negro, and to the recently enacted Black Codes as evidence of an intention to re-enslave him. Their leaders carried more conviction with the Northern electors than did Johnson, whose undignified outbursts during a speaking tour lost him much support. The result was a resounding victory for the Radicals, who obtained a two-thirds majority in both Houses of Congress. The way was now clear for them to carry out their own plan of Reconstruction, for they were strong enough to override the President's vetoes. A series of harsh and vengeful Reconstruction Acts was passed in 1867. The South was divided into five military districts, each under the command of a Federal Major-General. The former Confederacy was to be subjected to Army rule of the kind that Cromwell had once imposed on England. In order to be readmitted to the Union the Southern states were now required to ratify the Fourteenth Amendment and to frame state constitutions which provided for negro suffrage—and this in spite of the fact that very few of the Northern states had as yet granted the negro the vote.

Not content with these successes, the Radical leaders then tried to remove the President from office by impeachment. This would have suited them well, for as the law then stood Johnson would have been replaced by the President of the Senate, who was himself a leading Radical. According to the Constitution, the President could be thus dismissed on conviction for treason, bribery, or other high crimes and misdemeanours. Yet Johnson's opposition to Radical policies had never overstepped constitutional limits, and his enemies were put to some difficulty in framing charges against him. After vain endeavours to find any evidence of treason or corruptibility, the Radicals put forward as a pretext for his impeachment Johnson's effort, in August 1867, to rid himself of his Secretary of War, Edwin M. Stanton. This unscrupulous politician had long merited dismissal. He had been in the habit of passing on Cabinet secrets to the Radical leaders while professing the utmost loyalty to the President. But when Johnson demanded his resignation Stanton refused to comply. For some months he continued to conduct the business of the War Department, in which he finally barricaded himself. Stanton justified his conduct by reference to the Tenure of Office Act, a measure recently adopted over Johnson's veto as part of the Radical effort to diminish the powers of the Presidency. No Cabinet officers, the Act had declared, were to be dismissed without the consent of the Senate. Failure to obtain consent was punishable as a high crime.

Thus in March 1868 the Radical leaders were able to induce the House to adopt eleven articles impeaching Andrew Johnson at the bar of the Senate. The only concrete charge against him was his alleged violation of the Tenure of Office Act. Yet this measure was constitutionally doubtful, and its violation became a crime only because the Radicals said so. In spite of the weakness of their case they came within an ace of success. In the event they failed by a single vote to obtain the two-thirds majority in the Senate which they needed to convict the President. Seven Republican Senators, withstanding immense and prolonged pressure, refused to allow the impeachment process to be debased for party ends. They voted for acquittal.

By the narrowest possible margin a cardinal principle of the American Constitution, that of the separation of powers, was thus preserved. Had the impeachment succeeded the whole course of American constitutional development would have been changed. Power would henceforth have become concentrated solely in the legislative branch of the Government, and no President could have been sure of retaining office in the face of an adverse Congressional majority. Nevertheless the Radicals were strong enough in Congress during the rest of Johnson's term to be able to ignore his wishes. A further Republican victory at the polls in 1868 brought General Ulysses S. Grant to the White House. The triumph of the Radicals was now complete, for the ineptitude in high office of the victorious Union commander made him their tool.

The political reconstruction of the South ground forward in strict accordance with the harsh legislation of 1867. Under the superintendence of Federal military commanders elections were held in which the negro for the first time took part. Almost a million coloured men were enrolled on the voting lists. At the same time more than a hundred thousand Southern whites were disfranchised because they had been in rebellion. Negro voters were in a majority in five states. Yet the negro was merely the dupe of his ill-principled white leaders. These consisted either of Northern adventurers, known as "carpet-baggers," whose main purposes in going South were to make fortunes for themselves and to muster the negro vote for the Republican Party, or of Southern "scalawags," who were prepared, for the sake of office, to co-operate with a régime that most Southern whites detested. Between 1868 and 1871 "carpet-bag" and "scalawag" Governments, supported by the negro vote and by Federal bayonets, were installed in all the Southern states. When these states were deemed to have complied with the Radical requirements they were allowed to return to the Union.

Fraud, extravagance, and a humiliating racial policy were imposed upon the South by Radical rule. It could be maintained only by the drastic use of Federal power. To bolster up the "carpet-bag" Governments Congress initiated the Fifteenth Amendment, which laid down that suffrage could not be denied to any citizen on grounds of "race, colour, or previous condition of servitude." A series of laws placed Congressional elections under Federal management, and authorised the use of military force to suppress violence in the Southern states. These measures were prompted by the vigorous efforts of white Southerners, both by legal methods and by threats to negro voters from secret societies like the Ku Klux Klan, to overthrow the "carpet-bag" Governments and restore white supremacy. For a time repression achieved its purpose, but gradually state after state was recaptured by white voters. This success was partly due to the stubbornness of Southern resistance and partly to a change in Northern sentiment. By the early 1870's the ordinary Northerner had become fully alive to the political shortcomings of the negro and was scandalised by the corruption of the "carpet-bag" Governments. The Northern businessman wanted an end to unsettled conditions, which were bad for trade. Above all, Northerners became weary of upholding corrupt minority Governments by force. They began to withdraw their support from the Radical programme.

By 1875 the Radical Republicans had so far lost control that only South Carolina, Florida, and Louisiana were still in the hands of the "carpet-baggers." In the following year a way was opened for these states to recover control of their own affairs. After the Presidential election of 1876 disputes arose in these three states over the validity of the election returns. The matter was extremely important, since the nineteen electoral votes at stake were sufficient to decide the Presidential contest. The Democratic candidate, Samuel J. Tilden, had obtained 184 electoral votes, or one short of a majority. The Republican, Rutherford B. Hayes, therefore needed all the disputed nineteen. When the controversy was referred to the House of Representatives it was obvious that the Republican majority in that Assembly would decide in favour of Hayes. So as a sop to Democratic opinion generally, and to the South in particular, Hayes's supporters promised that Federal troops would be withdrawn from the South as soon as Hayes took office. Mollified by this concession, the South abandoned its opposition to Hayes. In April 1877, a month after Hayes assumed the Presidency, and twelve years after Lee's surrender at Appomattox, the last Federal garrisons left the South. The remaining "carpet-bag" Governments promptly collapsed, white supremacy was everywhere restored, and the period of Radical Reconstruction was over.

It had not been altogether an evil, for the "carpet-bag" legislatures promoted a number of long-overdue reforms and accomplished some good work in building roads and bridges. But it was on the whole a shameful and discreditable episode. In the judgment of an American historian, the "negro and carpet-bagger Governments were among the worst that have ever been known in any English-speaking land." Reconstruction left in the South a legacy of bitterness and hatred greater by far than that produced by four years of war. Remembering the Republicans as the party of negro rule, the white South for the next fifty years would vote almost to a man for the Democratic Party. The negro himself gained little lasting benefit from Reconstruction. His advancement had been the plaything of self-seeking and cynical men, and was set back for an incalculable period.

From the end of Reconstruction until the closing decade of the century American politics lacked interest. Memories of the Civil War remained fresh, especially in the South, and the passions aroused by it could still be revived. Indeed, they often were, especially by the Republican Party, which made a practice at election times of "waving the bloody shirt" and denouncing their Democratic opponents as rebels and traitors. Yet the issues of the war itself were dead, and unreplaced. No major questions divided the parties, no new policies were initiated, and scarcely a measure deserving the attention of the historian was placed on the Statute Book. Nor were the political personalities of the time any more exciting than the events in which they took part. A succession of worthy, mediocre men filled the Presidency, the chief virtue of their administrations being the absence of the corruption which had disgraced the two terms of the unfortunate General Grant. With few exceptions Congress too was filled with what one historian has called "sad, solemn fellows."

Yet if the politics of the period were insignificant its economic developments were of the first importance. Throughout the generation that followed the Civil War the pace of economic change quickened and the main outlines of modern America emerged. Between 1860 and 1900 the population of the Union soared from thirty·one to seventy-six millions. This increase was due in part to the heavy influx of European immigrants, who within forty years totalled fifteen millions. Cities grew fast. Great mineral deposits were discovered and exploited, giving rise to vast new industries. "No other generation in American history," it has been remarked, "witnessed changes as swift or as revolutionary as those which transformed the rural republic of Lincoln and Lee into the urban industrial empire of McKinley and Roosevelt."

Economic change transformed not only the regions which became great industrial centres, but the country as a whole. Even in the South a revolution was afoot. In Southern agriculture change was inevitable because of the disorganisation wrought by the war and the ending of slavery. Nearly all the great planters, impoverished by the war and crushed by taxation during the Reconstruction, were compelled to split their plantations and sell, often at absurdly low prices. Thousands of small farmers were thus able to increase the size of their holdings. An even greater number of Southern whites for the first time became landowners. The old sprawling plantations disappeared, and were replaced by an infinitely greater number of small farms, engaged for the most part in growing the same crops as before the war. Negroes, however, continued as in the days of slavery to provide the bulk of the labour for cotton cultivation. Because they lacked capital few of the coloured freedmen were able to buy farms or to pay rent. A novel form of tenantry known as "share-cropping" therefore came into being. Furnished by the farmer with land and equipment, the negro—and later the landless white—gave their labour in return for one-third of the crop they produced. By these means Southern agriculture slowly revived. But it was almost twenty years before the cotton crop of the former Confederate states reached the level of 1860. From then on expansion was rapid, and by 1900 the pre-war figures had been more than doubled.

This period saw also the beginnings of large-scale industry in the South. The Southern textile industry, very small before 1860, managed in time to recover and then to expand. Towards the end of the century the South, with its raw material at hand and its supply of cheap labour, possessed almost two million spindles and was daring to challenge New England's position in the home market. At the same time the tobacco industry flourished in North Carolina and Virginia, and the discovery of coal and iron deposits in Tennessee and Alabama led to the rise of a Southern iron industry. Yet the South remained predominantly agricultural, and the growth of Southern industry was insignificant compared with that of the North.

The Civil War had given a great impetus to Northern output. The Federal armies had needed huge quantities of arms and equipment, clothing and footwear. Fortified by Government contracts, Northern manufacturers embarked on large-scale production. Furthermore, in the absence of Southern representatives Congress passed into law the protective measures demanded by Northern industrialists and financiers. But the assistance thus afforded did no more than speed the coming of the American Industrial Revolution. The United States were, and still are, extraordinarily rich in mineral wealth. They possessed about two-thirds of the known coal deposits of the world, immense quantities of high-grade iron ore, equally great resources in petroleum, and, in the West, huge treasuries of gold, silver, and copper. Through their inventive ability and their aptitude for improving the inventions of others Americans grasped the power to turn their raw materials into goods. To this they added a magnificent transport system of railroads and canals which fed the factories and distributed their products. Moreover, America could look to Europe for capital as well as labour. The bulk of her industrial capital came from British, Dutch, and German investors. Much of the brawn and not a little of the brain that went into her making were also supplied by the great immigration from Europe.

Thus favoured, American industry forged swiftly ahead. Each decade saw new levels of output in the iron and steel mills of the Pittsburgh area, the oil refineries of Ohio, Pennsylvania, and elsewhere, the flour mills of Minneapolis and St. Paul, the meat-packing plants of Chicago and Cincinnati, the clothing and boot and shoe factories of New England, and the breweries of Milwaukee and St. Louis, to mention only the biggest of American industrial enterprises. In each of these fields great captains of industry arose, the most powerful of whom were Rockefeller in oil and Carnegie in steel. With untiring energy and skill, and with ruthless disregard for competitors, these men built up economic empires which gave them great wealth and a formidable power over the life of the community. Carnegie and Rockefeller, indeed, together with Morgan in finance and Vanderbilt and Harriman in railroads, became the representative figures of the age, in striking contrast to the colourless actors upon the political scene. Though the morality of their business methods has often been questioned, these men made industrial order out of chaos. They brought the benefits of large-scale production to the humblest home. By 1900, owing to their vigorous efforts, American industry was concentrated in a number of giant corporations, each practically a monopoly in its chosen field. This was a state of affairs presently to be challenged by Federal authority. But meanwhile the United States had ceased to depend on European manufactures; they were even invading Europe with their own. Thus America passed through a gilded age of which the millionaire seemed, at least to European eyes, the typical representative. Yet it was at the same time an age of unrest, racked by severe growing pains. There was much poverty in the big cities, especially among recent immigrants. There were sharp, sudden financial panics, causing loss and ruin, and there were many strikes, which sometimes broke into violence. Labour began to organise itself in Trade Unions and to confront the industrialists with a stiff bargaining power. These developments were to lead to a period of protest and reform in the early twentieth century. The gains conferred by large-scale industry were great and lasting, but the wrongs that had accompanied their making were only gradually righted. All this made for a lively, thrusting, controversial future.

CHAPTER 21

AMERICA AS
A WORLD-POWER

WHILE THE United States were growing into the world's leading industrial Power their people were busily completing the settlement of the continent. At the beginning of the Civil War, after two and a half centuries of westward advance from the Atlantic coast, the frontier of settlement had reached roughly the line of the 97th meridian, which runs through Nebraska, Kansas, Oklahoma, and Texas. Between this frontier and the towns and cities of the Pacific seaboard lay a thousand miles of wilderness. Here were the Great Plains, about a million square miles in extent, where roamed many Indian tribes, and little else except the immense herds of buffalo on which they lived. The sparse rainfall of the Great Plains and lack of timber had made them seem unsuitable for farming and unlikely ever to be peopled. Yet in less than a generation large parts of this huge area were settled by white men and the natural frontier disappeared. The population west of the Mississippi rose in thirty years from about five millions in 1860 to almost eighteen millions, while the number of states in the Union increased from thirty-three to forty-four. By 1890 only four more states remained to be carved out of the West. These were Utah, Oklahoma, New Mexico, and Arizona, all admitted to the Union by 1912, when the political shape of the country became complete.

White settlement of the Great Plains was first prompted by the discovery of precious metals. In 1859 gold was found at Pike's Peak, on the eastern slopes of the Rockies, and miners began to flock into Colorado. As fresh deposits of gold, silver, and copper came to light there was a rush to Nevada, Arizona, Idaho, and Montana, and finally to the

Black Hills of South Dakota. These sudden migrations in search of wealth did not always create lasting settlements, for many of the booms were short-lived. When precious ores ran low the whole population of the mining camps moved on elsewhere, leaving ghost towns to mark the site of their "diggings." Yet by speeding the political organisation of the West and encouraging the building of railroads the discovery of gold and silver did much to open up the Great Plains.

It was the railway indeed, more than any other factor, which threw wide the Plains to settlers. This was the great age of American railroad construction. At the close of the Civil War the United States had possessed about 35,000 miles of tracks, but in less than ten years that figure had been doubled, and by 1890 doubled again. The most prodigious feat was the building of a number of transcontinental railways. The first to cross the continent was completed in May 1869, when a link was made in Utah between the lines of the Union Pacific, stretching westward from Iowa, and the Central Pacific, reaching out eastward from California. This project was financed by a grant from Congress to the two companies of millions of acres of public land, a method which was also used elsewhere. Towards the end of the century three more transcontinental routes had been added, and other great lines had opened up the country. Many of the railroad companies took a direct part in peopling the West, for they realised that their lines could hardly pay until the country on either side of the tracks was settled. An extensive campaign to popularise the West was undertaken both in the Eastern States and in Europe. Because transport was cheap and land could be acquired on credit thousands of settlers were induced to seek new homes in the Great Plains.

Emigrants to the West could also buy land very cheaply from the state Governments, each of which had received from the Federal authorities large areas of the public domain. They could even obtain it free by virtue of the Homestead Act, which granted a quarter-section (160 acres) of public land to all white adult males who undertook to settle there. Although a loophole in the Act allowed land speculators to profit by it, this measure enabled large numbers of settlers, estimated in 1890 at more than a million, to obtain free farms for themselves, mostly to the west of the Mississippi.

The settlement of the West could only take place if the Indian barrier were removed. Already by the time of the Civil War the Indian had been obliged to retreat across half the continent in the face of white advance. Now, as the Red man was harried out of his last refuge, a further tragic chapter was added to his story. The threat to their hunting grounds, and indeed to their whole existence, delivered by the onrush of civilisation impelled the nomadic tribes of the Great Plains to resist the invaders with determination and savagery. From the Sioux and the Crows of the North to the Comanche and Apache of the South, these warlike tribesmen were magnificent horsemen and intrepid fighters. Their bows and arrows were much more effective than the muzzle-loading rifles with which the Federal troops were at first equipped. Yet their final defeat was inevitable. The introduction of the Winchester repeating rifle and the Colt revolver gave armed supremacy to the whites, who were already superior in organisation, numbers, and strategy. But the fatal blow was the wholesale slaughter of the buffalo, chiefly by professional hunters employed by Eastern leather manufacturers. By the early 1870's between two and three million buffalo were being killed annually for their hides, and ten years later a museum expedition seeking specimens could find only two hundred in the whole of the West. On the buffalo the Indian of the Plains had relied not only for food, but for a great variety of other things, from clothing to fuel. When the buffalo was virtually exterminated nomadic life became impossible. The Indians had to comply with the Government's plans and be herded into reservations.

Means had still to be found in the semi-arid West for making agriculture pay. The miner was at first succeeded not by the farmer but by the rancher, who for twenty years after the Civil War used the Great Plains as pasture for his cattle on the long drive from Texas to the Middle West. Although the journey involved passing through territory inhabited by hostile Indians, who frequently stampeded the cattle, vast herds were led each year from the ranches of the South-West to the cattle centres of Kansas and Nebraska. Then, after being fattened for market, the cattle were shipped to the stockyards and canneries of Kansas City or Chicago. But the farmer still hung back from the Great Plains. In this extensive grassland there were very few trees, and no lumber for building houses, barns, and fences. More serious still, the annual rainfall between the 98th meridian and the Rockies was usually below the 20-inch minimum needed for agriculture.

Science now stepped in. A technique known as dry farming was developed. Deep ploughing loosened the soil sufficiently to allow water to move upwards, and frequent harrowing prevented evaporation. New strains of wheat were introduced from Russia, which were resistant to drought and to the disease of wheat-rust, then common on the Plains. But it was large-scale industry that really made farming possible. A wide range of mechanical farm implements, reapers, harvesters, threshers, and improved types of plough enabled the Western farmer to cultivate large enough tracts of land to offset the low yield per acre. Moreover, the invention of barbed wire, though it ended the great cattle drives, solved the problem of fencing.

During the last quarter of the century large numbers of emigrant farmers were flowing into the Great Plains. By 1890 "the frontier"— which officially meant a region inhabited by more than two but less than six persons per square mile—had disappeared. The formerly un-settled area, the superintendent of the census explained, had now "been so broken into by isolated bodies of settlement that there [could] hardly be said to be a frontier line." The colonisation begun at Jamestown, Virginia, almost three centuries before was now complete. Hitherto the frontier had been America's safety-valve. Through it had passed ardent ambitions and bold, restless spirits. Now the safety-valve was shut, and the problems and pressures of dynamic growth within the United States were greatly intensified.

After slumbering since the end of Reconstruction American politics suddenly awoke. The alarm-clock was Populism. Sprung from deep-rooted discontent among farmers, this new movement made rapid headway. A climax was reached in 1896, when the Populists, merged by then with the Democratic Party, made a supreme effort at the polls. The Presidential campaign of that year was one of the fiercest and most spectacular in American history. It was concentrated on a single issue, namely, whether there should be both a gold and silver currency, or monometallism *versus* bimetallism. Known as the Battle of the Stan-dards, this contest was a passionate attempt by the farming interests to wrest control of the Federal Government from the financiers and in-dustrialists, who had enjoyed its favour since the Civil War.

Agriculture, like all other branches of American life, had grown im-mensely since the Civil War. Within forty years the number of farms and the acreage under cultivation about trebled. Production of wheat, corn, cotton, and other commodities rose in similar proportion. But life had also become more difficult for the farmer. As production rose farm prices steadily fell. At the same time farm costs were rising, and large numbers of farmers faced hardship. Many had to become ten-ants, and mortgages multiplied.

For this decline there were several reasons. In some areas, especially in the Old South and the Middle West, the soil was exhausted by waste-ful methods of cultivation. Elsewhere, as on the Great Plains, the farmer faced peculiar natural hazards. Yet these were difficulties which he had always had to endure, and the real explanation of his plight lay in another quarter. In spite of the rise in population, the growth of the cities, and the enormous demand for food, he always produced too much. Canada, South America, and Australia, all of which were experiencing similar agricultural booms, freely competed with the American farmer in the world market. Yet at home he had to buy his equipment and every essential of life in a protected market. The tariff policy of the Federal Government and the power of monopolies and trusts made the price of the manufactured goods he needed artificially high. He was exploited not only by the manufacturer but by the railroad companies. Dependent on a single line to carry his produce to market, the Western farmer was made to pay for the losses of the railroads in carrying industrial freight. The charges for farm products were so crushing that at one time it was cheaper to burn corn as fuel than to sell it. This and other railroad practices were strongly resented. Finally—and this seemed the most crippling burden—the high cost of money pressed heavily on a class which consisted overwhelmingly of debtors. More and more produce was needed to repay the same amount of money. Banking facilities in the West were inadequate, and this forced the farmer to borrow from Eastern financiers, whose interest rates ranged from 8 to 20 per cent. His grievances were inflamed by the deflationary fiscal policy of the Federal Government. At a time of unparalleled economic expansion the Government, in response to business interests which wanted a sound money policy, decided to contract the currency by ceasing to coin silver and withdrawing some of the "greenback" paper money issued during the Civil War.

Such consistent neglect of the farmers and their dependants by the Federal Government is surprising, since they still accounted for almost half the nation's population. But they were politically dis-united, and there remained a wide gulf between Westerners and Southerners because of the smouldering prejudices of the Civil War. The South was solidly Democratic, the West in general Republican. Until agrarian problems could be isolated from other political issues, there was little hope that the farmers could induce the Federal Government to pay any attention to their demands. Only if they formed their own organisations, as "big business" and the working man had already done, could they save themselves from exploitation by stronger economic groups.

Accordingly nation-wide farmers' organisations began to grow. The first of these, an order called the Patrons of Husbandry, or, more popularly, the Grange, was established in 1867. For some years membership was not large, but after the depression of 1873 the movement quickly gained ground. Two years later Granges had been established in almost every state and there were 20,000 lodges and 800,000 members. By this time the movement had ceased to be purely social in character, as had first been the case. Many state Granges ran co-operative business enterprises for marketing their produce and purchasing manufactured goods. By means of co-operative creameries, grain elevators, warehouses, loan agencies, and even factories, it was hoped to cut out the middleman's profit. In many states the Grange developed political offshoots, and Farmers' Parties under various names came into being in the Upper Mississippi valley. All this may seem far removed from the realms of high politics, but America was the first country openly to show in her home affairs that great national decisions must depend upon the matching and mating of small, local causes. When control of a number of state legislatures had been won laws were passed to check the malpractices of the railroads, but these so-called Granger laws were not very effective. It proved impossible to frame regulations that the railroads could not evade. Enforcement was difficult because the judiciary sympathised with the railroads, and in the 1880's a series of Supreme Court decisions severely limited the regulatory powers of the states.

The Grange went rapidly into decline during the improvement in farming conditions that came in the late 1870's. Thus the first attempt at united action by the farmers ended in failure. When bad times returned, as they soon did, new farm organisations, known as the Farmers' Alliances, began to appear in the North-West and in the South. The Alliances conducted much the same kind of social and economic activities as had the Grange, on which indeed they were largely modelled. But, unlike the Grange, the Alliances, almost from the outset, adopted a political programme which called for tariff reduction, currency inflation, and stricter regulation of railroads. As time went on the political emphasis of the movement grew sharper, until finally Populism was born.

The Populist outburst arose from the sharp agricultural depression that began in 1887 and steadily gained in intensity. Severe droughts caused widespread crop failures. There followed a wholesale foreclosing of mortgages and the bankruptcy of a large section of the farming community. Since it was now obvious to the farmers that they could hope for nothing from either of the two major parties, the Alliance movement spread far and wide and was itself transformed into Populism.

Though owing its origin, as well as the main body of its supporters, to farmers' discontent, the Populist Party came to include many other groups. The struggling trade union organisation known as the Knights of Labour, survivors of such short-lived political organisations as the Greenback and Union Labour Parties, and a host of fanatics ranging from suffragists to single-taxers, all joined in. Such groups brought to the movement a number of cranks, but the farmers themselves provided Populism with a full share of picturesque and eccentric figures. From "Pitchfork" Ben Tillman of South Carolina and Jerry Simpson of Kansas, who enjoyed the nickname of "Sockless Socrates," to the revivalist Mary Ellen Lease, who advised the Plains farmers to "raise less corn and more Hell," the leaders of the Populist revolt were of a kind that American politics had not experienced hitherto.

After sweeping triumphs in the state elections of 1890 the Populists had high hopes of success in the Presidential election two years later. Their candidate was James B. Weaver, a former leader of the now defunct Greenback Party. But, for all their hardships, many farmers were still unwilling to abandon their traditional party loyalties. Though Weaver polled a million votes the Democratic candidate, Grover Cleveland, was successful by a narrow majority over his Republican rival, Benjamin Harrison.

No sooner had Cleveland's second term begun—he had already been President from 1885 to 1889—than economic disaster befell. A financial panic led to countless failures in the business world and heavy unemployment in the great cities. There was an outbreak of violent strikes, and a further collapse of agricultural prices. Cleveland could find no means of ending the depression, and discontent spread among his supporters. Many of them disagreed with his tariff policy and with his use of Federal troops to break the great Pullman strike in Chicago in 1894, which had immobilised half the country's railroads. But it was his refusal to follow an inflationary policy that drove despairing Democrats into the ranks of the Populists. The President's offence in the eyes of the inflationists was his use of the patronage at his disposal to force the repeal of the Silver Purchase Act of 1890, a measure which by doubling the amount of silver to be coined had sought to increase the volume of currency in circulation and improve farm prices. Its failure to achieve either of these aims showed, according to the bimetallists, that the Act had not gone far enough and that the only remedy was the free and unlimited coinage of silver. Cleveland, on the other hand, believed that the Act had sparked the panic of 1893, and that accordingly the gold standard must be upheld.

The free silver question had been debated for some years before this, but the repeal of the Silver Purchase Act brought it into new prominence. Between 1893 and 1896 it gradually came to dwarf all other issues. The farmers, as we have seen, had long favoured inflation as a cure for low farm prices. Some of them had flirted earlier with the Greenback Party, which had promised inflation by printing more paper money. Now the agrarians hoped to restore prosperity by remonetising silver and coining all of the metal that the mines could yield. To business interests this seemed a sure road to bankruptcy, for inflation, they pointed out, was easier to start than to check. To them the gold standard seemed indispensable to stability. The next Presidential election was thus fought on the question of cheap money.

Whether the Populists would nominate a candidate of their own or amalgamate with the Democrats was at first in doubt. But the decision was given when the Democratic Convention met at Chicago in July 1896. With cheap-money men in control of the party machinery the Convention adopted a free-silver platform, and nominated as their candidate William Jennings Bryan, of Nebraska. Bryan's "Cross of Gold" speech to the Convention, containing an impassioned attack on the supporters of the gold standard, was to become one of the most celebrated examples of American oratory. Content with such a candidate and such a platform, the Populists endorsed Bryan. Though they did not entirely abandon their plans for a separate campaign, they marched with the Democrats against the Republican candidate, William J. McKinley, who stood for the gold standard. Bryan had formidable disadvantages to overcome. His own party was sharply split, and against him were ranged the Press and the business and financial elements. He embarked on a strenuous campaign, in which his great rhetorical powers were employed to the full. Yet all his efforts were unavailing. McKinley, who stayed at home throughout the campaign, won by more than half a million votes.

Having staked all on Bryan's election, the Populists found it difficult to re-establish themselves once he was defeated. Although the Populist movement did not formally disband until much later, its demise may be dated from this election. Most of the measures that its followers demanded were taken up by new reform movements in the twentieth century, and nearly all were passed into law. Free silver was never attained, but the farmers reached their objective by another road. Through the discovery of new deposits in the Klondike and South Africa the world's supply of gold rose sharply in the last years of the nineteenth century. The volume of money in circulation increased, and when in 1900 Congress passed a Currency Act to place the United States on the gold standard it met with hardly any opposition. The free-silver agitation was all but forgotten.

When Bryan again unsuccessfully opposed McKinley in the Presidential contest the passions aroused four years earlier were wholly absent. The depression was over and prosperity had returned. Home affairs were ignored and American eyes were fixed on larger horizons, for between the two elections the United States had begun to play in world affairs a part commensurate with their strength.

Since the fall of Napoleon the American people had been so engrossed in settling the continent and in exploiting its natural resources that foreign affairs had interested them little. Now, with the process of settlement complete, and the work of economic development well in hand, they sought fresh fields in which to labour. By the 1890's the idea of Empire had taken hold of all the great industrial Powers. Britain, France, and Germany were especially active in acquiring new colonies and new markets. This European example was not lost upon America. For these and other reasons a vigorous spirit of self-assertion developed, which first became manifest in the Venezuelan boundary dispute with Britain in 1895.

Ever since the end of the Civil War Anglo-American relations had been distinctly cool. In spite of the settlement of the *Alabama* claims by Gladstone's Government, Britain's sympathy for the South during the great conflict had left its mark upon the Union. Constant bickering agitated the two countries over such matters as seal-fishing in the Behring Sea, the rights of American fishermen in Canadian waters, and interpretations of the Clayton-Bulwer Treaty of 1850 about the proposed Panama Canal. But all these disputes paled before the question of the Venezuelan boundary. The frontier between this South American republic and British Guiana had long been unsettled, and although the United States had frequently offered mediation her advances had always been declined by Britain. In the summer of 1895 the American State Department made yet another move in a communication which President Cleveland described as "a twenty-inch gun note." Britain was accused of violating the Monroe Doctrine, and was required to give a definite answer as to whether she would accept arbitration. Lord Salisbury bided his time, waiting for passions to cool. He replied in November, rejecting arbitration and telling the American Government that its interpretation of the Monroe Doctrine was at fault. Meanwhile Cleveland sent Congress a message announcing that America would fix the boundary line independently and oblige the disputants to accept her decision.

For a few days war with Britain seemed possible, and even imminent.* But the first patriotic outburst in America soon gave way to more sober feelings. In Britain opinion had reacted less violently. At the

---

* I was returning from a visit to Cuba via America at this time and remember vividly looking at ships off the English coast and wondering which one would be our transport to Canada.—W. S. C.

height of the crisis news arrived of the Kaiser's telegram to President Kruger in South Africa, congratulating him on the repulse of the Jameson raid. These Imperial perplexities distracted attention in London. British wrath turned against Germany rather than the United States. Too involved in Europe and South Africa to think of quarrelling with America, the British Government agreed to arbitration. Their claims in Guiana were largely conceded by the tribunal. There followed a steady improvement in Anglo-American relations, chiefly because Britain was awakening to the dangers of her isolation. Her growing alarm at German naval expansion led her to make friendly overtures to which the United States were fully ready to respond.

The exuberant pride of Americans could not long be held in check. In the Cuban revolt against Spanish rule it found an outlet. Ever since this revolt began in 1895 American popular sentiment had sympathised with the rebel fight for independence. Tempers rose at tales of Spanish atrocities. General Weyler's policy of herding civilians into concentration camps, where thousands died of disease, was vehemently denounced. These atrocities, sensationally reported and embellished by two rival New York newspapers, led to demands for American intervention. In 1898 popular clamour for war with Spain reached its height. In February the American battleship *Maine,* sent to Cuba to protect American lives and property, was blown up by a mine in Havana harbour, with the loss of most of her crew. At this the Spanish Government hastily made concessions to the United States, which President McKinley was at first disposed to accept. But public indignation was too strong for him, and on April 11 war was declared.

The conflict lasted sixteen weeks, and was marked by a succession of overwhelming American victories. In Cuba an American expeditionary force, despite complaints about the mismanagement of the War Department and incompetent leadership in the field, won a series of rapid battles which brought about the surrender of all the Spanish forces in the island. At sea Commodore Dewey immobilised the main Spanish fleet in an engagement in Manila Bay on May 1. The Caribbean squadron of the Spanish Navy was sunk outside the Cuban port of Santiago. In August Spain sued for peace, and in December a treaty was signed at Paris whereby Cuba became independent. The United States acquired Puerto Rico, Guam, and the Philippines.

All this did much to heal the wounds remaining from the Civil War. In the wave of patriotism that swept the country Northerner and Southerner alike took pride in the achievements of their common country. Young men from both regions rushed to join the expeditionary force and fought side by side for San Juan Hill. The famous

Confederate cavalry leader Joe Wheeler exclaimed that a single battle for the Union flag was worth fifteen years of life. The venture also showed that the American people were now fully aware of their own strength as a world-Power. Their new colonial rôle was further stressed by the acquisition between 1898 and 1900 not only of the territory wrested from Spain, but of Hawaii, part of Samoa, and the vacant island of Wake in the Pacific. The United States, though not yet abandoning isolation, henceforward became less preoccupied by home affairs. They began to play an important rôle in the international scene. The Spanish War helped to promote a new and warmer friendship with Britain, for Britain, alone of the European nations, sympathised with the United States in the conflict. This the Americans appreciated, and as the nineteenth century drew to its end the foundations were laid for a closer concert between the two peoples in facing the problems of the world.

EPILOGUE 1

OLD BATTLEFIELDS OF VIRGINIA

In 1929, after an absence from America of nearly thirty years, Winston Churchill, in the course of an extended coast-to-coast visit, personally tramped across some of the Civil War battlefields of Virginia. He impressed as his guide an old man who, as a boy of eight, had witnessed some of the bloodiest fighting.

THE DAILY TELEGRAPH, DECEMBER 16, 1929

IT TAKES only a few hours by train or motor to go from Washington to Richmond, but we breathe a different air. It is another country. The scenes of bustling progress, of thriving and profuse prosperity, the echoes of the last word in modernity, have been left behind. We have exchanged the twentieth century for the nineteenth. We have crossed the mysterious boundary which separates the present from the past. More than that, we have crossed the frontiers which divide victory from defeat. We are in the rebel capital.

A mellow and yet a naughty light plays around long-beleaguered, valiantly defended, world-famous Virginia. The hum of Chicago, the rattle of Wall Street, the roar of New York, even the tranquil prosperity of California, all are absent. We have entered the domain of history. We march with Lee and Jackson, with Stuart, with Longstreet, and with Early through autumn woodlands, lonely in their leafy splendours of old gold and fading crimson. It is still a broken land.

"Lucifer, son of the morning, how art thou fallen!" Virginia, the proud Founder State of the American Union, the birthplace and home of its most renowned citizens, from Washington to Wilson, beaten down, trampled upon, disinherited, impoverished, riven asunder and flung aside while Northern wealth and power and progress strode on to Empire! And yet it had to be. Hardly even would the adherents of the lost cause wish it otherwise.

From noon till night, with guides excelling in every detail of military history, we chase McClellan through the Battle of the Seven Days. We begin with A. P. Hill in the two days' struggle at Beaver Dam Creek and

Gaines's Mill, while Jackson's marching columns, brought so swiftly and secretly from the Valley, cannot cope with the difficulties of the ground. It is not until late on the second day that the general attack of Lee's 45,000 Confederates can be launched against the Union right— 25,000 men isolated on the northern bank of the Chickahominy. Then a fierce struggle in the summer evening until darkness falls, and the Union troops magnificently resisting retreat by their five bridges across the river, sullenly covered by their heavy guns. And now a fatal day of uncertainty and delay. The fog of war! The silent woods! Where has McClellan gone? Will he hurl himself upon the denuded lines which cover Richmond, or will he recoil upon his base at White House? Either move loaded with desperate peril for both armies; a day of cruel suspense for Lee!

It is not until after dark on the third day that we know which course McClellan has taken. He has taken neither. With amazing decision and celerity he has thrown away his communications; he has severed himself from his base. He has established a new base on salt water; has ordered his fleet and store ships to meet him there, and is marching down the peninsula with his whole army in a long flank march across the front of the Richmond lines. Lee has not comprehended the meaning of seapower.

Swift, then, to strike him as he moves, we hurry back with Lee almost into Richmond, and leaving Jackson to follow the Federal tracks, pour down the roads which radiate from the capital, towards Savage Station, and White Oak Swamp. Now to cut the Union army in half as it toils along a single road! But our columns lag, the detour has been too much, the staff work is imperfect, the manoeuvre is too elaborate; we have not got the trained personnel to handle such complex affairs.

McClellan's flank guard holds firm, long enough to let the thirty-mile blue serpent—80,000 men, with all their wagons and artillery, marching in one column—slip past the hoped-for point of interception. We make another detour, and strike again furiously at Malvern Hill. But here he has entrenched again in full force, and a tremendous position. His left is impregnable, and before we have found out that his right can be turned, our own centre has attacked spontaneously—at half-cock as it were—and we are committed to general battle.

Again a bloody struggle; again late at night the Union positions are stormed; again McClellan retreats under the cover of darkness; and this time brings his whole army intact and in perfect order safely into his new base at Harrison's Landing on the James River, under the all-powerful guns of his fleet. We thought we had him to cut to pieces, and rounded up; but he had marched through the jaws of death. Never mind, we have driven him twenty miles further from Richmond, and we have gathered 35,000 good rifles from the battlefield. Important, this, because it is so difficult to fight without good rifles. Even the best generals and the bravest troops find it hard.

It was with deep interest that I followed these memorable operations. No one can understand what happened merely through reading books and studying maps. You must see the ground; you must cover the distances in person; you must measure the rivers, and see what the swamps were really like. It is difficult for the modern eye, accustomed to judge military positions in miles, to adjust itself to these battlefields, where the troops faced each other erect in solid lines at a few hundred yards range. And the Chickahominy River! What a surprise! It is little more than a woodland stream; and White Oak Swamp! a thicket with some puddles. These were the days when the greatest dramas were still played on miniature stages.

I was astonished also by the numerous traces which remain after nearly three-quarters of a century. The farmhouses and the churches still show the scars of shot and shell; the woods are full of trenches and rifle pits; the larger trees are full of bullets. Before the War Museum in Richmond still flies a tattered rebel flag. If you could read men's hearts, you would find that they, too, bear the marks.

We stay with Governor Byrd, where Jefferson Davis ruled, and see the Parliament Buildings where Lee received his commission and where Secession was declared. I decline a warm-hearted invitation to visit Yorktown, and take part in the celebration of the 163rd anniversary of the surrender of Lord Cornwallis. The Civil War makes better reading.

Accordingly, next day I motor sixty miles along the famous turnpike to Fredericksburg. Here, again, the battlefields tell their own story. Admirable descriptive iron plates, erected at the cost of Virginia, and inscribed by deeply instructed hands, fix almost every historical point. The stone wall and sunken road at Fredericksburg; the cemeteries of Union and Confederate soldiers; the trench lines trailing away through the deserted forest, revive the past with strange potency.

Here, south of the Rappahannock, is another wide area of battlefields, on which, perhaps, more soldiers have perished in an equal space than anywhere, excepting round Ypres and Verdun. Here the campaigns lie one upon the other; and Fredericksburg and Chancellorsville are overlaid by the Wilderness and Spotsylvania. The trenches crisscross one another; the monuments of dead commanders and shot-torn regiments are of different years. An earthly palimpsest of tragedy! Our guide observes, "My father was wounded here; he is still living in Richmond. His memory is perfect."

We are anxious to see the celebrated "Bloody Angle" in the salient of the Spotsylvania lines. The sandy tracks through this wild, wooded region are intricate. We stop at a farmhouse for information. The farmer, a tall man, hearty and strong, comes out of a substantial dwelling. "Yes; it is quite easy to get there. Turn off the high road half a mile back. Stay! I will go with you myself." We jolt along. "See, here is the line," he says; "the main trench is further on." "You know all this very well?" I remark. "I have lived here all my life. I was here when the battle was fought." "How old were you?" "Eight." "Tell me exactly what you remember."

So then he tells an unvarnished tale of how he and his father and two other children were in their farm (not this house, but a cottage a hundred yards away), and how suddenly one morning, very early, swarms of troops arrived, "like bees!" "The officer told us to pack up and clear out, for there was going to be a fight. My father told me to get them some water, which I did from the old well, while he put the horse in the cart and flung what he could snatch into it; and we drove off just as the cannon began and the shots whistled about. It was three or four days later when we came back. Our house was in ruins. There must have been a thousand dead men lying in that field below it. We had nothing left in the world. We were terribly hungry. We collected broken biscuits from among the dead."

The car stops. We alight and walk through sunlit glades of small oak, beech, and maple. "Here is the Angle," says our guide. "Here is where the dead lay thickest. Yes! in this trench they were piled in heaps, both sides together, blue and grey. We came here while the firing was still going on a mile or two away. My father scolded me for trying to take the boots off a dead soldier who lay here. See that little gully there? It was pouring with rain, and all the water running along it was red. You know," he adds, "a little blood goes a long way."

A small boy comes up with a basketful of bullets and regimental badges from the forgotten gleanings of a fearful harvest. We take some of these poor relics—all there is to show! Ah! No! Great causes have been settled. Destiny pivoting here has stamped the ground with a ruthless heel; the path of the world takes a different turn henceforward. Not in vain these deeds were done.

During the last few years Virginia and the Southern States have at last begun a decided recovery. Industries, particularly textiles, have shifted from the North. Motor roads lace the towns together. Swift cars fly to and fro, here and there skyscrapers shoot upwards. The population of Virginia is undergoing a rapid increase. The old inhabitants are going to get rich; their lands are rising in value. There is an influx of busy industrials from the North.

The Virginians take all this very coolly. "No doubt it will be nice to be rich and prosperous and go ahead, but still," they say, "we managed to get on all right before. We had a quiet life and culture of our own. Will it all be swamped by these new elements? We were knocked out of the world seventy years ago. We are not so very keen on going back. It may be progress, but it is Yankee progress. Now, in the old days before the war . . ."

EPILOGUE 2

IF LEE HAD NOT WON THE BATTLE OF GETTYSBURG

In 1930 Churchill wrote a marvellous "What if?" based on the supposition that Lee won at Gettysburg, then occupied Washington while Lincoln fled to New York. Finally Lee, all supreme, frees the slaves, eliminating the North's moral argument and the war ends with the South achieving independence. The Confederacy and United States co-exist uneasily until 1914, when world events drive them together and, along with Great Britain, they combine to prevent World War I!

He concludes by speculating what might have happened had Lee lost the Battle of Gettysburg. The Southern states, having lost the war and nursing a keen resentment, would have enacted all sorts of racist laws while carpet-baggers would have invaded the South. A powerful Confederacy would not have existed in 1914 and war in Europe would certainly have occurred. Who knows? War in 1914 might have produced a Red revolution in Russia and a Fascist dictatorship in Germany, with even graver implications for the world. And all this might have happened . . . had Lee not won the Battle of Gettysburg!

This moving and visionary piece was described by Shelby Foote, the great Civil War writer, as the only "What if?" he had ever admired.

SCRIBNER'S, DECEMBER 1930

THE QUAINT CONCEIT of imagining what would have happened if some important or unimportant event had settled itself differently has become so fashionable that I am encouraged to enter upon an absurd speculation. What would have happened if Lee had not won the Battle of Gettysburg? Once a great victory is won it dominates not only the future but the past. All the chains of consequence clink out as if they never could stop. The hopes that were shattered, the passions that were quelled, the sacrifices that were ineffectual are all swept out of the land of reality. Still it may amuse an idle hour, and perhaps serve as a corrective to undue complacency, if at this moment in the twentieth century—so rich in assurance and prosperity, so calm and buoyant—we meditate for a spell upon the debt we owe to those Confederate soldiers who by a deathless feat of arms broke the Union front at Gettysburg and laid open a fair future to the world.

It always amuses historians and philosophers to pick out the tiny things, the sharp agate points, on which the ponderous balance of destiny turns; and certainly the details of the famous Confederate victory of Gettysburg furnish a fertile theme. There can be at this date no conceivable doubt that Pickett's charge would have been defeated if Stuart with his encircling cavalry had not arrived in the rear of the Union position at the supreme moment. Stuart might have been arrested in his decisive swoop if any one of twenty commonplace incidents had occurred. If, for instance, General Meade had organized his lines of communication with posts for defence against raids, or if he had used his cavalry to scout upon his flanks, he would have received a timely warning. If General Warren had only thought of sending a battalion to hold Little Round Top the rapid advance of the masses of Confederate cavalry must have been detected. If only President Davis's letter to General Lee, captured by Captain Dahlgren, revealing the Confederacy plans had reached Meade a few hours earlier he might have escaped Lee's clutches.

Anything, we repeat, might have prevented Lee's magnificent combinations from synchronizing and, if so, Pickett's repulse was sure. Gettysburg would have been a great Northern victory. It might have well been a final victory. Lee might, indeed, have made a successful retreat from the field. The Confederacy, with its skilful generals and fierce armies, might have survived for another year, or even two, but once defeated decisively at Gettysburg, its doom was inevitable. The fall of Vicksburg, which happened only two days after Lee's immortal triumph, would in itself by opening the Mississippi to the river fleets of the Union, have cut the Secessionist States almost in half. Without wishing to dogmatize, we feel we are on solid ground in saying that the Southern States could not have survived the loss of a great battle in Pennsylvania and the almost simultaneous bursting open of the Mississippi.

However, all went well. Once again by the narrowest of margins the compulsive pinch of military genius and soldierly valour produced a perfect result. The panic which engulfed the whole left of Meade's massive army has never been made a reproach against the Yankee troops. Everyone knows they were stout fellows. But defeat is defeat, and rout is ruin. Three days only were required after the cannon at Gettysburg had ceased to thunder before General Lee fixed his headquarters in Washington. We need not here dwell upon the ludicrous features of the hurried flight to New York of all the politicians, place hunters, contractors, sentimentalists and their retinues, which was so successfully accomplished. It is more agreeable to remember how Lincoln, "greatly falling with a falling State," preserved the poise and dignity of a nation.

Never did his rugged yet sublime commonsense render a finer service to his countrymen. He was never greater than in the hour of fatal defeat.

But, of course, there is no doubt whatever that the mere military victory which Lee gained at Gettysburg would not by itself have altered the history of the world. The loss of Washington would not have affected the immense numerical preponderance of the Union States. The advanced situation of their capital and its fall would have exposed them to a grave injury, would no doubt have considerably prolonged the war; but standing by itself this military episode, dazzling though it may be, could not have prevented the ultimate victory of the North. It is in the political sphere that we have to look to find the explanation of the triumphs begun upon the battlefield.

Curiously enough, Lee furnishes an almost unique example of a regular and professional soldier who achieved the highest excellence both as a general and as a statesman. His ascendancy throughout the Confederate States on the morrow of his Gettysburg victory threw Jefferson Davis and his civil government irresistibly, indeed almost unconsciously, into the shade. The beloved and victorious commander, arriving in the capital of his mighty antagonists, found there the title deeds which enabled him to pronounce the grand decrees of peace. Thus it happened that the guns of Gettysburg fired virtually the last shots in the American Civil War.

The movement of events then shifted to the other side of the Atlantic Ocean. England—the name by which the British Empire was then commonly described—had been riven morally in twain by the drama of the American struggle. We have always admired the steadfastness with which the Lancashire cotton operatives, though starved of cotton by the Northern blockade—our most prosperous county reduced to penury, almost become dependent upon the charity of the rest of England—nevertheless adhered to the Northern cause. The British working classes on the whole judged the quarrel through the eyes of Disraeli and rested solidly upon the side of the abolition of slavery. Indeed, all Mr. Gladstone's democratic flair and noble eloquence would have failed, even upon the then restricted franchise, to carry England into the Confederate camp as a measure of policy. If Lee after his triumphal entry into Washington had merely been the soldier his achievements would have ended on the battlefield. It was his august declaration that the victorious Confederacy would pursue no policy towards the African negroes, which was not in harmony with the moral conceptions of Western Europe, that opened the high roads along which we are now marching so prosperously. . . .

A procession of tremendous events followed the Northern defeat at Gettysburg and the surrender of Washington. Lee's declaration abolishing slavery, coupled as it was with the inflexible resolve to secede from the American Union, opened the way for British intervention.

Within a month the formal treaty of alliance between the British Empire and the Confederacy had been signed. The terms of this alliance being both offensive and defensive, revolutionized the military and naval situation. The Northern blockade could not be maintained even for a day in the face of the immense naval power of Britain. The opening of the Southern ports released the pent-up cotton, restored the finances and replenished the arsenals of the Confederacy. The Northern forces at New Orleans were themselves immediately cut off and forced to capitulate. There could be no doubt of the power of the new allies to clear the Mississippi of Northern vessels throughout the whole of its course through the Confederate States. The prospect of a considerable British army embarking for Canada threatened the Union with a new military front.

But none of these formidable events in the sphere of arms and material force would have daunted the resolution of President Lincoln, or weakened the fidelity of the Northern States and armies. It was Lee's declaration abolishing slavery which by a single master-stroke gained the Confederacy an all-powerful ally and spread a moral paralysis far and wide through the ranks of their enemies. The North were waging war against Secession, but as the struggle had proceeded, the moral issue of slavery had first sustained and then dominated the political quarrel. Now that the moral issue was withdrawn, now that the noble cause which inspired the Union armies and the Governments behind them was gained, there was nothing left but a war of reconquest to be waged under circumstances infinitely more difficult and anxious than those which had already led to so much disappointment and defeat. Here was the South victorious, reinvigorated, reinforced, offering of her own free will to make a more complete abolition of the servile status on the American continent than even Lincoln had himself seen fit to demand. Was the war to continue against what soon must be heavy odds merely to assert the domination of one set of English-speaking people over another; was blood to flow indefinitely in an ever-broadening stream to gratify national pride or martial revenge?

It was this deprivation of the moral issue which undermined the obduracy of the Northern States. Lincoln no longer rejected the Southern appeal for independence. "If," he declared in his famous speech in Madison Square Gardens in New York, "our brothers in the South are willing faithfully to cleanse this continent of negro slavery, and if they will dwell beside us in neighbourly goodwill as an independent but friendly nation, it would not be right to prolong the slaughter on the question of sovereignty alone."

Thus peace came more swiftly than war had come. The Treaty of Harpers Ferry, which was signed between the Union and Confederate States on September 6, 1863, embodied the two fundamental propositions: that the South was independent, and the slaves were free. If the spirit of old John Brown had revisited the battle-scarred township which had been the scene of his life and death, it would have seen his cause victorious, but at a cost to the United States terrible indeed. Apart from the loss of blood and treasure, the American Union was riven in twain. Henceforth there would be two Americas in the same northern continent. One of them would have renewed in a modern and embattled form its old ties of kinship and affiliation with the Mother Country across the ocean. It was evident though peace might be signed and soldiers furl their flags, profound antagonisms, social, economic and military, underlay the life of the English-speaking world. Still slavery was abolished. As John Bright said, "At last after the smoke of the battlefield has cleared away, the horrid shape which had cast its shadow over the whole continent, had vanished and was gone for ever."

During the whole of the rest of the nineteenth century the United States of America, as the truncated Union continued to style itself, grew in wealth and population. An iron determination seemed to have taken hold of the entire people. By the 'eighties they were already cleared of their war debt, and indeed all traces of the war, except in the hearts of men, were entirely eradicated. But the hearts of men are strange things, and the hearts of nations are still stranger. Never could the American Union endure the ghastly amputation which had been forced upon it. Just as France after 1870 nursed for more than forty years her dream of *revanche,* so did the multiplying peoples of the American Union concentrate their thoughts upon another trial of arms.

And to tell the truth, the behaviour of the independent Confederacy helped but little in mitigating the ceaselessly fermenting wrath. The former Confederate States saw themselves possessed of a veteran army successful against numerous odds, and commanded by generals to whose military aptitude history has borne unquestioned tribute. To keep this army intact and—still more important—employed, became a high problem of state. To the south of the Confederacy lay Mexico, in perennial alternation between anarchy and dictatorship. Lee's early experiences in the former Mexican War had familiarized him with the military aspects of the country and its problems, and it was natural that he should wish to turn the bayonets of the army of northern Virginia upon this sporadically defended Eldorado. In spite of the pious protests of Mr. Disraeli's Liberal and pacifist Government of 1884, the Confederate States after three years' sanguinary guerrilla fighting conquered, subdued and reorganized the vast territories of Mexico. These proceedings involved a continuous accretion of Southern military forces. At the close of the Mexican War seven hundred thousand trained and well-tried soldiers were marshalled under what the North still called "the rebel flag." In the face of these potentially menacing armaments who can blame the Northern States for the precautions they took? Who can accuse them of provocation because they adopted the principle of compulsory military service? And when this was retorted by similar measures south of the Harpers Ferry Treaty line, can we be surprised that they increased the period of compulsory service from one year to two, and thereby turned their multitudinous militia into the cadres of an army "second to none." The Southern States, relying on their alliance with the supreme naval power of Britain, did not expend their money upon a salt-water navy. Their powerful ironclad fleet was designed solely for the Mississippi. Nevertheless, on land and water the process of armament and counter-armament proceeded ceaselessly over the whole expanse of the North American continent. Immense fortresses guarded the frontiers on either side and sought to canalize the lines of reciprocal invasion. The wealth of the Union States enabled them at enormous sacrifice at once to fortify their southern front and to maintain a strong fleet and heavy military garrison in the fortified harbours of the great lakes of the Canadian frontier. By the 'nineties North America bristled with armaments of every kind, and what with the ceaseless growth of the Confederate army—in which the reconciled negro population now formed a most important element—and the very large forces which England and Canada maintained in the North, it was computed that not less than two million armed men with trained reserves of six millions were required to preserve the uneasy peace of the North American continent. Such a process could not go on without a climax of tragedy or remedy.

The climax which came in 1905 was perhaps induced by the agitation of war excitement arising from the Russo-Japanese conflict. The roar of Asiatic cannon reverberated around the globe, and everywhere found immense military organizations in an actively receptive state. Never has the atmosphere of the world been so loaded with explosive forces. Europe and North America were armed camps, and a war of first magnitude was actually raging in Manchuria. At any moment, as the Dogger Bank incident* had shown, the British Empire might be involved in war with Russia. Indeed, we had been within the ace on that occasion. And apart from such accidents the British Treaty obligations towards Japan might automatically have drawn us in. The President of the United States had been formally advised by the powerful and highly competent American General Staff that the entry of Great Britain into such a war would offer in every way a favourable opportunity for settling once and for all with the Southern Republic. This fact was also obvious to most people. Thus at the same time throughout Europe and America precautionary measures of all kinds by land and sea were actively taken; and everywhere fleets and armies were assembled and arsenals clanged and flared by night and day.

Now that these awful perils have been finally warded off it seems to us almost incomprehensible that they could have existed. Nevertheless, it is horrible even to reflect that scarcely a quarter of a century ago English-speaking people ranged on opposite sides, watched each other with ceaseless vigilance and drawn weapons. By the end of 1905 the tension was such that nothing could long avert a fratricidal struggle on a gigantic scale, except some great melting of hearts, some wave of inspiration which should lift the dull, deadly antagonisms of the hour to a level so high that—even as a mathematical quantity passing through infinity changes its sign—they would become actual unities.

We must not underrate the strength of the forces which on both sides of the Atlantic Ocean and on both sides of the American continental frontiers were labouring faithfully and dauntlessly to avert the hideous doom which kindred races seemed resolved to prepare for themselves. But these deep currents of sanity and goodwill would not have been effective unless the decisive moment had found simultaneously in England and the United States leaders great enough to dominate events and marvellously placed upon the summits of national power. In President Roosevelt and Mr. Arthur Balfour, the British Prime Minister, were present two diverse personalities which together embodied all the qualities necessary alike for profound negotiation and for supreme decision.

After all, when it happened it proved to be the easiest thing in the world. In fact, it seemed as if it could not help happening, and we who look back upon it take it so much for granted that we cannot understand how easily the most beneficent Covenant of which human

---

* In 1904, during the Russo-Japanese War, a Russian fleet fired on the trawlers on the Dogger Bank, claiming that there were Japanese torpedo boats among them. A Commission of Inquiry was set up and Russia was ordered to pay compensation to the families of the victims.

records are witness might have been replaced by the most horrible conflict and world tragedy.

The Balfour-Roosevelt negotiations had advanced some distance before President Wilson, the enlightened Virginian chief of the Southern Republic, was involved in them. It must be remembered that whatever may be thought of Mr. Gladstone's cold-blooded *coup* in 1863, the policy of successive British Governments had always been to assuage the antagonism between North and South. At every stage the British had sought to promote good will and close association between her southern ally and the mighty northern power with whom she had so much in common. For instance, we should remember how in the Spanish-American War of 1895 the influence of Great Britain was used to the utmost and grave risks were run in order to limit the quarrel and to free the United States from any foreign menace. The restraining counsels of England on this occasion had led the Southern Republic to adopt a neutrality not only benevolent, but actively helpful. Indeed, in this war several veteran generals of the Confederate army had actually served as volunteers with the Union forces. So that one must understand that side by side with the piling up of armaments and the old antagonisms, there was an immense under-tide of mutual liking and respect. It is the glory of Balfour, Roosevelt and Wilson—this august triumvirate—that they were able so to direct these tides that every opposing circumstance or element was swept before them.

On Christmas Day, 1905, was signed the Covenant of the English-speaking Association. The essence of this extraordinary measure was crystal clear. The doctrine of common citizenship for all the peoples involved in the agreement was proclaimed. There was not the slightest interference with the existing arrangements of any member. All that happened was that henceforward the peoples of the British Empire and of what were happily called in the language of the line "The Re-United States," deemed themselves to be members of one body and inheritors of one estate. The flexibility of the plan which invaded no national privacy, which left all particularisms entirely unchallenged, which altered no institutions and required no elaborate machinery, was its salvation. It was, in fact, a moral and psychological rather than political reaction. Hundreds of millions of people suddenly adopted a new point of view. Without prejudice to their existing loyalties and sentiments, they gave birth in themselves to a new higher loyalty and a wider sentiment. The autumn of 1905 had seen the English-speaking world on the verge of catastrophe. The year did not die before they were associated by indissoluble ties for the maintenance of peace between themselves, for the prevention of war among outside Powers and for the economic development of their measureless resources and possessions.

The Association had not been in existence for a decade before it was called upon to face an emergency not less grave than that which had called it into being. Every one remembers the European crisis of August, 1914. The murder of the Archduke at Sarajevo, the disruption or decay of the Austrian and Turkish Empires, the old quarrel between Germany and France, and the increasing armaments of Russia—all taken together produced the most dangerous conjunction which Europe has ever known. Once the orders for Russian, Austrian, German and French mobilization had been given and twelve million soldiers were gathering upon the frontiers of their respective countries, it seemed that nothing could avert a war which might well have become Armageddon itself.

What the course and consequences of such a war would have been are matters upon which we can only speculate. M. Bloch in his thoughtful book published in 1909, indicated that such a war if fought with modern weapons would not be a short one.* He predicted that field operations would quickly degenerate into long lines of fortifications, and that a devastating stalemate with siege warfare, or trench warfare, lasting for years, might well ensue. We know his opinions are not accepted by the leading military experts of most countries. But, at any rate, we cannot doubt that a war in which four or five of the greatest European Powers were engaged might well have led to the loss of many millions of lives, and to the destruction of capital that twenty years of toil, thrift, and privation could not have replaced. It is no exaggeration to say that had the crisis of general mobilization of August, 1914, been followed by war, we might today in this island see income tax at four or five shillings in the pound (20 to 25 percent), and have two and a half million unemployed workmen on our hands. Even the United States far across the ocean might, against all its traditions, have been dragged into a purely European quarrel.

But in the nick of time friendly though resolute hands intervened to save Europe from what might well have been her ruin. It was inherent in the Covenant of the English-speaking Association that the ideal of mutual disarmament to the lowest point compatible with their joint safety should be adopted by the signatory members. It was also settled that every third year a Conference of the whole Association should be held in such places as might be found convenient. It happened that the third disarmament conference of the English-speaking Association— the E.S.A. as it is called for short—was actually in session in July, 1914.

---

* Jean Bloch (1836–1902), Polish financier and writer. His book *Is War Now Impossible?* was actually published in England in 1899.

The Association had found itself hampered in its policy of disarmament by the immense military and naval establishments maintained in Europe. Their plenipotentiaries were actually assembled to consider this problem when the infinitely graver issue burst upon them. They acted as men accustomed to deal with the greatest events. They felt so sure of themselves that they were able to run risks for others. On August 1, when the German armies were already approaching the frontiers of Belgium, when the Austrian armies had actually begun the bombardment of Belgrade, and when all along the Russian and French frontiers desultory picket firing had broken out, the E.S.A. tendered its friendly offices to all the mobilized Powers, counselling them to halt their armies within ten miles of their own frontiers, and to seek a solution of their differences by peaceful discussion. The memorable document added "that failing a peaceful outcome the Association must deem itself *ipso facto* at war with any Power in either combination whose troops invaded the territory of its neighbour."

Although this suave yet menacing communication was received with indignation in many quarters, it in fact secured for Europe the breathing space which was so desperately required. The French had already forbidden their troops to approach within ten miles of the German frontier, and they replied in this sense. The Czar eagerly embraced the opportunity offered to him. The secret wishes of the Kaiser and his emotions at this juncture have necessarily been much disputed. There are those who allege that, carried away by the excitement of mobilization and the clang and clatter of moving armies, he was not disposed to halt his troops already on the threshold of the Duchy of Luxembourg. Others avow that he received the message with a scream of joy and fell exhausted into a chair, exclaiming, "Saved! Saved! Saved!" Whatever may have been the nature of the Imperial convulsion, all we know is that the acceptance of Germany was the last to reach the Association. With its arrival, although there yet remained many weeks of anxious negotiation, the danger of a European war may be said to have passed away.

Most of us have been so much absorbed by the immense increases of prosperity and wealth, or by the commercial activity and scientific and territorial development and exploitation which have been the history of the English-speaking world since 1905, that we have been inclined to allow European affairs to fall into a twilight of interest. Once the perils of 1914 had been successfully averted and the disarmament of Europe had been brought into harmony with that already effected by the E.S.A., the idea of "A United States of Europe" was bound to occur continually. The glittering spectacle of the great English-speaking combination, its assured safety, its boundless power, the rapidity with which wealth was created and widely distributed within its bounds, the sense of buoyancy and hope which seemed to pervade the entire populations; all this pointed to European eyes a moral which none but the dullest could ignore. Whether the Emperor Wilhelm II will be successful in carrying the project of European unity forward by another important stage at the forthcoming Pan-European Conference at Berlin in 1932 is still a matter of prophecy. Should he achieve his purpose he will have raised himself to a dazzling pinnacle of fame and honour, and no one will be more pleased than the members of the E.S.A. to witness the gradual formation of another great area of tranquillity and cooperation like that in which we ourselves have learned to dwell. If this prize should fall to his Imperial Majesty, he may perhaps reflect how easily his career might have been wrecked in 1914 by the outbreak of a war which might have cost him his throne, and have laid his country in the dust. If today he occupies in his old age the most splendid situation in Europe, let him not forget that he might well have found himself eating the bitter bread of exile, a dethroned sovereign and a broken man loaded with unutterable reproach. And this, we repeat, might well have been his fate, if Lee had not won the Battle of Gettysburg.

PART II

AMERICA IN THE TWENTIETH CENTURY

*Selected Articles,
Broadcasts and
Speeches*

CHAPTER 1

THE CHICAGO
SCANDALS

After his first visit to Chicago, in the course of a lecture tour in 1901, the young Winston followed up five years later with a review of Upton Sinclair's The Jungle. *The piece highlights the plight of many of America's new immigrants—in this case a Lithuanian family driven out of their homeland by Russian pogroms—and is a devastating exposé of the darker side of unregulated capitalism as practised in the meat-packing factories of Chicago at the turn of the century.*

P.T.O. JUNE 16 & 23, 1906

WHEN I PROMISED to write a few notes on this book, I had an object—I hoped to make it better known. In the weeks that have passed that object has disappeared. The book has become famous. It has arrested the eye of a warm-hearted autocrat; it has agitated the machinery of a State department; and having passed out of the sedate columns of the reviewer into leading articles and "latest intelligence," has disturbed in the Old World and the New the digestions, and perhaps the consciences, of mankind.

Mr. Upton Sinclair is one of that active band of reformers, comprising some men of very great gifts and some men of very great wealth, whose energies are now directed in the United States to no less a task than the destruction or bodily capture of the Democratic party and the installation in its place of a thorough and unshrinking Socialist organization. His book is a tract in a swelling political agitation, and it takes the form of an indictment of the huge meat-packing business on the shores of Lake Michigan popularly called the great "Beef Trust." Nothing can exceed the skill and determination with which the author has marshalled his arguments. He is one of those debaters who stand no nonsense from their facts. He finds a place for each—even for the most contrary—in ingenious sequences which steadily approach his goal. All conditions of life—social, moral, political, economic, commercial, climatic, bacteriological—are assembled, drilled into order, arranged under their proper standards, and led by converging roads to the assault. No undisciplined statement is allowed to weaken the stability of their line. One purpose and one purpose alone animates the mind of the commander, and inspires his army down to the humblest item which marches silently in the ranks—to make the great Beef Trust stink in the nostrils of the world, and so to contaminate the system upon which it has grown to strength. Here in the compass of a few hundred pages has been collected all that can be said against the canning industry, all that will damage it before its servants and expose it to its customers.

The "packers" are brought to the bar. The goods they sell, the materials they use, the city they dwell in, the wages they pay—every circumstance, great and small, of their business, together with its consequences, direct or remote—are subjected to a pitiless and malevolent scrutiny.

The worst has been told, and only the worst; it has been told in the most effective way; and the reader is confronted—nay, overwhelmed—by concatenations of filthy, tragic, detestable details, which reduce him, however combative or incredulous, to a kind of horror-struck docility.

Let me say at once that people have no right to hold their noses and shut their eyes. If these things are true, all honour to him who has the power and skill to fasten world-wide attention upon them. If they be only half true, a great public service has been rendered. If only one-tenth part be true, there would still, I fancy, be some debt owing by society to Mr. Upton Sinclair. And there is, unhappily, good reason to believe—scarcely, indeed, any reason to doubt—that a very considerable body of undeniable and easily ascertainable truth sustains the charges that are made. Mr. Upton Sinclair has done for the "packers" what Mr. Henry Lloyd did some years ago in *Wealth against Commonwealth* for the Standard Oil Trust. The mood and the motive of both books are the same; but in one respect Mr. Sinclair's method has a great advantage over his forerunner. *Wealth against Commonwealth* was a laborious compilation. *The Jungle* is a human tragedy.

The thread on which all is strung is the gradual ruin, moral and physical, of a strong, brave, honest man. We are introduced abruptly to a family of Lithuanian peasants who have migrated to Chicago. The family is numerous. All relationships and all ages are included. There is Jurgis the hero, a mighty man, a Titan among workers. There is Ona, the girl to whom he is pledged, and for whose sake the great adventure of the ocean voyage has been made. There are her father and aunt, and his brother and his sister, Marija, and four or five small children of varying ages. All the grown-ups are thrifty, industrious, simple Lithuanian folk who, having massed their savings, have sailed for the

United States, and after being fleeced by every official into whose clutches their journey has led them, have arrived at length at Chicago, asking nothing better than to work from dawn to dusk at an honest trade.

The characters are drawn with care and feeling. We get to know them all. We get to like them all. We become swiftly interested in their domestic economy. How much is left to them of their slender stock of money, what are their prospects of employment, what wages are they bringing in each week, what debts and expenses have they to meet, what perils are in their path—all these petty, everyday matters are made real and important to us by a hundred pages of lively and elaborate art. Once this has been accomplished, Mr. Upton Sinclair has the reader very much at his mercy. He uses his advantage to the full. The utter destruction of this whole family in circumstances of misery and horrid degradation is the plan on which he proceeds, and which he carries out in an exquisite detail and with a ruthlessness of purpose which certainly leave nothing to be desired from an artistic point of view.

The scaffolding of this catastrophe may be set up within the compass of a few paragraphs. The family have very little money left when they arrive in Chicago, and what they have earned at European wages is swiftly draining away at American prices. They all seek work—not without success—and with them we enter the service of the great Beef Trust and of its auxiliary industries.

Jurgis, from his magnificent appearance, with the first flower of his manhood to sell, is at once selected from the huddling crowd of loafers and applicants at the gates of the killing sheds. Marija, his cousin, obtains a situation as a beef-boner. Ona is employed in a canning mill. Ona's father works underground in a pickling establishment. The unmarried brother finds a job. All this promises well. It is the summer time. Although living is dear, the wages are to them immense. They look with hope into the future—that hideous future towards which they are remorselessly drawn. Impelled by a leaflet of the "Why pay rent?" type, they buy a house on the instalment plan. Jurgis marries Ona, and in touching obedience to the old, generous traditions of Lithuania, the family entertain with rude hospitality all who may claim to share in their festivities. Then this one gleam of sunshine fades.

Throughout the whole narrative we study with care the surroundings. The mighty slaughter machine, which can slay during every hour of every single day four or five hundred cattle and a holocaust of hogs. We see an endless succession of pigs driven tirelessly forward on to the wheel of doom, mounting aloft swiftly, sliding, strung by the leg, along the overhead rail past the stickers, through the boiling vats, on, as hams and sausages, aye, and as curried prawns or potted woodcock, to the markets of the world. We see the whole process, its ugliness and its economy, its efficiency and its corruption:

All these industries were gathered into buildings near by, connected by galleries and railroads with the main establishment; and it was estimated that they had handled nearly a quarter of a billion of animals since the founding of the plant by the elder Durham a generation and more ago. If you counted with it the other big plants— and they were now really all one—it was, so Jokubas informed them, the greatest aggregation of labour and capital ever gathered in one place. It employed thirty thousand men; it supported directly two hundred and fifty thousand people in its neighbourhood, and indirectly it supported half a million. It sent its products to every country in the civilised world, and it furnished the food for no less than thirty million people. Most of the men here took a fearfully different view of the thing from Jurgis. He was quite dismayed when he first began to find it out—that most of the men hated their work. It seemed strange, it was even terrible, when you came to find out the universality of the sentiment; but it was certainly the fact—they hated their work. They hated the bosses and they hated the owners; they hated the whole place, the whole neighbourhood—even the whole city, with an all-inclusive hatred, bitter and fierce. Women and little children would fall to cursing about it; it was rotten, rotten as hell—everything was rotten. When Jurgis would ask them what they meant, they would begin to get suspicious, and content themselves with saying, "Never mind, you stay here and see for yourself."

Take this picture for economy and efficiency:

There was scarcely a thing needed in the business that Durham and Company did not make for themselves. There was a great steam-power plant and an electricity plant. There was a barrel factory, and a boiler-repair shop. There was a building to which the grease was piped, and made into soap and lard; and then there was a factory for making lard cans, and another for making soap boxes. There was a building in which the bristles were cleaned and dried, for the making of hair cushions and such things; there was a building where the skins were dried and tanned, there was another where heads and feet were made into glue, and another where bones were made into fertilizer. No tiniest particle of organic matter was wasted in Durham's. Out of the horns of the cattle they made combs, buttons, hair-pins and imitation ivory; out of the shin bones and other big bones they cut knife and tooth-brush handles, and mouthpieces for pipes; out of the hoofs they cut hair-pins and buttons, before they made the rest into glue. From such things as feet, knuckles, hide clippings, and sinews came such strange and unlikely products as gelatin, isinglass, and phosphorus, bone-black, shoe-blacking, and bone-oil. They had curled-hair works for the cattle tails, and a "wool-pullery" for the sheep skins; they made pepsin from the stomachs of the pigs, and albumen from the blood, and violin strings from the ill-smelling entrails. When there was nothing else to be done with a thing, they first put it into a tank and got out of it all the tallow and grease, and then they made it into fertilizer.

Now the companion picture—corruption:

There was never the least attention paid to what was cut up for sausage; there would come all the way back from Europe old sausage that had been rejected, and that was mouldy and white. It would be dosed with borax and glycerine, and dumped into the hoppers, and made over again for home consumption. There would be meat that had tumbled out on the floor, in the dirt and sawdust, where the workers had tramped and spit uncounted billions of consumption germs. There would be meat stored in great piles in rooms; and the water from leaky roofs would drip over it, and thousands of rats would race about on it. It was too dark in these storage places to see well, but a man could run his hand over these piles of meat and sweep off handfuls of the dried dung of rats. These rats were nuisances, and the packers would put poisoned bread out for them; they would die, and then rats, bread and meat would go into the hoppers together. This is no fairy story, and no joke; the meat would be shovelled into carts, and the man who did the shovelling would not trouble to lift out a rat even when he saw one—there were things that went into the sausage in comparison with which a poisoned rat was a tidbit. There was no place for the men to wash their hands before they ate their dinner, and so they made a practice of washing them in the water that was to be ladled into the sausage. There were the butt-ends of smoked meat, and the scraps of corned beef, and all the odds and ends of the waste of the plants, that would be dumped into old barrels in the cellar and left there.

There is no end to the dismal tale of fraud and cruelty:

It was late, almost dark, and the Government inspectors had all gone, and there were only a dozen or two of men on the floor. That day they had killed about four thousand cattle, and these cattle had come in freight trains from far States, and some of them had got hurt. There were some with broken legs, and some with gored sides; there were some that had died, from what cause no one could say; and they all had to be disposed of, here in darkness and silence. "Downers," the men called them, and the packing-house had a special elevator upon which they were raised to the killing-beds, where the gang proceeded to handle them, with an air of businesslike nonchalance which said plainer than any words that it was a matter of everyday routine.

Again:

> And shortly afterward one of these, a physician, made the discovery that the carcasses of steers which had been condemned as tubercular by the Government inspectors, and which therefore contained ptomaines which are deadly poisons, were left upon an open platform and carted away to be sold in the city; and so he insisted that these carcasses be treated with an injection of kerosene—and was ordered to resign the same week!

Winter comes on—winter in Chicago. Cold—dry, hard, cutting American cold—grips all men, stabbing with steel-blue daggers through their ribs at lungs and life. Blizzards scourge along the streets, and the snow drifts deep against the gimcrack houses. Each separate branch of the great packing industry develops some snare or danger of its own. There is short time in killing sheds. Marija is crippled by a cut which festers poisonously. Ona, who has gone to work within a week of having her baby, is afflicted with a woman's complaint which nevermore leaves her. The old father dies of the damp chills and poisonous fumes of the pickling cellar; his feet have first been eaten away by the acids on the floor. Instalments lag; debts accumulate; resources dwindle. Two children have to be withdrawn from school before the legal age, and driven to earn money as newsboys on the streets. The family emerge into the milder weather of the springtime as if they had been hunted and mauled by wolves. The unmarried brother takes himself off, and vanishes from the story.

> Their children were not as well as they had been at home; but how could they know that there was no sewer to their house, and that the drainage of fifteen years was in a cesspool under it? How could they know that the pale blue milk that they bought around the corner was watered, and doctored with formaldehyde besides? When the children were not well at home, Teta Elzbieta would gather herbs and

cure them; now she was obliged to go to the drug-store and buy extracts—and how was she to know that they were all adulterated? How could they find out that their tea and coffee, their sugar and flour, had been doctored; that their canned peas had been coloured with copper salts, and their fruit jams with aniline dyes? And even if they had known it, what good would it have done them, since there was no place within miles of them where any other sort was to be had? The bitter winter was coming, and they had to save money to get more clothing and bedding; but it would not matter in the least how much they saved, they could not get anything to keep them warm. All the clothing that was to be had in the stores was made of cotton and shoddy, which was made by tearing old clothes to pieces and weaving the fibre again.

The family, weakened, but surviving, suffer in summer as well as in the winter. Gone are the rude cabins of Lithuania, with their peasant ceremonies and peasant securities. We are in an atmosphere of fraud, stink, and electricity. Here is one cameo from their surroundings:

"Bubbly Creek" is an arm of the Chicago River, and forms the southern boundary of the yards; all the drainage of the square mile of packing-houses empties into it, so that it is really a great open sewer a hundred or two feet wide. One long arm of it is blind, and the filth stays there for ever and a day. The grease and chemicals that are poured into it undergo all sorts of strange transformations, which are the cause of its name; it is constantly in motion, as if huge fish were feeding in it, or great leviathans disporting themselves in its depths. Bubbles of carbonic acid gas will rise to the surface and burst, and make rings two or three feet wide. Here and there the grease and filth have caked solid, and the creek looks like a bed of lava; chickens walk about on it, feeding, and many times an unwary stranger has started to stroll across, and vanished temporarily. The packers used to leave the creek that way, till every now and then the surface would catch on fire and burn furiously, and the fire department would have to come and put it out. Once, however, an ingenious stranger came and started to gather this filth in scows, to make lard of; then the packers took the cue, and got out an injunction to stop him, and afterwards gathered it themselves. The banks of "Bubbly Creek" are plastered thick with hairs, and this also the packers gather and clean.

Mr. Sinclair has now accomplished his purpose so far as it relates to the methods of the packing industry. The human tragedy remains to be related.

The second winter proves fatal. For a time Jurgis struggles with almost superhuman strength. He meets every difficulty and every new expense by valiant answer, "I will work harder." Through blizzards and snow-drifts, in the darkness of the winter mornings, he carries the children to their work and Ona to the electric tramcar. At night he brings them all home. He works overtime. He denies himself every comfort. He faces the full blast of the storm.

We know the state of the family budget. We know the liabilities that must be met month by month. We know the wages earned and the mouths to feed. We calculate when the next instalment for the house will fall due. For a time we think he will conquer—maybe does conquer. He breaks the back of winter and emerges again—Atlas-like, bearing his world upon his shoulders.

Then, just as we are about to cheer his victory, he sprains his ankle on the slippery floor of the killing sheds. He will not give in. He is forced to give in. He is a cripple. He lies on his back for months and months helpless, mad with the sense of powerlessness. The family are without their support. Atlas has stumbled, and the world collapses. The earnings of delicate, ailing Ona at her canning factory, supple-mented by what the children can pick up—selling newspapers, raking in the ashpits for food—scarcely sustain the lives of our Lithuanian friends.

At length Jurgis is well. He returns to the killing beds only to find his place filled. This time he cannot get another. His bloom of manhood is gone. His vital energies are weakened. He is "past work." He walks with a slight limp. The days are coming when he will be mere industrial refuse—to be cast upon the rubbish-heap of labour. Machines need oil-ing and constant care. Horses must be fed and tended. But a man who is for the moment out of gear may be flung aside. He is cheap enough, and there are plenty more where he came from. Jurgis at last gets work of lower kind—work which no one will do except in desperation. He is employed in the "fertilizer plant." The reader must be referred to Mr. Upton Sinclair for a singularly complete account of the conditions pre-vailing in this industry.

While engaged in this employment Jurgis finds out that during his illness Ona has been seduced by the manager of the factory where she worked, under threat of being dismissed. He is dragged away to prison for a murderous assault before he has more than half-choked this ruf-fian. Thirty days later he returns. The house has been sold up for non-payment of the instalments. The children have taken to the streets.

Ona, prematurely confined, dies in a filthy lodging-house. Only one thing still links Jurgis with humanity. A few months later this frail monitor is drowned in a deep street puddle, and the hero of the story is hero no more. He curses God; but he does not die. He leaves the two women, Marija and Ona's aunt, to shift for themselves. He becomes a tramp. He prowls about the countryside seeking what he may devour. Another winter in Chicago, and he is a footpad. He commits highway robbery. He burgles. He garrottes. He falls still lower. He becomes a politician.

Mr. Upton Sinclair certainly introduces this faction with great skill and ingenuity. When in prison Jurgis has made friends with a good-natured desperado who seems to combine an habitual and conscientious war upon society with occasional divagations into politics. We see the hunted, starving Lithuanian carried off swiftly forward by events to an important position thus: Mike Scully, an Irishman, boss of the Chicago Democratic Party, has received a great sum of money on condition he will make a wealthy Jewish brewer Mayor of Chicago. He accepts the money, but not being sure whether his Jew, once elected, will play his game, he resolves to allow the Republican Party to win the election. A Republican "working man" candidate is needed to win such a contest, and such a candidate appears. Jurgis is called upon as a bona-fide labourer to urge his fellow to support the Republican against the forces of plutocracy. The doors of the great Beef Trust swing obediently open at Mike Scully's nod. Jurgis is at work again at good wages and on easy terms. For three or four months he organizes the Republican working class vote. The "working man" candidate is triumphantly elected, and plutocracy is abased in the person of the Jew, who has, in fact, paid the expenses of both parties in the contest. Jurgis, who has stolen, or, to use the idiom, "taken big graft," from the funds which had passed through his hands, is able to bank upwards of 300 dollars at the close of the fight.

___

One would think that this was the end. But there is yet another circle in Mr. Upton Sinclair's Inferno. Jurgis exchanges the rôle of politician for one, in the author's eyes, more base and vile than any in which he has appeared. The great Chicago strike breaks out. Maddened by suffering, the wretched folk of Packingtown rise against their master. Jurgis becomes a blackleg. He "jumps" the job of a "boss" who has struck. He is now earning a fine income. The strike ends, but by a breach of the conditions the old foreman is not restored. Jurgis seems on the high road to fortune. Far below him now are the squalid struggles of two years ago. He is a faithful myrmidon of the great Beef Trust. He is "in" with the "big graft" people. He has the political "pull." He may fairly look forward across a prosperous career to wealth, public banquets, and general complacency. He is reaching the position where he will be able to declare that he has found in America, to whose shores he had struggled an almost penniless immigrant, a land of hope and freedom—"a refuge for the oppressed of every race and of every clime."

But his fate is still malignant. Destiny and Mr. Upton Sinclair still hold him in their grip. One day, by pure chance, he encounters again the manager who had seduced his wife. He has lost every trace of his old virtue except the one remaining strain of virile ferocity. He pounces upon his foe. Again they tear him off; but not until he has torn away with his teeth a hideous mouthful of flesh and blood. This assault would not in itself have mattered. Jurgis, protected by his "pull," is bailed out at once. But to his horror he discovers that the man he has attacked is one of Mike Scully's most trusted agents. In Mr. Sinclair's compendious phrase, "his own 'pull' has run up against a bigger 'pull.' "

Down, then, once more to the depths—to shivering streets, to the crowded station-house, to the starving mob about the factory gates, and this time to rise no more. To rise no more, at least, in the unregenerate state. Salvation is at hand. He wanders to a Socialist meeting; he hears "the word" preached by a socialist orator. His soul—or is it his belly?—is saved. He becomes a convert to the terse creed of "Let the nation own the Trusts." The orthodoxy of his opinions procures him employment as hall porter at a Socialist hotel. We get one parting glimpse of Ona's cousin Marija—who was first made known to the reader as a kind of sturdy, rosy-cheeked Sarah Jane, the incarnation of rude, healthy peasant simplicity—as a morphia-doped prostitute in a raided brothel. The incongruity of this development adds finely to its repulsiveness. And then, with a few chapters on Socialistic revolutions, the curtain falls.

The reader will not, I think, be satisfied with this conclusion. After all that has happened, after all that has been suffered, he will look for some more complete consolation. Not so Mr. Upton Sinclair. This shrewd delineator of character, this painstaking and careful exponent of detail, appears sincerely unconscious of our disappointment. Consolation?—have we not the Socialist orator? Regeneration?—is not Jurgis fully instructed? Salvation?—who can doubt the earnestness of his convictions? What more can anyone require? Let us rejoice that through all this filth and agony one heart at least has been saved from error. There is one man more in Chicago who may be trusted to vote straight for the Socialist ticket. Hurrah!

In writing thus I do not mean to carp at the really excellent and valuable piece of work which this terrible book contains. It pierces the thickest skull and the most leathery heart. It forces people who never think about the foundations of society to pause and wonder. It enables those who sometimes think to understand. The justification of that vast and intricate fabric of Factory Law, of Health Acts, of Workmen's Compensation, upon which Parliament is swiftly and laboriously building year by year and month by month, is made plain, so that a child may see it, so that a fool may see it, so that a knave may see it. But I must frankly say that if the conditions of society in Chicago are such as Mr. Upton Sinclair depicts, no mere economic revolution would in itself suffice to purify and ennoble. A National or Municipal Beef Trust, with the United States Treasury at its back, might indeed give more regular employment at higher wages to its servants, and might sell cleaner food to its customers—at a price. But if evil systems corrupt good men, it is no less true that base men will dishonour any system, and while no bond of duty more exacting than that of material recompense regulates the relations of man and man, while no motion more lofty than that of self-interest animates the exertions of every class, and no hope beyond the limits of this fleeting world lights the struggles of humanity, the most admirable systems will merely succeed in transferring, under different forms and pretexts, the burden of toil, misery, and injustice from one set of human shoulders to another.

It is possible that this remarkable book may come to be considered a factor in far-reaching events. The indignation of millions of Americans has been aroused. That is a fire which has more than once burnt with a consuming flame. There are in the Great Republic in plentiful abundance all the moral forces necessary to such a purging process. The issue between Capital and Labour is far more cleanly cut today in the United States than in other communities or in any other age. It may be that in the next few years we shall be furnished with Transatlantic answers to many of the outstanding questions of economics and sociology upon whose verge British political parties stand in perplexity and hesitation. And that is, after all, an additional reason why English readers should not shrink from the malodorous recesses of Mr. Upton Sinclair's *Jungle*.

CHAPTER 2

PROHIBITION

Winston was not enamoured of Prohibition, and in the course of his 1929 tour of America, his eighteen-year-old son, Randolph, was placed in charge of assorted bottles of "medicine" to circumvent what he regarded as an unacceptable intrusion into the liberty of the individual.

THE DAILY TELEGRAPH, DECEMBER 2, 1929

BEFORE THE intense interest of the Great War died away, the far-seeing American people had provided themselves with another unfailing topic of conversation. The attempt of the Legislature to prevent by a stroke of the pen 120,000,000 persons from drinking spirits, wines, or even beer is the most amazing exhibition alike of the arrogance and of the impotence of a majority that the history of representative institutions can show.

The extreme self-assertion which leads an individual to impose his likes and dislikes upon others, the spasmodic workings of the electoral machine, the hysteria of wartime on the home front, and the rat-trap rigidity of the American Constitution have combined to produce on a gigantic scale a spectacle at once comic and pathetic.

Obviously there are limitations upon the power of legislative majorities. It is easy to pass a law. All you do is to organize the people who are keen upon it in every electoral area, and set to work to badger the local candidates and the local caucus till they make it a plank in their platform. Out of all these local platforms a high national structure is built up by the same methods, on the top of which is poised a statue of Uncle Sam, winking quizzically, above the inscription, "This is the Will of the Nation, and this is the Law of the Land." And all the people who have been walking about below, busy with their daily life, and making the country rich and strong, look up at the new monument and exclaim, "Fancy that; how funny!"

No folly is more costly than the folly of intolerant idealism. Follies which tend towards vice encounter at every stage in free and healthy communities enormous checks and correctives from the inherent good-ness and sanity of human nature; but follies sustained by lofty ideas go far, and set up strange and sinister reactions. When standards of con-duct or morals which are beyond the normal public sentiment of a great community are professed and enforced, the results are invariably eva-sion, subterfuge, and hypocrisy. In the end a lower standard is reached in practice than would have followed from a commonsense procedure.

The melancholy era which followed the victory of the North in the American Civil War affords a glaring example. Inspired by the noblest of ideals—the abolition of slavery—animated by fierce war hatred and party lust, the conquerors decreed that black and white should vote on equal terms throughout the Union, and the famous Fifteenth Amend-ment was added to the Constitution of the United States. Overwhelm-ing force was at their disposal, with every disposition to use it against the prostrate and disarmed Confederacy. The North were no more in-convenienced by the voting of a few handfuls of negroes scattered among their large population, and being outvoted on all occasions, than is a teetotaler by Prohibition.

But the South had different feelings. After years of waste, friction, and actual suffering the Fifteenth Amendment was reduced by the per-sistent will-power of the minority and through many forms of artifice and violence to a dead letter. The Southern negroes have the equal po-litical rights it was the boast of the Constitution to accord them; but for two generations it has been well understood that they are not to use them in any State or District where they would make any difference.

As with the Fifteenth, so will it be with the Eighteenth Amendment. A Chinese dignitary studying American life and law asked blandly, when Prohibition was explained to him, "When does it begin?" A more serious judgment was expressed to me by one well qualified to form an opinion, "There is less drinking, but there is worse drinking."

Ultimate decision upon the abstract rights and wrongs of Prohibi-tion depends upon the view which is held of the relation of the individ-ual to the State. Is the State, based upon majorities elected somehow, entitled to enforce its will upon all its individual members in every di-rection without limit; or is the State entitled to use its delegated powers only within such limits and for such purposes as have led individuals to band themselves together and submit themselves to its organization?

Has a majority—perhaps in fact a minority—a right to do anything which it can get voted by the legislature, or do its powers when ex-tended beyond a certain point degenerate into tyranny? Is it necessary for the purposes of "life, liberty, and the pursuit of happiness" that vast sums of money should be spent, and hordes of officials employed against sober and responsible citizens who wish to do no more than drink wine or beer as they would in any other country in the civilized world? Is not the State, on this question, exceeding its duties? Is it not needlessly and wrongfully interfering with the individual and with that very liberty which it has been called into existence to guard?

On the abstract merits there are, of course, two opinions, but on the practical results there can only be one. A law which does not carry with it the assent of public opinion or command the convictions of the leading elements in a community may endure, but cannot succeed; and under modern conditions in a democratic country it must, in the process of failure, breed many curious and dangerous evils.

To abstain from wine because one does not like it or need it is good; to abstain in order to set an example is better; to compel others to abstain because one has abstained oneself is, to say the least, bad manners; to indulge oneself while compelling others to abstain is contemptible. Yet this last has become one of the commonest features of American life. Millions of people of every class who vote dry, and thereby assume moral responsibility for all that the attempted enforcement of Prohibition involves, do not hesitate to procure and consume alcoholic beverages whenever they require them. Such a divorce between the civic act and private conduct would only be possible in a sphere where the vote of the legislative institution did not correspond to the moral convictions and deep-seated habits of the nation.

What of the cause of temperance meanwhile? Does it gain or lose by these violent measures? Has the progress of the United States, in combating the evils of drunkenness under Prohibition, been comparable with that, for instance, of Great Britain under a regulated freedom tempered by taxation? I was proud to tell Americans how our convictions for drunkenness had declined to a third of what they were before the war, and how each year, as Chancellor of the Exchequer, I had had to write the Budget down by three or four million pounds on account of the increasingly temperate habits of the British public, and how vast was the revenue still gathered to our national coffers, which in the United States flowed to the bootlegger or was squandered in a nightmare warfare to suppress him.

I was glad to point to the various experiments which are now being made with success and satisfaction in Canada. The Canadians, under the same unbalanced wartime emotion, decreed Prohibition. But when experience had taught them its evils, they still enjoyed the Constitutional power to retrace their steps. They have erected their new system around the impressive principle that no person shall have the slightest interest in the manufacture, transportation or sale of alcoholic liquor, and upon this firm foundation they have rallied the approval and the loyalty of the public.

Thoughtful Americans look wistfully across the Canadian border and across the Atlantic Ocean at Communities which seem to combine increasing sobriety with private liberty. They wonder how they are to escape from the rigid grip of their own political institutions and criss-cross party groupings. They are shocked at the growth of drunkenness and of the crimes and diseases of drunkenness in their midst. They resent the constant interference of the State with the private life of its citizens, and they blush at the choice they are often forced to make between irrational public duty and normal personal habits; but what can they do? Every avenue seems barred except the one by which the mighty bootlegging interest advances, with the tacit approval of public opinion, and in many cases with the corrupt connivance of the agents of Prohibition.

Yet, after all, the remedy is easy. Recognize the imperfections which vitiate even the best representative institutions; recognize that all citizens, majority or minority alike, have inherent rights; recognize that in the sphere of manners and morals the law must carry with it the real consent of the governed. Recur to those fundamental principles of personal liberty which Constitutions and States are created to defend, and strip from drunkenness and bootlegging the shelter of official interference with habits and customs as old as the world.

CHAPTER 3

1929: SPECULATION FEVER

In the course of his 1929 visit, Winston was in New York to witness the Great Crash on Wall Street and the panic it engendered. As he records, "Under my very window a gentleman cast himself down fifteen storeys and was dashed to pieces, causing wild commotions and the arrival of the fire brigade. . . ."

THE DAILY TELEGRAPH, DECEMBER 9, 1929

"THE DARK, narrow, crooked lane leading to the river and the graveyard," to quote the local description of Wall Street, has been, during the last few years, the cynosure of American eyes. No social or political topic, no foreign or domestic event, not the Presidential election, not even Prohibition itself, has been a serious competitor.

Everybody dabbles in stocks. Earned increments are sweet, but those unearned are sweeter. . . . Millions of men and women are in the market, all eager to supplement the rewards of energetic toil by "easy money." From every part of its enormous territories the American public follows the game. Horseracing, baseball, football, every form of sport or gambling cedes its place to a casino whose amplitude and splendours make Monte Carlo the meanest midget in Lilliput.

No pages of the innumerable newspapers which cater to the public taste are more prominently or carefully printed, more eagerly and more earnestly studied, than those which record the daily operations of the stock markets. Brokers abound on every side. The more enterprising hotels have a complete apparatus of tape machine and telephone facilities, and provide entire suites where, amid the clack and rattle of tickers, expert clerks chalk up from minute to minute the latest quotations, not only from New York, but from other important exchanges.

The housemaid who makes your bed is a stockholder on margin. Workmen of every class, brain or hand, the chauffeur, the tram conductor, the railwayman, the waiter, all have their open accounts, and so very often have their wives. Even the Transatlantic steamers have their floating migratory exchange, where seasick "bulls" and "bears" contend amid the heaves and lurches.

A speculative public, numbering in the United States alone many millions, is, of course, utterly novel. Nothing approaching it has ever been seen or dreamed of since the world began. Nothing can stop these enormous multitudes when they come in full of ardour. Nothing can even delay them when, swept by panic, they stream out. Nevertheless, the physical structure of the New York Stock Exchange has rules and regulations which have been framed with such massive strength and strictness that the perils of the situation are less formidable than would appear to European eyes.

London has never attempted to handle such masses. Our people have not the wealth, nor is our machinery adapted to such strains. The British workman bets and gambles on the turf, and finds his book-maker, legal or illegal, never far away. But the American public concentrates upon the stock markets, and it is as easy to buy shares, few or many on margin, as it is to buy a pound of tea, and far easier than to buy a motorcar or a gramophone upon the instalment system. The personal relation between broker and client, which is the staple of our old-world business, has been superseded in the United States by iron rules which, while they facilitate every form of speculation, have, nevertheless, enabled the brokers to weather, with scarcely a shipwreck the greatest financial hurricane that ever blew.

Before disparaging American methods, the English critic would do well to acquaint himself with the inherent probity and strength of the American speculative machine. It is not built to prevent crises, but to survive them.

The turbulent life-force of this community, its vast creative and productive effort and achievement, its sense of worlds to conquer, its unshakeable faith in a golden future, lead it naturally, perhaps inevitably, certainly uncontrollably, to anticipate the good days which are surely coming. "What," they ask, "can stop the United States?" Has it not rather only just got on the move?

Vast enterprises, acquiring momentum every day, science and organization smoothing and lighting the path, the very magnitude of every operation facilitating the next; a continent as raw material in the hands of industry, wealth abounding, and wealth diffused, millionaires multiplying, wages high and rising, seven million college students, motorcars, also by millions, food plentiful, clean and cheap, room to live, room to breathe, room to grow, room to kick, Socialism a European delusion, politics an occasional pastime, the Constitution a rock—why should they fear? Forward! Headlong! All will be well.

Was it wonderful that a population thus circumstanced and thus inspired should outstrip advancing reality, should prefer speculation to thrift, should try to live a year or two ahead of time, should consume and cast away, and make again? A blunder! We can repair it. Hideous losses! We can make them good. Ruins! Watch us rebuild them.

To write thus of the solidity of the speculative apparatus, or of the buoyancy of the speculative public, must not lead to any underrating of the disappointment and suffering which the recent violent collapse of values has brought to millions of American homes. The steady inflation of prices has gone on so long that ordinary people with busy lives and short views had readily and comfortably accepted its continuance as one of the regular conditions of life. The worker who had deposited his 35 per cent margin easily persuaded himself that he possessed one hundred units of capital. He felt himself doing business on a large scale like the great capitalists. Everyone round him was doing it too. It all seemed so good and sound; and behind it lay the broad United States.

And then—suddenly, the earth trembled, the chimney stacks fell crashing into the streets, and many dead and wounded were carried away. Then, when it was assumed that all was over, came other shocks, heavier and heavier, and the fronts of buildings cracked or fell out, spreading havoc and panic in the crowded streets, and thousands of millions of capital value were annihilated in ten days; and all the small stockholders were ruthlessly sold out. And the women said to their husbands: "Sell out at all costs," "Let it all go," "You have your job or your salary," "Let's keep the home." And the great popular stores said: "Halve the orders to be given out for Christmas and the spring." And several million families decided to make the old car do for another year.

The consuming power was grievously weakened. In opulent Fifth Avenue fur coats, already half-accepted by clients, came back in scores and dozens because they did not fit. Under my very window a gentleman cast himself down fifteen storeys and was dashed to pieces, causing a wild commotion and the arrival of the fire brigade. Quite a number of persons seem to have overbalanced themselves by accident in the same sort of way. A workman smoking his pipe on the girder of an unfinished building 400 ft. above the ground blocked the traffic of the street below, through the crowd, who thought he was a ruined capitalist waiting in a respectful and prudently withdrawn crescent for the final act.

And then the bankers arrived upon the scene and lectured the unfortunates who had lost their money, and preached the virtues of thrift and the immorality of speculation, and picked up the securities that were lying about the streets in baskets, and even in wagons, and took them home for safety to their vaults. Grim!

Still, after all, no one can say the public was not warned. Many times have the Federal Reserve authorities denounced speculation and raised the rate to check it. Repeatedly Mr. Mellon declared the position unsafe, and counselled investments in bonds. The British Chancellor of the Exchequer, with the profound knowledge of the Treasury behind him, stigmatized the proceedings as "an orgy." A certain Mr. Babson, whose firm advises the American public about the markets in much the same way as "Hotspur" tells our betting crowd about the Turf, had the prescience and, what is more remarkable, the courage to predict an imminent fall of at least 60 points in values. But all these warnings fell upon ears deaf to unwelcome tidings. The American public have certainly been cleaned out, but they cannot say that they have been hoodwinked.

I happened to be walking down Wall Street at the worst moment of the panic, and a perfect stranger who recognized me invited me to enter the gallery of the Stock Exchange. I expected to see pandemonium; but the spectacle that met my eyes was one of surprising calm and orderliness. There are only 1,200 members of the New York Stock Exchange, each of whom has paid over £100,000 for his ticket. These gentlemen are precluded by the strictest rules from running or raising their voices unduly. So there they were, walking to and fro like a slow-motion picture of a disturbed ant heap, offering each other enormous blocks of securities at a third of their old prices and half their present value, and for many minutes together finding no one strong enough to pick up the sure fortunes they were compelled to offer.

It was refreshing to exchange this scene of sombre and, for the moment, almost helpless liquidation for a window high in a titanic building. The autumn afternoon was bright and clear, and the noble scene stretched to far horizons. Below lay the Hudson and the East Rivers, dotted with numerous tugs and shipping of all kinds, and traversed by the ocean steamers from all over the world moving in and out of the endless rows of docks. Beyond lay all the cities and workshops of the New Jersey shore, pouring out their clouds of smoke and steam. Around towered the mighty buildings of New York, with here and there glimpses far below of streets swarming with human life.

No one who gazed on such a scene could doubt that this financial disaster, huge as it is, cruel as it is to thousands, is only a passing episode in the march of a valiant and serviceable people who by fierce experiment are hewing new paths for man, and showing to all nations much that they should attempt and much that they should avoid.

CHAPTER 4

CALIFORNIA

On his first visit to California, Winston was awestruck by the beauty of the scenery. In the California redwoods it took Winston, all his party, and several other visitors besides—fifteen in all—to encompass, with their arms stretched wide, "The Big Tree." Their travels took them to Hollywood and meetings with Charlie Chaplin and Harold Lloyd and, to his son Randolph's huge delight, such stars as Marion Davies, Colleen Moore, Anita Page, and Joan Crawford.

THE DAILY TELEGRAPH, DECEMBER 29 & 30, 1929

THE STATE OF CALIFORNIA has a coastline nearly 1,000 miles long, and I was assured that its whole population—man, woman, and child—could get into the motor cars they own and drive from one end of it to the other at any time they had the inclination. They would certainly be well advised to try the experiment, for a more beautiful region I have hardly ever seen.

The long strip of hilly or undulating country, rising often into mountain ranges, presents, through fifteen degrees of latitude, a smiling and varied fertility. Forests, vineyards, orange groves, olives, and every other form of cultivation that the natives desire, crowns or clothes the sunbathed peaks and valleys.

The Pacific laps the long-drawn shores, and assures at all seasons of the year an equable and temperate climate. The cool ocean and the warm land create in their contact a misty curtain which veils and mitigates the vigour of the sun. By a strange inversion you ascend the mountain to get warm, and descend to the sea level to get cool. Take it for all in all, the western slopes of the Rocky Mountains offer a spacious, delectable land, where man may work or play on every day in the year.

The prosperity arising from the calm fruitfulness of agriculture has been stimulated and multiplied by the flashing apparition of gold and oil, and is adorned by the gay tinsel of the Hollywood filmland. The people who have established themselves and are dominant in these thriving scenes represent what is perhaps the finest Anglo-Saxon stock to be found in the American Union. Blest with abundant food and pleasing dwellings, spread as widely as they may wish in garden cities, along the motor roads, or in their farms, the Californians have at their disposal all the natural and economic conditions necessary for health, happiness and culture.

Their easily gathered foods afford a diet in which milk, fruit, vegetables, and chicken predominate; while endless vineyards offer grape juice in unfermented, or even sometimes accidentally fermented, forms. A buoyancy of temperament, a geniality of manner, an unbounded hospitality, and a marked friendliness and respect towards Old England, her institutions and Empire, are the characteristics most easily discerned among them. Poverty as we know it in Europe, slums, congestion, and the gloomy abodes of concentrated industrialism are nowhere to be seen.

It was my good fortune to spend nearly a month in these agreeable surroundings and conditions, motoring through the country from end to end; and certainly it would be easy to write whole chapters upon the closely packed procession of scenes and sensations which saluted the journey. Here I can only give a few thumbnail sketches on which, however, the reader may care to cast an eye.

Entering California from the north, we travel along the celebrated Redwood Highway. The road undulates and serpentines ceaselessly. On either side from time to time are groves and forests of what one would call large fir trees. As we go on they get taller. The sense that each hour finds one amid larger trees only grows gradually. At length we stop to take stock of the scene, and one is surprised to see how small a car approaching round a bend a hundred yards away appears in relation to the trunks which rise, close together, in vast numbers on either side. Still full realization does not come. Another hour of swift progression! Now we are in the heart of the Redwoods. There is no mistake about it this time.

The road is an aisle in a cathedral of trees. Enormous pillars of timber tower up 200 ft. without leaf or twig to a tapering vault of sombre green and purple. So close are they together that the eye is arrested at a hundred yards distance by solid walls of timber. It is astonishing that so many vast growing organisms find in so small a space of air and soil the nourishment on which to dwell and thrive together. If a battle were fought in such a forest every bullet would be stopped within 200 yards, embedded in impenetrable stems. At the bases of these monsters men look like ants and motor cars look like beetles. Far above, the daylight twinkles through triangular and star-shaped openings. On the ground is vivid green or yellow bloom and leafage. These scenes repeat themselves at intervals for perhaps eighty or a hundred miles.

Suddenly we reach a notice with a finger-point: "The Big Tree." We turn off the well-oiled turnpike and jolt and bump eight miles through sandy tracks, surrounded by enormous trunks and ceilinged by brooding foliage. We walk gingerly across a river bed on a bridge formed by one fallen monster, and here at last is "The Big Tree." They tell us it is more than 400 ft. high. At its base some hospitable Californians are entertaining the petty officers from a British cruiser. We all join hands around the tree. It takes fifteen of us stretched to the full to compass it!

After compliments, jokes, and photographs, the guide remarks that this tree is certainly 4,000 years old. It has been growing all this time and is still full of life and vigour. Devastating fires have swept through the forest scores of times during its existence, and have licked up the undergrowth and all ordinary trees and vegetation, but they could not harm the giants. Sometimes a large ring of burnt wood from flames extinguished a thousand years ago is found when Redwood trees are cut down. They can survive everything and heal every wound they receive. These trees were already old "when the smoke of sacifice arose from the Pantheon and camelopards bounded in the Flavian amphitheatre," and, but for the timber companies, they may "still continue in undiminished vigour" when Macaulay's traveller from New Zealand "takes his stand upon a broken arch of London Bridge to sketch the ruins of St. Paul's." They will grow as long as the Californians allow them to grow.

Let me turn another page of my scrap book. I am at the top of the tallest building in San Francisco. Dizzy depths yawn beneath the window-sills. The Chairman of the Telephone Company has invited me to have ten minutes' talk with my wife in England. I take up the instrument. My wife speaks to me across one ocean and one continent— one of each. We hear each other as easily as if we were in the same room, or, not to exaggerate, say about half as well again as on an ordinary London telephone. I picture a well-known scene far off in Kent, 7,000 miles away. The children come to the telephone. I talk to them through New York and Rugby. They reply through Scotland and Canada. Why say the age of miracles is past? It is just beginning.

Turn over. We are in the Lick Observatory. A broad, squat cupola has been built by the munificence of a private citizen at the summit of a conical mountain 4,000 feet high. All is dark within the Observatory. The telescope, its girth not unworthy of the giant trees, peers through a slit of pale but darkening sky. The dome rotates, the floor sinks, then rises slightly.

I sit upon a ladder. The planet Saturn is about to set; but there is just time to observe him. Of course I know about the rings around Saturn. Pictures of them were shown in all the schools where I was educated.

But I was sceptical. We all know how astronomers have mapped the heavens out in the shape of animals. We can most of us—by a stretch of the imagination—recognize the Great Bear, but still one quite sympathizes with those who call it The Plough. Bear or Plough—one is as like it as the other. So I expected to see, when I looked at Saturn, a bright star with some smudges round it, which astronomers had dignified by the name of rings.

In this mood I applied myself to the eye-piece. I received the impression that some powerful electric light had been switched on by mistake in the Observatory and was in some way reflected in the telescope. I was about to turn and ask that it might be extinguished, when I realized that what I saw was indeed Saturn himself. A perfectly modelled globe, instinct with rotundity, with a clear-cut lifebuoy around its middle, all glowing with serene radiance. I gazed with awe and delight upon this sublime spectacle of a world 800 million miles away.

Again the dome rotates, and the floor rises or falls. I am told to look at the heavens with the naked eye. Can I see a very faint star amid several bright ones? It is very far off and quite an achievement to discern it. I see the faintest speck or rather blur of light. Now look through the telescope. Two pairs of lovely diamonds, dazzling in their limpid beauty, gleam on either side of the field of vision. "You are looking," says the astronomer, "at one of our best multiple stars. That faint speck you saw with the eye consists of these double twins, the stars in each pair revolving around the other pair!" Celestial jewellery! I forget how long they take to revolve, if indeed, it is yet known to man, or how far they are apart. Perhaps the light would pass from one to the other in four or five years. But it is all in the books.

Then we return swifter than light across the gulfs of space, and come to the moon, where dawn has just risen on the mountains, tipping them with flame, and casting their silhouettes in violet shadows upon the lunar craters. Thereafter for some time we talk about the heavens and my kindly teachers explain all—or perhaps not all—about nebulae and spiral nebulae.

It appears that outside our own universe, with its thousands of million suns, there are at least two million other universes, all gyrating and coursing through the heavens like dancers upon a stage. I had not heard of this before, and was inspired to many thoughts sufficiently commonplace to be omitted here. I was disturbed to think of all these universes which had not previously been brought to my attention. I hoped that nothing had gone wrong with them.

It is sixty miles from the Lick Observatory to Burlingame, the garden suburb of the San Francisco notables, where we were sheltered for the night. It was a relief, after thinking about two million universes and countless millions of suns, many complete with planets, moons, comets, meteoric streams, etc. and the incomprehensible distances which separate them, to take up the morning paper (which, according to American custom, is always published the evening before), and to read that the stock markets were still booming, that Mr. J. H. Thomas had a new idea (which he was keeping secret) about the unemployed, and that Mr. Snowden, by his firm stand for Britain had surrendered only half a million more of the taxpayers' money. And so to bed!

We follow from north to south the great road which runs the entire length of California. Our stages are sometimes as long as 250 miles. Night in the Redwoods is impressive. Every dozen miles or so rest camps—"motels," as they are called—have been built for the motorist population. Here simple and cheap accommodation is provided in clusters of detached cabins, and the carefree wanderers upon wheels gather round great fires singing or listening to the ubiquitous wireless music.

Great numbers motor for amusement, travelling very light, usually in couples, and thinking nothing of a thousand miles in their little cars. Continuous streams of vehicles flow up and down at speeds which rarely fall below forty miles an hour. The road by day recalls the French Corniche roads in character and beauty of scenery, but is often more crowded. Its ribbon surface follows in the main the mountainous coastline, now rising to a thousand feet or more, with awful gulfs and hairpin turns, now spinning along almost in the ocean spray. What with the traffic, the precipices, the turns, the ups and downs, and the high speeds, the journey is not dull, and the scenery is splendid.

As we progress the vegetation changes. The giant Redwoods die away; oak and other English-looking trees succeed them; and we flash across trout streams and rivers, much attenuated by the summer, and some even reduced to chains of pools. From the town of Eureka onwards I noticed the palm, and a hundred miles further south the vegetation and aspect of the landscape became Italian. We now come into the land of grapes and pause for luncheon at an immense wine factory. I forget how many millions of gallons of Californian wines are stored in the mighty vats of its warehouses.

Fermented! Certainly! Do not be alarmed, dear Miss Anna, it is "for sacramental purposes only." The Constitution of the United States, the God of Israel, and the Pope—an august combination—protect, with the triple sanctions of Washington, Jerusalem and Rome, this inspiring scene. Nevertheless, there is a fragrance in the air of which even the

Eighteenth Amendment cannot deprive us. Not to be tantalized, we hasten on, and fifty miles to the southward alight for refreshment before the verandahs and porticos of a pretty inn, whose advertisement proclaims, "Good Eats and Soft Drinks." Yielding to these allurements, I am supplied with a glass of "near beer." This excellent and innocent beverage is prepared in the following way:

Old-world beer is brewed, and thereafter all the alcohol in excess of one-half of 1 percent is eliminated, and cast to the dogs. The residue, when iced, affords a pleasant drink indistinguishable in appearance from the naughty article, and very similar in flavour. But, as the less regenerate inform us, "it lacks Authority." I was told that sometimes distressing accidents occur in the manufacture. Sometimes mistakes are made about the exact percentage, and on one melancholy occasion an entire brew was inadvertently released at the penultimate stage of manufacture, to spread its maddening poison through countless happy homes. But, needless to say, every precaution is taken.

I have not concealed my own views upon Prohibition, but candour compels me to say that, having been for two months for the first time in my life exposed to its full rigours, I have found the effects upon my constitution very much less disturbing than I had expected.

The shades of evening were already falling as we approached San Francisco. I had been dozing and awoke with a start to find myself in the midst of the ocean. As far as the eye could reach on all sides in the gathering dark nothing but water could be seen. The marvellous road was traversing an inlet of the sea, or perhaps an estuary, by a newly constructed bridge *seven miles long,* and only a few feet above the waves.

On either side the water reaches depths of eighty feet, and in the centre we climbed by easy gradients to a sort of Tower Bridge with bascules to allow the passage of shipping. This remarkable piece of engineering, brilliantly illuminated throughout its entire length, has been constructed to avoid the delays or inconvenience of detour or ferry. That the motor traffic—mainly pleasure traffic—should warrant the formidable outlay involved is a fair measure of the wealth and enterprise of California.

The City of San Francisco was, as everyone knows, destroyed by fire, not earthquake (this is important), at the beginning of the century. It has risen again from its ashes (not ruins) in quadrupled magnificence. Its forty-storey buildings tower above the lofty hog-backed promontory on which it is built. The sea mists which roll in and shroud it at frequent intervals rob it of sunshine, but ensure a cool temperate climate at most seasons of the year. I was eager to see the sea lions for which the bay is renowned, and made a special journey to view the rocks on which they are accustomed to bask. In this I was disappointed. The rocks were occupied only by large and dreary birds; and when I asked a bystander when the sea lions would appear, he replied gaily in Italian, "Damfino," meaning no doubt "in due course."

South of San Francisco we entered the latitude and vegetation of North Africa. The houses became increasingly Mauresque, the soil more sandy, and water—except, of course, for drinking purposes—scarce. Resting for a while at the seaside resorts of Pebble Beach and Santa Barbara, we draw by easy stages nearer to the latest city of the Pacific Coast, Los Angeles. Ignoring St. Augustine's famous pun, the inhabitants pronounce the "g" hard, as in "angle." A keen rivalry exists between Los Angeles and San Francisco. Each population exceeds a million, but by how much depends on which suburbs are included; and on this point there are disputes.

No two cities could present a greater contrast. San Francisco stretches up to the heavens; Los Angeles spreads more widely over the level shores than any city of equal numbers in the world. It is a gay and happy city, where everyone has room to live, where no one lacks a small, but sufficient dwelling, and every house stands separate in its garden. Poverty and squalor have never entered its broad avenues of palms. The distances are enormous. You motor ten miles to luncheon in one direction and ten miles to dinner in another. The streets by night are ablaze with electric lights and moving signs of every colour. A carnival in fairyland!

All this opulence and well-being is prominently supported by two twentieth-century industries. The first is oil. Everywhere scattered about in the city, all around it, on the beach, even in the sea itself, stand the pylon structures or derricks used for the finding and extraction of oil. At Calgary in Canada, where the oil lies a mile below the surface, these derricks are very tall; but in California they seem to average fifty or sixty feet. The hills to the south of the city are covered with them. They are packed so densely together as to look at a few miles' distance exactly like forests of fir-trees.

Democratic principles have shaped the laws governing this new-comer industry. Oilfields, like goldfields, are parcelled out in small holdings, almost in allotments. A multitude of small proprietors are pumping away in mad haste, lest their neighbours a few yards off should forestall them. There is an immense production of oil at cheap prices. For the present everyone is content, especially the consumers. Whether this system is the last word in the scientific utilization of oil resources is doubtful; that it will not last for ever is certain. It may well be that the natural oil age will synchronize with the twentieth century.

The second staple industry is found in the films associated with Hollywood. Here we enter a strange and an amusing world, the like of which has certainly never been seen before. Dozens of studios, covering together thousands of acres, and employing scores of thousands of very highly paid performers and technicians, minister to the gaiety of the world. It is like going behind the scenes of a theatre magnified a thousand-fold. Battalions of skilled workmen construct with magical quickness streets of London, of China, of India, jungles, mountains, and every conceivable form of scenery in solid and comparatively durable style. In a neighbouring creek pirate ships, Spanish galleons and Roman galleys ride at anchor.

This Peter Pan township is thronged with the most odd and varied of crowds that can be imagined. Here is a stream of South Sea Islanders, with sweet little nut-brown children, hurrying to keep their studio appointments. There is a corps-de-ballet which would rival the Moulin Rouge. Ferocious brigands, bristling with property pistols, cowboys, train robbers, heroines in distress of all descriptions, aged cronies stalk or stroll or totter to and fro. Twenty films are in the making at once. A gang of wild Circassian horsemen filters past a long string of camels from a desert caravan. Keen young men regulate the most elaborate processes of photography, and the most perfect installations for bridling light and sound. Competition is intense; the hours of toil are hard, and so are the hours of waiting. Youthful beauty claims her indisputable rights; but the aristocracy of the filmland found themselves on personality. It is a factory in appearance the queerest in the world, whose principal characteristics are hard work, frugality and discipline.

The apparition of the "talkies" created a revolution among the "movies." Hollywood was shaken to its foundations. No one could challenge the popularity of these upstarts. Their technique might be defective; their voices in reproduction rough and unmusical; their dialect weak; but talking films were what the public wanted; and what the public wants it has to get. So all is turned upside down, and new experts arrive with more delicate apparatus, and a far more complicated organization must be set up. Everywhere throughout filmland the characters must be made to talk as well as act. New values are established, and old favourites have to look to their laurels. Now that everyone is making talking pictures, not only darkness but perfect silence must be procurable whenever required, and balloons float above the studios to scare away the buzzings of wandering aeroplanes.

Alone among producers Charlie Chaplin remains unconverted, claiming that pantomime is the genius of drama, and that the imagination of the audience supplies better words than machinery can render, and prepared to vindicate the silent film by the glittering weapons of wit and pathos.

On the whole, I share his opinion.

CHAPTER 5

LAND OF CORN AND LOBSTERS

Winston delivers his verdict on American food, which he had ample occasion to savour in the course of his extensive coast-to-coast travels across the continent.

COLLIERS, AUGUST 5, 1933

I FEEL SHY about expressing my opinion about American food. I was everywhere received with such charming hospitality that to give any verdict of a critical character might seem churlish. However, as eating and drinking are matters in which the good taste of different people and different countries naturally and legitimately varies so widely, there may be no harm in my setting down a few general impressions. Then there is the danger that one may be thought greedy, and reproached for setting too much store by creature comfort and dwelling unduly upon trivialities. But here I fortify myself by Dr. Johnson's celebrated dictum: "I look upon it that he who does not mind his belly will hardly mind anything else."

So I will start out boldly with the assertion that Americans of every class live on lighter foods than their analogues in England. Fruit, vegetables and cereals play a much larger part in their bills of fare than with us, and they eat chicken much more often than meat—by which of course I mean beef and mutton. All this is no doubt very healthful, but personally I am a beef-eater, and I always expect my wife to provide me with butcher's meat once a day when I am at home.

Moreover, the American chicken is a small bird compared with the standard English fowl. Attractively served with rice and auxiliaries of all kinds, he makes an excellent dish. Still, I am on the side of the big chicken as regularly as Providence is on that of the big battalions. Indeed it seems strange in so large a country to find such small chickens. Conscious, perhaps, of their inferiority, the inhabitants call them "squabs." What an insulting title for a capon!

A dangerous, yet almost universal, habit of the American people is the drinking of immense quantities of iced water. This has become a ritual. If you go into a cafeteria or drug store and order a cup of coffee, a tumbler of iced water is immediately set before you. The bleak beverage is provided on every possible occasion; whatever you order, the man behind the counter will supply this apparently indispensible concomitant.

American meals nearly always start with a large slice of melon or grapefruit accompanied by iced water. This is surely a somewhat austere welcome for a hungry man at the midday or evening meal. Dessert, in my view, should be eaten at the end of the meal, not at the beginning. The influence of American customs is now so all-pervading that during the last few years I have noticed this habit creeping into England. It should be strongly repulsed.

The coffee in the United States is admirable, and a welcome contrast to the anaemic or sticky liquid which judicious Americans rightly resent in English provincial towns. The American Blue Point is a serious undertaking. On the other hand, the American lobster is unrivalled anywhere in the world; he has a succulence and a flavour which I have found nowhere else. Shad roe and terrapin I have eaten only in the United States; I find them both entertaining. Soft-shell crabs and corn on the cob are by no means unpalatable, but should not be eaten too often.

A very general custom in American society is to have a little preliminary repast before the company sits down at table. The guests arrive any time within half an hour of the nominal dinner hour, and stand about conversing, smoking cigarettes and drinking cocktails. There is, of course, the admirable tomato-juice cocktail. But this is not the one most commonly used. It was explained to me that nothing in the laws of the United States forbids the convivial consumption in a private house of any stores of liquor which happened to be in the host's private cellars before prohibition became effective in 1920. Many people must have had very large and well-stocked cellars in those distant days, and these supplies have lasted extremely well. Indeed one might almost believe that, like the widow's cruse, they miraculously replenish themselves.

Alcoholic liquor could therefore, without any illegality, enter into the composition of many kinds of cocktails and these short, hard, wet drinks may be freely enjoyed without any presumption of illegality. I am no devotee of cocktails, still I must admit that this preliminary festival while the guests are arriving is most agreeable. The cocktails are supported by all sorts of dainty, tasty little dishes continually handed round upon trays or displayed upon tables. This custom is nothing more nor less than the old custom of Imperial Russia called "the zakouski."

I remember as a child, nearly fifty years ago, being taken by my mother on a visit to the Duke of Edinburgh, who had married a Russian princess. There I saw exactly the same ritual, with kummel and vodka instead of the cocktails, and the same attractive, eatable kickshaws to keep them company. It was only after this was over that the regular dinner began. There is much to be said for this arrangement. No doubt it encourages unpunctuality, but on the other hand it protects those who have already arrived from starving helplessly till the late comers make their appearances.

I expect the practice has come to stay. It makes for sociability and good mixing, both of the guests and their refreshments. Indeed I should not be surprised if some day the formal sit-down dinner were dropped altogether and an ethereal generation contented themselves with cocktails, cigarettes and caviar, and then went off and danced for glee. I should not approve of this; but we live in a world of change, and who can control its oscillations?

The vast size of the United States and the imperative need of moving about have given the American an altogether different standard of distance from that which prevails in our small island. He thinks as little of a fourteen or fifteen hours' railway journey as we do of the hour and a half to Brighton or Oxford. He is no more balked by the prospect of travelling from New York to Palm Beach than we should be by going to Scotland. Even the mighty journey to California, from ocean to ocean, presents itself as quite an ordinary undertaking.

It is odd how quickly the visitor falls into this American order of ideas. A four or six hour journey by railway soon becomes a bagatelle. I have made three great journeys in the United States—the first separated from the two last (I am ashamed to say) by nearly thirty years. I dreaded the toil of travelling so much by railway, and it was a strong deterrent from undertaking a lecture tour. But I am bound to say that I did not find these long runs and this continuous travelling day after day, night after night, at all fatiguing on these later occasions. Indeed, I started for a journey of nearly six weeks soon after I had been struck by a taxi, very weak and frail, and with much misgivings as to my capacity to fulfil my engagements—but in fact I throve on it.

It was a fruitful convalescence, and I was much stronger at the end than at the beginning. The truth is that the trains are extremely comfortable: the enormous rolling stock, the weight of the metals and the steady pace maintained—even when interrupted occasionally by formidable bangs and jolts—give a sense of repose which I do not feel on our quick, tremulous, and comparatively light railways. In England, indeed, except for long journeys of four or five hours, I almost always go by motor car. In America one resigns oneself easily to many hours of train, and tranquilly settles down to work or reading without any feeling of impatience.

When in 1929 I traversed Canada from east to west and came back across the United States from California through Chicago to New York, and then down to the battlefields of the South, I had the wonderful experience of being transported (through the magnificent kindness of Canadian and American friends) entirely in a private car.* This rare and costly luxury gave a really joyous feeling. It was a home from home. And what a sense of power and choice, to be able to stop where you would and for as long as you would, and to sleep on till you wished to get up, and to hook onto any train when satiated with the wonders of the Yosemite Valley, or the Grand Canyon, or the roar of Niagara, or the clack and clutter of the Chicago stockyards! It was like marching and camping in wartime in enormous lands. Indeed, I meditated hiring a private car for my lecture tour. Alas, the cost! Twenty-four tickets were more than my business would bear.

Many English people do not like the long sleeping-cars in which strangers of both sexes are separated from one another only by curtains, and where the temperature is often tropical till you open the window, and artic when you do. Still, they are very practical once you are used to them. No one could require better accommodation than a drawing-room compartment all to oneself. Our sleeping-berths are nearly always at right angles to the train, and the beds are so narrow that one can hardly turn over in them. Moreover, the sheets and blankets are also on the narrow side, and at the slightest movement come untucked. The United States railway bed is a splendid soft, broad, affair. It lies lengthwise with the train, and I slept in one, night after night, as soundly as I should in any house.

Nowhere in the world have I seen such gargantuan meals as are provided upon American trains. Every plate would feed at least two people. I have always been amazed at the immense variety of foodstuffs which are carried in the dining-cars, and the skill and delicacy with which they are cooked even upon the longest journey through the very heart of the continent.

The black attendants with their soft voices and delightful drawl and courteous, docile, agreeable ways were an unfailing source not only of comfort but of perpetual amusement to me. In view of the results of the late presidential election, I may perhaps confess that, armed with a medical certificate, I somewhat anticipated the verdict of the American na-

---

* A railroad carriage.

tion upon the Eighteenth Amendment. But these discreet attendants never seemed to let their eyes stray upon any vessels or containers not officially brought to their notice. Indeed one would have thought that where liquids were concerned they were entirely colour-blind. One of them, however, shrouding with a napkin a gold-topped bottle which might well have contained ginger ale, when I returned to the compartment after a few moments' absence, made this memorable remark: "Yo' ought to be very careful with this, sah. Men will steal this who would not steal di'monds." It is pleasant to reflect that such a temptation will soon be forever removed from the weaker members of the American nation.

On one occasion only was there cause for alarm. A friend of mine when I left California in 1929 sent as a parting gift a good-sized suitcase, unlabelled, which at the last minute was thrust unostentatiously into my compartment. Unluckily something seemed to have gone wrong with its contents, and a very curious trickle had left its trail all along the station platform. However, no one said a word; and fortunately, on examination, the damage was found to be confined to only one of the articles which this mysterious, anonymous package contained.

Whenever I come to a new city I always make haste to climb the tallest building in it and examine the whole scene from this eagle's nest. They are wonderful, these bird's eye views; each one gives an impression of its own which lies in the memory like a well-known picture. I have heard the opinion expressed that all American cities are alike. I do not agree with this short-sighted view. The hotels are the same in their excellence and comfort, in their routine and service; but anyone who will not only perch himself on a pinnacle, but thread and circumnavigate the streets in a motor car, will soon perceive that each city has a panorama and a personality all its own.

Nothing of course can equal the world-famous silhouette of New York from the sea. It is a spectacle the magnificence of which is perhaps unsurpassed in the whole world and, though each building taken separately may have its failings, the entire mass of these vast structures is potent with grandeur and beauty. But San Francisco, earthquake-defying, makes a fine counterpart as it gazes on the Pacific. Nothing could be more different from San Francisco than Los Angeles, the one towering up under its cloud canopy, its buildings crowded together on the narrow promontory; the other spreading its garden villas over an enormous expanse, a system of rural townships basking in the sunlight.

From west to south! What lovely country surrounds the city of Atlanta! Its rich red soils, the cotton-quilted hills and uplands, the rushing, turgid rivers, are all alive with tragic memories of the Civil War. And who would miss Chattanooga, lying in its cup between the Blue

Ridge and Lookout Mountain? The scenery itself is exhilarating, but to it all is added the intense significance of history. All these rugged heights and peaks have their meaning in military topography: a short drive to the battlefield of Chickamauga, kept like a beautiful park, with many of the field batteries standing in the very positions where they fought, is enough to reward the visitor.

In Minneapolis amid its rolling plains my small party had its most affectionate welcome. Cincinnati, I thought, was the most beautiful of the inland cities of the Union. From the tower of its unsurpassed hotel the city spreads far and wide its pageant of crimson, purple and gold, laced by silver streams that are great rivers. There is a splendour in Chicago and a life-thrust that is all its own.

To me, Rochester makes a personal appeal. Here it was that my grandfather and his brother, having married two sisters, built two small, old-fashioned houses in what was then the best quarter of the town, and linked them by a bridge. Here they founded the newspaper which is still the leading daily.

· It would be easy to illustrate this theme further and recall the kind impressions of Boston, Cleveland, Pittsburgh, Philadelphia and a dozen others; but these examples suffice to convey the sense of variety and character which the great cities of America present to a sympathetic and inquiring eye.

For more than thirty years I have been accustomed to address the largest public audiences on all sorts of topics. A lecture tour as such, therefore, had no serious terrors for me. Still, to a stranger in a foreign land, it must always be something of an ordeal to come into the close, direct relationship of speaker and listener night after night, with thousands of men and women whose outlook and traditions are sundered from his own.

But American audiences yield to none in the interest, attention and good nature with which they follow a lengthy considered statement. These large assemblies always seemed to take particular pleasure in asking questions after my address was over. At every place I encouraged this, and sheaves of written questions were speedily composed and handed up, covering a discursive range of topics. The audiences appeared delighted when some sort of an answer was given immediately to each. Any fair retort, however controversial, was received with the greatest good humour. I remember, for instance, that I was asked: "What do you think of the dole?" I affected to misunderstand the question, and replied: "I presume you are referring to the Veterans' bonus." This gained an immediate success.

The most critical of my audiences was, of course, at Washington. Here one met the leading men of the Union, and the keen society of the political capital, with all its currents of organized, responsible opinion. But the most interesting, and in some ways the most testing, of all my experiences was not on the public platform.

A Washington hostess, in the centre of the political world, invited the British ambassador and me to a dinner of some forty or fifty persons. There were gathered many of the most important men and some of the most influential women in the United States. After the dinner was over, the whole company formed a half-circle round me, and then began one of the frankest and most direct political interrogations to which I have ever been subjected. The unspoken, but perfectly well-comprehended condition was that any question, however awkward, might be asked, and that any answer, however pointed, would be taken in good part.

For two hours we wrestled strenuously, unsparingly, but in the best of tempers, with one another, and when I was tired of defending Great Britain on all her misdeeds, I counter-attacked with a series of pretty direct questions of my own. Nothing was shirked on either side—debts, disarmament, naval parity, liquor legislation, the gold standard and the dole were all tackled on the dead level.

Nowhere else in the world, only between our two people, could such a discussion have proceeded. The priceless gift of a common language, and the pervading atmosphere of good sense and fellow feeling enabled us to rap all the most delicate topics without the slightest offense given or received. It was to me a memorable evening, unique in my experience, and it left in my mind enormous hopes of what will some day happen in the world when, no doubt, after most of us are dead and gone, the English-speaking peoples will really understand each other.

CHAPTER 6

ROOSEVELT
FROM AFAR

Here the future Prime Minister offers his assessment of the man who was shortly to become his close friend and valued comrade-in-arms when World War II broke out.

GREAT CONTEMPORARIES, 1937

THE LIFE and well-being of every country are influenced by the economic and financial policy of the United States. From the cotton spinners of Lancashire to the ryots of India; from the peasantry of China to the pawnbrokers of Amsterdam; from the millionaire financier watching the tape machine to the sturdy blacksmith swinging his hammer in the forge; from the monetary philosopher or student to the hard-headed business man or sentimental social reformer—all are consciously or unconsciously affected. For in truth Roosevelt is an explorer who has embarked on a voyage as uncertain as that of Columbus, and upon a quest which might conceivably be as important as the discovery of the New World. In those old days it was the gulf of oceans with their unknown perils and vicissitudes. Now in the modern world, just as mysterious and forbidding as the stormy waters of the Atlantic is the gulf between the producer, with the limitless powers of science at his command, and the consumer, with legitimate appetites which will never be satiated.

Plenty has become a curse. Bountiful harvests are viewed with dread which in the old times accompanied a barren season. The gift of well-organized leisure, which machines should have given to men, has only emerged in the hateful spectacle of scores of millions of able and willing workers kicking their heels by the hoardings of closed factories and subsisting upon charity, or as in England upon systematized relief. Always the peoples are asking themselves "Why should these things be? Why should not the new powers man has wrested from nature open the portals of a broader life to men and women all over the world?" And with increasing vehemence they demand that the thinkers and pioneers of humanity should answer the riddle and open these new possibilities to their enjoyment.

A single man whom accident, destiny, or Providence, has placed at the head of one hundred and twenty millions of active, educated, excitable and harassed people, has set out upon this momentous expedition. Many doubt if he will succeed. Some hope he will fail. Although the policies of President Roosevelt are conceived in many respects from a narrow view of American self-interest, the courage, the power and the scale of his effort must enlist the ardent sympathy of every country, and his success could not fail to lift the whole world forward into the sunlight of an easier and more genial age.

There is therefore a widespread desire to look at this man in the midst of his adventure. Trained to public affairs, connected with the modern history of the United States by a famous name, at forty-two he was struck down with infantile paralysis. His lower limbs refused their office. Crutches or assistance were needed for the smallest movement from place to place. To ninety-nine men out of a hundred such an affliction would have terminated all forms of public activity except those of the mind. He refused to accept this sentence. He fought against it with that same rebellion against commonly-adopted conventions which we now see in his policy. He contested elections: he harangued the multitude: he faced the hurly-burly of American politics in a decade when they were exceptionally darkened by all the hideous crimes and corruption of Gangsterdom which followed upon Prohibition. He beat down opponents in this rough arena. He sought, gained and discharged offices of the utmost labour and of the highest consequence. As Governor of New York State his administration, whatever its shortcomings, revealed a competent, purposeful personality. He stooped to conquer. He adapted himself to the special conditions and to the humiliations which had long obstructed the entry of the best of American manhood into the unsavoury world of politics. He subscribed to the Democratic ticket and made himself the mouthpiece of party aims without losing hold upon the larger objectives of American public life.

World events began to move. The Hoover administration could only gape upon the unheard-of problems of depression through glut. The long ascendancy of the Republican regime was clearly drawing to its close. The Presidency of the United States awaited a Democratic candidate. Five or six outstanding figures presented themselves, in busy scheming rivalry.

In the opinion of many of the shrewdest leaders of his party, Roosevelt was the weakest of these contestants. And there were for long those who considered that in hard common sense and genuine statecraft Roosevelt's former leader, Governor Al Smith, was unquestionably the strongest. But Roosevelt pulled his wires and played his cards in such a way that Fortune could befriend him. Fortune came along, not only as a friend or even as a lover, but as an idolator. There was one moment when his nomination turned upon as little as the spin of a coin. But when it fell there was no doubt whose head was stamped upon it.

He arrived at the summit of the greatest economic community in the world at the moment of its extreme embarrassment. Everybody had lost faith in everything. Credit was frozen. Millions of unemployed without provision filled the streets or wandered despairing about the vast spaces of America. The rotten foundations of the banks were simultaneously undermined and exposed. A universal deadlock gripped the United States. The richest man could not cash the smallest cheque. People possessing enormous intrinsic assets in every kind of valuable security found themselves for some days without the means to pay a hotel bill or even a taxi fare. We must never forget that this was the basis from which he started. Supreme power in the Ruler, and a clutching anxiety of scores of millions who demanded and awaited orders.

Since then there has been no lack of orders. Although the Dictatorship is veiled by constitutional forms, it is none the less effective. Great things have been done, and greater attempted. To compare Roosevelt's effort with that of Hitler is to insult not Roosevelt but civilization. The petty persecutions and old-world assertions of brutality in which the German idol has indulged only show their smallness and squalor compared to the renaissance of creative effort with which the name of Roosevelt will always be associated.

The President's second momentous experiment is an attempt to reduce unemployment by shortening the hours of labour of those who are employed and spreading the labour more evenly through the wage-earning masses. Who can doubt that this is one of the paths which will soon be trodden throughout the world? If it is not to be so, we may well ask what is the use to the working masses of invention and science. Are great discoveries in organization or processes only to mean that fewer labourers will produce more than is required during the same long hours, while an ever larger proportion of their mates are flung redundant upon the labour market? If that were so, surely the poor English Luddites of a hundred years ago were right in attempting to break up the new machines. Alone through the establishment of shorter hours can the wage-earners enjoy the blessings of modern mass production; and indeed without shorter hours those blessings are but a curse.

Thus the Roosevelt adventure claims sympathy and admiration from all of those in England, and in foreign countries, who are convinced that the fixing of a universal measure of value based not upon the rarity or plenty of any single commodity, but conforming to the advancing powers of mankind, is the supreme achievement which at this time lies before the intellect of Man. But very considerable misgivings must necessarily arise when a campaign to attack the monetary problem becomes intermingled with, and hampered by, the elaborate processes of social reform and the struggles of class warfare. In Great Britain we know a lot about trade unions. It is now nearly a century since they began to play a part in our life. It is half a century since Lord Beaconsfield, a Conservative Prime Minister at the head of an aristocratic and bourgeois Parliament, accorded them exceptional favour before the law and protected them from being sued in their corporate capacity. We have dwelt with British trade unionism ever since. It has introduced a narrowing element into our public life. It has been a keenly-felt impediment to our productive and competitive power. It has become the main foundation of a socialist political party, which has ruled the State greatly to its disadvantage, and will assuredly do so again. It reached a climax in a general strike, which if it had been successful would have subverted the Parliamentary constitution of our island.

But when all is said and done, there are very few well-informed persons in Great Britain, and not many employers of labour on a large scale, who would not sooner have to deal with the British trade unions as we know them, than with the wild vagaries of communist-agitated and totally unorganized labour discontent. The trade unions have been a stable force in the industrial development of Britain in the last fifty years. They have brought steadily to the front the point of view of the toiler and the urgent requirements of his home, and have made these vital matters imprint themselves upon the laws and customs of our country. They have been a steadying force which has counterbalanced and corrected the reckless extravagances of the Red intelligentsia. Over and over again in thirty years we have heard employers say, "We might easily go further than the trade union leaders and fare a good deal worse"; and in the Great War, the sturdy patriotism of the trade unionists and the masculine common sense of their officials gave us an invaluable and, as it proved, unbreakable basis upon which to carry forward the struggle for national self-preservation.

But when one sees an attempt made within the space of a few months to lift American trade unionism by great heaves and bounds to the position so slowly built up—and even then with much pain and loss—in Great Britain, we cannot help feeling grave doubts. One wonders whether the struggle of American industrial life—its richness and fertility, its vivid possibilities to brains and brawn, to handicraft and industry, the whole spread over so vast a continent with such sharp contrasts in conditions and climate—may not result in a general crippling of that enterprise and flexibility upon which not only the wealth, but the happiness of modern communities depends. One wonders whether the rigid and hitherto comparatively modest structure of American trade unionism will be capable of bearing the immense responsibilities for national well-being and for the production of necessaries of all kinds for the people of the United States which the power now given to them implies. If anything like a beer racket or any other racket broke in upon the responsible leaders of American trade unions, the American democracy might easily wander in a very uncomfortable wilderness for ten or twenty years. Our trade unions have grown to manhood and power amid an enormous network of counter-checks and consequential corrections; and to raise American trade unionism from its previous condition to industrial sovereignty by a few sweeping decrees may easily confront both the trade unions and the United States with problems which for the time being will be at once paralysing and insoluble.

A second danger to President Roosevelt's valiant and heroic experiments seems to arise from the disposition to hunt down rich men as if they were noxious beasts. It is a very attractive sport, and once it gets started quite a lot of people everywhere are found ready to join in the chase. Moreover, the quarry is at once swift and crafty, and therefore elusive. The pursuit is long and exciting, and everyone's blood is infected with its ardour. The question arises whether the general well-being of the masses of the community will be advanced by an excessive indulgence in this amusement. The millionaire or multi-millionaire is a highly economic animal. He sucks up with sponge-like efficiency money from all quarters. In this process, far from depriving ordinary people of their earnings, he launches enterprise and carries it through, raises values, and he expands that credit without which on a vast scale no fuller economic life can be opened to the millions. To hunt wealth is not to capture commonwealth.

This money-gathering, credit-producing animal can not only walk—he can run. And when frightened he can fly. If his wings are clipped, he can dive or crawl. When in the end he is hunted down, what is left but a very ordinary individual apologizing volubly for his mistakes, and particularly for not having been able to get away?

But meanwhile great constructions have crumbled to the ground. Confidence is shaken and enterprise chilled, and the unemployed queue up at the soup-kitchens or march out upon the public works with ever-growing expense to the taxpayer and nothing more appetizing to take home to their families than the leg or the wing of what was once a millionaire. One quite sees that people who have got interested in this fight will not accept such arguments against their sport. What they will have to accept is the consequences of ignoring such arguments. It is indispensable to the wealth of nations and to the wage and life standards of labour, that capital and credit should be honoured and cherished partners in the economic system. If this is rejected there is always, of course, the Russian alternative. But no one can suppose that the self-reliant population of the United States, which cut down the forests and ploughed up the soil and laced the continent with railways, and carried wealth-getting and wealth-diffusing to a higher point than has ever been reached by mankind, would be content for a week with the dull brutish servitude of Russia.

It was a prudent instinct that led Mr. Roosevelt to discard those attempts at legal price-fixing which have so often been made in old-world countries, and have always, except in time of war or in very circumscribed localities, broken down in practice. Such measures are appropriate to break monopolies or rings, but can never be accepted as a humdrum foundation for economic life. There can never be good wages or good employment for any length of time without good profits, and the sooner this is recognized, the sooner the corner will be turned.

Writing as a former Chancellor of the British Exchequer for nearly five years, I find myself very much astonished by a law recently passed in the United States that all returns of income for the purposes of taxation must be made public. Such a rule would seem highly obstructive to commercial revival, as well—though this is minor—as being objectionable in the sphere of personal relations. In Great Britain we plume ourselves on collecting effectually the largest possible revenues from wealth upon as high a scheme of graduated taxation as will not defeat its own purpose. Our income and super-tax payers have frequently been paid tributes by foreign observers for the thoroughness and punctuality with which they meet their dues. Even our own Socialist ministers have testified to this. But it has always been accepted that the relations of the taxpayer, rich or poor, are with the State and the State alone, and that neither his employees nor his trade rivals, neither his neighbours nor his creditors, neither his enemies nor his friends, should know what has passed between him and the Treasury. To ask a trader or manufacturer engaged in productive enterprise, with all the hazards attendant thereupon, to reveal not only to the collectors of the public revenue but to all and sundry his income for the year, must be an impediment to national business almost measureless in its irritation, and in its mischief. It seems to me to be only another variant of that hideous folly of prohibition from which the wisdom and virility of the United States by a patient but irresistible heave of broad shoulders so lately shook itself free.

No one could write in this sense without at the same time feeling the justification there is for the anger of the American public against many of their great leaders of finance. The revelations and exposures which have flowed in a widening stream, and even flood, during the last four years, have laid many prominent persons open to prejudice and public censure, apart altogether from the law. The passionate desire of the struggling wage-earner with a family at home and many applicants for his job, with the vultures of ill-health and bad luck hovering above him and those dear to him, is for clean hands in the higher ranks, and for a square deal even if it be only a raw deal.

A thousand speeches could be made on this. The important question is whether American democracy can clear up scandals and punish improprieties without losing its head, and without injuring the vital impulses of economic enterprise and organization. It is no use marching up against ordinary private business men, working on small margins, as if they were the officials of Government departments, who so long as they have attended at their offices from ten to four in a respectable condition, have done their job. There are elements of contrivance, of housekeeping, and of taking risks which are essential to all profitable activity. If these are destroyed the capitalist system fails, and some other system must be substituted. No doubt the capitalist system is replete with abuses and errors and inequities like everything else in our imperfect human life; but it was under it that only a few years ago the United States produced the greatest prosperity for the greatest numbers that has ever been experienced in human record. It is not illogical to say: "Rather than condone these faults and these abuses we will sweep this system away no matter what it costs in our material well-being. We will replace it by the only other system which enables large organizations and developments to be undertaken, namely, nationalization of all the means of production, distribution, credit and exchange." It is, however, irrational to tear down or cripple the capitalist system without having the fortitude of spirit and ruthlessness of action to create a new communist system.

There, it seems to foreign observers, lies the big choice of the United States at the present time. If the capitalist system is to continue, with its rights of private property, with its pillars of rent, interest and profit, and the sanctity of contracts recognized and enforced by the State, then it must be given a fair chance. It is the same for us in the Old World. If we are to continue in the old leaky lifeboat amid these stormy seas, we must do our best to keep it bailed, to keep it afloat, and to steer for port. If we decide to take to the rafts of a new system, there also we are vociferously assured there is a chance of making land. But the Siberian coast is rugged and bleak, and there are long, cruel frosts in the Arctic Ocean.

It is a very open question, which any household may argue to the small hours, whether it is better to have equality at the price of poverty, or well-being at the price of inequality. Life will be pretty rough, anyhow. Whether we are ruled by tyrannical bureaucrats or self-seeking capitalists, the ordinary man who has to earn his living, and tries to make provision for old age and for his dear ones when his powers are exhausted, will have a hard pilgrimage through this dusty world. The United States was built upon property, liberty and enterprise, and certainly it has afforded the most spacious and ample life to the scores of millions that has ever yet been witnessed. To make an irrevocable departure into the Asiatic conceptions would be a serious step, and should be measured with a steady eye at the outset.

We must then hope that neither the tangles of the N.R.A. nor the vague, ethereal illusions of sentimentalists or doctrinaires will prevent President Roosevelt from testing and plumbing the secrets of the monetary problem. If he succeeds all the world will be his debtor: if he fails he will at any rate have made an experiment for mankind on a scale which only the immense strength of the United States could sustain. It would be a thousand pities if this tremendous effort by the richest nation in the world to expand consciously and swiftly the bounds of the consuming power should be vitiated by being mixed up with an ordinary radical programme and a commonplace class fight. If failure there be, which God forfend, it will be taken for a generation as proof positive that all efforts to procure prosperity by currency and credit inflation are doomed to failure.

But the President has need to be on his guard. To a foreign eye it seems that forces are gathering under his shield which at a certain stage may thrust him into the background and take the lead themselves. If that misfortune were to occur, we should see the not-unfamiliar spectacle of a leader running after his followers to pull them back. It is to be hoped and indeed believed that the strong common sense, the sturdy individualism and the cold disillusioned intelligence of the American people will protect their leader from such inglorious experiences.

However we may view the Presidency which has reached half its natural span,* it is certain that Franklin Roosevelt will rank among the

---

* Written in 1934.

greatest of men who have occupied that proud position. His generous sympathy for the underdog, his intense desire for a nearer approach to social justice, place him high among the great philanthropists. His composure combined with activity in time of crisis class him with famous men of action. His freeing the United States from prohibition and the vigour of his administrative measures of relief and credit expansion proclaim him a statesman of world renown. He has known how to gain the confidence and the loyalty of the most numerous and the most ebullient of civilized communities, and all the world watches his valiant effort to solve their problems with an anxiety which is only the shadow of high hope.

Will he succeed or will he fail? That is not the question we set ourselves, and to prophesy is cheap. But succeed or fail, his impulse is one which makes towards the fuller life of the masses of the people in every land, and which as it glows the brighter may well eclipse both the lurid flames of German Nordic national self-assertion and the baleful unnatural lights which are diffused from Soviet Russia.

CHAPTER 7

CAN AMERICA KEEP OUT OF WAR?

At this point Churchill had no doubt that Europe was heading remorselessly toward war. He knew that only the full-hearted commitment of the United States on the side of the democracies could prevent it. He was sufficiently a realist to know that this was not going to happen. The following is just one of many impassioned pleas he made in an effort to alert the United States to the dangers posed by the dictators Hitler and Mussolini.

COLLIERS, OCTOBER 2, 1937

THE LAMENTABLE EVENTS now taking place in the Far East bring this question into the arena of practical and current politics.* The United States, like Great Britain, has enormous interests, commercial, moral and cultural, in China. These interests have been built up over several generations. The construction by Japan of her modern navy has during the last twenty years completely transformed the position in the Yellow Sea and upon the Asiatic side of the Pacific Ocean. Unless at some future date the position in Europe is so secure and the feeling in the United States is so strong that joint Anglo-American action with a very serious purpose behind it becomes possible, we must expect in common with the other European nations to suffer a ceaseless encroachment upon our interests.

Japan is in the hands of leaders who are themselves controlled, under pain of imminent death, by a military secret society whose ideas are far removed from a modern conception. Remorseless conquest and subjugation, apart from China, by Japan will be driven forward by these primordial forces.

The spectacle will not be pleasant to witness nor the experience agreeable to endure. Nevertheless, it is not likely that the present renewed Japanese inroad upon China will lead to a world conflagration. On the contrary, the fact that Japan finds the moment opportune to ex-

---

* The Japanese had overrun Manchuria in 1931 and infiltrated N.E. China. In July, 1937, they launched a full-scale invasion and within the year Japan had taken all the Eastern Provinces and had set up puppet governments at Peking and Nanking.

pand her energy and entangle her troops in China looks as if her military men do not expect a major war this year. The great danger to the world at the present time still lies not in the Far East, but in the heart of Christendom and Europe.

European politics change with kaleidoscopic rapidity. Every crisis brings into being a new alignment of forces. The bickering of avowed enemies has its counterpart in the secret suspicions and rivalries of those who find themselves temporarily in the same camp. Antagonisms flare up and are resolved. Over a large part of the continent there is no permanence either in feuds or friendships.

But there is tension always. At any moment may come an explosion. And the peoples are afraid.

They have every reason for fear. War is not inevitable. It may be avoided. I believe that if a sufficient number of nations have the will to peace and the courage of their good intentions, there will be no war. But, up to the present, the danger is more apparent than the effort to avoid it. There are no guarantors of peace whose strength and purpose are undoubted. Aggression, fully armed, grows bolder with easy successes.

It would be idle optimism to underestimate the menace of such a situation. And there are two factors above all others which underline the threat. One is dissatisfaction with the territorial settlements which followed the war of 1914–18. The other is the identification of great states with principles of autocratic government to which has been given a religious or semi-religious authority.

It is one of the characteristics that distinguish man from the brute creation that man is prepared to kill or be killed for the sake of an idea. All ideas are, in a sense, explosive. But the idea which is independent of reasoning, which is held as an article of faith, is the most dangerous of all. In Germany, Italy and Russia we see today such ideas rampant and in arms.

The main cause which has brought war in Europe nearer, which has dispersed the dreams of those who thought that the age of brutal violence was ended, is to be found in the rearmament of mighty Germany. The concentration of the whole life and strength of the German people, with all their intelligence and valour, upon military preparations, dominates the mind of Europe and fills the whole continent with lively alarm and dark suspicions. More than that, it produces reactions in the shape of counterarmament and political and military combinations among all the states who are neighbors of Germany. I am not now concerned whether Germany should be blamed or not blamed, but only with the result. While the great wheels revolve in the German Fatherland, while her redoubtable manhood tramps the gravel of the parade grounds, while every conceivable instrument of war and preparations for war are being made to the last ounce of the strength of the people, all the neighbours of Germany are plunged in increasing anxiety and counterpreparation.

But even this might run its course with no worse harm than the unproductive expenditure of vast sums of money. Worse lies behind. The dictator-ruled countries, especially Germany, Italy and Japan, are suffering from acute economic strain. In Germany, the most formidable, this strain has reached a very high degree of intensity. The life, the liberty, the comforts, the food of the whole people are already under conditions almost equal to those of war. The world remains at peace; but the internal strain upon the German people grows with every month that passes. Their patriotism, their docility, their helplessness in the hands of a powerful propaganda and strong party machinery lead them to continue on this sombre path of sacrifice. But at any moment trouble may rise in the interior of Germany. Beneath the smooth surface and well-ordered parade of Nazidom there stir and smoulder all the passions of a great people. Protestant pastors, the Catholic hierarchy, the tormented Jewish race, Communists, Socialists, Liberals, Trade Unionists, Monarchists who see the old régime apparently relegated to permanent obscurity, Saxons, Bavarians, Wurttembergers who find their state rights completely absorbed, wealthy men and great industrialists who find little more consideration for property in Nazi Germany than they would in Soviet Russia—all these forces are silent, obedient, but at the same time awake. There are many in Germany who say: "Wait till the Day comes. Then we may regain our freedom."

But what is the régime to do in the face of all these difficulties? They promised to cure unemployment. They have largely done so, but how? Only by a process of rearmament and of ever more severe national discipline which cannot be kept up perpetually. To relax their grip may be at the same time to release avenging forces. Dictators and those who immediately sustain them cannot quit their offices with the easy disdain—or more often relief—with which an American President or a British Prime Minister submits himself to an adverse popular verdict. For a dictator the choice may well be the throne or the grave. The character of the men who have raised themselves from obscurity to these positions of fierce, dazzling authority does not permit us to believe that they would bow their heads meekly to the stroke of fate. One has the feeling they would go down or conquer fighting, and play the fearful stakes which are in their hands.

The position of the German dictator and his associates is indeed grim. Rearmament in its industrial aspect will soon reach its culminating point. To stop or slow down the great wheels is not only to enable alarmed rivals to catch up but to deprive of employment millions of hard-pressed men, hitherto placated only by state work and already restive under grievous physical privations. How to dismount from the tiger? Alas, we cannot see the way! The dangerous ride cannot be indefinitely prolonged. Food is running short. Raw material is with difficulty purchased across the exchange. Credit is almost dead. There is a steel famine in the world. The period of high prices into which we have entered is full of danger, even to the best organized and most prosperous nations. But to Germany, and in a lesser degree to Italy, the increasing world-squeeze of raw materials and the sinister rise in the price of foodstuffs can only spell a check on armament production and a spur to political discontent.

Thus we are confronted with a situation in Europe abhorrent to its peoples, including the great mass of German and Italian peoples, in which bands of competent, determined men under ruthless leadership find themselves alike unable to go or to stop. It may well be that the choice before Germany is a choice between an internal and an external explosion. But it is not Germany that will really choose. It is only that band of politicians who have obtained this enormous power, whose movements are guided by two or three men, who will decide the supreme issue of peace or war. To this horrible decision they cannot come unbiased. Economic and political ruin may stare them in the face, and the only means of escape may be victory in the field. They have the power to make war. They have the incentive to make war; nay, it may well be almost compulsion.

Such is the danger to Europe. I am far from convinced that it may not be averted, but that it is dire, imminent, growing, none can doubt. I survey this scene as an Englishman. Our only interest is peace. We have nothing to gain by war. We have much to lose by victory, and everything to lose by defeat. Yet if there should be a resumption of the general war in Europe we might well, in spite of our dearest wishes, be compelled to take part in it.

But why, it may well be asked, should the United States, with all the Atlantic between it and this scene, with the Pacific guarding its opposite flank—why should it be involved in so hideous a catastrophe if it should occur, which God forbid? In later years I have become more closely acquainted with the thought and feeling of the American people. I understand something of their point of view. If I had had an American father instead of an American mother, I have little doubt I should share it. I cannot now conceive any argument which could be addressed to them if the European war suddenly began again, which should lead them to seek to take part in it.

Although the loss of American life in the Great War was spared by its victorious close in the winter of 1918, and the homes of the United States did not suffer the same horrible depletion as those of Britain and France, nevertheless, precious life was lost, vast expenditure was incurred, money was lent in billions which have never been repaid. Reproaches, recriminations and belittlings were the aftermath of victory. The only trophies were disappointment and disillusion. One cannot doubt what would be the reply of the American people to any argument, however cogent, and any appeal, however impassioned, which might be addressed to them from Britain or from France, to enter once again this European maelstrom.

However, great wars and those who take part in them are not decided by debate and division in elected assemblies, nor by the ordinary processes of reason. There are tides and floods in human affairs before which such dikes and dams which mankind has yet been able to build have been swept away. The day may come, perhaps it has already dawned, when human precautions and organizations will be strong enough to prevent the vast senseless carnage and destruction of war. If the power of the United States were joined to that of the League of Nations, perhaps we could say with confidence that the world we live in would not suffer the supreme misfortune. We must take it, however, as settled that nothing of this kind will occur at present. Whether a world war breaks out or not will depend almost entirely upon such forces of restraint and control as Great Britain and France can bring to bear.

But what happens if these forces fail? The movement of opinion in the United States toward trading in time of war is remarkable. The doctrine of the freedom of the seas which produced the miserable quarrel of 1812, and which gave cause to grave anxieties in 1915 and 1916, has been discarded. So resolved are the American people not to be drawn into any future war in Europe that they are prepared to deny to their countrymen all right of trading in American ships with belligerent countries. There is to be an embargo upon the export of war material, and American vessels, adventurers or traders who put to sea, must do so at their own risk.

Certainly, upon the basis that the United States is a neutral, we in Great Britain would be bound to concur in American decisions about blockading. The principle of naval parity between the two English-speaking nations would make it impossible for Great Britain ever to enforce a blockade which the United States was determined to resist. But it may well be that the United States, although a neutral, would sympathize strongly with those powers which were declared by the Tribunal of Europe to be the victims of unprovoked aggression.

But even if no question arose about the freedom of the seas, if the citizens of the United States in their desire to avoid war suspended altogether ocean traffic, may there not be other causes even more potent which would overwhelm the most invincible neutrality? Would the complete domination of Europe by a Nazi régime be compatible with the safety of the American Republic? Could the United States afford to see, for instance, the subjugation of the British Isles and the transference of all the immense territories of the British Empire to the control of the European conqueror? There are many people on the continent who consider that the most suitable area for Teutonic racial expansion lies in South America, and especially in Brazil, the Argentine and Chile. At present, Britain and her navy stand as an obstacle so serious that such ideas seem fantastic. But if Britain were either crushed into surrender or forced (even, perhaps, without a war) to enter the vast Nordic system, then, for the first time, the New World, with all its hopes of freedom, would stand face to face with the Old World and its armed ambitions.

Naturally, all these issues are only to be discussed as vague and remote contingencies. But it is sometimes well to peer ahead into the mysteries of the future, and so dispose one's thoughts and arrangements as to promote good tendencies rather than bad, thus preventing nightmares from being translated into tragedies. To adopt a humble metaphor: "A stitch in time saves nine." In proportion as the United States can lend even an indirect encouragement to the forces which are at work to establish a reign of law through the instrumentality of President Wilson's great conception, the League of Nations, so will increase, step by step, the assurances against a renewal of general war. The sympathy which the United States Ambassador in Paris has recently expressed with the ideals of free democracy has in itself exercised a steadying influence by the agencies both of warning to some and encouragement to others. No one would expect the Government of the United States to commit itself to any form of European entanglement or adventure. But, on the other hand, declarations of total indifference to anything that may occur outside the American continent will not, in fact, be founded upon truth, and might well in effect stimulate the very dangers which sane and virtuous men and women throughout the world have the greatest interest in avoiding.

Nor is this period of increasing anxiety through which Europe is passing necessarily permanent. The bad conjunction which has brought it about is the rise of the Nazi spirit of armed intolerance, coupled and synchronizing with the development of the airplane as a terrible and possibly supreme engine of war. Navies cannot invade at all: armies cannot invade by surprise. A long period of mobilization and assembly lies as a merciful time-pad between even the most highly organized military powers. The vast masses of conscript populations might refuse to take part in wars of aggression, if only some interlude could be provided. But the air power is at once the most sudden and the most irresponsible. It involves the use of comparatively small numbers of highly trained persons. It can be set in motion by the gesture of a single man. Its action is at once instantaneous and irrevocable.

A capital city might be laid in ashes before even a diplomatic dispute, let alone an ultimatum or formal declaration of war, had occurred. Then that nation whose air force had committed this awful crime would be told that the action taken by their government had forestalled in the nick of time a similar attack about to be made on them. It is this volatile power of an air force acting at the caprice or dark design of a handful of individuals in response to the will of a single despot that has made this hideous addition to the older perils.

But will this air power last for ever? There are many who say it is exaggerated even now. There are high experts in many countries who contend that though an air force might start a war at a moment's notice it could not bring it to a conclusion, and that it would not be a decisive weapon. As to that, we can only hope that no proof will ever be afforded. But meanwhile, the march of science proceeds along the earth as well as in the sky. The day will almost certainly come, perhaps in ten years, perhaps even in less, when the ground will have regained indisputable superiority over the air, and when the raiding airplane will be clawed down in flaming ruin with sufficient certainty to impose an effective deterrent on those who would use it. If, therefore, peace can be maintained during this intervening period, we may hope that far greater reassurances of its maintenance will be secured, and that the curse which threatens the world may give place to the splendid opportunities, joys and glories which science and freedom offer to modern man.

All the more, then, it is indispensable that the whole influence of the United States should be consciously and continuously exerted to maintain stability during this era of hazardous transition, and thus gain the blessings alike of the unslain and of the unborn.

CHAPTER 8

THE UNION OF THE ENGLISH-SPEAKING PEOPLES

Winston Churchill, reflecting on his American mother, Jennie Jerome of Brooklyn, New York, once remarked that he was himself "an English-speaking union." Indeed, it could be said that this was the prime theme running through his long life, spanning some sixty-five years in politics. It was his innermost conviction that if the British and American peoples marched together, all would be well.

NEWS OF THE WORLD, MAY 15, 1938

IT IS A RELIEF to turn from the quarrels and jealousies of distracted Europe to contemplate the majestic edifice of Anglo-American friendship.

But let us not deceive ourselves. Look more closely. In places the facing stone has been eaten away by acids in the atmosphere. There are cracks in the pillars that support the mighty dome. Pierce to the foundations. Beneath a crust that sometimes seems all too thin are bitter waters of suspicion, a marsh of misunderstanding. No one is really afraid that the building will collapse. Something stronger than any masonry holds it together—a cement of the spirit. But it would be well to strengthen the foundations; to grout and bind and buttress till the great structure is indeed secure.

We can best serve the cause of Anglo-American friendship if we understand clearly the factors that threaten and diminish it. And to do that we must examine the past as well as the present. As a nation, we have short memories. We fight and forget. But others remember. The founders of America fled from Britain to escape persecution. Tyranny—or what can be more disastrous than tyranny, a purblind, pettifogging legalism—pursued them across the Atlantic. Taxed by men they had never seen, sitting in a Parliament in whose deliberations they had no voice, the descendants of the Pilgrim Fathers and the Virginian Cavaliers raised, together, the standard of revolt.

But we forget—and America remembers—that the first shots in the

War of Independence were fired by British troops—"unmolested and unprovoked," says the contemporary Massachusetts *Spy*—on men who offered no resistance. The long war, in which German mercenaries were lavishly, if unsuccessfully, employed, was ended by a grudging peace.

Suspicion and bitterness remained. France beheaded a King—and crowned an Emperor whose armies trampled the map of Europe. At death-grips with Napoleon, Britain blockaded the coast of the United States, seized American ships, and pressed American sailors into service on her men-o'-war. The resulting war of 1812 to 1815 was to Britain only a vexatious diversion. But it was a life-and-death struggle to the United States, and its incidents left an indelible impress on the American mind. Indian tribes, fighting as allies of England, killed and ravaged. Fort Dearborn, on the site where Chicago now stands, was stormed by painted savages and the entire garrison massacred. Women and children were murdered. A British fleet sailed up the Potomac to Washington, burned the Capitol and the Government offices and the President's house.

It is doubtful if one in ten thousand of our population has ever heard of that raid of reprisals. But we should remember—vividly—for centuries after the event, if London were, even for a day, in the hands of an American force that destroyed Buckingham Palace, the Houses of Parliament, Whitehall and Downing Street. True, we should also remember the strong ties of blood and race that bound the Americans and ourselves. But might not these make the injury all the worse?

In the American Civil War, again, it seemed to the North that we thought more of cotton than of principles. A majority of Englishmen, including Mr. Gladstone, believed that it was impossible to maintain the Union by force of arms, and were prepared—at any rate at one point in the struggle—to recognize the Confederate States. There was a moment when Britain and America almost blundered into a war which would inevitably have established the independence of the South and perpetuated the shame of slavery.

During the early stages of the Great War many awkward incidents arose from differing interpretations of neutral rights. But for the U-boat campaign and its atrocities, the blockade of Germany might have led to a grave crisis in Anglo-American relations. In the long series of quarrels and disputes Britain was not always in the wrong, nor America always in the right. Usually, at the root of our differences there was the clash of incompatible rights, or sheer misunderstanding. We have done terrible things to each other through misunderstanding. Odious chapters of our common history are stained with blood and the hatreds that are fed by blood. Wrongs, revenges, insults, calumnies, battles and executions crowd the pages, with noble suffering, or conquering figures silhouetted against the dull red haze.

To us, however, these conflicts have, as a rule, been side-issues. That has helped us to forget. And sometimes we have wanted to forget because we were ashamed. But America was concerned more vitally, and some of the most glorious episodes of her history are bound up with these tragic happenings. So Americans have a double reason to remember. The cheers of vanished armies, the rumbling of long-silenced cannonades, still come down to them today.

Turn from those old unhappy events to our present situation. Although the ideals of the two countries are similar, their interests in some respects diverge. Their industries are competitive in the world market. Every instinct of America is to keep out of European affairs; Britain cannot do so even if she wished.

The question of the War Debt rankles. In the eyes of the great bulk of the American people, war debts are on exactly the same footing as private or commercial indebtedness. They cannot understand the difficulties in the way of payment, or the strain which it would put on the delicate machinery of international exchange. To them, given the ability and the willingness to meet an obligation, there is no difference between payment across the exchange and across the ocean, and payment across the counter. They have no doubt about our ability to pay. Why should they? They contrast our balanced Budget with the chaos of their own national finances. So they brand Britain as a defaulter—a dishonest debtor.

Yet the fact is that, apart from shipments of gold (which is not available in sufficient quantity and, in any case, is not wanted), there are only two ways in which we can discharge our debt. One is by selling more goods and services to the United States. But America cannot receive these without injury to her own nationals. That method, therefore, is ruled out by the Americans' decision. The second way is to reduce our purchases from the United States and to tax such commodities—cotton, for instance—as we must buy and America must sell, to create dollar credits from which debt payments might be made. Such a process would be equally injurious to both countries, and it could not fail to raise an increasing friction between them. Yet while this ugly and irritating business of the War Debt remains in suspense it is a real barrier to Anglo-American friendship.

We must also remember that for over a century America has attracted immigrants not only from Britain, but from all Europe. There is a great German population in the Middle West. Swedes and Italians are to be found everywhere. Of every hundred American citizens nine are negroes. Practically every nation on earth has contributed its quota to this vast melting-pot. These foreign elements may learn to speak English, but will they think English thoughts? Though those of European stock may be fused into the nation of their adoption and become "hundred per cent Americans," it can only be by processes which tend to separate the American mind from ours.

Another factor—though, happily, fading—must be taken into account: the powerful and highly organized Irish-American community. They have taken with them across the ocean a burning and deep-rooted hatred of the English name. They are irreconcilable enemies of the British Empire.

When we talk of collaboration between the two great branches of the English-speaking peoples and of Anglo-American friendship, these are facts which we must face. Otherwise we shall merely be repeating our wishes in the form of platitudes. Yet, when all has been urged and weighed, it still remains true that the conceptions which unite us are incomparably stronger than those that divide; that they are vital, not morbid; that they embrace the future rather than the past. The mischances of history have riven and sundered us, but our roots lie deep in the same rich soil. The great Republic of the West, no less than the British Empire, sprang from the loins of Shakespeare's England. The beginnings of American history are to be found, not across the Atlantic, but where the Thames flows between green lawns and woodlands down to a grey sea. Britain and America are joint sharers in a great inheritance of law and letters. Our political institutions, under the mask of outward difference, bear the marks of a common origin and a common aim. We are both democracies—and today our countries are, with France, the last great strongholds of Parliamentary government and individual liberty. It is the English-speaking nations who, almost alone, keep alight the torch of Freedom. These things are a powerful incentive to collaboration.

With nations, as with individuals, if you care deeply for the same things, and these things are threatened, it is natural to work together to preserve them.

The greatest tie of all is *language*. There is nothing like that. Ancient alliances, solemn treaties, faithful services given and repaid, important mutual interests—not all these taken together are equal, or nearly equal, to the bond of a common tongue. Words are the only things that last for ever. The most tremendous monuments or prodigies of engineering crumble under the hand of Time. The Pyramids moulder, the bridges rust, the canals fill up, grass covers the railway track; but words spoken two or three thousand years ago remain with us now, not as mere relics of the past, but with all their pristine vital force. Leaping across the gulf of Time, they light the world for us today. It is this power of words—words written in the past; words spoken at this moment; words printed in the newspapers; words sent speeding through the ether in a Transatlantic broadcast; the flashing interchange of thought—that is our principal agency of union. Its work must continue indefinitely—will continue, indeed, on an ever larger scale. With every new school that is opened, with every book that is printed, with every improvement in travel, with every film, with every record, identity of language gathers greater power and applies its processes more often to more people.

Of course, there is the other side. There is always the other side. A common language may become a vehicle of quarrel. I remember that sometimes trouble arose in France between British and American soldiers that would not have arisen had one party been French or Italian. But such troubles blow over. They are, no doubt, to be expected after so many generations of misunderstanding.

But as British and American troops stood in the line together, shoulder to shoulder, in a common cause, the bitterness gradually melted away. So far as these men were concerned the sponge was drawn across the scores of the past. It is for us to see that this great lever of a common language is rightly used. We must employ it to explore and, so far as possible, compose the differences between us, and to bring to the surface our underlying identity of outlook and purpose. Above all, we must use it to understand each other.

We, on this side of the Atlantic, know too little of American history. Not only are we ignorant of the full extent of our past quarrels with the United States, but we have only the most superficial comprehension of that great Westward drive which carried civilization across a Continent. We have heard of Buffalo Bill. Thanks to "The Plainsman" we have now been introduced to Wild Bill Hickok. But we see the story through a reducing-glass. The Odyssey of a people has been an individual adventure; the epic has been dwarfed to the proportions of a fairy-tale. We talk glibly of the Monroe Doctrine. How many of us understand it? How many of us realize when we criticize America as selfishly holding aloof from the League of Nations, that for over a hundred years the United States has been the guarantor of the whole of the Western Hemisphere against aggression from without? Such is the practical effect of the Monroe Doctrine.

I should like to see American history taught in our schools concurrently with our own Island story. It might help to correct the popular idea of the United States as a land of money-grubbers and multiple divorces. But that conception should also be assailed directly. No doubt there is a certain excuse for it. It is easier to secure a divorce in certain American States than it is here. But the American divorce law is merely the logical development of ideas held nearly 400 years ago by the first Protestant Archbishop of Canterbury and, in the seventeenth century, by the English Puritans.

Divorce, however, may be available for those who desire it without affecting the permanence of marriage. For the vast majority of Americans, as for the vast majority of British people, marriage is a contract for life, a partnership which only death dissolves.

The charge of money-grubbing arises directly from the needs and circumstances of a dynamically expanding society. The great tasks which Americans have set themselves for a century have been in the economic field. Washington, Hamilton, Jefferson, Jackson, Adams and Marshall—these men, soldiers, statesmen, lawyers, made a nation. They fashioned the instruments of government and established the broad lines on which American politics were to develop. But when they leave the stage, the searchlight of history wheels—save for the years of the Civil War—to the struggle to subdue and utilize a Continent.

That struggle has necessarily and rightly taken the first place in the life of the American people. So business to the American is more than the means of earning a living or making a fortune; it is that career of interest, ambition, possibly even glory, which in the older world is afforded by the learned professions and State services, military and civilian.

A young American, wishing to play a worthy part in the control of affairs, directs himself instinctively towards the managing of factories, railroads, banks, stores, or some other of the thousand-and-one varieties of industrial or commercial enterprise. Practically all the prizes of American life are to be gained in business. There, too, is the main path of useful service to the nation. Nearly all that is best and most active in the manhood and ability of the United States goes into business with the same sense of serving the country as a son of an old family in England might enter Parliament. It is this concentration of American talent on business that has gained for the United States the title, "The Land of the Dollar." But for the best type of Americans, dollars have been a by-product in business activity rather than its main aim.

On the other hand, dollars have played too great a part in American politics, left, as they have been, very largely to men of inferior moral and intellectual calibre. It is as a result of this that today, when the phase of intensive economic expansion is over, the flower of American manhood still regards the political scene with suspicion and distaste. We, in this country, must try to understand these things, just as we must seek to correct American misconceptions of England.

Some of these, however, are already being corrected by pressures arising from the slump. Americans have learned by bitter experience that to provide for the casualties of civilization by means of social insurance is not necessarily the sign of an effete society. They are being forced in this matter to follow the pathways we have opened.

There are, indeed, many ways in which both countries might, with advantage, learn from each other. For instance, Americans ought to pay more attention to their politics and we to our business. The process has begun. There is a new sense of reality in American politics. And in current political controversies there are frequent appeals to English examples. We, on our side, are studying American business organization. And the conception of business as a form of public service is taking root strongly among us.

It is encouraging also that so many American books are being read in England and so many English books in America. The literature of a nation is the best interpreter of its spirit. Reading each other's books, we come to appreciate more clearly our fundamental kinship, and to see our differences in truer perspective. The best British and American films carry this work of mutual illumination a stage further.

But direct personal contact is still of the first importance. We cannot dispense with it. British lecture tours in America have been of immense value in this respect. They have taken a number of people from this side of the Atlantic—myself among them—over a considerable part of the American Continent, and enabled them to meet large numbers of American citizens of varying types. These Americans have thus learned something of England; the lecturers have brought home with them a new and truer picture of America. The lecture habit has not been developed in English as in American life, but there are great provincial cities in which, every winter, men and women of national reputation may be heard on the lecture platform. It would be an excellent thing if the societies which arrange these matters would include American speakers in their programmes more frequently.

Private visits also play their part. Every year thousands of Americans come to this country. As yet we do not return these visits to a sufficient extent. But increasing numbers of our people are learning the delights of travel, and its field widens every year. I look forward to the day when British holiday-makers who now spend a fortnight or three weeks on the Continent will be able to visit America with equal ease. I can conceive of nothing better calculated to remove prejudices. The friendliness of Americans to the traveller from Britain, their unfailing kindliness, their generous hospitality, are something to marvel at. I am afraid that we do not always extend the same welcome to American visitors to our shores. Yet, in spite of "British reserve," some of us manage to make friends. Ties are formed strong enough to defy time and distance. We cherish pleasant memories of American homes, and they of ours. Such friendships make a notable contribution to the cause of Anglo-American understanding. It is in the homes, not the hotels, of a nation that we each can learn the truth about our people.

Here I might make an appeal to those British businessmen who have dealings with the United States. When Americans call upon you over here, don't be content with purely business contacts. Ask them to your homes and your clubs, so that they may see something of the real England. The social life of America is built mainly around business. When an Englishman crosses the Atlantic on a commercial mission, his business card opens to him a whole world of American social life. Let us respond in kind.

In these various ways the two great divisions of the English-speaking race may be drawn closer together. Private contacts and friendships between individuals, by increasing the area of understanding and good will, pave the way for a closer understanding between the two nations and their Governments, with all that this would mean to the peace of the world.

Britain and America both desire peace. God knows we have had enough of war! And though we are both arming today, we are arming only for defence. We have all we want in territory. We seek no aggrandisement; we have no old scores to wipe out. We know we have more to lose by war than any two human organizations that have ever existed. We have learned that our security and honour are most surely to be found in reconciling and identifying our several national interests with the general interests of the world. We believe that the prosperity of others makes for our prosperity; that their peace is our safety, that their progress smooths our path.

Ought we not, then, to take counsel with one another? Ought we not, when necessary, to be prepared to act together? One great stumbling-block is the determination of the American people to keep clear of European entanglements and to many Americans Britain is primarily a European Power. We cannot, indeed, cut ourselves adrift from Europe. But we are primarily not a European, but a World Power. Our commerce is carried on all the oceans; great lands in every continent are proud to be parts of the British Empire. That Empire, indeed, unites the Old World with the New. Its existence makes it difficult, if not impossible, for America to maintain a rigidly isolationist attitude. In any great war of the future in which the British Empire was engaged is it conceivable that the mandatory embargo of the Neutrality Act would be, or could be, enforced against Canada? And suppose that Canada were invaded or attacked, would there be no appeal to the spirit of the Monroe Doctrine? Apart from any sentiment of friendship towards England, here are powerful forces which, in any such situation, would tend to modify American neutrality policy in favour of the British Empire.

But need such a situation arise? If Britain and the United States were agreed to act together the risk would be slight. These two great kindred Powers in collaboration could prevent—or at least localize and limit—almost any quarrel that might break out among men. They could do this, almost certainly, without any resort to force themselves, by moral, economic and financial power, provided that in reserve there were armaments of sufficient strength to ensure that moral, economic and financial powers were not violently ruptured and suspended.

Collaboration of this kind does not imply any formal union of the English-speaking peoples. It is a union of spirit, not of forms, that we seek. There need not even be an alliance. All that is necessary is a willingness to consult together, an understanding that Britain and America shall pursue, side by side, their mutual good and the good of the whole world. There would be nothing in such an understanding that need arouse fears elsewhere. Collaboration of the English-speaking peoples threatens no one. It might safeguard all.

Here, then, is the goal towards which we should work and the spirit in which we should pursue it. And hopeful signs are not wanting. In spite of all impediments, Britain and America have never been closer in aim and purpose than now, or nearer to full mutual understanding. Our ways have diverged in the past. I believe that, increasingly, they will lie together in the future. We shall certainly follow the path of our joint destiny more prosperously, and far more safely, if we tread it together like good companions.

CHAPTER 9

DEFENCE OF FREEDOM AND PEACE

Following the infamous Munich Agreement, by which the British and French governments sold out the Czechoslovak Republic to the Nazis, Churchill again renewed his warnings of the imminence of war and his efforts to alert the people of America while time remained.

BROADCAST TO THE UNITED STATES
FROM LONDON, OCTOBER 16, 1938

I AVAIL MYSELF with relief of the opportunity of speaking to the people of the United States. I do not know how long such liberties will be allowed. The stations of uncensored expression are closing down; the lights are going out; but there is still time for those to whom freedom and Parliamentary government mean something, to consult together. Let me, then, speak in truth and earnestness while time remains.

The American people have, it seems to me, formed a true judgment upon the disaster which has befallen Europe. They realize, perhaps more clearly than the French and British publics have yet done, the far-reaching consequences of the abandonment and ruin of the Czechoslovak Republic. I hold to the conviction I expressed some months ago, that if in April, May or June, Great Britain, France and Russia had jointly declared that they would act together upon Nazi Germany if Herr Hitler committed an act of unprovoked aggression against this small state, and if they had told Poland, Yugoslavia and Rumania what they meant to do in good time, and invited them to join the combination of peace-defending Powers, I hold that the German Dictator would have been confronted with such a formidable array that he would have been deterred from his purpose. This would also have been an opportunity for all the peace-loving and moderate forces in Germany, together with the chiefs of the German Army, to make a great effort to re-establish something like sane and civilized conditions in their own country. If the risks of war which were run by France and Britain at the last moment had been boldly faced in good time, and plain declarations made, and meant, how different would our prospects be today!

But all these backward speculations belong to history. It is no good using hard words among friends about the past, and reproaching one fertile progress that has appeared in the world since the Mongol invasions of the thirteenth century.

The culminating question to which I have been leading is whether the world as we have known it—the great and hopeful world of before the war, the world of increasing hope and enjoyment for the common man, the world of honored tradition and expanding science—should meet this menace by submission or by resistance. Let us see, then, whether the means of resistance remain to us today. We have sustained an immense disaster; the renown of France is dimmed. In spite of her brave, efficient army, her influence is profoundly diminished. No one has a right to say that Britain, for all her blundering, has broken her word—indeed, when it was too late, she was better than her word. Nevertheless, Europe lies at this moment abashed and distracted before the triumphant assertions of dictatorial power. In the Spanish Peninsula, a purely Spanish quarrel has been carried by the intervention, or shall I say the "non-intervention" (to quote the current jargon), of Dictators into the region of a world cause. But it is not only in Europe that these oppressions prevail. China is being torn to pieces by a military clique in Japan; the poor, tormented Chinese people there are making a brave and stubborn defence. The ancient empire of Ethiopia has been overrun. The Ethiopians were taught to look to the sanctity of public law, to the tribunal of many nations gathered in majestic union. But all failed; they were deceived, and now they are winning back their right to live by beginning again from the bottom a struggle on primordial lines. Even in South America, the Nazi regime begins to undermine the fabric of Brazilian society.

Far away, happily protected by the Atlantic and Pacific Oceans, you, the people of the United States, to whom I now have the chance to speak, are the spectators; and, I may add, the increasingly involved spectators of these tragedies and crimes. We are left in no doubt where American conviction and sympathies lie; but will you wait until British freedom and independence have succumbed, and then take up the cause when it is three-quarters ruined, yourselves alone? I hear that they are saying in the United States that, because England and France have failed to do their duty, therefore the American people can wash their hands of the whole business. This may be the passing mood of many people, but there is no sense in it. If things have got much worse, all the more must we try to cope with them.

For, after all, survey the remaining forces of civilization; they are overwhelming. If only they were united in a common conception of right and duty, there would be no war. On the contrary, the German people, industrious and faithful, valiant, but alas! lacking in the proper spirit of civic independence, liberated from their present nightmare would take their honored place in the vanguard of human society. Alexander the Great remarked that the people of Asia were slaves because they had not learned to pronounce the word "No." Let that not be the epitaph of the English-speaking peoples or of Parliamentary democracy, or of France, or of the many surviving Liberal states of Europe.

There, in one single word, is the resolve which the forces of freedom and progress, of tolerance and good will, should take. It is not in the power of one nation, however formidably armed, still less is it in the power of a small group of men, violent, ruthless men, who have always to cast their eyes back over their shoulders, to cramp and fetter the forward march of human destiny. The preponderant world forces are upon our side; they have but to be combined to be obeyed. We must arm. Britain must arm. America must arm. If, through an earnest desire for peace, we have placed ourselves at a disadvantage, we must make up for it by redoubled exertions, and, if necessary, by fortitude in suffering. We shall, no doubt, arm. Britain, casting away the habits of centuries, will decree national service upon her citizens. The British people will stand erect, and will face whatever may be coming.

But arms—instrumentalities, as President Wilson called them—are not sufficient by themselves. We must add to them the power of ideas. People say we ought not to allow ourselves to be drawn into a theoretical antagonism between Nazidom and democracy; but the antagonism is here now. It is this very conflict of spiritual and moral ideas which gives the free countries a great part of their strength. You see these dictators on their pedestals, surrounded by the bayonets of their soldiers and the truncheons of their police. On all sides they are guarded by masses of armed men, cannons, aeroplanes, fortifications, and the like—they boast and vaunt themselves before the world, yet in their hearts there is unspoken fear. They are afraid of words and thoughts: words spoken abroad, thoughts stirring at home—all the more powerful because forbidden—terrify them. A little mouse of thought appears in the room, and even the mightiest potentates are thrown into panic. They make frantic efforts to bar out thoughts and words; they are afraid of the workings of the human mind. Cannons, aeroplanes, they can manufacture in large quantities; but how are they to quell the natural promptings of human nature, which after all these centuries of trial and progress has inherited a whole armory of potent and indestructible knowledge?

Dictatorship—the fetish worship of one man—is a passing phase. A state of society where men may not speak their minds, where children denounce their parents to the police, where a business man or small shopkeeper ruins his competitor by telling tales about his private opinions—such a state of society cannot long endure if brought into contact with the healthy outside world. The light of civilized progress with its tolerances and co-operation, with its dignities and joys, has often in the past been blotted out. But I hold the belief that we have now at last got far enough ahead of barbarism to control it, and to avert it, if only we realize what is afoot and make up our minds in time. We shall do it in the end. But how much harder our toil for every day's delay!

Is this a call to war? Does anyone pretend that preparation for resistance to aggression is unleashing war? I declare it to be the sole guarantee of peace. We need the swift gathering of forces to confront not only military but moral aggression; the resolute and sober acceptance of their duty by the English-speaking peoples and by all the nations, great and small, who wish to walk with them. Their faithful and zealous comradeship would almost between night and morning clear the path of progress and banish from all our lives the fear which already darkens the sunlight to hundreds of millions of men.

CHAPTER 10

"GIVE US THE TOOLS"

In early 1941 President Franklin D. Roosevelt sent a letter to Churchill (Prime Minister since May 10, 1940), introducing his Republican opponent in the recent presidential elections, Wendell Willkie. The President quoted some moving lines by Longfellow to which the Prime Minister replied with one of his famous wartime broadcasts.

EXTRACT OF A BROADCAST, LONDON, FEBRUARY 9, 1941

THE OTHER DAY, President Roosevelt gave his opponent in the late Presidential Election [Mr. Wendell Willkie] a letter of introduction to me, and in it he wrote out a verse, in his own handwriting, from Longfellow, which he said, "applies to you people as it does to us." Here is the verse:

> *. . . Sail on, O Ship of State!*
> *Sail on, O Union, strong and great!*
> *Humanity with all its fears,*
> *With all the hopes of future years,*
> *Is hanging breathless on thy fate!*

What is the answer that I shall give, in your name, to this great man, the thrice-chosen head of a nation of a hundred and thirty millions? Here is the answer which I will give to President Roosevelt: Put your confidence in us. Give us your faith and your blessing, and, under Providence, all will be well.

We shall not fail or falter; we shall not weaken or tire. Neither the sudden shock of battle, nor the long-drawn trials of vigilance and exertion will wear us down. Give us the tools, and we will finish the job.

THE WHITE HOUSE
WASHINGTON

*Jan 20
'941*

Dear Churchill

Wendell Willkie will give you
this — He is truly helping to keep
politics out over here.

I think this verse applies to your
people as it does to us:

"Sail on, Oh Ship of State!
Sail on Oh Union strong and great.
Humanity with all its fears,
With all the hope of future years
Is hanging breathless on thy fate"

As ever yours
Franklin D Roosevelt

*Franklin Delano Roosevelt's "Ship of State" letter
to Churchill, January 19, 1941.*

CHAPTER 11

"WESTWARD, LOOK, THE LAND IS BRIGHT"

With German forces overrunning the Balkans and Greece with devastating speed—and with the United States still six months away from entry into the conflict—Churchill placed his faith in the growing flow of military equipment and supplies from across the Atlantic to sustain Britain's war effort and, indeed, provide the very means of survival for a nation facing starvation from the U-boat menace.

BROADCAST, LONDON, APRIL 27, 1941

DURING THE LAST YEAR we have gained by our bearing and conduct a potent hold upon the sentiments of the people of the United States. Never, never in our history, have we been held in such admiration and regard across the Atlantic Ocean. In that great Republic, now in much travail and stress of soul, it is customary to use all the many valid, solid arguments about American interests and American safety, which depend upon the destruction of Hitler and his foul gang and even fouler doctrines. But in the long run—believe me, for I know—the action of the United States will be dictated, not by methodical calculations of profit and loss, but by moral sentiment, and by that gleaming flash of resolve which lifts the hearts of men and nations, and springs from the spiritual foundations of human life itself.

It was with indescribable relief that I learned of the tremendous decisions lately taken by the President and people of the United States. The American Fleet and flying boats have been ordered to patrol the wide waters of the Western Hemisphere, and to warn the peaceful shipping of all nations outside the combat zone of the presence of lurking U-boats or raiding cruisers belonging to the two aggressor nations. We British shall therefore be able to concentrate our protecting forces far more upon the routes nearer home, and to take a far heavier toll of the U-boats there. I have felt for some time that something like this was bound to happen. The President and Congress of the United States, having newly fortified themselves by contact with their electors, have solemnly pledged their aid to Britain in this war because they deem our cause just, and because they know their own interests and safety would be endangered if we were destroyed. They are taxing themselves heavily. They have passed great legislation. They have turned a large part of their gigantic industry to making the munitions which we need. They have even given us or lent us valuable weapons of their own. I could not believe that they would allow the high purposes to which they have set themselves to be frustrated and the products of their skill and labour sunk to the bottom of the sea. U-boat warfare as conducted by Germany is entirely contrary to international agreements freely subscribed to by Germany only a few years ago. There is no effective blockade, but only a merciless murder and marauding over wide, indiscriminate areas utterly beyond the control of the German seapower. When I said ten weeks ago: "Give us the tools and we will finish the job," I meant, *give* them to us: put them within our reach—and that is what it now seems the Americans are going to do. And that is why I feel a very strong conviction that though the Battle of the Atlantic will be long and hard, and its issue is by no means yet determined, it has entered upon a more grim but at the same time a far more favourable phase. When you come to think of it, the United States are very closely bound up with us now, and have engaged themselves deeply in giving us moral, material, and, within the limits I have mentioned, naval support.

It is worth while therefore to take a look on both sides of the ocean at the forces which are facing each other in this awful struggle, from which there can be no drawing back. No prudent and far-seeing man can doubt that the eventual and total defeat of Hitler and Mussolini is certain, in view of the respective declared resolves of the British and American democracies. There are less than seventy million malignant Huns—some of whom are curable and others killable—many of whom are already engaged in holding down Austrians, Czechs, Poles, French, and the many other ancient races they now bully and pillage. The peoples of the British Empire and of the United States number nearly two hundred millions in their homelands and in the British Dominions alone. They possess the unchallengeable command of the oceans, and will soon obtain decisive superiority in the air. They have more wealth, more technical resources, and they make more steel, than the whole of the rest of the world put together. They are determined that the cause of freedom shall not be trampled down, nor the tide of world progress turned backwards, by the criminal Dictators.

While therefore we naturally view with sorrow and anxiety much that is happening in Europe and in Africa, and may happen in Asia, we must not lose our sense of proportion and thus become discouraged or alarmed. When we face with a steady eye the difficulties which lie before us, we may derive new confidence from remembering those we have already overcome. Nothing that is happening now is comparable in gravity with the dangers through which we passed last year. Nothing that can happen in the East is comparable with what is happening in the West.

Last time I spoke to you I quoted the lines of Longfellow which President Roosevelt had written out for me in his own hand. I have some other lines which are less well known but which seem apt and appropriate to our fortunes to-night, and I believe they will be so judged wherever the English language is spoken or the flag of freedom flies:

> For while the tired waves, vainly breaking,
> Seem here no painful inch to gain,
> Far back, through creeks and inlets making,
> Comes silent, flooding in, the main.
> And not by eastern windows only,
> When daylight comes, comes in the light;
> In front the sun climbs slow, how slowly!
> But westward, look, the land is bright.

CHAPTER 12

THE ATLANTIC CHARTER

The Prime Minister reports to the British people following his meeting with President Roosevelt at Placentia Bay, Newfoundland, two weeks earlier on board HMS Prince of Wales, *at which the Atlantic Charter was signed.*

BROADCAST, LONDON, AUGUST 24, 1941

I THOUGHT YOU would like me to tell you something about the voyage which I made across the ocean to meet our great friend, the President of the United States. Exactly where we met is a secret, but I don't think I shall be indiscreet if I go so far as to say that it was "somewhere in the Atlantic."

In a spacious, landlocked bay which reminded me of the West Coast of Scotland, powerful American warships protected by strong flotillas and far-ranging aircraft awaited our arrival, and, as it were, stretched out a hand to help us in. Our party arrived in the newest, or almost the newest, British battleship, the *Prince of Wales,* with a modern escort of British and Canadian destroyers, and there for three days I spent my time in company, and I think I may say in comradeship, with Mr. Roosevelt; while all the time the chiefs of the staff and the naval and military commanders both of the British Empire and of the United States sat together in continual council.

President Roosevelt is the thrice-chosen head of the most powerful state and community in the world. I am the servant of King and Parliament at present charged with the principal direction of our affairs in these fateful times, and it is my duty also to make sure, as I have made sure, that anything I say or do in the exercise of my office is approved and sustained by the whole British Commonwealth of Nations. Therefore this meeting was bound to be important, because of the enormous forces at present only partially mobilized but steadily mobilizing which are at the disposal of these two major groupings of the human family: the British Empire and the United States, who, fortunately for the

The Prime Minister aboard the HMS Prince of Wales, *surrounded by*
sailors from the USS Augusta *at Placentia Bay, Newfoundland,*
for the Atlantic Charter meeting, August 9, 1941.

progress of mankind, happen to speak the same language, and very
largely think the same thoughts, or anyhow think a lot of the same
thoughts.

The meeting was therefore symbolic. That is its prime importance. It
symbolizes, in a form and manner which everyone can understand in
every land and in every clime, the deep underlying unities which stir
and at decisive moments rule the English-speaking peoples throughout
the world. Would it be presumptuous for me to say that it symbolizes
something even more majestic—namely, the marshalling of the good
forces of the world against the evil forces which are now so formidable
and triumphant and which have cast their cruel spell over the whole of
Europe and a large part of Asia?

This was a meeting which marks for ever in the pages of history the
taking-up by the English-speaking nations, amid all this peril, tumult
and confusion, of the guidance of the fortunes of the broad toiling
masses in all the continents; and our loyal effort without any clog of
selfish interest to lead them forward out of the miseries into which they
have been plunged back to the broad highroad of freedom and justice.
This is the highest honour and the most glorious opportunity which
could ever have come to any branch of the human race.

When one beholds how many currents of extraordinary and terrible

events have flowed together to make this harmony, even the most sceptical person must have the feeling that we all have the chance to play
our part and do our duty in some great design, the end of which no
mortal can foresee. Awful and horrible things are happening in these
days. The whole of Europe has been wrecked and trampled down by
the mechanical weapons and barbaric fury of the Nazis; the most
deadly instruments of war-science have been joined to the extreme re-
finements of treachery and the most brutal exhibitions of ruthlessness,
and thus have formed a combine of aggression the like of which has
never been known, before which the rights, the traditions, the characteristics and the structure of many ancient honoured states and peoples
have been laid prostate and are now ground down under the heel and
terror of a monster. The Austrians, the Czechs, the Poles, the Norwegians, the Danes, the Belgians, the Dutch, the Greeks, the Croats and
the Serbs, above all the great French nation, have been stunned and
pinioned. Italy, Hungary, Rumania, Bulgaria have bought a shameful
respite by becoming the jackals of the tiger, but their situation is very
little different and will presently be indistinguishable from that of his
victims. Sweden, Spain and Turkey stand appalled, wondering which
will be struck down next.

Here, then, is the vast pit into which all the most famous states and
races of Europe have been flung and from which unaided they can
never climb. But all this did not satiate Adolf Hitler; he made a treaty
of non-aggression with Soviet Russia, just as he made one with Turkey,
in order to keep them quiet till he was ready to attack them, and then,
nine weeks ago today, without a vestige of provocation, he hurled millions of soldiers, with all their apparatus, upon the neighbour he had
called his friend, with the avowed object of destroying Russia and tearing her in pieces. This frightful business is now unfolding day by day before our eyes. Here is a devil who, in a mere spasm of his pride and lust
for domination, can condemn two or three millions, perhaps it may be
many more, of human beings, to speedy and violent death. "Let Russia
be blotted out—Let Russia be destroyed. Order the armies to advance."
Such were his decrees. Accordingly from the Arctic Ocean to the Black
Sea, six or seven millions of soldiers are locked in mortal struggle. Ah,
but this time it was not so easy.

This time it was not all one way. The Russian armies and all the peoples of the Russian Republic have rallied to the defence of their hearths
and homes. For the first time Nazi blood has flowed in a fearful torrent.
Certainly 1,500,000, perhaps 2,000,000 of Nazi cannon-fodder have bit
the dust of the endless plains of Russia. The tremendous battle rages
along nearly 2,000 miles of front. The Russians fight with magnificent

devotion; not only that, our generals who have visited the Russian front line report with admiration the efficiency of their military organization and the excellence of their equipment. The aggressor is surprised, startled, staggered. For the first time in his experience mass murder has become unprofitable. He retaliates by the most frightful cruelties. As his armies advance, whole districts are being exterminated. Scores of thousands—literally scores of thousands—of executions in cold blood are being perpetrated by the German police-troops upon the Russian patriots who defend their native soil. Since the Mongol invasions of Europe in the sixteenth century, there has never been methodical, merciless butchery on such a scale, or approaching such a scale. And this is but the beginning. Famine and pestilence have yet to follow in the bloody ruts of Hitler's tanks. We are in the presence of a crime without a name.

But Europe is not the only continent to be tormented and devastated by aggressions. For five long years the Japanese military factions, seeking to emulate the style of Hitler and Mussolini, taking all their posturing as if it were a new European revelation, have been invading and harrying the 500,000,000 inhabitants of China. Japanese armies have been wandering about that vast land in futile excursions, carrying with them carnage, ruin and corruption and calling it the "Chinese Incident." Now they stretch a grasping hand into the southern seas of China; they snatch Indo-China from the wretched Vichy French; they menace by their movements Siam; menace Singapore, the British link with Australia; and menace the Philippine Islands under the protection of the United States. It is certain that this has got to stop. Every effort will be made to secure a peaceful settlement. The United States are labouring with infinite patience to arrive at a fair and amicable settlement which will give Japan the utmost reassurance for her legitimate interests. We earnestly hope these negotiations will succeed. But this I must say: that if these hopes should fail we shall of course range ourselves unhesitatingly at the side of the United States.

And thus we come back to the quiet bay somewhere in the Atlantic where misty sunshine plays on great ships which carry the White Ensign, or the Stars and Stripes. We had the idea, when we met there—the President and I—that without attempting to draw up final and formal peace aims, or war aims, it was necessary to give all peoples, especially the oppressed and conquered peoples, a simple, rough-and-ready wartime statement of the goal towards which the British Commonwealth and the United States mean to make their way, and thus make a way for others to march with them upon a road which will certainly be painful, and may be long!

There are, however, two distinct and marked differences in this joint declaration from the attitude adopted by the Allies during the latter part of the last war; and no one should overlook them. The United States and Great Britain do not now assume that there will never be any more war again. On the contrary, we intend to take ample precautions to prevent its renewal in any period we can foresee by effectively disarming the guilty nations while remaining suitably protected ourselves.

The second difference is this: that instead of trying to ruin German trade by all kinds of additional trade barriers and hindrances as was the mood of 1917, we have definitely adopted the view that it is not in the interests of the world and of our two countries that any large nation should be unprosperous or shut out from the means of making a decent living for itself and its people by its industry and enterprise. These are far-reaching changes of principle upon which all countries should ponder. Above all, it was necessary to give hope and the assurance of final victory to those many scores of millions of men and women who are battling for life and freedom, or who are already bent down under the Nazi yoke. Hitler and his confederates have for some time past been adjuring, bullying and beseeching the populations whom they have wronged and injured, to bow to their fate, to resign themselves to their servitude, and for the sake of some mitigations and indulgences, to "collaborate"—that is the word—in what is called the New Order in Europe.

What is this New Order which they seek to fasten first upon Europe and if possible—for their ambitions are boundless—upon all the continents of the globe? It is the rule of the *Herrenvolk*—the master-race—who are to put an end to democracy, to parliaments, to the fundamental freedoms and decencies of ordinary men and women, to the historic rights of nations; and give them in exchange the iron rule of Prussia, the universal goose-step, and a strict, efficient discipline enforced upon the working-class by the political police, with the German concentration camps and firing parties, now so busy in a dozen lands, always handy in the background. There is the New Order.

Napoleon in his glory and his genius spread his Empire far and wide. There was a time when only the snows of Russia and the white cliffs of Dover with their guardian fleets stood between him and the dominion of the world. Napoleon's armies had a theme: they carried with them the surges of the French Revolution. Liberty, Equality and Fraternity—that was the cry. There was a sweeping away of outworn medieval systems and aristocratic privilege. There was the land for the people, a new code of law. Nevertheless, Napoleon's Empire vanished like a dream. But Hitler, Hitler has no theme, naught but mania, appetite and exploitation. He has, however, weapons and machinery for grinding down and for holding down conquered countries which are the product, the sadly perverted product, of modern science.

The ordeals, therefore, of the conquered peoples will be hard. We must give them hope; we must give them the conviction that their sufferings and their resistances will not be in vain. The tunnel may be dark and long, but at the end there is light. That is the symbolism and that is the message of the Atlantic meeting. Do not despair, brave Norwegians: your land shall be cleansed not only from the invader but from the filthy quislings who are his tools. Be sure of yourselves, Czechs: your independence shall be restored. Poles, the heroism of your people standing up to cruel oppressors, the courage of your soldiers, sailors and airmen, shall not be forgotten: your country shall live again and resume its rightful part in the new organization of Europe. Lift up your heads, gallant Frenchmen: not all the infamies of Darlan and of Laval shall stand between you and the restoration of your birthright. Tough, stout-hearted Dutch, Belgians, Luxembourgers, tormented, mishandled, shamefully castaway peoples of Yugoslavia, glorious Greece, now subjected to the crowning insult of the rule of the Italian jackanapes; yield not an inch! Keep your souls clean from all contact with the Nazis; make them feel even in their fleeting hour of brutish triumph that they are the moral outcasts of mankind. Help is coming; mighty forces are arming in your behalf. Have faith. Have hope. Deliverance is sure.

There is the signal which we have flashed across the water; and if it reaches the hearts of those to whom it is sent, they will endure with fortitude and tenacity their present misfortunes in the sure faith that they, too, are still serving the common cause, and that their efforts will not be in vain.

You will perhaps have noticed that the President of the United States and the British representative, in what is aptly called the "Atlantic Charter," have jointly pledged their countries to the final destruction of the Nazi tyranny. That is a solemn and grave undertaking. It must be made good; it will be made good. And, of course, many practical arrangements to fulfil that purpose have been and are being organized and set in motion.

The question has been asked: how near is the United States to war? There is certainly one man who knows the answer to that question. If Hitler has not yet declared war upon the United States, it is surely not out of his love for American institutions; it is certainly not because he could not find a pretext. He has murdered half a dozen countries for far less. Fear of immediately redoubling the tremendous energies now being employed against him is no doubt a restraining influence. But the real reason is, I am sure, to be found in the method to which he has so faithfully adhered and by which he has gained so much.

What is that method? It is a very simple method. One by one: that is his plan; that is his guiding rule; that is the trick by which he has enslaved so large a portion of the world. Three and a half years ago I appealed to my fellow countrymen to take the lead in weaving together a strong defensive union within the principles of the League of Nations, a union of all the countries who felt themselves in ever-growing danger. But none would listen; all stood idle while Germany rearmed. Czechoslovakia was subjugated; a French Government deserted their faithful ally and broke a plighted word in that ally's hour of need. Russia was cajoled and deceived into a kind of neutrality or partnership, while the French Army was being annihilated. The Low Countries and the Scandinavian countries, acting with France and Great Britain in good time, even after the war had begun, might have altered its course, and would have had, at any rate, a fighting chance. The Balkan States had only to stand together to save themselves from the ruin by which they are now engulfed. But one by one they were undermined and overwhelmed. Never was the career of crime made more smooth.

Now Hitler is striking at Russia with all his might, well knowing the difficulties of geography which stand between Russia and the aid which the Western Democracies are trying to bring. We shall strive our utmost to overcome all obstacles and to bring this aid. We have arranged for a conference in Moscow between the United States, British and Russian authorities to settle the whole plan. No barrier must stand in the way. But why is Hitler striking at Russia, and inflicting and suffering himself or, rather, making his soldiers suffer, this frightful slaughter? It is with the declared object of turning his whole force upon the British Islands, and if he could succeed in beating the life and the strength out of us, which is not so easy, then is the moment when he will settle his account, and it is already a long one, with the people of the United States and generally with the Western Hemisphere. One by one, there is the process; there is the simple, dismal plan which has served Hitler so well. It needs but one final successful application to make him the master of the world. I am devoutly thankful that some eyes at least are fully opened to it while time remains. I rejoiced to find that the President saw in their true light and proportion the extreme dangers by which the American people as well as the British people are now beset. It was indeed by the mercy of God that he began eight years ago that revival of the strength of the American Navy without which the New World today would have to take its orders from the European dictators, but with which the United States still retains the power to marshal her gigantic strength, and in saving herself to render an incomparable service to mankind.

We had a church parade on the Sunday in our Atlantic bay. The President came on to the quarter-deck of the *Prince of Wales,* where there were mingled together many hundreds of American and British sailors and marines. The sun shone bright and warm while we all sang the old hymns which are our common inheritance and which we learned as children in our homes. We sang the hymn founded on the psalm which John Hampden's soldiers sang when they bore his body to the grave, and in which the brief, precarious span of human life is contrasted with the immutability of Him to Whom a thousand ages are but as yesterday, and as a watch in the night. We sang the sailors' hymn "For those in peril"—and there are very many—"on the sea." We sang "Onward Christian Soldiers." And indeed I felt that this was no vain presumption, but that we had the right to feel that we were serving a cause for the sake of which a trumpet has sounded from on high.

When I looked upon that densely-packed congregation of fighting men of the same language, of the same faith, of the same fundamental laws and the same ideals, and now to a large extent of the same interests, and certainly in different degrees facing the same dangers, it swept across me that here was the only hope, but also the sure hope, of saving the world from measureless degradation.

And so we came back across the ocean waves, uplifted in spirit, fortified in resolve. Some American destroyers which were carrying mails to the United States marines in Iceland happened to be going the same way, too, so we made a goodly company at sea together.

And when we were right out in mid-passage one afternoon a noble sight broke on the view. We overtook one of the convoys which carry the munitions and supplies of the New World to sustain the champions of freedom in the Old. The whole broad horizon seemed filled with ships; seventy or eighty ships of all kinds and sizes, arrayed in fourteen lines, each of which could have been drawn with a ruler, hardly a wisp of smoke, not a straggler, but all bristling with cannons and other precautions on which I will not dwell, and all surrounded by their British escorting vessels, while overhead the far-ranging Catalina air-boats soared—vigilant, protecting eagles in the sky. Then I felt that—hard and terrible and long drawn-out as this struggle may be—we shall not be denied the strength to do our duty to the end.

CHAPTER 13

THE WHITE HOUSE CHRISTMAS TREE

On December 7, 1941, Japanese forces attacked the U.S. fleet in Pearl Harbor. Churchill lost no time in arranging forthwith a visit to the United States, which was now Britain's comrade-in-arms. President and Mrs. Roosevelt invited him to join them as their guest for Christmas at the White House. For Churchill it was a joyous occasion: though he knew that much sacrifice and peril lay ahead, there was no longer any doubt in his mind of the ultimate victory of the Allied cause.

BROADCAST, WASHINGTON, D.C., DECEMBER 24, 1941

I SPEND this anniversary and festival far from my country, far from my family, yet I cannot truthfully say that I feel far from home. Whether it be the ties of blood on my mother's side, or the friendships I have developed here over many years of active life, or the commanding sentiment of comradeship in the common cause of great peoples who speak the same language, who kneel at the same altars and, to a very large extent, pursue the same ideals, I cannot feel myself a stranger here in the centre and at the summit of the United States. I feel a sense of unity and fraternal association which, added to the kindliness of your welcome, convinces me that I have a right to sit at your fireside and share your Christmas joys.

This is a strange Christmas Eve. Almost the whole world is locked in deadly struggle, and, with the most terrible weapons which science can devise, the nations advance upon each other. Ill would it be for us this Christmastide if we were not sure that no greed for the land or wealth of any other people, no vulgar ambition, no morbid lust for material gain at the expense of others, had led us to the field. Here, in the midst of war, raging and roaring over all the lands and seas, creeping nearer to our hearts and homes, here, amid all the tumult, we have tonight the peace of the spirit in each cottage home and in every generous heart. Therefore we may cast aside for this night at least the cares and dangers which beset us, and make for the children an evening of happiness in a world of storm. Here, then, for one night only, each home throughout the English-speaking world should be a brightly-lighted island of happiness and peace.

Let the children have their night of fun and laughter. Let the gifts of Father Christmas delight their play. Let us grown-ups share to the full in their unstinted pleasures before we turn again to the stern task and the formidable years that lie before us, resolved that, by our sacrifice and daring, these same children shall not be robbed of their inheritance or denied their right to live in a free and decent world.

And so, in God's mercy, a happy Christmas to you all.

CHAPTER 14

"A LONG HARD WAR"

This was Churchill's first address to Congress. He could not resist teasing the senators and congressmen present with the thought that had his father been American and his mother British "I might have got here on my own!"

ADDRESS TO A JOINT SESSION OF THE U.S. CONGRESS,
DECEMBER 26, 1941

I FEEL GREATLY HONOURED that you should have invited me to enter the United States Senate Chamber and address the representatives of both branches of Congress. The fact that my American forebears have for so many generations played their part in the life of the United States, and that here I am, an Englishman, welcomed in your midst, makes this experience one of the most moving and thrilling in my life, which is already long and has not been entirely uneventful. I wish indeed that my mother, whose memory I cherish across the vale of years, could have been here to see. By the way, I cannot help reflecting that if my father had been American and my mother British, instead of the other way round, I might have got here on my own. In that case, this would not have been the first time you would have heard my voice. In that case I should not have needed any invitation, but if I had, it is hardly likely it would have been unanimous. So perhaps things are better as they are. I may confess, however, that I do not feel quite like a fish out of water in a legislative assembly where English is spoken.

I am a child of the House of Commons. I was brought up in my father's house to believe in democracy. "Trust the people"—that was his message. I used to see him cheered at meetings and in the streets by crowds of working men way back in those aristocratic Victorian days when, as Disraeli said, the world was for the few, and for the very few. Therefore I have been in full harmony all my life with the tides which have flowed on both sides of the Atlantic against privilege and monopoly, and I have steered confidently towards the Gettysburg ideal of "government of the people by the people for the people." I owe my advancement entirely to the House of Commons, whose servant I am. In my country, as in yours, public men are proud to be the servants of the State and would be ashamed to be its masters. On any day, if they thought the people wanted it, the House of Commons could by a simple vote remove me from my office. But I am not worrying about it at all. As a matter of fact, I am sure they will approve very highly of my journey here, for which I obtained the King's permission in order to meet the President of the United States and to arrange with him all that mapping-out of our military plans, and for all those intimate meetings of the high officers of the armed services of both countries, which are indispensable to the successful prosecution of the war.

I should like to say first of all how much I have been impressed and encouraged by the breadth of view and sense of proportion which I have found in all quarters over here to which I have had access. Anyone who did not understand the size and solidarity of the foundations of the United States might easily have expected to find an excited, disturbed, self-centred atmosphere, with all minds fixed upon the novel, startling, and painful episodes of sudden war as they hit America. After all, the United States have been attacked and set upon by three most powerfully-armed dictator States. The greatest military power in Europe, the greatest military power in Asia, Germany and Japan, Italy, too, have all declared, and are making, war upon you, and a quarrel is opened, which can only end in their overthrow or yours. But here in Washington, in these memorable days, I have found an Olympian fortitude which, far from being based upon complacency, is only the mask of an inflexible purpose and the proof of a sure and well-grounded confidence in the final outcome. We in Britain had the same feeling in our darkest days. We, too, were sure in the end all would be well. You do not, I am certain, underrate the severity of the ordeal to which you and we have still to be subjected. The forces ranged against us are enormous. They are bitter, they are ruthless. The wicked men and their factions who have launched their peoples on the path of war and conquest know that they will be called to terrible account if they cannot beat down by force of arms the peoples they have assailed. They will stop at nothing. They have a vast accumulation of war weapons of all kinds. They have highly-trained, disciplined armies, navies, and air services. They have plans and designs which have long been tried and matured. They will stop at nothing that violence or treachery can suggest.

It is quite true that, on our side, our resources in man-power and materials are far greater than theirs. But only a portion of your resources is as yet mobilized and developed, and we both of us have much to learn in the cruel art of war. We have therefore, without doubt, a time of tribulation before us. In this time some ground will be lost which it will be hard and costly to regain. Many disappointments and unpleasant surprises await us. Many of them will afflict us before the full marshalling of our latent and total power can be accomplished. For the best part of twenty years the youth of Britain and America have been taught that war is evil, which is true, and that it would never come again, which has been proved false. For the best part of twenty years the youth of Germany, Japan and Italy have been taught that aggressive war is the noblest duty of the citizen, and that it should be begun as soon as the necessary weapons and organization had been made. We have performed the duties and tasks of peace. They have plotted and planned for war. This, naturally, has placed us in Britain and now places you in the United States at a disadvantage which only time, courage, and strenuous, untiring exertions can correct.

We have indeed to be thankful that so much time has been granted to us. If Germany had tried to invade the British Isles after the French collapse in June, 1940, and if Japan had declared war on the British Empire and the United States at about the same date, no one could say what disasters and agonies might not have been our lot. But now at the end of December, 1941, our transformation from easy-going peace to total war efficiency has made very great progress. The broad flow of munitions in Great Britain has already begun. Immense strides have been made in the conversion of American Industry to military purposes, and now that the United States are at war it is possible for orders to be given every day which a year or eighteen months hence will produce results in war power beyond anything that has yet been seen or foreseen in the dictator States. Provided that every effort is made, that nothing is kept back, that the whole man-power, brain-power, virility, valour, and civic virtue of the English-speaking world with all its galaxy of loyal, friendly, associated communities and States—provided all that is bent unremittingly to the simple and supreme task, I think it would be reasonable to hope that the end of 1942 will see us quite definitely in a better position than we are now, and that the year 1943 will enable us to assume the initiative upon an ample scale.

Some people may be startled or momentarily depressed when, like your President, I speak of a long and hard war. But our peoples would rather know the truth, sombre though it be. And after all, when we are doing the noblest work in the world, not only defending our hearths and homes but the cause of freedom in other lands, the question of whether deliverance comes in 1942, 1943, or 1944 falls into its proper place in the grand proportions of human history. Sure I am that this day—now—we are the masters of our fate; that the task which has been set us is not above our strength; that its pangs and toils are not beyond our endurance. As long as we have faith in our cause and an unconquerable will-power, salvation will not be denied us. In the words of the Psalmist, "He shall not be afraid of evil tidings; his heart is fixed, trusting in the Lord." Not all the tidings will be evil.

On the contrary, mighty strokes of war have already been dealt against the enemy; the glorious defence of their native soil by the Russian armies and people have inflicted wounds upon the Nazi tyranny and system which have bitten deep, and will fester and inflame not only in the Nazi body but in the Nazi mind. The boastful Mussolini has crumbled already. He is now but a lackey and serf, the merest utensil of his master's will. He has inflicted great suffering and wrong upon his own industrious people. He has been stripped of his African empire, Abyssinia has been liberated. Our armies in the East, which were so weak and ill-equipped at the moment of French desertion, now control all the regions from Teheran to Benghazi, and from Aleppo and Cyprus to the sources of the Nile.

For many months we devoted ourselves to preparing to take the offensive in Libya. The very considerable battle, which has been proceeding for the last six weeks in the desert, has been most fiercely fought on both sides. Owing to the difficulties of supply on the desert flanks, we were never able to bring numerically equal forces to bear upon the enemy. Therefore we had to rely upon a superiority in the numbers and quality of tanks and aircraft, British and American. Aided by these, for the first time, we have fought the enemy with equal weapons. For the first time we have made the Hun feel the sharp edge of those tools with which he has enslaved Europe. The armed forces of the enemy in Cyrenaica amounted to about 150,000, of whom about one-third were Germans. General Auchinleck set out to destroy totally that armed force. I have every reason to believe that his aim will be fully accomplished. I am glad to be able to place before you, members of the Senate and of the House of Representatives, at this moment when you are entering the war, proof that with proper weapons and proper organization we are able to beat the life out of the savage Nazi. What Hitler is suffering in Libya is only a sample and foretaste of what we must give him and his accomplices, wherever this war shall lead us, in every quarter of the globe.

There are good tidings also from blue water. The life-line of supplies which joins our two nations across the ocean, without which all might fail, is flowing steadily and freely in spite of all the enemy can do. It is a fact that the British Empire, which many thought eighteen months ago was broken and ruined, is now incomparably stronger, and is growing stronger with every month. Lastly, if you will forgive me for saying it, to me the best tidings of all is that the United States, united as never before, have drawn the sword for freedom and cast away the scabbard.

All these tremendous facts have led the subjugated peoples of Europe to lift up their heads again in hope. They have put aside for ever the shameful temptation of resigning themselves to the conqueror's will. Hope has returned to the hearts of scores of millions of men and women, and with that hope there burns the flame of anger against the brutal, corrupt invader, and still more fiercely burn the fires of hatred and contempt for the squalid quislings whom he has suborned. In a dozen famous ancient States now prostrate under the Nazi yoke, the masses of the people of all classes and creeds await the hour of liberation, when they too will be able once again to play their part and strike their blows like men. That hour will strike, and its solemn peal will proclaim that the night is past and that the dawn has come.

The onslaught upon us so long and so secretly planned by Japan has presented both our countries with grievous problems for which we could not be fully prepared. If people ask me—as they have a right to ask me in England—why is it that you have not got ample equipment of modern aircraft and Army weapons of all kinds in Malaya and in the East Indies, I can only point to the victories General Auchinleck has gained in the Libyan campaign. Had we divested and dispersed our gradually growing resources between Libya and Malaya, we should have been found wanting in both theatres. If the United States have been found at a disadvantage at various points in the Pacific Ocean, we know well that it is to no small extent because of the aid you have been giving us in munitions for the defence of the British Isles and for the Libyan campaign, and, above all, because of your help in the battle of the Atlantic, upon which all depends, and which has in consequence been successfully and prosperously maintained. Of course it would have been much better, I freely admit, if we had had enough resources of all kinds to be at full strength at all threatened points; but considering how slowly and reluctantly we brought ourselves to large-scale preparations, and how long such preparations take, we had no right to expect to be in such a fortunate position.

The choice of how to dispose of our hitherto limited resources had to be made by Britain in time of war and by the United States in time of peace; and I believe that history will pronounce that upon the whole—and it is upon the whole that these matters must be judged—the choice made was right. Now that we are together, now that we are linked in a righteous comradeship of arms, now that our two considerable nations, each in perfect unity, have joined all their life energies in a common resolve, a new scene opens upon which a steady light will glow and brighten.

Many people have been astonished that Japan should in a single day have plunged into war against the United States and the British Empire. We all wonder why, if this dark design, with all its laborious and intricate preparations, had been so long filling their secret minds, they did not choose our moment of weakness eighteen months ago. Viewed quite dispassionately, in spite of the losses we have suffered and the further punishment we shall have to take, it certainly appears to be an irrational act. It is, of course, only prudent to assume that they have made very careful calculations and think they see their way through. Nevertheless, there may be another explanation. We know that for many years past the policy of Japan has been dominated by secret societies of subalterns and junior officers of the Army and Navy, who have enforced their will upon successive Japanese Cabinets and Parliaments by the assassination of any Japanese statesman who opposed, or who did not sufficiently further, their aggressive policy. It may be that these societies, dazzled and dizzy with their own schemes of aggression and the prospect of early victories, have forced their country against its better judgment into war. They have certainly embarked upon a very considerable undertaking. For after the outrages they have committed upon us at Pearl Harbour, in the Pacific Islands, in the Philippines, in Malaya, and in the Dutch East Indies, they must now know that the stakes for which they have decided to play are mortal.

When we consider the resources of the United States and the British Empire compared to those of Japan, when we remember those of China, which has so long and valiantly withstood invasion and when also we observe the Russian menace which hangs over Japan, it becomes still more difficult to reconcile Japanese action with prudence or even with sanity. What kind of a people do they think we are? Is it possible they do not realize that we shall never cease to persevere against them until they have been taught a lesson which they and the world will never forget?

Members of the Senate and members of the House of Representatives, I turn for one moment more from the turmoil and convulsions of the present to the broader basis of the future. Here we are together facing a group of mighty foes who seek our ruin; here we are together defending all that to free men is dear. Twice in a single generation the catastrophe of world war has fallen upon us; twice in our lifetime has the long arm of fate reached across the ocean to bring the United

States into the forefront of the battle. If we had kept together after the last War, if we had taken common measures for our safety, this renewal of the curse need never have fallen upon us.

Do we not owe it to ourselves, to our children, to mankind tormented, to make sure that these catastrophes shall not engulf us for the third time? It has been proved that pestilences may break out in the Old World, which carry their destructive ravages into the New World, from which, once they are afoot, the New World cannot by any means escape. Duty and prudence alike command first that the germ-centres of hatred and revenge should be constantly and vigilantly surveyed and treated in good time, and, secondly, that an adequate organization should be set up to make sure that the pestilence can be controlled at its earliest beginnings before it spreads and rages throughout the entire earth.

Five or six years ago it would have been easy, without shedding a drop of blood, for the United States and Great Britain to have insisted on fulfilment of the disarmament clauses of the treaties which Germany signed after the Great War; that also would have been the opportunity for assuring to Germany those raw materials which we declared in the Atlantic Charter should not be denied to any nation, victor or vanquished. That chance has passed. It is gone. Prodigious hammer-strokes have been needed to bring us together again, or if you will allow me to use other language, I will say that he must indeed have a blind soul who cannot see that some great purpose and design is being worked out here below, of which we have the honour to be the faithful servants. It is not given to us to peer into the mysteries of the future. Still, I avow my hope and faith, sure and inviolate, that in the days to come the British and American peoples will for their own safety and for the good of all walk together side by side in majesty, in justice, and in peace.

CHAPTER 15

"HEAVIER WORK LIES AHEAD"

By May 13, 1943, the Allies had succeeded in defeating the German-Italian army in North Africa commanded by Field Marshal Erwin Rommel. Churchill addressed Congress for the second time as the Allies stood poised to launch their assault on Italy and to intensify the strategic bombing of Germany.

ADDRESS TO A JOINT SESSION OF
THE U.S. CONGRESS, MAY 19, 1943

SEVENTEEN MONTHS have passed since I last had the honour to address the Congress of the United States. For more than 500 days, every day a day, we have toiled and suffered and dared shoulder to shoulder against the cruel and mighty enemy. We have acted in close combination or concert in many parts of the world, on land, on sea, and in the air. The fact that you have invited me to come to Congress again a second time, now that we have settled down to the job, and that you should welcome me in so generous a fashion, is certainly a high mark in my life, and it also shows that our partnership has not done so badly.

I am proud that you should have found us good allies, striving forward in comradeship to the accomplishment of our task without grudging or stinting either life or treasure, or, indeed, anything that we have to give. Last time I came at a moment when the United States was aflame with wrath at the treacherous attack upon Pearl Harbour by Japan, and at the subsequent declarations of war upon the United States made by Germany and Italy. For my part I say quite frankly that in those days, after our long—and for a whole year lonely—struggle, I could not repress in my heart a sense of relief and comfort that we were all bound together by common peril, by solemn faith and high purpose, to see this fearful quarrel through, at all costs, to the end.

That was the hour of passionate emotion, an hour most memorable in human records, an hour, I believe, full of hope and glory for the future. The experiences of a long life and the promptings of my blood have wrought in me the conviction that there is nothing more important for the future of the world than the fraternal association of our two peoples in righteous work both in war and peace.

So in January, 1942, I had that feeling of comfort, and I therefore prepared myself in a confident and steadfast spirit to bear the terrible blows which were evidently about to fall on British interests in the Far East, which were bound to fall upon us, from the military strength of Japan during a period when the American and British fleets had lost, for the time being, the naval command of the Pacific and Indian Oceans.

One after another, in swift succession, very heavy misfortunes fell upon us, and upon our Allies, the Dutch, in the Pacific theatre. The Japanese have seized the lands and islands they so greedily coveted. The Philippines are enslaved, the lustrous, luxuriant regions of the Dutch East Indies have been overrun. In the Malay Peninsula and at Singapore we ourselves suffered the greatest military disaster, or at any rate the largest military disaster, in British history.

Mr. President, Mr. Speaker, all this has to be retrieved, and all this and much else has to be repaid. And here let me say this: let no one suggest that we British have not at least as great an interest as the United States in the unflinching and relentless waging of war against Japan. And I am here to tell you that we will wage that war, side by side with you, in accordance with the best strategic employment of our forces, while there is breath in our bodies and while blood flows in our veins.

A notable part in the war against Japan must, of course, be played by the large armies and by the air and naval forces now marshalled by Great Britain on the eastern frontiers of India. In this quarter there lies one of the means of bringing aid to hard-pressed and long-tormented China. I regard the bringing of effective and immediate aid to China as one of the most urgent of our common tasks.

It may not have escaped your attention that I have brought with me to this country and to this conference Field-Marshal Wavell and the other two Commanders-in-Chief from India. Now, they have not travelled all this way simply to concern themselves about improving the health and happiness of the Mikado of Japan. I thought it would be good that all concerned in this theatre should meet together and thrash out in friendly candour, heart to heart, all the points that arise; and there are many.

You may be sure that if all that was necessary was for an order to be given to the great armies standing ready in India to march towards the Rising Sun and open the Burma Road, that order would be given this afternoon. The matter is, however, more complicated, and all movement or infiltration of troops into the mountains and jungles to the

North-East of India is very strictly governed by what your American military men call the science of logistics.

But, Mr. President, I repudiate, and I am sure with your sympathy, the slightest suspicion that we should hold anything back that could be usefully employed, or that I and the Government I represent are not as resolute to employ every man, gun and airplane that can be used in this business, as we have proved ourselves ready to do in other theatres of the war.

In our conferences in January, 1942, between the President and myself, and between our high expert advisers, it was evident that, while the defeat of Japan would not mean the defeat of Germany, the defeat of Germany would infallibly mean the ruin of Japan. The realisation of this simple truth does not mean that both sides should not proceed together, and indeed the major part of the United States forces is now deployed on the Pacific fronts. In the broad division which we then made of our labours, in January, 1942, the United States undertook the main responsibility for prosecuting the war against Japan, and for helping Australia and New Zealand to defend themselves against a Japanese invasion, which then seemed far more threatening than it does now.

On the other hand, we took the main burden on the Atlantic. This was only natural. Unless the ocean life-line which joins our two peoples could be kept unbroken, the British Isles and all the very considerable forces which radiate therefrom would be paralysed and doomed. We have willingly done our full share of the sea work in the dangerous waters of the Mediterranean and in the Arctic convoys to Russia, and we have sustained, since our alliance began, more than double the losses in merchant tonnage that have fallen upon the United States.

On the other hand, again, the prodigious output of new ships from the United States building-yards has, for six months past, overtaken, and now far surpasses, the losses of both Allies, and if no effort is relaxed there is every reason to count upon the ceaseless progressive expansion of Allied shipping available for the prosecution of the war.

Our killings of the U-boat, as the Secretary of the Navy will readily confirm, have this year greatly exceeded all previous experience, and the last three months, and particularly the last three weeks, have yielded record results. This of course is to some extent due to the larger number of U-boats operating, but it is also due to the marked improvement in the severity and power of our measures against them, and of the new devices continually employed.

While I rate the U-boat danger as still the greatest we have to face, I have a good and sober confidence that it will not only be met and contained but overcome. The increase of shipping tonnage over sinkings provides, after the movement of vital supplies of food and munitions has been arranged, that margin which is the main measure of our joint war effort.

We are also conducting from the British Isles the principal air offensive against Germany, and in this we are powerfully aided by the United States Air Force in the United Kingdom, whose action is chiefly by day as ours is chiefly by night. In this war numbers count more and more, both in night and day attacks. The saturation of the enemy's *flak,* through the multiplicity of attacking planes and the division and diversion of his fighter protection by the launching of several simultaneous attacks, are rewards which will immediately be paid from the substantial increases in British and American numbers which are now taking place.

There is no doubt that the Allies already vastly outnumber the hostile air forces of Germany, Italy, and Japan, and still more does the output of new aeroplanes surpass the output of the enemy. In this air war, in which both Germany and Japan fondly imagined that they would strike decisive and final blows, and terrorise nations great and small into submission to their will—in this air war it is that these guilty nations have already begun to show their first real mortal weakness. The more continuous and severe the air fighting becomes, the better for us, because we can already replace casualties and machines far more rapidly than the enemy, and we can replace them on a scale which increases month by month.

Progress in this sphere is swift and sure, but it must be remembered that the preparation and development of airfields, and the movement of the great masses of ground personnel on whom the efficiency of modern air squadrons depends, however earnestly pressed forward, are bound to take time.

Opinion, Mr. President, is divided as to whether the use of air power could by itself bring about a collapse in Germany or Italy. The experiment is well worth trying, so long as other measures are not excluded. Well, there is certainly no harm in finding out. But however that may be, we are all agreed that the damage done to the enemy's war potential is enormous.

The condition to which the great centres of German war industry, and particularly the Ruhr, are being reduced, is one of unparalleled devastation. You have just read of the destruction of the great dams which feed the canals, and provide the power to the enemy's munition works. That was a gallant operation, costing eight out of the nineteen Lancaster bombers employed, but it will play a very far-reaching part in reducing the German munitions output.

It is the settled policy of our two Staffs and war-making authorities to make it impossible for Germany to carry on any form of war industry on a large or concentrated scale, either in Germany, in Italy, or in the enemy-occupied countries. Wherever these centres exist or are developed, they will be destroyed, and the munitions populations will be dispersed. If they do not like what is coming to them, let them disperse beforehand on their own. This process will continue ceaselessly with ever-increasing weight and intensity until the German and Italian peoples abandon or destroy the monstrous tyrannies which they have incubated and reared in their midst.

Meanwhile, our air offensive is forcing Germany to withdraw an ever larger proportion of its war-making capacity from the fighting fronts in order to provide protection against air attack. Hundreds of fighter aircraft, thousands of anti-aircraft cannon, and many hundreds of thousands of men, together with a vast share of the output of the war factories, have already been assigned to this purely defensive function. All this is at the expense of the enemy's power of new aggression, and of his power to resume the initiative.

Surveying the whole aspect of the air war, we cannot doubt that it is a major factor in the process of victory. That I think is established as a solid fact. It is agreed between us all that we should, at the earliest moment, similarly bring our joint air power to bear upon the military targets in the home lands of Japan. The cold-blooded execution of the United States airmen by the Japanese Government is a proof, not only of their barbarism, but of the dread with which they regard this possibility.

It is the duty of those who are charged with the direction of the war to overcome at the earliest moment the military, geographical, and political difficulties, and begin the process, so necessary and desirable, of laying the cities and other munitions centres of Japan in ashes, for in ashes they must surely lie before peace comes back to the world.

That this objective holds a high place in the present conference is obvious to thinking men, but no public discussion would be useful upon the method or sequence of events which should be pursued in order to achieve it. Let me make it plain, however, that the British will participate in this air attack on Japan in harmonious accord with the major strategy of the war. That is our desire. And the cruelties of the Japanese enemy make our airmen all the more ready to share the perils and sufferings of their American comrades.

At the present time, speaking more generally, the prime problem which is before the United States, and to a lesser extent before Great Britain, is not so much the creation of armies or the vast output of munitions and aircraft. These are already in full swing, and immense progress, and prodigious results, have been achieved. The problem is rather the application of those forces to the enemy in the teeth of U-boat resistance across the great ocean spaces, across the narrow seas, or on land through swamps, mountains, and jungles in various quarters of the globe.

That is our problem. All our war plans must, therefore, be inspired, pervaded, and even dominated by the supreme object of coming to grips with the enemy under favourable conditions, or at any rate tolerable conditions—we cannot pick and choose too much—on the largest scale, at the earliest possible moment, and of engaging that enemy wherever it is profitable, and indeed I might say wherever it is possible, to do so. Thus, in this way, shall we make our enemies in Europe and in Asia burn and consume their strength on land, on sea, and in the air with the maximum rapidity.

Now you will readily understand that the complex task of finding the maximum openings for the employment of our vast forces, the selection of the points at which to strike with the greatest advantage to those forces, and the emphasis and priority to be assigned to all the various enterprises which are desirable, is a task requiring constant supervision and adjustment by our combined Staffs and Heads of Governments.

This is a vast, complicated process, especially when two countries are directly in council together, and when the interests of so many other countries have to be considered, and the utmost good will and readiness to think for the common cause, the cause of all the United Nations, are required from everyone participating in our discussions. The intricate adjustments and arrangements can only be made by discussion between men who know all the facts, and who are and can alone be held accountable for success or failure. Lots of people can make good plans for winning the war if they have not got to carry them out. I dare say if I had not been in a responsible position I should have made a lot of excellent plans, and very likely should have brought them in one way or another to the notice of the executive authorities.

But it is not possible to have full and open argument about these matters. It is an additional hardship to those in charge that such questions cannot be argued out and debated in public except with enormous reticence, and even then with very great danger that the watching and listening enemy may derive some profit from what he overhears. In these circumstances, in my opinion, the American and British Press and public have treated their executive authorities with a wise and indulgent consideration, and recent events have vindicated their self-restraint. Mr. President, it is thus that we are able to meet here to-day in all faithfulness, sincerity, and friendship.

Geography imposes insuperable obstacles to the continuous session of the combined Staff and Executive chiefs, but as the scene is constantly changing, and lately I think I may say constantly changing for the better, repeated conferences are indispensable if the sacrifices of the fighting troops are to be rendered fruitful, and if the curse of war which lies so heavily upon almost the whole world is to be broken and swept away within the shortest possible time.

I therefore thought it my duty, with the full authority of His Majesty's Government, to come here again with our highest officers in order that the combined Staffs may work in the closest contact with the chief executive power which the President derives from his office, and in respect of which I am the accredited representative of Cabinet and Parliament.

The wisdom of the founders of the American Constitution led them to associate the office of Commander-in-Chief with that of the Presidency of the United States. In this they were following the precedents which were successful in the days of George Washington. It is remarkable that after more than 150 years this combination of political and military authority has been found necessary, not only in the United States, but in the case of Marshal Stalin in Russia and of Generalissimo Chiang Kai-shek in China. Even I, as Majority Leader in the House of Commons—one branch of the Legislature—have been drawn from time to time, not perhaps wholly against my will, into some participation in military affairs.

Modern war is total, and it is necessary for its conduct that the technical and professional authorities should be sustained and if necessary directed by the Heads of Government, who have the knowledge which enables them to comprehend not only the military but the political and economic forces at work, and who have the power to focus them all upon the goal.

These are the reasons which compelled the President to make his long journey to Casablanca, and these are the reasons which bring me here. We both earnestly hope that at no distant date we may be able to achieve what we have so long sought—namely, a meeting with Marshal Stalin and if possible with Generalissimo Chiang Kai-shek. But how and when and where this is to be accomplished is not a matter upon which I am able to shed any clear ray of light at the present time, and if I were I should certainly not shed it.

In the meanwhile we do our best to keep the closest association at every level between all the authorities of all the Allied countries engaged in the active direction of the war. It is my special duty to promote and preserve this intimacy and concert between all parts of the British Commonwealth and Empire, and especially with the great self-governing Dominions, like Canada, whose Prime Minister is with us at this moment, whose contribution is so massive and invaluable. There could be no better or more encouraging example of the fruits of our consultations than the campaign in North-West Africa, which has just ended so well.

One morning in June last, when I was here, the President handed me a slip of paper which bore the utterly unexpected news of the fall of Tobruk, and the surrender, in unexplained circumstances, of its garrison of 25,000 men. That indeed was a dark and bitter hour for me, and I shall never forget the kindness and the wealth of comradeship which our American friends showed me and those with me in such adversity. Their only thought was to find the means of helping to restore the situation, and never for a moment did they question the resolution or fighting quality of our troops. Hundreds of Sherman tanks were taken from the hands of American divisions and sent at the utmost speed round the Cape of Good Hope to Egypt. When one ship carrying fifty tanks was sunk by torpedo, the United States Government replaced it and its precious vehicles before we could even think of asking them to do so. The Sherman was the best tank in the desert in the year 1942, and the presence of these weapons played an appreciable part in the ruin of Rommel's army at the battle of Alamein and in the long pursuit which chased him back to Tunisia.

And at this time, June of last year, when I was here last, there lighted up those trains of thought and study which produced the memorable American and British descent upon French North-West Africa, the results of which are a cause of general rejoicing. We have certainly a most encouraging example here of what can be achieved by British and Americans working together heart and hand. In fact one might almost feel that if they could keep it up there is hardly anything that they could not do, either in the field of war or in the not less tangled problems of peace.

History will acclaim this great enterprise as a classic example of the way to make war. We used the weapon of sea power, the weapon in which we were strongest, to attack the enemy at our chosen moment and at our chosen point. In spite of the immense elaboration of the plan, and of the many hundreds, thousands even, who had to be informed of its main outlines, we maintained secrecy and effected surprise.

We confronted the enemy with a situation in which he had either to lose invaluable strategical territories, or to fight under conditions most costly and wasteful to him. We recovered the initiative, which we still retain. We rallied to our side French forces which are already a brave and will presently become a powerful army under the gallant General Giraud. We secured bases from which violent attacks can and will be delivered by our Air power on the whole of Italy, with results no one can measure, but which must certainly be highly beneficial to our affairs.

We have made an economy in our strained and straitened shipping position worth several hundreds of great ships, and one which will give us the advantage of far swifter passage through the Mediterranean to the East, to the Middle East, and to the Far East. We have struck the enemy a blow which is the equal of Stalingrad, and most stimulating to our heroic and heavily-engaged Russian allies. All this gives the lie to the Nazi and Fascist taunt that Parliamentary democracies are incapable of waging effective war. Presently we shall furnish them with further examples.

Still, I am free to admit that in North Africa we builded better than we knew. The unexpected came to the aid of the design and multiplied the results. For this we have to thank the military intuition of Corporal Hitler. We may notice, as I predicted in the House of Commons three months ago, the touch of the masterhand. The same insensate obstinacy which condemned Field-Marshal von Paulus and his army to destruction at Stalingrad has brought this new catastrophe upon our enemies in Tunisia.

We have destroyed or captured considerably more than a quarter of a million of the enemy's best troops, together with vast masses of material, all of which had been ferried across to Africa after paying a heavy toll to British submarines and British and United States aircraft. No one could count on such follies. They gave us, if I may use the language of finance, a handsome bonus after the full dividend had been earned and paid.

At the time when we planned this great joint African operation, we hoped to be masters of Tunisia even before the end of last year; but the injury we have now inflicted upon the enemy, physical and psychological, and the training our troops have obtained in the hard school of war, and the welding together of the Anglo-American Staff machine— these are advantages which far exceed anything which it was in our power to plan. The German lie factory is volubly explaining how valuable is the time which they bought by the loss of their great armies. Let them not delude themselves. Other operations which will unfold in due course, depending as they do upon the special instruction of large numbers of troops and upon the provision of a vast mass of technical apparatus, these other operations have not been in any way delayed by the obstinate fighting in Northern Tunisia.

Mr. President, the African war is over. Mussolini's African Empire and Corporal Hitler's strategy are alike exploded. It is interesting to compute what these performances have cost these two wicked men and those who have been their tools or their dupes. The Emperor of Abyssinia sits again upon the throne from which he was driven by Mussolini's poison gas. All the vast territories from Madagascar to Morocco, from Cairo to Casablanca, from Aden to Dakar, are under British, American, or French control. One continent at least has been cleansed and purged for ever from Fascist or Nazi tyranny.

The African excursions of the two Dictators have cost their countries in killed and captured 950,000 soldiers. In addition nearly 2,400,000 gross tons of shipping have been sunk and nearly 8,000 aircraft destroyed, both of these figures being exclusive of large numbers of ships and aircraft damaged. There have also been lost to the enemy 6,200 guns, 2,550 tanks and 70,000 trucks, which is the American name for lorries, and which, I understand, has been adopted by the combined staffs in North-West Africa in exchange for the use of the word petrol in place of gasolene.

These are the losses of the enemy in the three years of war, and at the end of it all what is it that they have to show? The proud German Army has by its sudden collapse, sudden crumbling and breaking up, unexpected to all of us, the proud German Army has once again proved the truth of the saying, "The Hun is always either at your throat or at your feet," and that is a point which may have its bearing upon the future. But for us, arrived at this milestone in the war, we can say: "One Continent redeemed."

The North-West African campaign, and particularly its Tunisian climax, is the finest example of the co-operation of the troops of three different countries and of the combination under one supreme commander of the sea, land, and air forces which has yet been seen: in particular the British and American Staff work, as I have said, has matched the comradeship of the soldiers of our two countries striding forward side by side under the fire of the enemy.

It was a marvel of efficient organisation which enabled the Second American Corps, or rather Army, for that was its size, to be moved 300 miles from the Southern sector, which had become obsolete through the retreat of the enemy, to the Northern coast, from which, beating down all opposition, they advanced and took the fortress and harbour of Bizerta. In order to accomplish this march of 300 miles, which was covered in twelve days, it was necessary for this very considerable Army, with its immense modern equipment, to traverse at right angles all the communications of the British First Army, which was already engaged or about to be engaged in heavy battle; and this was achieved without in any way disturbing the hour-to-hour supply upon which that Army depended. I am told that these British and American officers worked together without the slightest question of what country they belonged to, each doing his part in the military organisation which must henceforward be regarded as a most powerful and efficient instrument of war.

There is honour, Mr. President, for all; and I shall at the proper time and place pay my tribute to the British and American commanders by land and sea who conducted or who were engaged in the battle. This only will I say now: I do not think you could have chosen any man more capable than General Eisenhower of keeping his very large, heterogeneous force together, through bad times as well as good, and of creating the conditions of harmony and energy which were the indispensable elements of victory.

I have dwelt in some detail, but I trust not at undue length, upon these famous events; and I shall now return for a few minutes to the general war, in which they have their setting and proportion. It is a poor heart that never rejoices; but our thanksgiving, however fervent, must be brief.

Heavier work lies ahead, not only in the European, but, as I have indicated, in the Pacific and Indian spheres; and the President and I, and the combined Staffs, are gathered here in order that this work may be, so far as lies within us, well conceived, and thrust forward without losing a day.

Not for one moment must we forget that the main burden of the war on land is still being borne by the Russian armies. They are holding at the present time no fewer than 190 German divisions and 28 satellite divisions on their front. It is always wise, while doing justice to one's own achievements, to preserve a proper sense of proportion; and I therefore mention that the figures of the German forces opposite Russia compare with the equivalent of about 15 divisions which we have destroyed in Tunisia, after a campaign which has cost us about 50,000 casualties. That gives some measure of the Russian effort, and of the debt which we owe to her.

It may well be that a further trial of strength between the German and Russian armies is impending. Russia has already inflicted injuries upon the German military organism which will, I believe, prove ultimately mortal; but there is little doubt that Hitler is reserving his supreme gambler's throw for a third attempt to break the heart and spirit and destroy the armed forces of the mighty nation which he has already twice assaulted in vain.

He will not succeed. But we must do everything in our power that is sensible and practicable to take more of the weight off Russia in 1943. I do not intend to be responsible for any suggestion that the war is won, or that it will soon be over. That it will be won by us I am sure. But how and when cannot be foreseen, still less foretold.

I was driving the other day not far from the field of Gettysburg which I know well, like most of your battlefields. It was the decisive battle of the American Civil War. No one after Gettysburg doubted which way the dread balance of war would incline, yet far more blood was shed after the Union victory at Gettysburg than in all the fighting which went before. It behoves us, therefore, to search our hearts and brace our sinews and take the most earnest counsel, one with another, in order that the favourable position which has already been reached both against Japan and against Hitler and Mussolini in Europe shall not be let slip.

If we wish to abridge the slaughter and ruin which this war is spreading to so many lands and to which we must ourselves contribute so grievous a measure of suffering and sacrifice, we cannot afford to relax a single fibre of our being or to tolerate the slightest abatement of our efforts. The enemy is still proud and powerful. He is hard to get at. He still possesses enormous armies, vast resources, and invaluable strategic territories. War is full of mysteries and surprises. A false step, a wrong direction, an error in strategy, discord or lassitude among the Allies, might soon give the common enemy power to confront us with new and hideous facts. We have surmounted many serious dangers, but there is one grave danger which will go along with us till the end; that danger is the undue prolongation of the war. No one can tell what new complications and perils might arise in four or five more years of war. And it is in the dragging-out of the war at enormous expense, until the democracies are tired or bored or split, that the main hopes of Germany and Japan must now reside. We must destroy this hope, as we have destroyed so many others, and for that purpose we must beware of every topic however attractive and every tendency however natural which turns our minds and energies from this supreme objective of the general victory of the United Nations. By singleness of purpose, by steadfastness of conduct, by tenacity and endurance such as we have so far displayed—by these, and only by these, can we discharge our duty to the future of the world and to the destiny of man.

CHAPTER 16

ANGLO-AMERICAN UNITY

In America once again for discussions with President Roosevelt on the next phase of the war—the great buildup to the Normandy landings, which were to take place some nine months later—Churchill travelled to Harvard to receive an honorary degree.

SPEECH AT HARVARD UNIVERSITY, SEPTEMBER 6, 1943

THE LAST TIME I attended a ceremony of this character was in the spring of 1941, when, as Chancellor of Bristol University, I conferred a degree upon the United States Ambassador, Mr. Winant, and *in absentia* upon [Harvard's] President Conant, who is here today and presiding over this ceremony. The blitz was running hard at that time, and the night before, the raid on Bristol had been heavy. Several hundreds had been killed and wounded. Many houses were destroyed. Buildings next to the University were still burning and many of the University authorities who conducted the ceremony had pulled on their robes over uniforms begrimed and drenched; but all was presented with faultless ritual and appropriate decorum, and I sustained a very strong and invigorating impression of the superiority of man over the forces that can destroy him.

Here now, today, I am once again in academic groves—groves is, I believe, the right word—where knowledge is garnered, where learning is stimulated, where virtues are inculcated and thought encouraged. Here, in the broad United States, with a respectable ocean on either side of us, we can look upon the world in all its wonder and in all its woe. But what is this that I discern as I pass through your streets, as I look around this great company?

I see uniforms on every side. I understand that nearly the whole energies of the University have been drawn into the preparation of American youth for the battlefield. For this purpose all classes and courses have been transformed, and even the most sacred vacations have been swept away in a round-the-year and almost round-the-clock drive to make warriors and technicians for the fighting fronts.

Twice in my lifetime the long arm of destiny has searched across the oceans and involved the entire life and manhood of the United States in a deadly struggle. There was no use in saying "We don't want it; we won't have it; our forebears left Europe to avoid these quarrels; we have founded a new world which has no contact with the old." There was no use in that. The long arm reaches out remorselessly, and everyone's existence, environment, and outlook undergo a swift and irresistible change. What is the explanation, Mr. President, of these strange facts, and what are the deep laws to which they respond? I will offer you one explanation—there are others, but one will suffice. The price of greatness is responsibility. If the people of the United States had continued in a mediocre station, struggling with the wilderness, absorbed in their own affairs, and a factor of no consequence in the movement of the world, they might have remained forgotten and undisturbed beyond their protecting oceans: but one cannot rise to be in many ways the leading community in the civilized world without being involved in its problems, without being convulsed by its agonies and inspired by its causes.

If this has been proved in the past, as it has been, it will become indisputable in the future. The people of the United States cannot escape world responsibility. Although we live in a period so tumultuous that little can be predicted we may be quite sure that this process will be intensified with every forward step the United States make in wealth and in power. Not only are the responsibilities of this great republic growing, but the world over which they range is itself contracting in relation to our powers of locomotion at a positively alarming rate.

We have learned to fly. What prodigious changes are involved in that new accomplishment. Man has parted company with his trusty friend the horse and has sailed into the azure with the eagles, eagles being represented by the infernal [*loud laughter*]—I mean internal—combustion engine. Where, then, are those broad oceans, those vast staring deserts? They are shrinking beneath our very eyes. Even elderly Parliamentarians like myself are forced to acquire a high degree of mobility.

But to the youth of America, as to the youth of Britain, I say "You cannot stop." There is no halting-place at this point. We have now reached a stage in the journey where there can be no pause. We must go on. It must be world anarchy or world order. Throughout all this ordeal and struggle which is characteristic of our age, you will find in the British Commonwealth and Empire good comrades to whom you are united by other ties besides those of State policy and public need. To a large extent, they are the ties of blood and history. Naturally, I, a child of both worlds, am conscious of these.

Law, language, literature—these are considerable factors. Common conceptions of what is right and decent, a marked regard for fair play, especially to the weak and poor, a stern sentiment of impartial justice, and above all the love of personal freedom, or as Kipling put it: "Leave to live by no man's leave underneath the law"—these are common conceptions on both sides of the ocean among the English-speaking peoples. We hold to these conceptions as strongly as you do.

We do not war primarily with races as such. Tyranny is our foe, whatever trappings or disguise it wears, whatever language it speaks, be it external or internal, we must for ever be on our guard, ever mobilized, ever vigilant, always ready to spring at its throat. In all this, we march together. Not only do we march and strive shoulder to shoulder at this moment under the fire of the enemy on the fields of war or in the air, but also in those realms of thought which are consecrated to the rights and the dignity of man.

At the present time we have in continual vigorous action the British and United States Combined Chiefs of Staff Committee, which works immediately under the President and myself as representative of the British War Cabinet. This committee, with its elaborate organization of Staff officers of every grade, disposes of all our resources and, in practice, uses British and American troops, ships, aircraft, and munitions just as if they were the resources of a single State or nation.

I would not say there are never divergences of view among these high professional authorities. It would be unnatural if there were not. That is why it is necessary to have plenary meeting of principals every two or three months. All these men now know each other. They trust each other. They like each other, and most of them have been at work together for a long time. When they meet they thrash things out with great candour and plain, blunt speech, but after a few days the President and I find ourselves furnished with sincere and united advice.

This is a wonderful system. There was nothing like it in the last war. There never has been anything like it between two allies. It is reproduced in an even more tightly-knit form at General Eisenhower's headquarters in the Mediterranean, where everything is completely intermingled and soldiers are ordered into battle by the supreme commander or his deputy, General Alexander, without the slightest regard to whether they are British, American, or Canadian, but simply in accordance with the fighting need.

Now in my opinion it would be a most foolish and improvident act on the part of our two Governments, or either of them, to break up this smooth-running and immensely powerful machinery the moment the war is over. For our own safety, as well as for the security of the rest of the world, we are bound to keep it working and in running order after the war—probably for a good many years, not only until we have set up some world arrangement to keep the peace but until we know that it is an arrangement which will really give us that protection we must have from danger and aggression, a protection we have already had to seek across two vast world wars.

I am not qualified, of course, to judge whether or not this would become a party question in the United States, and I would not presume to discuss that point. I am sure, however, that it will not be a party question in Great Britain. We must not let go of the securities we have found necessary to preserve our lives and liberties until we are quite sure we have something else to put in their place which will give us an equally solid guarantee.

The great Bismarck—for there were once great men in Germany—is said to have observed towards the close of his life that the most potent factor in human society at the end of the nineteenth century was the fact that the British and American peoples spoke the same language. That was a pregnant saying. Certainly it has enabled us to wage war together with an intimacy and harmony never before achieved among allies.

The gift of a common tongue is a priceless inheritance and it may well some day become the foundation of a common citizenship. I like to think of British and Americans moving about freely over each other's wide estates with hardly a sense of being foreigners to one another. But I do not see why we should not try to spread our common language even more widely throughout the globe and, without seeking selfish advantage over any, possess ourselves of this invaluable amenity and birthright.

Some months ago I persuaded the British Cabinet to set up a committee of Ministers to study and report upon Basic English. Here you have a plan. There are others, but here you have a very carefully wrought plan for an international language capable of a very wide transaction of practical business and interchange of ideas. The whole of it is comprised in about 650 nouns and 200 verbs or other parts of speech—no more indeed than can be written on one side of a single sheet of paper.

What was my delight when, the other evening, quite unexpectedly, I heard the President of the United States suddenly speak of the merits of Basic English, and is it not a coincidence that, with all this in mind, I should arrive at Harvard, in fulfillment of the long-dated invitations to receive this degree with which President Conant has honoured me? For Harvard has done more than any other American university to promote the extension of Basic English. The first work on Basic English was written by two Englishmen, Ivor Richards, now of Harvard, and C. K. Ogden, of Cambridge University, England, working in association.

The Harvard Commission on English Language Studies is distinguished both for its research and its practical work, particularly in introducing the use of Basic English in Latin America; and this Commission, your Commission, is now, I am told, working with secondary schools in Boston on the use of Basic English in teaching the main language to American children and in teaching it to foreigners preparing for citizenship.

Gentlemen, I make you my compliments. I do not wish to exaggerate, but you are the head-stream of what might well be a mighty fertilizing and health-giving river. It would certainly be a grand convenience for us all to be able to move freely about the world—as we shall be able to do more freely than ever before as the science of the world develops—be able to move freely about the world, and be able to find everywhere a medium, albeit primitive, of intercourse and understanding. Might it not also be an advantage to many races, and an aid to the building-up of our new structure for preserving peace? All these are great possibilities, and I say: "Let us go into this together. Let us have another Boston Tea Party about it."

Let us go forward as with other matters and other measures similar in aim and effect—let us go forward in malice to none and good will to all. Such plans offer far better prizes than taking away other people's provinces or lands or grinding them down in exploitation. The empires of the futures are the empires of the mind.

It would, of course, Mr. President, be lamentable if those who are charged with the duty of leading great nations forward in this grievous and obstinate war were to allow their minds and energies to be diverted from making the plans to achieve our righteous purposes without needless prolongation of slaughter and destruction.

Nevertheless, we are also bound, so far as life and strength allow, and without prejudice to our dominating military tasks, to look ahead to those days which will surely come when we shall have finally beaten down Satan under our feet and find ourselves with other great allies at once the masters and the servants of the future. Various schemes of achieving world security while yet preserving national rights, tradition and customs are being studied and probed.

We have all the fine work that was done a quarter of a century ago by those who devised and tried to make effective the League of Nations after the last war. It is said that the League of Nations failed. If so, that is largely because it was abandoned, and later on betrayed: because those who were its best friends were till a very late period infected with a futile pacifism: because the United States, the originating impulse, fell out of the line: because, while France had been bled white and England was supine and bewildered, a monstrous growth of aggression sprang up in Germany, in Italy and Japan.

We have learned from hard experiences that stronger, more efficient, more rigorous world institutions must be created to preserve peace and to forestall the causes of future wars. In this task the strongest victorious nations must be combined, and also those who have borne the burden and heat of the day and suffered under the flail of adversity; and, in this task, this creative task, there are some who say: "Let us have a world council and under it regional or continental councils," and there are others who prefer a somewhat different organization.

All these matters weigh with us now in spite of the war, which none can say has reached its climax, which is perhaps entering for us, British and Americans, upon its most severe and costly phase. But I am here to tell you that, whatever form your system of world security may take, however the nations are grouped and ranged, whatever derogations are made from national sovereignty for the sake of the large synthesis, nothing will work soundly or for long without the united effort of the British and American peoples.

If we are together nothing is impossible. If we are divided all will fail. I therefore preach continually the doctrine of the fraternal association of our two peoples, not for any purpose of gaining invidious material advantages for either of them, not for territorial aggrandisement or the vain pomp of earthly domination, but for the sake of service to mankind and for the honour that comes to those who faithfully serve great causes.

Here let me say how proud we ought to be, young and old alike, to live in this tremendous, thrilling, formative epoch in the human story, and how fortunate it was for the world that when these great trials came upon it there was a generation that terror could not conquer and brutal violence could not enslave. Let all who are here remember, as the words of the hymn we have just sung suggest, let all of us who are here remember that we are on the stage of history, and that whatever our station may be, and whatever part we have to play, great or small, our conduct is liable to be scrutinized not only by history but by our own descendants.

Let us rise to the full level of our duty and of our opportunity, and let us thank God for the spiritual rewards he has granted for all forms of valiant and faithful service.

CHAPTER 17

THE DEATH OF PRESIDENT ROOSEVELT

As the hour of victory approached, Churchill paid tribute to his comrade-in-arms, whom he saluted as "the greatest American friend we have ever known."

STATEMENT TO THE HOUSE OF COMMONS, APRIL 17, 1945

I BEG TO MOVE:

That an humble Address be presented to His Majesty to convey to His Majesty the deep sorrow with which this House has learned of the death of the President of the United States of America, and to pray His Majesty that in communicating his own sentiments of grief to the United States Government, he will also be generously pleased to express on the part of this House their sense of the loss which the British Commonwealth and Empire and the cause of the Allied nations have sustained, and their profound sympathy with Mrs. Roosevelt and the late President's family, and with the Government and people of the United States of America.

My friendship with the great man to whose work and fame we pay our tribute today began and ripened during this war. I had met him, but only for a few minutes, after the close of the last war, and as soon as I went to the Admiralty in September 1939, he telegraphed inviting me to correspond with him direct on naval or other matters if at any time I felt inclined. Having obtained the permission of the Prime Minister, I did so. Knowing President Roosevelt's keen interest in sea warfare, I furnished him with a stream of information about our naval affairs, and about the various actions, including especially the action of the Plate River, which lighted the first gloomy winter of the war.

When I became Prime Minister, and the war broke out in all its hideous fury, when our own life and survival hung in the balance, I was already in a position to telegraph to the President on terms of an association which had become most intimate and, to me, most agreeable. This continued through all the ups and downs of the world struggle until Thursday last, when I received my last messages from him. These messages showed no falling off in his accustomed clear vision and vigour upon perplexing and complicated matters. I may mention that this correspondence which, of course, was greatly increased after the United States entry into the war, comprises to and fro between us, over 1,700 messages. Many of these were lengthy messages, and the majority dealt with those more difficult points which come to be discussed upon the level of heads of Governments only after official solutions have not been reached at other stages. To this correspondence there must be added our nine meetings—at Argentia, three in Washington, at Casablanca, at Teheran, two at Quebec and, last of all, at Yalta, comprising in all about 120 days of close personal contact, during a great part of which I stayed with him at the White House or at his home at Hyde Park or in his retreat in the Blue Mountains, which he called Shangri-la.

I conceived an admiration for him as a statesman, a man of affairs, and a war leader. I felt the utmost confidence in his upright, inspiring character and outlook, and a personal regard—affection I must say— for him beyond my power to express today. His love of his own country, his respect for its constitution, his power of gauging the tides and currents of its mobile public opinion, were always evident, but added to these were the beatings of that generous heart which was always stirred to anger and to action by spectacles of aggression and oppression by the strong against the weak. It is, indeed, a loss, a bitter loss to humanity that those heart-beats are stilled for ever.

President Roosevelt's physical affliction lay heavily upon him. It was a marvel that he bore up against it through all the many years of tumult and storm. Not one man in ten millions, stricken and crippled as he was, would have attempted to plunge into a life of physical and mental exertion and of hard, ceaseless political controversy. Not one in ten millions would have tried, not one in a generation would have succeeded, not only in entering this sphere, not only in acting vehemently in it, but in becoming indisputable master of the scene. In this extraordinary effort of the spirit over the flesh, of will-power over physical infirmity, he was inspired and sustained by that noble woman his devoted wife, whose high ideals marched with his own, and to whom the deep and respectful sympathy of the House of Commons flows out today in all fullness.

There is no doubt that the President foresaw the great dangers closing in upon the pre-war world with far more prescience than most well-informed people on either side of the Atlantic, and that he urged forward with all his power such precautionary military preparations as peacetime opinion in the United States could be brought to accept. There never was a moment's doubt, as the quarrel opened, upon which side his sympathies lay. The fall of France, and what seemed to most people outside this island, the impending destruction of Great Britain, were to him an agony, although he never lost faith in us. They were an agony to him not only on account of Europe, but because of the serious perils to which the United States herself would have been exposed had we been overwhelmed or the survivors cast down under the German yoke. The bearing of the British nation at that time of stress, when we were all alone, filled him and vast numbers of his countrymen with the warmest sentiments towards our people. He and they felt the blitz of the stern winter of 1940–41, when Hitler set himself to rub out the cities of our country, as much as any of us did, and perhaps more indeed, for imagination is often more torturing than reality. There is no doubt that the bearing of the British and, above all, of the Londoners, kindled fires in American bosoms far harder to quench than the conflagrations from which we were suffering. There was also at that time, in spite of General Wavell's victories—all the more, indeed, because of the reinforcements which were sent from this country to him—the apprehension widespread in the United States that we should be invaded by Germany after the fullest preparation in the spring of 1941. It was in February that the President sent to England the late Mr. Wendell Willkie, who, although a political rival and an opposing candidate, felt as he did on many important points. Mr. Willkie brought a letter from Mr. Roosevelt, which the President had written in his own hand, and this letter contained the famous lines of Longfellow:

> . . . Sail on, O ship of State!
> Sail on, O Union, strong and great!
> Humanity with all its fears,
> With all the hopes of future years,
> Is hanging breathless on thy fate!

At about that same time he devised the extraordinary measure of assistance called Lend-Lease, which will stand forth as the most unselfish and unsordid financial act of any country in all history. The effect of this was greatly to increase British fighting power, and for all the purpose of the war effort to make us, as it were, a much more numerous community. In that autumn I met the President for the first time during the war at Argentia in Newfoundland, and together we drew up the declaration which has since been called the Atlantic Charter, and which will, I trust, long remain a guide for both our peoples and for other people of the world.

All this time in deep and dark and deadly secrecy, the Japanese were preparing their act of treachery and greed. When next we met in Washington, Japan, Germany and Italy had declared war upon the United States, and both our countries were in arms, shoulder to shoulder. Since then we have advanced over the land and over the sea through many difficulties and disappointments, but always with a broadening measure of success. I need not dwell upon the series of great operations which have taken place in the Western Hemisphere, to say nothing of that other immense war proceeding on the other side of the world. Nor need I speak of the plans which we made with our great ally, Russia, at Teheran, for these have now been carried out for all the world to see.

But at Yalta I noticed that the President was ailing. His captivating smile, his gay and charming manner, had not deserted him, but his face had a transparency, an air of purification, and often there was a far-away look in his eyes. When I took my leave of him in Alexandria harbour I must confess that I had an indefinable sense of fear that his health and his strength were on the ebb. But nothing altered his inflexible sense of duty. To the end he faced his innumerable tasks unflinching. One of the tasks of the President is to sign maybe a hundred or two State papers with his own hand every day, commissions and so forth. All this he continued to carry out with the utmost strictness. When death came suddenly upon him "he had finished his mail." That portion of his day's work was done. As the saying goes, he died in harness, and we may well say in battle harness, like his soldiers, sailors, and airmen, who side by side with ours are carrying on their task to the end all over the world. What an enviable death was his! He had brought his country through the worst of its perils and the heaviest of its toils. Victory had cast its sure and steady beam upon him.

In the days of peace he had broadened and stabilized the foundations of American life and union. In war he had raised the strength, might and glory of the great Republic to a height never attained by any nation in history. With her left hand she was leading the advance of the conquering Allied armies into the heart of Germany, and with her right, on the other side of the globe, she was irresistibly and swiftly breaking up the power of Japan. And all the time ships, munitions, supplies, and food of every kind were aiding on a gigantic scale her allies, great and small, in the course of the long struggle.

But all this was no more than worldly power and grandeur, had it not been that the causes of human freedom and of social justice, to which so much of his life had been given, added a lustre to this power and pomp and warlike might, a lustre which will long be discernible among men. He has left behind him a band of resolute and able men handling the numerous interrelated parts of the vast American war machine. He has left a successor who comes forward with firm step and sure conviction to carry on the task to its appointed end. For us, it remains only to say that in Franklin Roosevelt there died the greatest American friend we have ever known, and the greatest champion of freedom who has ever brought help and comfort from the new world to the old.

CHAPTER 18

TRIBUTE TO GENERAL EISENHOWER

On May 8, 1945, Germany signed an act of unconditional surrender, but the war against Japan still had a further two months to run. On the occasion of General Dwight D. Eisenhower being accorded the Freedom of the City of London, the Prime Minister paid tribute to the man who had led Allied forces to victory in Western Europe.

SPEECH AT THE MANSION HOUSE, LONDON, JUNE 12, 1945

I HAVE BEEN BROUGHT very closely in contact with General Eisenhower since the day early in 1942 when we first met at the White House after the attack on Pearl Harbour, and all the grave matters of the direction of the armies to the landings in French North Africa and all the great efforts which were called for a year ago had to be discussed and examined, and I had the opportunity of seeing at close quarters General "Ike"—for that is what I call him—in action. I saw him at all sorts of times, because in war things do not always go as we wish. Another will breaks in, and there is a clash, and questions arise. Never have I seen a man so staunch in pursuing the purpose in hand, so ready to accept responsibility for misfortune, or so generous in victory.

There is one moment I would dwell on. It was just about a little more than a year ago that he had to decide whether to go across the Channel or put it off for, it might be, eleven days. It was a terrible decision. The Army had gathered. A million men in the front line had gathered, and thousands of crafts and tens of thousands of aircraft, and the great ships were all arranged. You could not hold it. It was like trying to hold an avalanche in leash. Should it be launched or should it not be launched?

There were a great many people who had a chance of expressing their opinions. I was not one of them, because it was purely a technical matter. A great many generals and admirals were gathered in the High Command to express their opinions and views, but there was only one man on whom the awful brunt fell of saying "Go" or "Stay." To say "Stay" meant keeping hundreds of thousands of men cooped up in wired enclosures so that the plans they had been told of might not leak out. It meant the problem of hundreds of thousands of men on board ship who had to be provided for and found accommodation. It might have meant that the air could not cover the landing or that the water was too rough for the many boats that were needed.

It was one of the most terrible decisions, and this decision was taken by this man—this very great man [*prolonged applause*].

It is one of many decisions he has taken. Had he not said "Go," and eleven days had passed, the weather would have smiled, and all the groups of meteorologists would have been happy. The expedition would have started; and two days later the worst gale for forty years at that season of the year fell upon the beaches in Normandy. Not only did he take the risk and arrive at the fence, he cleared it in magnificent style.

There are many occasions when that kind of decision falls on the Supreme Commander. Many fearful tales come from the front line. A great deal of anxiety is felt by populations at home. Do we go forward? Do we fight in this area? Are we to push on? These decisions all resolved themselves into an "Aye" or a "No," and all I can say about our guest is that in very many most important decisions history will acclaim his decisions as right, and that the bias, the natural bias, that moved him in these matters was very much more in favour of "Aye" than of "No."

I could go on for a very long time about your guest. There is no doubt whatever that we have among us to-day one of the greatest Americans who have reached our shores and dwelt a considerable time among us. We honour him very much for his invariable consideration of the British point of view, for his impartial treatment of all the officers under his command. I know he will tell you when he rises that he never gave an order to a British officer which he could not immediately obey.

We also have made our contribution to the battles on the Continent, and I am quite sure that the influence he will wield in the world will be one always of bringing our countries together in the much more difficult task of peace, in the same way as he brought them together in the grim and awful cataclysm of war. I have had personal acquaintance with him now for three years. It is not much, but three years of this sort may seem five-and-twenty. I feel we have here a great creative, constructive and combining genius, one from our sister nation across the ocean, one who will never speak evil but will always cherish his contact with the British people, and to whom I feel we should at this moment give the most cordial testimony in our power of our admiration, of our affection, and of our heartfelt good wishes for everything that may happen to him in the future.

CHAPTER 19

THE ATOMIC BOMB

Earlier the same day, President Truman had announced that American and British scientists, working under conditions of the greatest secrecy at Los Alamos, had produced the atomic bomb and that the first had that day been dropped on Hiroshima. This dramatic development was to have the effect of cutting short the war in the Far East by at least a year and is credited with saving the lives of an estimated one million American and British servicemen, which would otherwise have been lost in the intended invasion of Japan.

Churchill, reeling from the shock of being rejected by the British electorate in the recent General Election, wrote the following statement before quitting 10 Downing Street. It was issued by his successor as Prime Minister, Clement Attlee.

STATEMENT, 10 DOWNING STREET, AUGUST 6, 1945

BY THE YEAR 1939 it had become widely recognized among scientists of many nations that the release of energy by atomic fission was a possibility. The problems which remained to be solved before this possibility could be turned into practical achievement were, however, manifold and immense; and few scientists would at that time have ventured to predict that an atomic bomb could be ready for use by 1945. Nevertheless, the potentialities of the project were so great that His Majesty's Government thought it right that research should be carried on in spite of the many compelling claims on our scientific man-power. At this stage the research was carried out mainly in our Universities, principally Oxford, Cambridge, London (Imperial College), Liverpool, and Birmingham. At the time of the formation of the Coalition Government, responsibility for co-ordinating the work and pressing it forward lay with the Ministry of Aircraft Production, advised by a committee of leading scientists presided over by Sir George Thomson.

At the same time, under the general arrangements then in force for the pooling of scientific information, there was a full interchange of ideas between the scientists carrying out this work in the United Kingdom and those in the United States.

Such progress was made that by the summer of 1941 Sir George Thomson's committee was able to report that, in their view, there was a reasonable chance that an atomic bomb could be produced before the end of the war. At the end of August, 1941, Lord Cherwell, whose duty it was to keep me informed on all these and other technical developments, reported the substantial progress which was being made. The general responsibility for the scientific research carried on under the various technical committees lay with the then Lord President of the Council, Sir John Anderson. In these circumstances (having in mind also the effect of ordinary high explosive, which we had recently experienced), I referred the matter on August 30, 1941, to the Chiefs of Staff Committee in the following minute:

> General Ismay, for Chiefs of Staff Committee: Although personally I am quite content with the existing explosives, I feel we must not stand in the path of improvement, and I therefore think that action should be taken in the sense proposed by Lord Cherwell, and that the Cabinet Minister responsible should be Sir John Anderson. I shall be glad to know what the Chiefs of Staff Committee think.

The Chiefs of the Staff recommended immediate action with the maximum priority.

It was then decided to set up within the Department of Scientific and Industrial Research a special division to direct the work, and Imperial Chemical Industries Limited agreed to release Mr. W. A. Akers to take charge of this directorate, which we called, for purposes of secrecy, the Directorate of "Tube Alloys." After Sir John Anderson had ceased to be Lord President and became Chancellor of the Exchequer I asked him to continue to supervise this work, for which he has special qualifications. To advise him, there was set up under his chairmanship a consultative council composed of the President of the Royal Society, the Chairman of the Scientific Advisory Committee of the Cabinet, the Secretary of the Department of Scientific and Industrial Research, and Lord Cherwell. The Minister of Aircraft Production, at that time Lord Brabazon, also served on this committee.

Under the chairmanship of Mr. Akers there was also a technical committee, on which sat the scientists who were directing the different sections of the work and some others. This committee was originally composed of Sir James Chadwick, Professor Peierls, and Drs. Halban, Simon and Slade. Later it was joined by Sir Charles Darwin and Professors Cockcroft, Oliphant and Feather. Full use was also made of university and industrial laboratories.

On October 11, 1941, President Roosevelt sent me a letter suggesting that any extended efforts on this important matter might usefully be co-ordinated, or even jointly conducted. Accordingly, all British and

American efforts were joined, and a number of British scientists concerned proceeded to the United States. Apart from these contacts, complete secrecy guarded all these activities, and no single person was informed whose work was not indispensable to progress.

By the summer of 1942 this expanded programme of research had confirmed with surer and broader foundations the promising forecasts which had been made a year earlier, and the time had come when a decision must be made whether or not to proceed with the construction of large-scale production plants. Meanwhile it had become apparent from the preliminary experiments that these plants would have to be on something like the vast scale described in the American statements which have been published today.

Great Britain at this period was fully extended in war production, and we could not afford such grave interference with the current munitions programmes on which our warlike operations depended. Moreover, Great Britain was within easy range of German bombers, and the risk of raiders from the sea or air could not be ignored. The United States, however, where parallel or similar progress had been made, was free from these dangers. The decision was therefore taken to build the full-scale production plants in America.

In the United States the erection of the immense plants was placed under the responsibility of Mr. Stimson, United States Secretary of War, and the American Army Administration, whose wonderful work and marvellous secrecy cannot be sufficiently admired. The main practical effort and virtually the whole of its prodigious cost now fell upon the United States authorities, who were assisted by a number of British scientists. The relationship of the British and American contributions was regulated by discussion between the late President Roosevelt and myself, and a combined policy committee was set up.

The Canadian Government, whose contribution was most valuable, provided both indispensable raw material for the project as a whole and also necessary facilities for the work on one section of the project, which has been carried out in Canada by the three Governments in partnership.

The smoothness with which the arrangements for co-operation which were made in 1943 have been carried into effect is a happy augury for our future relations, and reflects great credit on all concerned—on the members of the combined policy committee which we set up; on the enthusiasm with which our scientists and technicians gave of their best—particularly Sir James Chadwick, who gave up his work at Liverpool to serve as technical adviser to the United Kingdom members of the policy committee and spared no effort; and, not least, on the generous spirit with which the whole United States organization welcomed our men and made it possible for them to make their contribution.

By God's mercy British and American science outpaced all German efforts. These were on a considerable scale, but far behind. The possession of these powers by the Germans at any time might have altered the result of the war, and profound anxiety was felt by those who were informed. Every effort was made by our Intelligence Service and by the Air Force to locate in Germany anything resembling the plants which were being created in the United States. In the winter of 1942–43 most gallant attacks were made in Norway on two occasions by small parties of volunteers from the British Commandos and Norwegian forces, at very heavy loss of life, upon stores of what is called "heavy water," an element in one of the possible processes. The second of these two attacks was completely successful.

The whole burden of execution, including the setting-up of the plants and many technical processes connected therewith in the practical sphere, constitutes one of the greatest triumphs of American—or indeed human—genius of which there is record. Moreover, the decision to make these enormous expenditures upon a project which, however hopefully established by American and British research, remained nevertheless a heart-shaking risk, stands to the everlasting honour of President Roosevelt and his advisers.

It is now for Japan to realize, in the glare of the first atomic bomb which has smitten her, what the consequences will be of an indefinite continuance of this terrible means of maintaining a rule of law in the world.

This revelation of the secrets of nature, long mercifully withheld from man, should arouse the most solemn reflections in the mind and conscience of every human being capable of comprehension. We must indeed pray that these awful agencies will be made to conduce to peace among the nations, and that instead of wreaking measureless havoc upon the entire globe they may become a perennial fountain of world prosperity.

CHAPTER 20

THE SINEWS OF PEACE

Churchill's famous "Iron Curtain" speech was delivered in the heart of the American Midwest, because Churchill knew that he would be speaking at the feet of the President of the United States, Harry Truman, who was to introduce him. The speech was a "call to arms" to the United States—not to fight a new war, but to join with the nations of Europe in defending the peace. Churchill, now Leader of the Opposition and seventy-one years of age, delivered an impassioned plea to America not to repeat the mistakes of the previous generation which, following World War I, had turned its back on Europe and retreated into isolationism with disastrous consequences for both Europe and America.

He spoke at a time when Western Europe lay in ruins and when the Red Army of the Soviet Union had overrun half the continent. Only the creation of a new alliance, underpinned by the United States with its newly acquired monopoly of the atomic bomb, could prevent the onward roll of Russian tanks to the English Channel—and could do so without a shot being fired. That Churchill's remarks did not fall on stony ground is evidenced by the fact that within three years the NATO alliance had come into being.

WESTMINSTER COLLEGE, FULTON, MISSOURI, MARCH 5, 1946

I AM GLAD to come to Westminster College this afternoon, and I am complimented that you should give me a degree. The name "Westminster" is somehow familiar to me. I seem to have heard of it before. Indeed, it was at Westminster that I received a very large part of my education in politics, dialectic, rhetoric, and one or two other things. In fact we have both been educated at the same, or similar, or, at any rate, kindred establishments.

It is also an honour, perhaps almost unique, for a private visitor to be introduced to an academic audience by the President of the United States. Amid his heavy burdens, duties, and responsibilities—unsought but not recoiled from—the President has travelled a thousand miles to dignify and magnify our meeting here to-day and to give me an opportunity of addressing this kindred nation, as well as my own countrymen across the ocean, and perhaps some other countries too. The President has told you that it is his wish, as I am sure it is yours, that I should have full liberty to give my true and faithful counsel in these anxious and baffling times. I shall certainly avail myself of this freedom, and feel the more right to do so because any private ambitions I may have cherished in my younger days have been satisfied beyond my wildest dreams. Let me, however, make it clear that I have no official mission or status of any kind, and that I speak only for myself. There is nothing here but what you see.

I can therefore allow my mind, with the experience of a lifetime, to play over the problems which beset us on the morrow of our absolute victory in arms, and to try to make sure with what strength I have that what has been gained with so much sacrifice and suffering shall be preserved for the future glory and safety of mankind.

The United States stands at this time at the pinnacle of world power. It is a solemn moment for the American Democracy. For with primacy in power is also joined an awe-inspiring accountability to the future. If you look around you, you must feel not only the sense of duty done but also you must feel anxiety lest you fall below the level of achievement. Opportunity is here now, clear and shining for both our countries. To reject it or ignore it or fritter it away will bring upon us all the long reproaches of the after-time. It is necessary that constancy of mind, persistency of purpose, and the grand simplicity of decision shall guide and rule the conduct of the English-speaking peoples in peace as they did in war. We must, and I believe we shall, prove ourselves equal to this severe requirement.

When American military men approach some serious situation they are wont to write at the head of their directive the words "over-all strategic concept." There is wisdom in this, as it leads to clarity of thought. What then is the over-all strategic concept which we should inscribe today? It is nothing less than the safety and welfare, the freedom and progress, of all the homes and families of all the men and women in all the lands. And here I speak particularly of the myriad cottage or apartment homes where the wage-earner strives amid the accidents and difficulties of life to guard his wife and children from privation and bring the family up in the fear of the Lord, or upon ethical conceptions which often play their potent part.

To give security to these countless homes, they must be shielded from the two giant marauders, war and tyranny. We all know the frightful disturbances in which the ordinary family is plunged when the curse of war swoops down upon the bread-winner and those for whom he works and contrives. The awful ruin of Europe, with all its vanished glories, and of large parts of Asia glares us in the eyes. When the designs of wicked men or the aggressive urge of mighty States dissolve over large areas the frame of civilised society, humble folk are confronted with difficulties with which they cannot cope. For them all is distorted, all is broken, even ground to pulp.

When I stand here this quiet afternoon I shudder to visualise what is actually happening to millions now and what is going to happen in this period when famine stalks the earth. None can compute what has been called "the unestimated sum of human pain." Our supreme task and duty is to guard the homes of the common people from the horrors and miseries of another war. We are all agreed on that.

Our American military colleagues, after having proclaimed their "over-all strategic concept" and computed available resources, always proceed to the next step—namely, the method. Here again there is widespread agreement. A world organisation has already been erected for the prime purpose of preventing war, UNO, the successor of the League of Nations, with the decisive addition of the United States and all that that means, is already at work. We must make sure that its work is fruitful, that it is a reality and not a sham, that it is a force for action, and not merely a frothing of words, that it is a true temple of peace in which the shields of many nations can some day be hung up, and not merely a cockpit in a Tower of Babel. Before we cast away the solid assurances of national armaments for self-preservation we must be certain that our temple is built, not upon shifting sands or quagmires, but upon the rock. Anyone can see with his eyes open that our path will be difficult and also long, but if we persevere together as we did in the two world wars—though not, alas, in the interval between them—I cannot doubt that we shall achieve our common purpose in the end.

I have, however, a definite and practical proposal to make for action. Courts and magistrates may be set up but they cannot function without sheriffs and constables. The United Nations Organisation must immediately begin to be equipped with an international armed force. In such a matter we can only go step by step, but we must begin now. I propose that each of the Powers and States should be invited to delegate a certain number of air squadrons to the service of the world organisation. These squadrons would be trained and prepared in their own countries, but would move around in rotation from one country to another. They would wear the uniform of their own countries but with different badges. They would not be required to act against their own nation, but in other respects they would be directed by the world organisation. This might be started on a modest scale and would grow as confidence grew. I wished to see this done after the first world war, and I devoutly trust it may be done forthwith.

It would nevertheless be wrong and imprudent to entrust the secret knowledge or experience of the atomic bomb, which the United States,

Great Britain, and Canada now share, to the world organisation, while it is still in its infancy. It would be criminal madness to cast it adrift in this still agitated and un-united world. No one in any country has slept less well in their beds because this knowledge and the method and the raw materials to apply it, are at present largely retained in American hands. I do not believe we should all have slept so soundly had the positions been reversed and if some Communist or neo-Fascist State monopolised for the time being these dread agencies. The fear of them alone might easily have been used to enforce totalitarian systems upon the free democratic world, with consequences appalling to human imagination. God has willed that this shall not be and we have at least a breathing space to set our house in order before this peril has to be encountered: and even then, if no effort is spared, we should still possess so formidable a superiority as to impose effective deterrents upon its employment, or threat of employment, by others. Ultimately, when the essential brotherhood of man is truly embodied and expressed in a world organisation with all the necessary practical safeguards to make it effective, these powers would naturally be confided to that world organisation.

Now I come to the second danger of these two marauders which threatens the cottage, the home, and the ordinary people—namely, tyranny. We cannot be blind to the fact that the liberties enjoyed by individual citizens throughout the British Empire are not valid in a considerable number of countries, some of which are very powerful. In these States control is enforced upon the common people by various kinds of all-embracing police governments. The power of the State is exercised without restraint, either by dictators or by compact oligarchies operating through a privileged party and a political police. It is not our duty at this time when difficulties are so numerous to interfere forcibly in the internal affairs of countries which we have not conquered in war. But we must never cease to proclaim in fearless tones the great principles of freedom and the rights of man which are the joint inheritance of the English-speaking world and which through Magna Carta, the Bill of Rights, the Habeas Corpus, trial by jury, and the English common law find their most famous expression in the American Declaration of Independence.

All this means that the people of any country have the right, and should have the power by constitutional action, by free unfettered elections, with secret ballot, to choose or change the character or form of government under which they dwell; that freedom of speech and thought should reign; that courts of justice, independent of the executive, unbiased by any party, should administer laws which have received the broad assent of large majorities or are consecrated by time and custom. Here are the title deeds of freedom which should lie in every cottage home. Here is the message of the British and American peoples to mankind. Let us preach what we practise—let us practise what we preach.

I have now stated the two great dangers which menace the homes of the people: War and Tyranny. I have not yet spoken of poverty and privation which are in many cases the prevailing anxiety. But if the dangers of war and tyranny are removed, there is no doubt that science and co-operation can bring in the next few years to the world, certainly in the next few decades, newly taught in the sharpening school of war, an expansion of material well-being beyond anything that has yet occurred in human experience. Now, at this sad and breathless moment, we are plunged in the hunger and distress which are the aftermath of our stupendous struggle; but this will pass and may pass quickly, and there is no reason except human folly or sub-human crime which should deny to all the nations the inauguration and enjoyment of an age of plenty. I have often used words which I learned fifty years ago from a great Irish-American orator, a friend of mine, Mr. Bourke Cockran. "There is enough for all. The earth is a generous mother; she will provide in plentiful abundance food for all her children if they will but cultivate her soil in justice and in peace." So far I feel that we are in full agreement.

Now, while still pursuing the method of realising our over-all strategic concept, I come to the crux of what I have travelled here to say. Neither the sure prevention of war, nor the continuous rise of world organisation will be gained without what I have called the fraternal association of the English-speaking peoples. This means a special relationship between the British Commonwealth and Empire and the United States. This is no time for generalities, and I will venture to be precise. Fraternal association requires not only the growing friendship and mutual understanding between our two vast but kindred systems of society, but the continuance of the intimate relationship between our military advisers, leading to common study of potential dangers, the similarity of weapons and manuals of instructions, and to the interchange of officers and cadets at technical colleges. It should carry with it the continuance of the present facilities for mutual security by the joint use of all Naval and Air Force bases in the possession of either country all over the world. This would perhaps double the mobility of the American Navy and Air Force. It would greatly expand that of the British Empire Forces and it might well lead, if and as the world calms down, to important financial savings. Already we use together a large number of islands; more may well be entrusted to our joint care in the near future.

The United States has already a Permanent Defence Agreement with the Dominion of Canada, which is so devotedly attached to the British Commonwealth and Empire. This Agreement is more effective than many of those which have often been made under formal alliances. This principle should be extended to all British Commonwealths with full reciprocity. Thus, whatever happens, and thus only, shall we be secure ourselves and able to work together for the high and simple causes that are dear to us and bode no ill to any. Eventually there may come—I feel eventually there will come—the principle of common citizenship, but that we may be content to leave to destiny, whose outstretched arm many of us can already clearly see.

There is however an important question we must ask ourselves. Would a special relationship between the United States and the British Commonwealth be inconsistent with our over-riding loyalties to the World Organisation? I reply that, on the contrary, it is probably the only means by which that organisation will achieve its full stature and strength. There are already the special United States relations with Canada which I have just mentioned, and there are the special relations between the United States and the South American Republics. We British have our twenty years Treaty of Collaboration and Mutual Assistance with Soviet Russia. I agree with Mr. Bevin, the Foreign Secretary of Great Britain, that it might well be a fifty years Treaty so far as we are concerned. We aim at nothing but mutual assistance and collaboration. The British have an alliance with Portugal unbroken since 1384, and which produced fruitful results at critical moments in the late war. None of these clash with the general interest of a world agreement, or a world organisation; on the contrary they help it. "In my father's house are many mansions." Special associations between members of the United Nations which have no aggressive point against any other country, which harbour no design incompatible with the Charter of the United Nations, far from being harmful, are beneficial and, as I believe, indispensable.

I spoke earlier of the Temple of Peace. Workmen from all countries must build that temple. If two of the workmen know each other particularly well and are old friends, if their families are inter-mingled, and if they have "faith in each other's purpose, hope in each other's future and charity towards each other's shortcomings"—to quote some good words I read here the other day—why cannot they work together at the common task as friends and partners? Why cannot they share their tools and thus increase each other's working powers? Indeed they must do so or else the temple may not be built, or, being built, it may collapse, and we shall all be proved again unteachable and have to go and try to learn again for a third time in a school of war, incomparably more rigorous than that from which we have just been released. The dark ages may return, the Stone Age may return on the gleaming wings of science, and what might now shower immeasurable material blessings upon mankind, may even bring about its total destruction. Beware, I say; time may be short. Do not let us take the course of allowing events to drift along until it is too late. If there is to be a fraternal association of the kind I have described, with all the extra strength and security which both our countries can derive from it, let us make sure that that great fact is known to the world, and that it plays its part in steadying and stabilising the foundations of peace. There is the path of wisdom. Prevention is better than cure.

A shadow has fallen upon the scenes so lately lighted by the Allied victory. Nobody knows what Soviet Russia and its Communist International organisation intends to do in the immediate future, or what are the limits, if any, to their expansive and proselytising tendencies. I have a strong admiration and regard for the valiant Russian people and for my wartime comrade, Marshal Stalin. There is deep sympathy and goodwill in Britain—and I doubt not here also—towards the peoples of all the Russias and a resolve to persevere through many differences and rebuffs in establishing lasting friendships. We understand the Russian need to be secure on her western frontiers by the removal of all possibility of German aggression. We welcome Russia to her rightful place among the leading nations of the world. We welcome her flag upon the seas. Above all, we welcome constant, frequent and growing contacts between the Russian people and our own people on both sides of the Atlantic. It is my duty however, for I am sure you would wish me to state the facts as I see them to you, to place before you certain facts about the present position in Europe.

From Stettin in the Baltic to Trieste in the Adriatic, an iron curtain has descended across the Continent. Behind that line lie all the capitals of the ancient states of Central and Eastern Europe. Warsaw, Berlin, Prague, Vienna, Budapest, Belgrade, Bucharest and Sofia, all these famous cities and the populations around them lie in what I must call the Soviet sphere, and all are subject in one form or another, not only to Soviet influence but to a very high and, in many cases, increasing measure of control from Moscow. Athens alone—Greece with its immortal glories—is free to decide its future at an election under British, American and French observation. The Russian-dominated Polish Government has been encouraged to make enormous and wrongful inroads upon Germany, and mass expulsions of millions of Germans on a scale grievous and undreamed-of are now taking place. The Communist parties, which were very small in all these Eastern States of Europe, have been raised to pre-eminence and power far beyond their numbers and are seeking everywhere to obtain totalitarian control. Police governments are prevailing in nearly every case, and so far, except in Czechoslovakia, there is no true democracy.

Turkey and Persia are both profoundly alarmed and disturbed at the claims which are being made upon them and at the pressure being exerted by the Moscow Government. An attempt is being made by the Russians in Berlin to build up a quasi-Communist party in their zone of Occupied Germany by showing special favours to groups of left-wing German leaders. At the end of the fighting last June, the American and British Armies withdrew westwards, in accordance with an earlier agreement, to a depth at some points of 150 miles upon a front of nearly four hundred miles, in order to allow our Russian allies to occupy this vast expanse of territory which the Western Democracies had conquered.

If now the Soviet Government tries, by separate action, to build up a pro-Communist Germany in their areas, this will cause new serious difficulties in the British and American zones, and will give the defeated Germans the power of putting themselves up to auction between the Soviets and the Western Democracies. Whatever conclusions may be drawn from these facts—and facts they are—this is certainly not the Liberated Europe we fought to build up. Nor is it one which contains the essentials of permanent peace.

The safety of the world requires a new unity in Europe, from which no nation should be permanently outcast. It is from the quarrels of the strong parent races in Europe that the world wars we have witnessed, or which occurred in former times, have sprung. Twice in our own lifetime we have seen the United States, against their wishes and their traditions, against arguments, the force of which it is impossible not to comprehend, drawn by irresistible forces, into these wars in time to secure the victory of the good cause, but only after frightful slaughter and devastation had occurred. Twice the United States has had to send several millions of its young men across the Atlantic to find the war; but now war can find any nation, wherever it may dwell between dusk and dawn. Surely we should work with conscious purpose for a grand pacification of Europe, within the structure of the United Nations and in accordance with its Charter. That I feel is an open cause of policy of very great importance.

In front of the iron curtain which lies across Europe are other causes for anxiety. In Italy the Communist Party is seriously hampered by having to support the Communist-trained Marshal Tito's claims to former Italian territory at the head of the Adriatic. Nevertheless the future of Italy hangs in the balance. Again one cannot imagine a regenerated Europe without a strong France. All my public life I have worked for a strong France and I never lost faith in her destiny, even in the darkest hours. I will not lose faith now. However, in a great number of countries, far from the Russian frontiers and throughout the world, Communist fifth columns are established and work in complete unity and absolute obedience to the directions they receive from the Communist centre. Except in the British Commonwealth and in the United States where Communism is in its infancy, the Communist parties or fifth columns constitute a growing challenge and peril to Christian civilisation. These are sombre facts for anyone to have to recite on the morrow of a victory gained by so much splendid comradeship in arms and in the cause of freedom and democracy; but we should be most unwise not to face them squarely while time remains.

The outlook is also anxious in the Far East and especially in Manchuria. The Agreement which was made at Yalta, to which I was a party, was extremely favourable to Soviet Russia, but it was made at a time when no one could say that the German war might not extend all through the summer and autumn of 1945 and when the Japanese war was expected to last for a further 18 months from the end of the German war. In this country you are all so well-informed about the Far East, and such devoted friends of China, that I do not need to expatiate on the situation there.

I have felt bound to portray the shadow which, alike in the west and in the east, falls upon the world. I was a high minister at the time of the Versailles Treaty and a close friend of Mr. Lloyd-George, who was the head of the British delegation at Versailles. I did not myself agree with many things that were done, but I have a very strong impression in my mind of that situation, and I find it painful to contrast it with that which prevails now. In those days there were high hopes and unbounded confidence that the wars were over, and that the League of Nations would become all-powerful. I do not see or feel that same confidence or even the same hopes in the haggard world at the present time.

On the other hand I repulse the idea that a new war is inevitable; still more that it is imminent. It is because I am sure that our fortunes are still in our own hands and that we hold the power to save the future, that I feel the duty to speak out now that I have the occasion and the opportunity to do so. I do not believe that Soviet Russia desires war. What they desire is the fruits of war and the indefinite expansion of their power and doctrines. But what we have to consider here to-day while time remains, is the permanent prevention of war and the establishment of conditions of freedom and democracy as rapidly as possible in all countries. Our difficulties and dangers will not be removed by closing our eyes to them. They will not be removed by mere waiting to see what happens; nor will they be removed by a policy of appeasement. What is needed is a settlement, and the longer this is delayed, the more difficult it will be and the greater our dangers will become.

From what I have seen of our Russian friends and Allies during the war, I am convinced that there is nothing they admire so much as strength, and there is nothing for which they have less respect than for weakness, especially military weakness. For that reason the old doctrine of a balance of power is unsound. We cannot afford, if we can help it, to work on narrow margins, offering temptations to a trial of strength. If the Western Democracies stand together in strict adherence to the principles of the United Nations Charter, their influence for furthering those principles will be immense and no one is likely to molest them. If however they become divided or falter in their duty and if these all-important years are allowed to slip away then indeed catastrophe may overwhelm us all.

Last time I saw it all coming and cried aloud to my own fellow-countrymen and to the world, but no one paid any attention. Up till the year 1933 or even 1935, Germany might have been saved from the awful fate which has overtaken her and we might all have been spared the miseries Hitler let loose upon mankind. There never was a war in all history easier to prevent by timely action than the one which has just desolated such great areas of the globe. It could have been prevented in my belief without the firing of a single shot, and Germany might be powerful, prosperous and honoured to-day; but no one would listen and one by one we were all sucked into the awful whirlpool. We surely must not let that happen again. This can only be achieved by reaching now, in 1946, a good understanding on all points with Russia under the general authority of the United Nations Organisation and by the maintenance of that good understanding through many peaceful years, by the world instrument, supported by the whole strength of the English-speaking world and all its connections. There is the solution which I respectfully offer to you in this Address to which I have given the title "The Sinews of Peace."

Let no man underrate the abiding power of the British Empire and Commonwealth. Because you see the 46 millions in our island harassed about their food supply, of which they only grow one half, even in wartime, or because we have difficulty in restarting our industries and export trade after six years of passionate war effort, do not suppose that we shall not come through these dark years of privation as we have come through the glorious years of agony, or that half a century from now, you will not see 70 or 80 millions of Britons spread about the world and united in defence of our traditions, our way of life, and of the world causes which you and we espouse. If the population of the English-speaking Commonwealths be added to that of the United States with all that such co-operation implies in the air, on the sea, all over the globe and in science and in industry, and in moral force, there will be no quivering, precarious balance of power to offer its temptation to ambition or adventure. On the contrary, there will be an overwhelming assurance of security. If we adhere faithfully to the Charter of the United Nations and walk forward in sedate and sober strength seeking no one's land or treasure, seeking to lay no arbitrary control upon the thoughts of men; if all British moral and material forces and convictions are joined with your own in fraternal association, the highroads of the future will be clear, not only for us but for all, not only for our time, but for a century to come.

CHAPTER 21

IF I WERE
AN AMERICAN

*Alive to the fierce debate raging in America between the forces of isola-
tionism and those who would have the United States play a leading role on
the world stage, Churchill boldly addresses the question—as alive today as
it was half a century ago—as to whether or not it is in America's interest to
be the "world's policeman."*

LIFE, APRIL 14, 1947

IT IS BARELY a year since I spoke at Fulton at the desire of the
President of the United States. I read over again last night
what I then said. I was surprised that such mild, mellifluous, carefully
shaped and guarded sentiments should have caused so much commotion, not only in America and in my own country but elsewhere. In
sum, all I said was that the United Nations organization was the
supreme hope of the future; that the United States should take the lead
in this; that they should not share the secrets of the atomic bomb till international progress had been made; that the "Fraternal Association"
of the United States and the British Empire and Commonwealth of
Nations—the English-speaking world—should not only be maintained
but developed; that they should share bases and have similar weapons,
and that they should work for the ideals which they have in common, in
menace to none and for the safety of all.

It is true that I said:

"From Stettin in the Baltic to Trieste in the Adriatic an 'Iron Curtain' has descended across the Continent. Behind that line lie all the
capitals of the ancient states of Central and Eastern Europe. Warsaw,
Berlin, Prague, Vienna, Budapest, Belgrade, Bucharest and Sofia, all
these famous cities and the populations around them lie in the Soviet
sphere and all are subject in one form or another, not only to Soviet influence but to a very high and increasing measure of control from
Moscow. . . . Athens alone, with its immortal glories, is free to decide
its future at an election under British, American and French observation."

Statements of this character are not seriously challenged in any part of the world today, outside the vast Communist or Communist-controlled regions. They have been endorsed by the overwhelming weight of American public opinion and, not less important, by the policy of the United States government. Not only has the Communist peril been recognized as the gravest that now overhangs the world, but a series of measures of a resolute character has been taken to resist further encroachments and expansion by the Russian Soviet State in Europe and in Asia. In Europe these measures have hitherto been especially concerned with Germany, Austria and Hungary, and in Asia with Persia and China. Now, by the momentous declaration of President Truman, supported by the leading American statesmen of both Democratic and Republican parties, they are focused directly upon the Eastern Mediterranean. The President has made it plain that vital American interests and duties exist in these waters and throughout the Middle East, and that the United States government will not suffer such interests to be molested or undermined, nor these duties flinched from or neglected. Should Congress confirm the policy and action recommended by the President, a new situation will be created in the Mediterranean, full of hope for the future of the Middle East and also to the future peace of the world and the United Nations organization newly created to maintain it. Greece and Turkey are the two countries primarily affected.

In his evidence before the House of Representatives Foreign Affairs Committee, Mr. Dean Acheson, the United States Acting Secretary of State, is reported to have testified on 21 March, 1947 as follows:

"A Communist-dominated government in Greece would be considered dangerous to United States security."

This is precisely the issue which broke upon us in Athens in December, 1944, when I was at the head of His Majesty's Government. It fell to me to take important executive action. I must emphasize that I acted with the full authority and agreement of my colleagues in the British National War Cabinet. We *also* felt at that time, like Mr. Dean Acheson now, and I do not doubt the opinion is maintained by the present Labour-Socialist Cabinet, that "a Communist-dominated Government in Greece would be dangerous to *British* security," and to the general cause of Freedom, for which we had contended so long. In December, 1944, however, the case was aggravated and rendered urgent in the last degree, by the imminence of a Communist *coup d'etat* enforced by methods of bloody violence on a formidable scale.

As the fighting in Athens developed, two or three British divisions moved gradually into the city. For 40 days of street fighting we battled for the life and soul of Athens. Ward by ward, district by district, almost house by house, the Communist intruders were driven back and finally out, with heavy losses. In their withdrawal, they murdered at least 20,000 men, women and children whom they did not like or who got in their way. But eventually, in spite of a storm of Left-Wing criticism, which, having a good conscience, I bore without vexation, the city of Athens and the Greek nation were saved from becoming a Communist totalitarian state. After much labour and exertion, they were even allowed a free vote about what kind of country they wanted to be, and what kind of government they wanted to have. Both at the elections and in the plebiscite the Greeks voted as I had always believed and predicted. There is no part of my work of the righteousness of which I am more profoundly convinced than the British conduct toward Greece in the winter of 1944 and 1945. And it is upon the foundation of this work that the United States is able to take its stand today.

Let us now pass from Greek episodes to the other and larger dynamic questions raised by President Truman's declaration of 12 March, 1947. This involves the decision of the United States to take a leading part, so far as it is necessary to world peace, in the Eastern Mediterranean, or what is commonly called the Middle East.

I understand and have never underrated the weighty arguments of former days in favour of American isolationism. If my father had been an American citizen instead of my mother, I should have hesitated a long time before getting mixed up with Europe and Asia and that sort of thing. Why, I should have asked myself, should my forebears have gone across the Atlantic Ocean in little ships with all the perils of wind and weather to make a new home in a vast, unexplored continent? Why should they have left class and feudal systems of society, or actual tyrannies which denied them religious freedom, to encounter the unknown? Why should they have struggled on through hard bleak generations cutting down the forests, cultivating the land, fighting the Red Indians, climbing over the mountains, wending across the prairies, driving their covered wagons and presently their railways, to the misty and mysterious Pacific, in order to find, create and consolidate "the land of the free and the home of the brave"—why all this, if it was not to find self-expression in isolation? Why, then, I should have asked myself, have I got to go back to Europe and to Asia, just because they showed me maps of these continents when I was at school? Are not the oceans broad and have we not got one on each side of us? It would have taken me a lot to get over this.

However, there has been a lot, and it is needful to look around upon it all. The United States has become the most powerful force in the world, and at this same moment all the ancient nations and races of Europe and Asia, except only the Union of Soviet Socialist Republics and Great Britain and her Commonwealth, have been for the time being exhausted in the aftermath of their horrible struggles. More than that, the fundamental principles which have governed the growth of American democracy, are also challenged, not only in Europe and Asia, but in every country throughout the world. The doctrine that all men are created free and equal and are entitled to life, liberty and the pursuit of happiness, is confronted bluntly and menacingly with the to-talitarian conception that the State is all and the individual is a slave or a pawn. The remaining free, democratic countries are also preyed upon from within by a sect which has no national loyalties and obeys blindly the orders which it receives from the supreme Communist oligarchy in the Kremlin. This also raises new and far-reaching issues.

It would seem to force thoughtful and patriotic Americans to ask themselves why millions of Americans should be taken from their homes and farms and businesses from which they get their living and rear their families, to go across the ocean every 25 years or so and shed their blood in wars, in the making of which they have had no say, in the preventing of which they have so far been no use. Why should the American people pour out its life and treasure generation after genera-tion to try to put things right across the oceans *after* they have watched them all go wrong?

These are the questions which I would have pondered over, and per-haps said something about, if I had been born a citizen of the United States. But I should also have memories and comprehension of what had happened in the last 30 years or more. I should see this shattered, convulsive, quivering Europe as a source of great danger to me in my home state—which I might have been elected to represent in Washing-ton (you never know). When I reflected on the strength of the United States, its freedoms and its many virtues, all the toils, sacrifices, costs and burdens cast upon it, I might well have come to the conclusion that the United States has no choice but to lead or fall. It is certainly not strange that American opinion should be greatly influenced by Presi-dent Truman, General Marshall, Mr. Bernard Baruch, Senator Van-denberg, Governor Dewey and other champions of peace and progress in trying to nip evil in the bud, quench fire at its outbreak, and stop pestilence by timely inoculation.

And then there are other facts. There is this awful thing they call Sci-ence. It never will leave you alone—not even after conquering the Red

Indians and the forest and the prairies. Facts, obnoxious and persistent, come reaching out their claws, upsetting the lives of homes from Boston to San Francisco, from Chicago to New Orleans. Detestable facts arising from muddle and disaster thousands of miles away, or from terrible discoveries and inventions, but facts none the less, that all can see and have lately felt. These are facts that must be mastered and controlled. And not only are there these ugly facts, there are the calls of duty inseparable from world-power and its responsibilities. I am not surprised that many Americans ask whether it would not be worthwhile. Would not it indeed be a measure of ordinary prudence, would it not also indeed be a high moral duty to take a little interest between whiles in matters which make so great a difference to the ordinary life and welfare of the American common man? It must be the interest as well as honour for every man in every free country to see whether these unrelenting, recurring dangers cannot be so governed by a world organization as to make things better for all humanity.

As I said at Fulton, "half a century from now, there will be at least eighty millions of Britons spread about the Globe, united in defense of our traditions, our way of life, and of the world themes to which we and the United States have long been faithful." But Britain and the British Commonwealth as a whole will welcome the establishment of American power in the Middle East and will give her potent aid by every means. Americans should not hesitate to march forward unswervingly upon the path to which Destiny has called them, guided by the principles of the Declaration of Independence, expressed so carefully and so pregnantly in the balanced, well-shaped language of the 18th Century, by the founders of the greatest State in the world. All is there, nothing can be abandoned; nothing need be added, nothing should be denied.

Let us then go forward together in all understanding and amity. Divided all may be destroyed piecemeal; united, in the United Nations, we may save freedom, civilization and democracy—and perhaps even roll away the curse of war forever from mankind.

CHAPTER 22

THE NORTH ATLANTIC TREATY

The NATO treaty, which Churchill's "Iron Curtain" speech had foreshadowed three years earlier, had been signed on April 24. It was to prove a sure defence and bulwark to the nations of Europe, forestalling Soviet expansionism, guaranteeing fifty years of peace at the highest level, and, ultimately, being the rock upon which the structure of the Soviet Union eventually crashed to destruction, lacking an economy that could support the burden of the arms race.

SPEECH IN THE HOUSE OF COMMONS, MAY 12, 1949

THE HOUSE will not be surprised if I begin by saying that I find myself in very general agreement with the sombre speech which the Foreign Secretary has just made. I am glad that the lifting by the Soviet Government of the blockade of Berlin has not been taken by him as an occasion for proclaiming that an important peace gesture has been made. Before the last war, I do remember how, every time Herr Hitler made some reassuring statement, such as "This is my last territorial demand," people came to me and said, "There, now, you see how wrong you have been; he says it is his last territorial demand"; but the bitter experience we have all gone through in so many countries, on this side and on the other side of the Atlantic, has made us more wary of these premature rejoicings upon mere words and gestures. We give our cordial welcome to the Atlantic Pact. We give our thanks to the United States for the splendid part they are playing in the world. As I said when over there the other day:

> Many nations have risen to the summit of world affairs, but here is a great example where new-won supremacy has not been used for self-aggrandizement, but only further sacrifices.

The sacrifices are very great. In addition to the enormous sums sent to Europe under Marshall Aid, the Atlantic Pact entails further subsidies for military supplies which are estimated at over $1,000,000,000 up to the year 1950. All this has to be raised by taxation from the annual production of the hard-working American people, who are not all Wall

Street millionaires, but are living their lives in very different parts of the country than Wall Street. I say that nothing like this process of providing these enormous sums for defence and assistance to Europe—nothing like this has ever been seen in all history. We acknowledge it with gratitude, and we must continue to play our part as we are doing in a worthy manner and to the best of our abilities.

Our differences with the Soviet Government began before the war ended. Their unfriendly attitude to the Western Allies was obvious before the end of 1945, and, at the meeting of the United Nations organization in London in January 1946, Anglo-Russian relations had already reached a point where the Foreign Secretary had to give the word "lie" in open conference to Mr. Vyshinsky. I was impressed with that indication, which I read in the newspapers, and I was also very much impressed with the statements made at that time by Mr. Vandenberg, that great American statesman, as I will not hesitate to call him. His whole career in recent years has been to carry world security and righteous causes far above the level of the fierce and repeated American political contentions and elections.

I have always myself looked forward to the fraternal association of the English-speaking world and also to the union of Europe. It is only in this way, in my view, that the peace and progress of mankind can be maintained. I gave expression to these views at Fulton in March 1946, after the remarks to which I have referred had shown the differences which had arisen with Russia. Although what I said then reads very tamely today, and falls far short of what has actually been done, and far short of what the House actually has to vote at the present time, a Motion of Censure against me was placed on the Order Paper in the name of the hon. Member for Luton [Mr. Warbey] in the following terms:

> World Peace and Security—That this House considers that proposals for a military alliance between the British Commonwealth and the United States of America for the purpose of combating the spread of Communism, such as were put forward in a speech at Fulton, Missouri, USA, by the right hon. Gentleman the Member for Woodford are calculated to do injury to good relations between Great Britain, USA and the USSR, and are inimical to the cause of world peace.

That is the operative part. It is quite unusual, when a Private Member is out of office, that a Motion of that kind should be placed upon the Order Paper with regard to a speech made on his own responsibility, but no fewer than 105 hon. Members of the party opposite put their names to it. I do not see them all here today; some of them are here, but, of course, I feel that there has been a large-scale process of conversion, and, naturally, I welcome converts, and so do His Majesty's Government. They say that there is more joy over one sinner who repenteth than over ninety and nine just persons who need no repentance. Here, we have got about a hundred in a bunch, so far as I can make out, although some of them have emphasized the change of heart which they have gone through by a suitable act of penance by abstaining from attending this Debate.

Mr. Sydney Silverman [Nelson and Colne] *rose*—

Mr. Churchill: Far be it from me to refuse an opportunity to a penitent.

Mr. Silverman: I was only going to say in all humility to the right hon. Gentleman that because a number of people are prepared to support the calling in of the fire brigade, that does not mean that they withdraw one word of censure from those who contributed to the setting of the house on fire.

Mr. Churchill: I did not expect that such a condemnation of the Soviet Government's policy would be forthcoming from the hon. Gentleman. For all these reasons, it is most certainly true that the occasion is not entirely unmingled with joy, for the country sees so many who have changed their courses, but I say that we are now asked to approve this Atlantic Pact, and the only opposition to it is expected from that small band of Communists, crypto-Communists and fellow-travellers whose dimensions have been very accurately ascertained in recent times. In all this matter, the policy of the Foreign Secretary has been wise and prudent. We have given it our fullest support, and we shall continue to do so. There is, of course, a difference between what a private Member of Parliament may say, even if his words carry far, and what a Minister has to do. To perceive a path and to point it out is one thing, but to blaze the trail and labour to construct the path is a harder task, and, personally, I do not grudge the right hon. Gentleman any credit for the contribution which he has made to bringing about the Atlantic Pact. It entitles him, and the Government he represents, to the congratulations of the House which will be formally signified tonight by the passing of this Motion.

We must not, however, lose sight of the fact that the prime agent is the United States. I agree with what the Foreign Secretary said, that if the United States had acted in this way at an earlier period in their history they might well have averted the first world war, and could certainly, by sustaining the League of Nations from its birth, have warded off the second. The hope of mankind is that by their present valiant and self-sacrificing policy they will be the means of preventing a third world war. The future is, however, shrouded in obscurity.

As I have said on former occasions, we are dealing with absolutely incalculable factors in dealing with the present rulers of Russia. No one knows what action they will take, or to what internal pressures they will respond. He would be a bold, and, I think, an imprudent man who embarked upon detailed prophecies about what will be the future course of events. But it is absolutely certain that the strengthening by every means in our power of the growing ties which unite the signatories of the Atlantic Pact, of the Brussels Treaty, and the signatories of the Statute of the Council of Europe—on all of which there is overwhelming agreement in this House—is our surest guarantee of peace and safety. Now we must persevere faithfully and resolutely along these courses.

While I like the strong note which was struck by the Foreign Secretary in his speech this afternoon, we must persevere along these courses. It has been said that democracy suffers from the weakness of chopping and changing, that it can never pursue any course for any length of time, especially Parliamentary democracy. But I think that may prove to be a phase from which we are shaking ourselves free. At any rate, persistence at this time and a perseverance which is emphasized in the speech of the Foreign Secretary is, we on this side are quite certain, the safest course for us to follow and also the most right and honourable course for us to follow. It has been said that the Atlantic Pact and the European Union are purely defensive conceptions. The Foreign Secretary has claimed that they are not aggressive in any way. How could they be? When we consider the great disparity of military strength on the continent of Europe, no one can doubt that these measures are of a defensive and non-aggressive character. The military forces of the Soviet Union are at least three or four times as great as those which can be set against them on land. Besides this, they have their fifth column in many countries, waiting eagerly for the moment when they can play the quisling and pay off old scores against the rest of their fellow countrymen. Nothing that can be provided in the Atlantic Pact or the Western Union Agreement on land can make our position and policy other than purely defensive. It remains the first duty of all the signatory Powers to do their utmost to make Europe, and for us here to make Britain, self-supporting and independently secure. For this we must all labour.

This may be an occasion for satisfaction, but it is not an occasion for triumph or for exultation. We are on the eve of the Four-Power Conference out of which we may hope a peace treaty with Germany may come. We must give that conference the best possible chance and be careful not to use language at this juncture which would hamper its discussions or compromise its chances of success. At the same time, I am glad that the Foreign Secretary is not under any illusions and that we shall not be deceived by gestures unaccompanied by action. It is deeds, not words, which are wanted. Any deed done by the Russian Soviet Government which really makes for the peaceful and friendly intercourse of mankind will have its immediate response, but mere manœuvres must be watched with the utmost vigilance.

Moreover, there can be no assurance of permanent peace in Europe while Asia is on the Elbe or while so many ancient States and famous capitals of Eastern Europe are held in the grip of the thirteen men who form the oligarchy of the Kremlin. The Communist gains in China and the disturbances, all springing from the same source, which are causing so much misery in South-East Asia, all bring home to us the magnitude of the great struggle for freedom which is going on under the conditions of what is called the "cold war." We are confronted with a mighty oligarchy disposing not only of vast armies and important armaments by sea and in the air, but which has a theme, almost a religion, in the Communist doctrine and propaganda which claims its devotees in so many countries and makes them, over a large portion of the globe, the enemies of the lands of their birth.

There is this fear which the Soviet dictators have of a friendly intercourse with the Western democracies and their hitherto inflexible resolve to isolate the enormous populations they control. They even fear words on the broadcast. Everyone in this country is free to tune in to the Russian broadcasts at any hour of the day, and I am bound to say I am very glad that they should be free to do so. It would be a terrible thing if we were afraid of anything that might be said about us on the broadcasts. It is a woeful admission of a guilty conscience or a defective political system when you are afraid to let your people listen to what goes on abroad. We soon got used to "Lord Haw-Haw" during the war, and we never feared what he might have said about us. It is astonishing that there should be this terror in the hearts of these men, wielding such immense material and physical power, merely of words let out by our fairly harmless BBC upon the ether. They must have very poor nerves to get alarmed by that. But the fact remains that there is this fear—fear of friendship and fear of words, and it acts upon men who wield the most terrible agencies of military force.

The situation is, therefore, from many points of view unprecedented and incalculable. Over the whole scene reigns the power of the atomic bomb, ever growing in the hands of the United States. It is this, in my view, and this alone that has given us time to take the measures of self-protection and to develop the units which make those measures possible, one of which is before us this afternoon. I have said that we must rise above that weakness of democratic and Parliamentary Governments, in not being able to pursue a steady policy for a long time, so as to get results. It is surely our plain duty to persevere steadfastly, irrespective of party feelings or national diversities, for only in this way have we good chances of securing that lasting world peace under a sovereign world instrument of security on which our hearts are set. We shall, therefore, support His Majesty's Government in the Motion which the right hon. Gentleman has just commended to us.

CHAPTER 23

"WE MUST NOT LOSE HOPE"

This was Churchill's third and final address to Congress. Less than three months before, on October 26, 1951, at the age of seventy-six, he had been returned as Prime Minister for the second time. The menace posed by the Soviet Union, which by now had acquired nuclear weapons, was grave. Meanwhile, war was raging in Korea, where American forces, supported by British and Commonwealth troops, were resisting the onslaught not only of North Korea but also of the Communist Chinese. The Prime Minister turned once again to his theme of Anglo-American unity, reiterating Bismarck's declaration that the supreme fact of the nineteenth century was that "Britain and the United States spoke the same language."

ADDRESS TO A JOINT SESSION OF
THE U.S. CONGRESS, JANUARY 17, 1952

THIS IS the third time it has been my fortune to address the Congress of the United States upon our joint affairs. I am honoured indeed by these experiences which I believe are unique for one who is not an American citizen. It is also of great value to me, on again becoming the head of His Majesty's Government, to come over here and take counsel with many trusted friends and comrades of former anxious days. There is a lot for us to talk about together so that we can understand each other's difficulties, feelings and thoughts, and do our best for the common cause. Let us, therefore, survey the scene this afternoon with cool eyes undimmed by hate or passion, guided by righteous inspiration and not uncheered by hope.

I have not come here to ask you for money to make life more comfortable or easier for us in Britain. Our standards of life are our own business and we can only keep our self-respect and independence by looking after them ourselves. During the war we bore our share of the burden and fought from first to last, unconquered—and for a while alone—to the utmost limits of our resources. Your majestic obliteration of all you gave us under Lend-Lease will never be forgotten by this generation in Britain, or by history.

After the war—unwisely as I contended, and certainly contrary to American advice—we accepted as normal debts nearly £4,000 million sterling of claims by countries we had protected from invasion, or had otherwise aided, instead of making counter-claims which would at least have reduced the bill to reasonable proportions. The £1,000 million loan we borrowed from you in 1946, and which we are now repaying, was spent, not on ourselves, but mainly in helping others. In all, since the war, as the late Government affirmed, we have lent or given to European or Asian countries £1,300 million in the form of unrequited exports. This, added to the cost of turning over our industry from war to peace, and rebuilding homes shattered by bombardment was more than we could manage without an undue strain upon our life-energies for which we shall require both time and self-discipline to recover.

Why do I say all this? Not to compare our financial resources with yours—we have but a third your numbers, and much less than a third your wealth. Not to claim praise or rewards, but to convince you of our native and enduring strength, and that our true position is not to be judged by the present state of the dollar exchange or by sterling area finance. Our production is half as great again as it was before the war, our exports are up by two-thirds. Recovery, while being retarded, has been continuous, and we are determined that it shall go on.

As I said at Fulton in Missouri six years ago, under the auspices of President Truman, "let no man underrate the abiding power of the British Commonwealth and Empire. Do not suppose we shall not come through these dark years of privation as we came through the glorious years of agony, or that a half century from now you will not see seventy or eighty millions of Britons spread about the world and united in defence of our traditions, our way of life and of the world causes which you and we espouse. If the population of the English-speaking Commonwealth be added to that of the United States, with all that such co-operation implies, in the air, on the sea and all over the globe, and in science, industry and moral force, there will be no quivering, precarious balance of power to offer its temptation to ambition or adventure." I am very glad to be able to say the same to you here today.

It is upon this basis of recovery, in spite of burdens, that the formidable problem of the new rearmament has fallen upon us. It is the policy of the United States to help forward in many countries the process of rearmament. In this, we, who contribute ourselves two-thirds as much as the rest of Europe put together, require your aid if we are to realize in good time the very high level of military strength which the Labour Government boldly aimed at, and to which they committed us. It is for you to judge to what extent United States' interests are involved; whether you aid us much or little we shall continue to do our utmost in the common cause. But, Members of the Congress, our contribution will perforce be limited by our own physical resources, and thus the combined strength of our two countries, and also of the free world, will be somewhat less than it might be. That is why I have come here to ask, not for gold, but for steel; not for favours but equipment, and that is why many of our requests have been so well and generously met.

At this point I will venture, if I may, to make a digression. After a lot of experience I have learned it is not a good thing to dabble in the internal politics of another country. It's hard enough to understand one's own. But I will tell you something about our British politics all the same. In our island we indulge from time to time in having Elections. I believe you sometimes have them over here. We have had a couple in twenty months, which is quite a lot, and quite enough for the time being. We now look forward to a steady period of administration in accordance with the mandates we have received. Like you we tend to work on the two-party system. The differences between parties on our side of the Atlantic, and perhaps elsewhere between British parties, are often less than they appear to outsiders. In modern Britain the dispute is between a form of Socialism which has hitherto respected political liberty, on the one hand, and on the other hand, free enterprise regulated by law and custom. These two systems of thought between political opponents, fortunately overlap quite a lot in practice. Our complicated society would be deeply injured if we did not practise and develop what is called in the United States the bi-partisan habit of mind, which divides, so far as possible, what is done to make a party win and bear in their turn the responsibility of office, and what is done to make the nation live and serve high causes.

I hope here, Members of Congress, you will allow me to pay a tribute to the late Senator Vandenberg. I had the honour to meet him on several occasions. His final message in these anxious years gave a feeling that in this period of United States leadership and responsibility, all the great Americans should work together for all the things that matter most. That at least is the spirit which we shall try to maintain among British leaders in our own country. And that was the spirit which alone enabled us to survive the perils of the late war.

But now let me return to my theme of the many changes that have taken place since I was last here. There is a jocular saying: "To improve is to change; to be perfect is to have changed often." I had to use that once or twice in my long career. But if that were true everyone ought to be getting on very well. The changes that have happened since I last spoke to Congress are indeed astounding. It is hard to believe we are living in the same world. Former allies have become foes. Former foes have become allies. Conquered countries have been liberated. Liberated nations have been enslaved by Communism. Russia, eight years ago our brave ally, has cast away the admiration and goodwill her soldiers had gained for her by their valiant defence of their own country. It is not the fault of the Western Powers if an immense gulf has opened between us. It took a long succession of deliberate and unceasing works and acts of hostility to convince our peoples—as they are now convinced—that they have another tremendous danger to face and that they are now confronted with a new form of tyranny and aggression as dangerous and as hateful as that which we overthrew.

When I visited Washington during the war I used to be told that China would be one of the Big Four Powers among the nations, and most friendly to the United States. I was always a bit sceptical, and I think it is now generally admitted that this hopeful vision has not yet come true. But I am by no means sure that China will remain for generations in the Communist grip. The Chinese said of themselves several thousand years ago: "China is a sea that salts all the waters that flow into it." There's another Chinese saying about their country which is much more modern—it dates only from the fourth century. This is the saying: "The tail of China is large and will not be wagged." I like that one. The British democracy approves the principles of movable party heads and unwaggable national tails. It is due to the working of these important forces that I have the honour to be addressing you at this moment.

You have wisely been resolute, Members of the Congress, in confronting Chinese Communist aggression. We take our stand at your side. We are grateful to the United States for bearing nine-tenths, or more, of the burden in Korea which the United Nations have morally assumed. I am very glad that whatever diplomatic divergencies there may be from time to time about procedure you do not allow the Chinese anti-Communists on Formosa to be invaded and massacred from the mainland. We welcome your patience in the armistice negotiations and our two countries are agreed that if the truce we seek is reached, only to be broken, our response will be prompt, resolute and effective. What I have learnt over here convinces me that British and United States policy in the Far East will be marked by increasing harmony.

I can assure you that our British hearts go out in sympathy to the families of the hundred thousand Americans who have given their lives or shed their blood in Korea. We also suffer these pangs for the loss of our own men there, and not only there but in other parts of Asia also under the attack by the same enemy. Whatever course events in Korea may take in the near future, and to prophesy would be difficult—much too difficult for me to embark upon it—I am sure our soldiers, and your soldiers, have not made their sacrifice in vain. The cause of world law has found strong and invaluable defence, and the foundations of the world instrument for preserving peace, justice and freedom among the nations have been deepened and strengthened. They stand now, not on paper but on rock.

Moreover, the action which President Truman took in your name, and with your full support in his stroke against aggression in Korea, has produced consequences far beyond Korea; consequences which may well affect the destiny of mankind. The vast process of American rearmament in which the British Commonwealth and Empire and the growing power of United Europe will play their part to the utmost of their strength, this vast process has already altered the balance of the world and may well, if we all persevere steadfastly and loyally together, avert the danger of a Third World War, or the horror of defeat and subjugation should one come upon us. Mr. President and Mr. Speaker, I hope the mourning families throughout the great Republic will find some comfort and some pride in these thoughts.

Another extraordinary change has taken place in the Far East since I last addressed you. Peace has been made with Japan; there indeed I congratulate you upon the policy which in wise and skilful hands has brought the Japanese nation from the woe and shame of defeat in their wicked war back to that association with the Western democracies upon which the revival of their traditions, dignity and happiness can alone be regained and the stability of the Far East assured. In the anxious and confused expanses of South-East Asia there is another sphere where our aims and interests, and those of the French, who are fighting bravely at heavy cost to their strength in Europe, may find a fertile field for agreement on policy. I feel sure that the conversations we have had between our two Foreign Secretaries—between Mr. Eden and Mr. Acheson—men whose names and experience are outstanding throughout the world, will help to place the problems of South-East Asia in their right setting. It would not be helpful to the common cause, for our evils all spring from one centre, if an effective truce in Korea led only to a transference of Communist aggression to these other fields. Our problems will not be solved unless they are steadily viewed and acted upon as a whole in their integrity as a whole.

In the Middle East enormous changes have also taken place since I was last in power in my own country. When the war ended the Western nations were respected and predominant throughout these ancient lands, and there were quite a lot of people who had a good word to say about Great Britain. Today it is a sombre and confusing scene; yet there is still some sunshine as well as shadow. From the days of the Balfour

Declaration I have desired that the Jews should have a national home, and I have worked for that end. I rejoice to pay my tribute here to the achievements of those who have founded the Israelite State, who have defended themselves with tenacity, and who offer asylum to great numbers of Jewish refugees. I hope that with their aid they may convert deserts into gardens; but if they are to enjoy peace and prosperity they must strive to renew and preserve their friendly relations with the Arab world without which widespread misery might follow for all.

Britain's power to influence the fortunes of the Middle East and guard it from aggression is far less today, now that we have laid aside our Imperial responsibility for India and its armies. It is no longer for us alone to bear the whole burden of maintaining the freedom of the famous waterway of the Suez Canal. That has become an international rather than a national responsibility. I welcome the statesmanlike conception of the Four-Power approach to Egypt, announced by the late British Government, in which Britain, the United States, France and Turkey may share with Egypt in the protection of the world interests involved, among which Egypt's own interests are paramount.

Such a policy is urgent. Britain is maintaining over fifty thousand troops in the Suez Canal Zone, who again might be well employed elsewhere, not for national vainglory or self-seeking advantage, but in the common interest of all nations. We do not seek to be masters of Egypt; we are there only as the servants and guardians of the commerce of the world. It would enormously aid us in our task if even token forces of the other partners in the Four-Power proposal were stationed in the Canal Zone as a symbol of the unity of purpose which inspires us. And I believe it is no exaggeration to state that such token forces would probably bring into harmony all that movement by which the Four-Power policy may be made to play a decisive part by peaceful measures, and bring to an end the wide disorders of the Middle East in which, let me assure you, there lurk dangers not less great than those which the United States has stemmed in Korea.

Now I come to Europe where the greatest of all our problems and dangers lie. I have long worked for the cause of a United Europe, and even of a United States of Europe, which would enable that Continent, the source of so much of our culture, ancient and modern, and the parent of the New World, to resume and revive its former splendours. It is my sure hope and conviction that European unity will be achieved, and that it will not ultimately be limited only to the countries at present composing Western Europe. I said at Zurich in 1946 that France should take Germany by the hand and lead her back into the family of nations, and thus end a thousand-year quarrel which has torn Europe to pieces and finally plunged the whole world twice over into slaughter and havoc.

Real and rapid progress is being made towards European unity, and it is both the duty and the policy of both Great Britain and her Commonwealth, and of the United States, to do our utmost, all of us, to help and speed it. As a forerunner of United Europe there is the European Army, which could never achieve its necessary strength without the inclusion of Germany. If this necessary and urgent object is being achieved by the fusion of the forces of the Continental nations outside what I have called in former times, the Iron Curtain, that great operation deserves our fullest support. But, Members of Congress, fusion is not the only way in which the defence of Western Europe can be built. The system of a grand alliance such as has been created by the North Atlantic Treaty Organization is no bar to the fusion of as many of its members as wish for this closer unity. And the United States, British and Canadian troops will stand, indeed are already standing, shoulder to shoulder with their European comrades in defence of the civilization and freedom of the West. We stand together under General Eisenhower to defend the common cause from violent aggression.

What matters most is not the form of fusion, or melding—a word I learned over here—but the numbers of divisions, and of armoured divisions and the power of the air forces, and their weapons available for unified action under the Supreme Commander. We, in Britain, have denuded our island of military formations to an extent I have never seen before, and I cannot accept the slightest reproach from any quarter that we are not doing our full duty, because the British Commonwealth of Nations, spread all over the world, is not prepared to become a State or a group of States in any Continental federal system on either side of the Atlantic. The sooner strong enough forces can be assembled in Europe under united command the more effective will be the deterrents against a Third World War. The sooner, also, will our sense of security, and the fact of our security, be seen to reside in valiant, resolute and well-armed manhood, rather than in the awful secrets which science has wrested from nature. These are at present, it must be recognized—these secrets—the supreme deterrent against a Third World War, and the most effective guarantee of victory in it.

If I may say this, Members of Congress, be careful above all things, therefore, not to let go of the atomic weapon until you are sure, and more than sure, that other means of preserving peace are in your hands. It is my belief that by accumulating deterrents of all kinds against aggression we shall, in fact, ward off the fearful catastrophe, the fears of which darken the life and mar the progress of all the peoples of the globe. We must persevere steadfastly and faithfully in the task to which, under United States leadership, we have solemnly bound ourselves. Any weakening of our purpose, any disruption of our organization would bring about the very evils which we all dread, and from which we should all suffer, and from which many of us would perish.

We must not lose patience, and we must not lose hope. It may be that presently a new mood will reign behind the Iron Curtain. If so it will be easy for them to show it, but the democracies must be on their guard against being deceived by a false dawn. We seek or covet no one's territory; we plan no forestalling war; we trust and pray that all will come right. Even during these years of what is called the "cold war," material production in every land is continually improving through the use of new machinery and better organization and the advance of peaceful science. But the great bound forward in progress and prosperity for which mankind is longing cannot come till the shadow of war has passed away. There are, however, historic compensations for the stresses which we suffer in the "cold war." Under the pressure and menace of Communist aggression the fraternal association of the United States with Britain and the British Commonwealth, and the new unity growing up in Europe—nowhere more hopeful than between France and Germany—all these harmonies are being brought forward, perhaps by several generations in the destiny of the world. If this proves true—and it has certainly proved true up to date—the architects in the Kremlin may be found to have built a different and a far better world structure than what they planned.

Members of the Congress, I have dwelt today repeatedly upon many of the changes that have happened throughout the world since you last invited me to address you here and I am sure you will agree that it is hardly possible to recognize the scene or believe it can truly have come to pass. But there is one thing which is exactly the same as when I was here last. Britain and the United States are working together and working for the same high cause. Bismarck once said that the supreme fact of the nineteenth century was that Britain and the United States spoke the same language. Let us make sure that the supreme fact of the twentieth century is that they tread the same path.

CHAPTER 24

HONORARY UNITED STATES CITIZENSHIP

President John F. Kennedy and the U.S. Congress decided to confer upon Winston Churchill the supreme accolade of honorary U.S. citizenship. Churchill, now in his eighty-ninth year, was too frail to make the journey to Washington, but deputed his son, Randolph, to read the following statement on his behalf at a ceremony in the Rose Garden of the White House. It was with great pride that I accompanied my father to Washington for the occasion.

WASHINGTON, D.C., APRIL 9, 1963

MR. PRESIDENT, I have been informed by Mr. David Bruce that it is your intention to sign a Bill conferring upon me Honorary Citizenship of the United States.

I have received many kindnesses from the United States of America, but the honour which you now accord me is without parallel. I accept it with deep gratitude and affection.

I am also most sensible of the warm-hearted action of the individual States who accorded me the great compliment of their own honorary citizenships as a prelude to this Act of Congress.

It is a remarkable comment on our affairs that the former Prime Minister of a great sovereign state should thus be received as an honorary citizen of another. I say "great sovereign state" with design and emphasis, for I reject the view that Britain and the Commonwealth should now be relegated to a tame and minor role in the world. Our past is the key to our future, which I firmly trust and believe will be no less fertile and glorious. Let no man underrate our energies, our potentialities and our abiding power for good.

I am, as you know, half American by blood, and the story of my association with that mighty and benevolent nation goes back nearly ninety years to the day of my Father's marriage. In this century of storm and tragedy I contemplate with high satisfaction the constant factor of the interwoven and upward progress of our peoples. Our comradeship and our brotherhood in war were unexampled. We stood together, and because of that fact the free world now stands. Nor has our partnership any exclusive nature: the Atlantic community is a dream that can well be fulfilled to the detriment of none and to the enduring benefit and honour of the great democracies.

Mr. President, your action illuminates the theme of unity of the English-speaking peoples, to which I have devoted a large part of my life. I would ask you to accept yourself, and to convey to both Houses of Congress, and through them to the American people, my solemn and heartfelt thanks for this unique distinction, which will always be proudly remembered by my descendants.

The White House, April 9, 1963.

PART III

AMERICA'S ENGLISH HERITAGE

In conclusion, I append the following three chapters, taken from Sir Winston Churchill's A History of the English-Speaking Peoples *(Vol. I), to explain the English origins of America's legal system and Congress, which imbues so much of the judicial and political life of America to this day.*

CHAPTER 1

THE ENGLISH COMMON LAW

It may strike modern-day Americans as strange, but it is nonetheless fact that American judges and lawyers spend much of their careers reading the decisions of long-dead British judges in search of answers to live American problems. Nowhere has this been more evident than in the recent impeachment proceedings against President William Jefferson Clinton, in which the outcome depended in large measure on what ancient British jurists meant when they first used the words "high crimes and misdemeanours"—just one of the many phrases in the American constitution taken directly from prior British law. The evolution of the English Common Law thus has a direct bearing on American law as practised today.

THE PLANTAGENET DYNASTY of Kings—England's Norman conquerors—were rough masters, and the temper of the age was violent. It was the violence however of vigour, not of decadence. England has had greater soldier-kings and subtler diplomatists than Henry II, but no man has left a deeper mark upon our laws and institutions. His strange outbursts of frenzied energy did not exhaust themselves in politics, war, and the chase. Like his Norman predecessors and his sons, Henry II possessed an instinct for the problems of government and law, and it is here that his achievement lies. The names of his battles have vanished with their dust, but his fame will live with the English Constitution and the English Common Law.

This great King was fortunate in his moment. William the Conqueror and Henry I had brought to England or preserved there all those instruments through which their successor was to work. They themselves could move but slowly and with caution. The land must settle itself to its new rules and rulers. In 1154 however Henry of Anjou had come to a country which nearly twenty years of anarchy had prepared for the acceptance of a strong hand at the centre. Himself a Frenchman, the ruler of more than half France, he brought to his task the qualities of vision, wide experience, and a strength that did not scruple to stoop to cunning. The disasters of Stephen's reign determined Henry not only to curb baronial independence and regain the ground lost by his predecessor, but to go much further. In place of a multitude of manorial courts where local magnates dispensed justice whose quality and character varied with the customs and temper of the neighbourhood, he planned a system of royal courts which would administer a law common to all England and all men.

The policy was not without peril. The King was wise enough to avoid a direct assault, for he knew, as the Conqueror had known, that to lay a finger upon the sanctity of customary rights would provoke disaster. Faced with this barrier, Henry shrewdly opposed custom to custom and cloaked innovation in the respected garb of conservatism. He was careful to respect existing forms. His plan was to stretch old principles to take on new meanings. In an unwritten Constitution the limits of the King's traditional rights were vaguely defined. This opened a shrewd line of advance. For centuries before the Conquest Church and King had been the enemies of seigneurial anarchy, but there had been no question of swiftly extending the Crown's jurisdiction. Fastening upon the elastic Saxon concept of the King's Peace, Henry used it to draw all criminal cases into his courts. Every man had his own Peace, which it was a crime to break, and the more important the man the graver the breach. The King's Peace was the most important of all, and those who broke it could be tried in the King's court. But the King's Peace was limited, and often embraced only offences committed in the King's presence or on the King's highway or land. When the King died his Peace died with him and men might do as they willed. Cautiously and quietly Henry began to claim that the King's Peace extended over all England, and that no matter where it was broken offenders should be tried in the King's courts. Civil cases he attracted by straining a different principle, the old right of the King's court to hear appeals in cases where justice had been refused and to protect men in possession of their lands. He did not brandish what he was about; the changes that he made were introduced gradually and without legislation, so that at first they were hardly perceived. Rarely is it possible to state the date at which any innovation was made; yet at the King's death a clever man might have looked back and seen how much had been altered in the thirty-five years that Henry II had sat on the English throne.

But if Henry was to pose as a conservative in the legal sphere he must be consistent. Compulsion could play little part in his programme; it had to be the first principle of his policy to attract cases to his courts rather than to compel them. A bait was needed with which to draw litigants to the royal courts; the King must offer them better justice than they could have at the hands of their lords. Henry accordingly threw open to litigants in the royal courts a new procedure for them—trial by jury. *Regale quoddam beneficium* a contemporary called it—a royal boon; and the description illuminates both the origin of the jury and the part it played in the triumph of the Common Law. Henry did not invent the jury; he put it to a new purpose. The idea of the jury is the one great contribution of the Franks to the English legal system, for, unknown in England before the Conquest, the germ of it lies far back in the practice of the Carolingian kings. In origin the jury was a royal instrument of administrative convenience: the King had the right to summon a body of men to bear witness under oath about the truth of any question concerning the royal interest. It was through this early form of jury that William the Conqueror had determined the Crown rights in the great Domesday survey. The genius of Henry II, perceiving new possibilities in such a procedure, turned to regular use in the courts an instrument which so far had only been used for administrative purposes.

Only the King had the right to summon a jury. Henry accordingly did not grant it to private courts, but restricted it to those who sought justice before the royal judges. It was an astute move. Until this time both civil and criminal cases had been decided through the oath, the ordeal, or the duel. The court would order one of the litigants to muster a body of men who would swear to the justice of his cause and whom it was hoped God would punish if they swore falsely; or condemn him, under the supervision of a priest, to carry a red-hot iron, or eat a morsel of bread, or be plunged in a pool of water. If the iron did not burn or the bread choke or the water reject him, so that he could not sink, then Divine Providence was adjudged to have granted a visible sign that the victim was innocent. The duel, or trial by battle, was a Norman innovation based on the modern theory that the God of Battles will strengthen the arm of the righteous, and was at one time much favoured for deciding disputes about land. Monasteries and other substantial landowners took the precaution however of assisting the Almighty by retaining professional champions to protect their property and their rights. All this left small room for debate on points of law. In a more rational age men were beginning to distrust such antics, and indeed the Church refused to sanction the ordeal during the same year that Magna Carta was sealed. Thus trial by jury quickly gained favour. But the old processes were long in dying. If a defendant preferred to take his case before God man could not forbid him, and the ordeal therefore was not abolished outright. Hence a later age was to know the horrors of the *peine forte et dure*—the compulsion of the accused by slow pressure to death to agree to put himself before a jury. Time swept this away; yet so late as 1818 a litigant nonplussed the judges by an appeal to trial by battle and compelled Parliament to abolish this ancient procedure.

The jury of Henry II was not the jury that we know. There were various forms of it; but in all there was this essential difference: the jurymen were witnesses as well as judges of the facts. Good men and true were picked, not yet for their impartiality, but because they were the men most likely to know the truth. The modern jury, which knows nothing about the case till it is proved in court, was slow in coming. The process is obscure. A jury summoned to Westminster from distant parts might be reluctant to come. The way was long, the roads unsafe, and perhaps only three or four would arrive. The court could not wait. An adjournment would be costly. To avoid delay and expense the parties might agree to rely on a jury *de circumstantibus,* a jury of bystanders. The few jurors who knew the truth of the matter would tell their tale to the bystanders, and then the whole body would deliver their verdict. In time the jurors with local knowledge would cease to be jurors at all and become witnesses, giving their evidence in open court to a jury entirely composed of bystanders. Such, we may guess, or something like it, was what happened. Very gradually, as the laws of evidence developed, the change came. By the fifteenth century it was under way; yet the old idea lingered, and as early as the Tudor kings jurymen might be tried for perjury if they gave a wrongful verdict.

The jury system has come to stand for all we mean by English justice, because so long as a case has to be scrutinised by twelve honest men defendant and plaintiff alike have a safeguard from arbitrary perversion of the law. It is this which distinguishes the law administered in English courts from Continental legal systems based on Roman law. Thus amidst the great process of centralisation the old principle was preserved, and endures to this day, that law flows from the people, and is not given by the King.

These methods gave good justice. Trial by jury became popular. Professional judges removed from local prejudice, whose outlook ranged above the interested or ignorant lord or his steward, armed with the King's power to summon juries, secured swifter decisions, and a strong authority to enforce them. Henry accordingly had to build up almost from nothing a complete system of royal courts, capable of absorbing a great rush of new work. The instrument to which he turned was the royal Council, the organ through which all manner of governmental business was already regularly carried out. It was to be the common parent of Chancery and Exchequer, of Parliament, of the Common Law courts, and those Courts of Prerogative on which the Tudors and Stuarts relied. At the outset of Henry II's reign it dealt almost indiscriminately with every kind of administrative business. On the judicial side the Court of the Exchequer, which tried cases affecting the royal revenue, was beginning to take shape; but in the main the Council in this aspect was scarcely more than the King's feudal court, where he did justice, like any other lord, among his vassals. Under Henry II all this was changed. The functions of the King's justices became more and more specialised. During the reigns of his sons the Council began to divide into two great courts, the King's Bench and the Common Pleas. They did not become fully separate till a century later. Thereafter, with the Court of the Exchequer, they formed the backbone of the Common Law system down to the nineteenth century. In addition, travelling justices—"justices in eyre"—were from time to time appointed to hear all manner of business in the shires, whose courts were thus drawn into the orbit of royal justice.

But all this was only a first step. Henry also had to provide means whereby the litigant, eager for royal justice, could remove his case out of the court of his lord into the King's court. The device which Henry used was the royal writ. At all costs baronial rights must be formally respected; but by straining the traditional rights of the Crown it was possible to claim that particular types of case fell within the King's province. Upon this principle Henry evolved a number of set formulæ, or writs, each fitted to a certain type of case; and any man who could by some fiction fit his own case to the wording of one of the royal writs might claim the King's justice. The wording of writs was rigid, but at this date new forms of writ might still be given. For about eighty years they increased in number, and with each new form a fresh blow was struck at the feudal courts. It was not until de Montfort's revolt against the third Henry in the thirteenth century that the multiplication of writs was checked and the number fixed at something under two hundred. This system then endured for six hundred years. However the times might change, society had to adapt itself to that unbending framework. Inevitably English law became weighted with archaisms and legal fictions. The whole course of a case might depend on the writ with which it was begun, for every writ had its special procedure, mode of trial, and eventual remedy. Thus the Saxon spirit of formalism survived. Henry II had only been able to break down the primitive methods of the early courts by fastening upon the law a procedure which became no less rigid. Yet, cumbersome though it was, the writ system gave to English law a conservative spirit which guarded and preserved its continuity from that time on in an unbroken line.

It is a maxim of English law that legal memory begins with the accession of Richard I in 1189. The date was set for a technical reason by a statute of Edward I. It could scarcely have been more appropriately chosen however, for with the close of the reign of Henry II we are on the threshold of a new epoch in the history of English law. With the establishment of a system of royal courts, giving the same justice all over the country, the old diversity of local law was rapidly broken down, and a law common to the whole land and to all men soon took its place. A modern lawyer, transported to the England of Henry's predecessor, would find himself in strange surroundings; with the system that Henry bequeathed to his son he would feel almost at home. That is the measure of the great King's achievement. He had laid the foundations of the English Common Law, upon which succeeding generations would build. Changes in the design would arise, but its main outlines were not to be altered.

It was in these fateful and formative years that the English-speaking peoples began to devise methods of determining legal disputes which survive in substance to this day. A man can only be accused of a civil or criminal offence which is clearly defined and known to the law. The judge is an umpire. He adjudicates on such evidence as the parties choose to produce. Witnesses must testify in public and on oath. They are examined and cross-examined, not by the judge, but by the litigants themselves or their legally qualified and privately hired representatives. The truth of their testimony is weighed not by the judge but by twelve "good men and true," and it is only when this jury has determined the facts that the judge is empowered to impose sentence, punishment, or penalty according to law. All this might seem very obvious, even a platitude, until one contemplates the alternative system which still dominates a large portion of the world. Under Roman law, and systems derived from it, a trial in those turbulent centuries, and in some countries even to-day, is often an inquisition. The judge makes his own investigation into the civil wrong or the public crime, and such investigation is largely uncontrolled. The suspect can be interrogated in private. He must answer all questions put to him. His right to be represented by a legal adviser is restricted. The witnesses against him can testify in secret and in his absence. And only when these processes have been accomplished is the accusation or charge against him formulated and published. Thus often arise secret intimidation, enforced confessions, torture, and blackmailed pleas of guilty. These sinister dangers were extinguished from the Common Law of England more than six centuries ago. By the time Henry II's great-grandson, Edward I, had died English criminal and civil procedure had settled into a mould and a tradition which in the mass govern the English-speaking peoples to-day. In all claims and disputes, whether they concerned the grazing lands of the Middle West, the oilfields of California, the sheep-runs and gold-mines of Australia, or the territorial rights of the Maoris, these rules have obtained, at any rate in theory, according to the procedure and mode of trial evolved by the English Common Law.

Nor was this confined to how trials were conducted. The law that was applied to such multitudinous problems, some familiar, others novel, was in substance the Common Law of England. The law concerning murder, theft, the ownership of land, and the liberty of the individual was all transported, together with much else, to the New World, and, though often modified to suit the conditions and temper of the times, descends in unbroken line from that which governed the lives and fortunes of twelfth-century Englishmen.

Most of it was then unwritten, and in England much still remains so. The English statutes, for example, still contain no definition of the crime of murder, for this, like much other law, rested on the unwritten custom of the land as declared by the inhabitants and interpreted, developed, and applied by the judges. Lawyers could only ascertain it by studying reports and records of ancient decisions. For this they had already in this early age made their own arrangements. A century after Henry's death they began to group themselves into professional communities in London, the Inns of Court, half colleges, half law-schools, but predominantly secular, for the presence of clerics learned in the laws of Rome and the Canon Law of the Roman Church was not encouraged, and here they produced annual law reports, or "Year Books," as they were then called, whose authority was recognised by the judges, and which continued in almost unbroken succession for nearly three centuries. In all this time however only one man attempted a general and comprehensive statement of the English Common Law. About the year 1250 a Judge of Assize named Henry of Bracton produced a book of nearly nine hundred pages entitled *A Tract on the Laws and Customs of England.* Nothing like it was achieved for several hundred years, but Bracton's method set an example, since followed throughout the English-speaking world, not so much of stating the Common Law as of explaining and commenting on it, and thus encouraging and helping later lawyers and judges to develop and expand it. Digests and codes imposed in the Roman manner by an omnipotent state on a subject people were alien to the spirit and tradition of England. The law was already there, in the customs of the land, and it was only a matter of discovering it by diligent study and comparison of recorded decisions in earlier cases and applying it to the particular dispute before the court. In the course of time the Common Law changed. Lawyers of the reign of Henry II read into the statements of their predecessors of the tenth century meanings and principles which their authors never intended, and applied them to the novel conditions and problems of their own day. No matter. Here was a precedent. If a judge could be shown that a custom or something like it had been recognised and acted upon in an earlier and similar case he would be more ready, if it accorded with his sense of what was just and with the current feelings of the community, to follow it in the dispute before him. This slow but continuous growth of what is popularly known as "case law" ultimately achieved much the same freedoms and rights for the individual as are enshrined in other countries by written instruments such as the Declarations of the Rights of Man and the spacious and splendid provisions of the American Declaration of Independence and constitutional guarantees of civil rights. But English justice advanced very cautiously. Even the framers of Magna Carta did not attempt to lay down new law or proclaim any broad general principles. This was because both sovereign and subject were in practice bound by the Common Law, and the liberties of Englishmen rested not on any enactment of the State, but on immemorial slow-growing custom declared by juries of free men who gave their verdicts case by case in open court.

CHAPTER 2

MAGNA CARTA

On June 15, 1215, by the banks of the River Thames at Runnymede, the barons of England required King John to sign the Great Charter, or Magna Carta, as it was known. The significance of this rests in the fact that the Kings of England, who hitherto had claimed supreme power by Divine right, were for the first time required to acknowledge that they ruled by consent of the governed. While the King might be above other mortals, yet even he is beneath the law. The Founding Fathers of the American Constitution ensured that what applied to the Kings of England holds good to this day even for the most powerful man in the world—the President of the United States. The notion that even Kings or Presidents are answerable for their actions before the highest court in the land goes back to that day, nearly eight centuries ago, when the Magna Carta was signed at Runnymede.

THE CHARACTER of the prince who now ascended the throne of England and became lord of Normandy, Anjou, Touraine, and Maine, claimant to Brittany and heir to Queen Eleanor's Aquitaine, was already well known. Richard had embodied the virtues which men admire in the lion, but there is no animal in nature that combines the contradictory qualities of John. He united the ruthlessness of a hardened warrior with the craft and subtlety of a Machiavellian. Although from time to time he gave way to furious rages, in which "his eyes darted fire and his countenance became livid," his cruelties were conceived and executed with a cold, inhuman intelligence. Monkish chroniclers have emphasised his violence, greed, malice, treachery, and lust. But other records show that he was often judicious, always extremely capable, and on occasions even generous. He possessed an original and inquiring mind, and to the end of his life treasured his library of books. In him the restless energy of the Plantagenet race was raised to a furious pitch of instability. A French writer, Taine, it is true, has tried to throw the sombre cloak of madness over his moral deformities, but a study of his actions shows John gifted with a deep and persistent sagacity, with patience and artifice, and with an unshakable resolve, which he fulfilled, to maintain himself upon the throne while the breath was in his body. The difficulties with which he contended, on the whole with remarkable success, deserve cool and attentive study. Moreover, when the long tally is added it will be seen that the British nation and the English-speaking world owe far more to the vices of John than to the labours of virtuous sovereigns; for it was through the union of many forces against him that the most famous milestone of our rights and freedom was in fact set up. . . .

The very success of Henry II in re-establishing order and creating an efficient central administration had left new difficulties for those who came after him. Henry II had created an instrument so powerful that it needed careful handling. He had restored order only at the cost of offending privilege. His fiscal arrangements were original, and drastic in their thoroughness. His work had infringed feudal custom at many points. All this had been accepted because of the King's tactful management and in the reaction from anarchy. Richard I, again, had left England in the hands of able administrators, and the odium of their strict government and financial ingenuity fell on them directly, and stopped short of the King, radiant in the halo of a Crusader and fortunate in his absence. John was at hand to bear the brunt in person.

John, like William Rufus, pressed to logical limits the tendencies of his father's system. There were arrears in the payment of scutage from Richard's reign, and more money was needed to fight the French king, Philip Augustus. But a division had opened in the baronage. The English barons of John's reign had become distinct from his Norman feudatories and not many families now held lands on both sides of the Channel. Even King Richard had met with refusals from his English nobles to fight abroad. Disputes about foreign service and payment of scutage lay at the root of the baronial agitation. By systematic abuse of his feudal prerogatives John drove the baronage to violent resistance. English society was steadily developing. Class interests had assumed sharper definition. Many barons regarded attendance or suit at Court as an opportunity for exerting influence rather than for rendering dutiful service. The sense of Church unity grew among the clergy, and corporate feeling in the municipalities. All these classes were needed by the new centralised Government; but John preferred to emphasise the more ruthless aspects of the royal power. . . .

The war with the French king was continued, and John's demands in money and service kept the barons' anger hot. In 1214 an English expedition which John had led to Poitou failed. In Northern France the army commanded by his nephew, Otto of Saxony, and by the Earl of Salisbury, was defeated by King Philip at Bouvines. This battle destroyed in a day the whole Continental combination on which John's hopes had been based. Here again was the opportunity of the King's domestic enemies. They formed plans to restrain the rule of a despotic and defeated King, and openly threatened revolt unless their terms were accepted. Left to themselves, they might have ruined their cause by rancorous opposition and selfish demands, but Archbishop Langton, anxious for a just peace, exercised a moderating influence upon them. Nor could the King, as a Papal vassal, openly disregard Langton's advice. . . .

The barons, encouraged by the King's defeat abroad, persisted in their demands. A great party in the Church stood with them. In vain did John manœuvre, by the offer to grant freedom of election to the Church, to separate the clergy from the barons. Armed revolt seemed the only solution. Although in the final scene of the struggle the Archbishop showed himself unwilling to go to the extreme of civil war, it was he who persuaded the barons to base their demands upon respect for ancient custom and law, and who gave them some principle to fight for besides their own class interests. After forty years' experience of the administrative system established by Henry II the men who now confronted John had advanced beyond the magnates of King Stephen's time. They had learned to think intelligently and constructively. In place of the King's arbitrary despotism they proposed, not the withering anarchy of feudal separatism, but a system of checks and balances which would accord the monarchy its necessary strength, but would prevent its perversion by a tyrant or a fool. The leaders of the barons in 1215 groped in the dim light towards a fundamental principle. Government must henceforward mean something more than the arbitrary rule of any man, and custom and the law must stand even above the King. It was this idea, perhaps only half understood, that gave unity and force to the barons' opposition and made the Charter which they now demanded imperishable.

On a Monday morning in June, between Staines and Windsor, the barons and Churchmen began to collect on the great meadow at Runnymede. An uneasy hush fell on them from time to time. Many had failed to keep their tryst; and the bold few who had come knew that the King would never forgive this humiliation. He would hunt them down when he could, and the laymen at least were staking their lives in the cause they served. They had arranged a little throne for the King and a tent. The handful of resolute men had drawn up, it seems, a short document on parchment. Their retainers and the groups and squadrons of horsemen in sullen steel kept at some distance and well in the background. For was not armed rebellion against the Crown the supreme feudal crime? Then events followed rapidly. A small cavalcade appeared from the direction of Windsor. Gradually men made out the faces of the King, the Papal Legate, the Archbishop of Canterbury, and several bishops. They dismounted without ceremony. Someone, probably the Archbishop, stated briefly the terms that were suggested. The King declared at once that he agreed. He said the details should be arranged immediately in his chancery. The original "Articles of the Barons" on which Magna Carta is based exist to-day in the British Museum. They were sealed in a quiet, short scene, which has become one of the most famous in our history, on June 15, 1215. Afterwards the King returned to Windsor. Four days later, probably, the Charter itself was engrossed. In future ages it was to be used as the foundation of principles and systems of government of which neither King John nor his nobles dreamed.

At the beginning of the year 1216 there had seemed to be every chance that John would still defeat the baronial opposition and wipe out the humiliation of Runnymede. Yet before the summer was out the King was dead, and the Charter survived the denunciation of the Pope and the arbitrament of war. In the next hundred years it was reissued thirty-eight times, at first with a few substantial alterations, but retaining its original characteristics. Little more was heard of it until the seventeenth century. After more than two hundred years a Parliamentary Opposition struggling to check the encroachments of the Stuarts upon the liberty of the subject rediscovered it and made of it a rallying cry against oppression. Thus was created the glorious legend of the "Charter of an Englishman's liberties."

If we set aside the rhetorical praise which has been so freely lavished upon the Charter and study the document itself we may find it rather surprising reading. It is in a form resembling a legal contract, and consists of sixty-one clauses, each dealing either with the details of feudal administration and custom or with elaborate provisions for securing the enforcement of the promises which it embodies. It is entirely lacking in any spacious statement of the principles of democratic government or the rights of man. It is not a declaration of constitutional doctrine, but a practical document to remedy current abuses in the feudal system. In the forefront stand the questions of scutage, of feudal reliefs and of wardship. The word "freeman" was a technical feudal term, and it is doubtful whether it included even the richer merchants, far less the bondmen or humbler classes who make up the bulk of a nation. It implies on the King's part a promise of good government for the future, but the terms of the promise are restricted to the observance of the customary privileges and interests of the baronial class. The barons on their part were compelled to make some provision for their tenants, the limits forced on John being vaguely applied to the tenants-in-chief as well; but they did as little as they safely and decently could. The villeins, in so far as they were protected, received such solicitous attention as befitted valuable chattels attached to the manor and not as free citizens of the realm.

The thirteenth century was to be a great age of Parliamentary development and experiment, yet there is no mention in Magna Carta of Parliament or representation of any but the baronial class. The great watchwords of the future here find no place. The actual Charter is a redress of feudal grievances extorted from an unwilling king by a discontented ruling class insisting on its privileges, and it ignored some of the most important matters which the King and baronage had to settle, such as the terms of military service.

Magna Carta must not however be dismissed lightly, in the words of a modern writer, as "a monument of class selfishness." Even in its own day men of all ranks above the status of villeins had an interest in securing that the tenure of land should be secure from arbitrary encroachment. Moreover, the greatest magnate might hold, and often did hold, besides his estate in chief, parcels of land under the most diverse tenures, by knight service, by the privileges of "socage," or as a tenant at will. Therefore in securing themselves the barons of Runnymede were in fact establishing the rights of the whole landed class, great and small—the simple knight with two hundred acres, the farmer or small yeoman with sixty. And there is evidence that their action was so understood throughout the country. In 1218 an official endeavoured to upset by writ a judgment given in the county court of Lincolnshire. The victim was a great landowner, but the whole county rallied to his cause and to the "liberty sworn and granted," stating in their protest that they acted "with him, and for him, and for ourselves, and the community of the whole realm."

If the thirteenth-century magnates understood little and cared less for popular liberties or Parliamentary democracy, they had all the same laid hold of a principle which was to be of prime importance for the future development of English society and English institutions. Throughout the document it is implied that here is a law which is above the King and which even he must not break. This reaffirmation of a supreme law and its expression in a general charter is the great work of Magna Carta; and this alone justifies the respect in which men have held it. The reign of Henry II, according to the most respected authorities, initiates the rule of law. But the work as yet was incomplete: the Crown was still above the law; the legal system which Henry had created could become, as John showed, an instrument of oppression.

Now for the first time the King himself is bound by the law. The root principle was destined to survive across the generations and rise paramount long after the feudal background of 1215 had faded in the past.

The Charter became in the process of time an enduring witness that the power of the Crown was not absolute.

The facts embodied in it and the circumstances giving rise to them were buried or misunderstood. The underlying idea of the sovereignty of law, long existent in feudal custom, was raised by it into a doctrine for the national State. And when in subsequent ages the State, swollen with its own authority, has attempted to ride roughshod over the rights or liberties of the subject it is to this doctrine that appeal has again and again been made, and never, as yet, without success.

CHAPTER 3

THE MOTHER OF PARLIAMENTS

The Congress of the United States today is the direct progeny of the English Parliament, which has been meeting at Westminster for nigh on 750 years. As Senator George J. Mitchell recently remarked: "The Parliament building at Westminster is one of the most visible symbols in the world of self-governance, of individual liberty, of a free and vibrant people. These are British values which, I am proud to say, have become American values."

T HE LATER YEARS of Henry III's troubled reign were momentous in their consequences for the growth of English institutions. This may perhaps be called the seed-time of our Parliamentary system, though few participants in the sowing could have foreseen the results that were eventually to be achieved. The commission for reform set about its work seriously, and in 1258 its proposals were embodied in the Provisions of Oxford, supplemented and extended in 1259 by the Provisions of Westminster. This baronial movement represented something deeper than dislike of alien counsellors. The two sets of Provisions, taken together, represent a considerable shift of interest from the standpoint of Magna Carta. The Great Charter was mainly concerned to define various points of law, whereas the Provisions of Oxford deal with the overriding question of by whose advice and through what officials royal government should be carried on. Many of the clauses of the Provisions of Westminster moreover mark a limitation of baronial rather than of royal jurisdiction. The fruits of Henry II's work were now to be seen; the nation was growing stronger, more self-conscious and self-confident. The notable increase in judicial activity throughout the country, the more frequent visits of the judges and officials—all of them dependent upon local co-operation—educated the country knights in political responsibility and administration. This process, which shaped the future of English institutions, had its first effects in the thirteenth century.

The staple of the barons' demand was that the King in future should govern by a Council of Fifteen, to be elected by four persons, two from the baronial and two from the royal party. It is significant that the King's proclamation accepting the arrangement in English as well as French is the first public document to be issued in both languages since the time of William the Conqueror. For a spell this Council, animated and controlled by Simon de Montfort, governed the land. They held each other in proper check, sharing among themselves the greater executive offices and entrusting the actual administration to "lesser men," as was then widely thought to be desirable. The magnates, once their own class interests were guarded, and their rights—which up to a certain point were the rights of the nation—were secure, did not wish to put the levers of power in the hands of one or two of their number. This idea however of a Cabinet of politicians, chosen from the patriciate, with highly trained functionaries of no political status operating under them, had in it a long vitality and many resurrections.

It is about this time that the word "Parlement"—Parliament—began to be current. In 1086 William the Conqueror had "deep speech" with his wise men before launching the Domesday inquiry. In Latin this would have appeared as *colloquium;* and "colloquy" is the common name in the twelfth century for the consultations between the King and his magnates. The occasional colloquy "on great affairs of the Kingdom" can at this point be called a Parliament. But more often the word means the permanent Council of officials and judges which sat at Westminster to receive petitions, redress grievances, and generally regulate the course of the law. By the thirteenth century Parliament establishes itself as the name of two quite different, though united, institutions.

If we translate their functions into modern terms we may say that the first of these assemblies deals with policy, the second with legislation and administration. The debate on the Address at the beginning of a session is very like a colloquy, while the proceedings of "Parliament" have their analogue in the committee stage of a Bill. In the reign of Henry III, and even of Edward I, it was by no means a foregone conclusion that the two assemblies would be amalgamated. Rather did it look as if the English Constitution would develop as did the French Constitution, with a King in Council as the real Government, with the magnates reduced to a mere nobility, and "Parlement" only a clearing-house for legal business. Our history did not take this course. In the first place the magnates during the century that followed succeeded in mastering the Council and identifying their interests with it. Secondly, the English counties had a life of their own, and their representatives at Westminster were to exercise increasing influence. But without the powerful impulse of Simon de Montfort these forces might not have combined to shape a durable legislative assembly.

The King, the Court party, and the immense foreign interests associ-ated therewith had no intention of submitting indefinitely to the thral-dom of the Provisions. Every preparation was made to recover the lost ground. In 1259 the King returned with hopes of foreign aid from Paris, where he had been to sign a treaty of peace with the French. His son Edward was already the rising star of all who wished to see a strong monarchy. Supporters of this cause appeared among the poor and tur-bulent elements in London and the towns. The enthusiasm of the revo-lution—for it was nothing less—had not been satisfied by a baronial victory. Ideas were afoot which would not readily be put to sleep. It is the merit of Simon de Montfort that he did not rest content with a vic-tory by the barons over the Crown. He turned at once upon the barons themselves. If the King should be curbed, so also must they in their own spheres show respect for the general interest. Upon these issues the claims of the middle classes, who had played a great part in carrying the barons to supremacy, could not be disregarded. The "apprentice" or bachelor knights, who may be taken as voicing the wishes of the country gentry, formed a virile association of their own entitled "the Community of the Bachelors of England." Simon de Montfort became their champion. Very soon he began to rebuke great lords for abuse of their privileges. He wished to extend to the baronial estates the reforms already undertaken in the royal administration. He addressed himself pointedly to Richard, Earl of Gloucester, who ruled wide estates in the South-West and in South Wales. He procured an ordinance from the Council making it plain that the great lords were under the royal au-thority, which was again—though this he did not stress—under the Council. Here was dictatorship in a new form. It was a dictatorship of the Commonwealth, but, as so often happens to these bold ideas, it ex-pressed itself inevitably through a man and a leader. These develop-ments split the baronial party from end to end; and the King and his valiant son Edward, striking in with all their own resources upon their divided opponents, felt they might put the matter to the proof.

At Easter in 1261 Henry, freed by the Pope from his oath to accept the Provisions of Oxford and Westminster, deposed the officials and Ministers appointed by the barons. There were now two Governments with conflicting titles, each interfering with the other. The barons sum-moned the representatives of the shires to meet them at St. Albans; the King summoned them to Windsor. Both parties competed for popular support. The barons commanded greater sympathy in the country, and only Gloucester's opposition to de Montfort held them back from sharp action. After the death of Gloucester in July 1262 the baronial party rallied to de Montfort's drastic policy. Civil war broke out, and Simon and his sons, all of whom played vigorous parts, a moiety of barons, the middle class, so far as it had emerged, and powerful allies in Wales together faced in redoubtable array the challenge of the Crown.

Simon de Montfort was a general as well as a politician. Nothing in his upbringing or circumstances would naturally have suggested to him the course he took. It is ungratefully asserted that he had no real conception of the ultimate meaning of his actions. Certainly he builded better than he knew. By September 1263 a reaction against him had become visible: he had succeeded only too well. Edward played upon the discontent among the barons, appealed to their feudal and selfish interest, fomented their jealousy of de Montfort, and so built up a strong royalist party. At the end of the year de Montfort had to agree to arbitration by Louis IX, the French king. The decision went against him. Loyal to his monarchical rank, the King of France defended the prerogative of the King of England and declared the Provisions to be illegal. As Louis was accepted as a saint in his own lifetime this was serious. Already however the rival parties had taken up arms. In the civil war that followed the feudal party more or less supported the King. The people, especially the towns, and the party of ecclesiastical reform, especially the Franciscans, rallied to de Montfort. New controls were improvised in many towns to defeat the royalist sympathies of the municipal oligarchies. In the summer of 1264 de Montfort once again came South to relieve the pressure which Henry and Edward were exerting on the Cinque Ports.

The King and Prince Edward met him in Sussex with a superior power. At Lewes a fierce battle was fought. In some ways it was a forerunner of Edgehill. Edward, like Rupert four hundred years later, conquered all before him, pursued incontinently, and returned to the battlefield only to find that all was lost. Simon had, with much craft and experience of war, laid a trap to which the peculiar conditions of the ground lent themselves, whereby when his centre had been pierced his two wings of armoured cavalry fell upon the royal main body from both flanks and crushed all resistance. He was accustomed at this time owing to a fall from his horse to be carried with the army in a sumptuous and brightly decorated litter, like the coach of an eighteenth-century general. In this he placed two or three hostages for their greater security, and set it among the Welsh in the centre, together with many banners and emblems suggesting his presence. Prince Edward, in his charge, captured this trophy, and killed the unlucky hostages from his own party who were found therein. But meanwhile the King and all his Court and principal supporters were taken prisoners by de Montfort, and the energetic prince returned only to share their plight.

Simon de Montfort was now in every respect master of England, and if he had proceeded in the brutal manner of modern times in several European countries by the wholesale slaughter of those who were in his grip he might long have remained so. In those days however, for all their cruelty in individual cases, nothing was pushed to the last extreme. The influences that counted with men in contest for power at the peril of their lives were by no means only brutal. Force, though potent, was not sovereign. Simon made a treaty with the captive King and the beaten party, whereby the rights of the Crown were in theory respected, though in practice the King and his son were to be subjected to strict controls. The general balance of the realm was preserved, and it is clear from Simon's action not only that he felt the power of the opposing forces, but that he aimed at their ultimate unification. He saw himself, with the King in his hands, able to use the authority of the Crown to control the baronage and create the far broader and better political system which, whether he aimed at it or not, must have automatically followed from his success. Thus he ruled the land, with the feeble King and the proud Prince Edward prisoners in his hands. This opens the third and final stage in his career.

All the barons, whatever party they had chosen, saw themselves confronted with an even greater menace than that from which they had used Simon to deliver them. The combination of Simon's genius and energy with the inherent powers of a Plantagenet monarchy and the support of the middle classes, already so truculent, was a menace to their class privileges far more intimate and searching than the misgovernment of John or the foreign encumbrances of Henry III. Throughout these struggles of lasting significance the English barony never deviated from their own self-interest. At Runnymede they had served national freedom when they thought they were defending their own privilege. They had now no doubt that Simon was its enemy. He was certainly a despot, with a king in his wallet and the forces of social revolution at his back. The barons formed a hard confederacy among themselves, and with all the forces of the Court not in Simon's hands schemed night and day to overthrow him.

For the moment de Montfort was content that the necessary steps should be taken by a Council of nine who controlled expenditure and appointed officials. Any long-term settlement could be left until the Parliament which he had summoned for 1265. The Earl's autocratic position was not popular, yet the country was in such a state of confusion that circumstances seemed to justify it. In the North and along the Welsh Marches the opposition was still strong and reckless; in France the Queen and the earls Hugh Bigod and Warenne intrigued for support; the Papacy backed the King. De Montfort kept command of the Narrow Seas by raising a fleet in the Cinque Ports and openly encouraging privateering. In the West however he lost the support of Gilbert de Clare, Earl of Gloucester and the son of his former rival Richard de Clare. Without openly joining the royalists Clare conspired with them and revived his father's quarrel with de Montfort. Summoned to the Parliament of 1265, he replied by accusing the Earl of appropriating for himself and his sons the revenues of the Crown and the confiscated property of the opposition nobles. There was some truth in these accusations, but Clare's main objection appears to have been that he did not share the spoils.

In January 1265 a Parliament met in London to which Simon summoned representatives both from the shires and from the towns. Its purpose was to give an appearance of legality to the revolutionary settlement, and this, under the guidance of de Montfort, it proceeded to do. Its importance lay however more in its character as a representative assembly than in its work. The constitutional significance which was once attached to it as the first representative Parliament in our history is somewhat discounted by modern opinion. The practical reason for summoning the strong popular element was de Montfort's desire to weight the Parliament with his own supporters: among the magnates only five earls and eighteen barons received writs of summons. Again he fell back upon the support of the country gentry and the burgesses against the hostility or indifference of the magnates. In this lay his message and his tactics.

The Parliament dutifully approved of de Montfort's actions and accepted his settlement embodied in the Provisions. But Clare's withdrawal to the West could only mean the renewal of war. King Henry III abode docilely in Simon's control, and was treated all the time with profound personal respect. Prince Edward enjoyed a liberty which could only have been founded upon his parole not to escape. However, as the baronial storm gathered and many divisions occurred in Simon's party, and all the difficulties of government brought inevitable unpopularity in their train, he went out hunting one day with a few friends, and forgot to return as in honour bound. He galloped away through the woodland, first after the stag and then in quest of larger game. He at once became the active organising head of the most powerful elements in English life, to all of which the destruction of Simon de Montfort and his unheard-of innovations had become the supreme object. By promising to uphold the Charters, to remedy grievances and to expel the foreigners, Edward succeeded in uniting the baronial party and in cutting away the ground from under de Montfort's feet. The Earl now appeared as no more than the leader of a personal faction, and his alliance with Llewellyn, grandson of Llewellyn the Great, by which he recognised the claims of the Welsh prince to territory and independence, compromised his reputation. Out-manœuvred politically by Edward, he had also placed himself at a serious military disadvantage. While Edward and the Marcher barons, as they were called, held the Severn valley de Montfort was penned in, his retreat to the east cut off, and his forces driven back into South Wales. At the beginning of August he made another attempt to cross the river and to join the forces which his son, Simon, was bringing up from the south-east. He succeeded in passing by a ford near Worcester, but his son's forces were trapped by Edward near Kenilworth and routed. Unaware of this disaster, the Earl was caught in turn at Evesham; and here on August 4 the final battle took place.

It was fought in the rain and half-darkness of a sudden storm. The Welsh broke before Edward's heavy horse, and the small group around de Montfort were left to fight desperately until sheer weight of numbers overwhelmed them. De Montfort died a hero on the field. The Marchers massacred large numbers of fugitives and prisoners and mutilated the bodies of the dead. The old King, a pathetic figure, who had been carried by the Earl in all his wanderings, was wounded by his son's followers, and only escaped death by revealing his identity with the cry, "Slay me not! I am Henry of Winchester, your King."

The great Earl was dead, but his movement lived widespread and deep throughout the nation. The ruthless, haphazard granting away of the confiscated lands after Evesham provoked the bitter opposition of the disinherited. In isolated centres at Kenilworth, Axholme, and Ely the followers of de Montfort held out, and pillaged the countryside in sullen despair. The Government was too weak to reduce them. The whole country suffered from confusion and unrest. The common folk did not conceal their partisanship for de Montfort's cause, and rebels and outlaws beset the roads and forests. Foreign merchants were forbidden in the King's name to come to England because their safety could not be guaranteed. A reversion to feudal independence and consequent anarchy appeared imminent. In these troubles Pope Clement IV and his Legate Ottobon enjoined moderation; and after a six-months' unsuccessful siege of Kenilworth Edward realised that this was the only policy. There was strong opposition from those who had benefited from the confiscations. The Earl of Gloucester had been bitterly disillusioned by Edward's repudiation of his promises of reform. Early in 1267 he demanded the expulsion of the aliens and the re-enactment of the Provisions. To enforce his demands he entered London with general acceptance. His action and the influence of the Legate secured pardon and good terms for the disinherited on the compromise principle of "No disinheritance, but repurchase." Late in 1267 the justices were sent out through the country to apply these terms equitably. The records testify to the widespread nature of the disturbances and to the fact that locally the rebellion had been directed against the officials, that it had been supported by the lower clergy, with not a few abbots and priors, and that a considerable number of the country gentry not bound to the baronial side by feudal ties had supported de Montfort.

In the last years of his life, with de Montfort dead and Edward away on Crusade, the feeble King enjoyed comparative peace. More than half a century before, at the age of nine, he had succeeded to the troubled inheritance of his father in the midst of civil war. At times it had seemed as if he would also die in the midst of civil war. At last however the storms were over: he could turn back to the things of beauty that interested him far more than political struggles. The new Abbey of Westminster, a masterpiece of Gothic architecture, was now dedicated; its consecration had long been the dearest object of Henry III's life. And here in the last weeks of 1272 he was buried.

The quiet of these last few years should not lead us to suppose that de Montfort's struggle and the civil war had been in vain. Among the common people he was for many years worshipped as a saint, and miracles were worked at his tomb. Their support could do nothing for him at Evesham, but he had been their friend, he had inspired the hope that he could end or mend the suffering and oppression of the poor; for this they remembered him when they had forgotten his faults. Though a prince among administrators, he suffered as a politician from overconfidence and impatience. He trampled upon vested interests, broke with all traditions, did violence to all forms, and needlessly created suspicion and distrust. Yet de Montfort had lighted a fire never to be quenched in English history. Already in 1267 the Statute of Marlborough had re-enacted the chief of the Provisions of Westminster. Not less important was his influence upon his nephew, Edward, the new King, who was to draw deeply upon the ideas of the man he had slain. In this way de Montfort's purposes survived both the field of Evesham and the reaction which succeeded it, and in Edward I the great Earl found his true heir.

ACKNOWLEDGEMENTS

I wish to express my gratitude to Piers Brendon, Keeper of the Churchill Archives, Churchill College, Cambridge, England, together with his colleagues Alan Kucia and Jenny Mountain, for their assistance.

My thanks are also due to Richard Langworth, President of the Churchill Center (www.winstonchurchill.org), for his guidance in locating some of my grandfather's lesser-known articles on America, as well as to my editor at Random House, Scott Moyers, and his team for their unfailing courtesy and enthusiasm.

I wish also to thank my secretaries, Mrs. Caroline Rodaway and Miss Penelope Tay, for their invaluable contribution.

Finally, I wish to express my special appreciation of the encouragement given by my wife, Luce, in the completion of this project.

THE CHURCHILL CENTER

Headquartered in Washington, D.C., but active internationally, the Churchill Center works to encourage study of the life and thought of Sir Winston Spencer Churchill; to foster research about his speeches, writings and deeds; to advance knowledge of his example as a statesman; and, by programmes of teaching and publishing, to impart that learning to men, women and young people around the world. It has an active membership in America and also in Great Britain, Canada and Australia through the associated International Churchill Societies. Together, the Center and Societies publish the quarterly *Finest Hour,* the biannual *Churchill Proceedings* and other specialty publications; sponsor international conferences and tours; and offer an expansive internet website (www.winstonchurchill.org).

The Churchill Center has helped bring about re-publication of over twenty of Sir Winston Churchill's long-out-of-print books and launched the campaign for completion of the Companion Volumes of the official biography. More recently, the Center has sponsored three academic symposia in America and Britain; seminars where students and scholars discuss Churchill's books; scholarships for young Churchill scholars at the University of Edinburgh and the University of Dallas; and important reference works. In 1998 it launched the Churchill Lecture, in which prominent world figures apply Sir Winston's experience to the world today.

The Churchill Center is embarked on an endowment campaign to enable it to expand with a headquarters building, a standard Churchill library, and computer facilities linked to the major Churchill archives.

In addition, it aims to provide video programmes for schoolchildren, college and graduate level courses on the career of Churchill, fellowships to assist graduate students, and visiting professorships and academic chairs. The overall aim is to "teach statesmanship," using the greatest teacher of that craft the twentieth century produced.

Membership in the Churchill Center and Societies is available for a modest subscription, with discounts to students. For further information please contact:

USA: The Churchill Center, PO Box 385-W, Hopkinton, NH 03229; telephone toll-free (888) WSC-1874

UK: International Churchill Society, PO Box 1257, Melksham, Wilts. SN12 6GQ

Canada: International Churchill Society, 3256 Rymal Rd., Mississauga, Ont. L4Y 3C1

Australia: International Churchill Society, 181 Jersey Street, Wembley, WA 6014

INDEX

ABOUT THE AUTHOR

SIR WINSTON CHURCHILL is one of the greatest men of our century. Best known for his courageous leadership as Prime Minister of Great Britain during World War II, he was also a prolific author and won the Nobel Prize for literature in 1953 for his *History of the English-Speaking Peoples,* from which the greater part of this work is drawn. Churchill died at the age of ninety in 1965.

ABOUT THE EDITOR

WINSTON SPENCER CHURCHILL is the grandson of Sir Winston Churchill and the son of Randolph Churchill and Ambassador Pamela Harriman. For many years he was a journalist and war correspondent for such newspapers as *The Times, The Evening Standard,* and *The Daily Telegraph,* reporting on conflicts in Africa, the Middle East, and Vietnam. He is the author of five books, and from 1970 to 1997 served as a Conservative Member of Parliament. Winston Churchill lives in London.

ABOUT THE TYPE

This book was set in Times Roman, designed by Stanley Morison specifically for *The Times* of London. The typeface was introduced in the newspaper in 1932. Times Roman had its greatest success in the United States as a book and commercial typeface, rather than one used in newspapers.